The Bureaucratic

Phenomenon

The Bureaucratic Phenomenon

MICHEL CROZIER

THE UNIVERSITY OF CHICAGO PRESS

Translated by the author from *Le phénomène bureau-cratique: Essai sur les tendances bureaucratiques des systèmes d'organisations modernes et sur leurs relations en France avec le système social et culturel.*
Paris: Editions du Seuil, 1963

ISBN: 0-226-12165-8 (Clothbound) ; 0-226-12166-6 (Paperbound)

THE UNIVERSITY OF CHICAGO PRESS, CHICAGO 60637
Tavistock Publications, London E.C.4

Printed in the United States of America

ACKNOWLEDGMENTS

The two research projects which served as starting points for this new discussion of the theory of bureaucracy were accomplished under a grant from the French Commissariat Général à la Productivité. I want to express thanks to M. Francis Raison now director of the productivity division of the Commissariat Général au Plan for the help he gave me.

A number of people have helped me temporarily in these two projects and I cannot thank them all here, but I want to express my most grateful thanks to Mrs. Colette Barreau, who was my assistant during three years for the second study, on the Industrial Monopoly. Her contribution was always enriching and many of the ideas to be found here originated during our discussions.

It has been necessary to hide the names of the organizations studied and I must therefore thank anonymously the managers and executives, the trade union officials and local secretaries, whose help was decisive in securing the approval of the work community. I want to express my gratefulness especially, of course, to all the interviewees, workers and supervisors, whose good will and active co-operation we could enjoy for a kind of activity which was completely new in France at the time.

The first idea of the new theory of bureaucracy came out of my thoughts and discussion at the Center for Advanced Study in the Behavioral Sciences at Palo Alto, California, in 1959–60. I owe very much to the environment and stimulation such an institution provides, and I want to thank my colleagues of that year, especially Conrad Arensberg, Sigmund Diamond, and Herbert Kaufmann, for their comments and criticisms.

The first draft of this book was written originally in English, with the help, for chapters 3, 4, and 5, of Miss Miriam Gallagher. It was then rewritten completely in French. For the final editing of the present English version I owe very much to Mrs. Erika Langmuir, who struggled patiently with my French colloquialisms.

CONTENTS

PART FOUR

BUREAUCRACY AS A CULTURAL PHENOMENON: THE FRENCH CASE

INTRODUCTION

We are all aware of the importance which large organizations have assumed, and will increasingly assume, in modern societies. Most of us are employed, more or less directly, by large organizations; most of the goods we consume are mass-produced by these same organizations. Our leisure and even our cultural life are dominated by other large organizations: the cities in which we reside are themselves large organizations whose complexity is beyond our understanding. In order to exercise effectively our rights of dissent and representation we must employ, at least in part, the large organization—a mode of action essential to modern man.

Evolution in this direction has always evoked fears. The term "large organization" makes one think "bureaucracy"—i.e., unnecessary complications, constraining standardization, the stifling of individual personality. These seeming concomitants of the development of large organizations, and their spreading into all phases of human activity frighten many people.

We constantly associate large organization with bureaucracy, speaking, for example, of "the menace of bureaucracy." Is the association a legitimate one? Does it not involve a confusion of vocabulary that permits us to describe any large organization as a "bureaucracy" and to designate as "bureaucratization" the evolution of modern societies to an economic and social system dominated by large organizations? The growing utilization of complex organizations is a means of action indispensable to modern man. But does this really condemn us to endure more and more "bureaucratic" practices, in the popular pejorative sense of the term?

Questions such as these, which should certainly have been considered as open, have been ignored until the present.[1] Attention has been called to the accelerated growth of large organizations and, in particular, to the extent to which their internal government differs

---

[1] This generalization, like all generalizations, is in fact only partially true. Numerous references will be made in this study to the work of our predecessors who have more or less directly touched upon this problem.

from the democratic ideal. The problem thus posed could not be a problem of diagnosis, but one of remedy only. And the debate has mainly been limited to the passionate interventions of scholars, revolutionaries, reformists, and traditionalists, who seek above all to convince us that their prescriptions constitute the only efficient means of fighting against the conformity, sterility, and dehumanization which threaten modern man.

Personally, we believe that such discussions are premature. Remedies cannot profitably be argued before we have gained a more thorough knowledge of the disease. To understand this malady of bureaucracy better, we must for the time being abandon the anecdotal history of its vicissitudes and devote ourselves to a scientific— i.e., functional—study. It is the basic objective of the present work to provide such a study. We shall examine the bureaucratic phenomenon, as it is found within the context of human activities, at the core of organizations which characterize our present world. Thus we hope to provide an indispensable factual basis from which, perhaps, later studies can discuss in more realistic terms than heretofore the consequences for civilization and for modern man of the growth of large organizations and the development of new forms of organization.

To achieve this, we shall first present at length the especially significant case studies of two French administrative organizations —about whose "bureaucratic" character (in the pejorative sense of the term) everyone is agreed. Our orientation, at the same time empirical and abstract, is very different from the traditional ideological ones. Nevertheless, it produces, no less than they, some highly ambitious—perhaps overambitious—projects. On the basis of our first analyses, we intend to elaborate a theory of the bureaucratic phenomenon that may be inserted both into a general theory of the functioning of organizations and into a general theory of cultural systems. Such an enterprise remains hazardous to the extent to which it is difficult to confront, on the still very uncertain ground of the bureaucratic phenomenon, two different theories at very different levels of conceptualization. But it is essential. The problems of human relations posed by the study of bureaucratic practices can be understood only if both the needs inherent to the functioning of complex organizations, and also the cultural givens to which all participants of the bureaucratic game, in a given society, must subscribe, are taken into account.

After a first relatively rigorous theoretical generalization on the functioning of organizations, we shall therefore propose a broader primary synthesis that integrates a series of cultural elements. This synthesis will be more in the nature of a tentative hypothesis than a systematic theory. However, it will permit us to formulate some answers to the fundamental questions which we have posed.

Such a program calls for certain preliminary explanations, both of the area delimited for study and of method and objectives. Let us first attempt to state precisely the nature and limits of our subject. We will not begin with a narrow definition of the bureaucratic phenomenon. In launching our research, we have deliberately chosen not to depart from an a priori definition. On the contrary, we shall analyze, in their real complexity and as they are currently experienced, facts and behavior which are generally considered bureaucratic, in order to discover what theoretical model they may fit. It would be contrary to this spirit to define the problem precisely in advance: the analysis itself aims at a delimitation of it. In the perspective which we have chosen, elaborating a theory consists of arriving at a more scientific definition of a phenomenon; and the act of defining becomes the goal, not the point of departure, of the research.

If we cannot here define the bureaucratic phenomenon, however we can trace, at least in rough outline, the area of our study, its objectives, and the type of contribution we wish to make. The term "bureaucratic," as we have already remarked, is vague and lends itself to confusion. Three main uses of it seem to have become distinct in the social sciences.

The first and the most traditional usage corresponds to a concept of political science: bureaucracy is government by bureaus. In other words, it is government by departments of the state staffed by appointed and not elected functionaries, organized hierarchically, and dependent on a sovereign authority. Bureaucratic power, in this sense, implies the reign of law and order, but, at the same time, government without the participation of the governed. The second usage originates with Max Weber and has been propagated especially by sociologists and historians: bureaucratization is the rationalization of collective activities. This bureaucratization is brought about by, among other means, the inordinate concentration of the units of production and in general of all organizations and the development within these of a system of impersonal rules, as much for the definition of functions and the repartition of responsibilities as for the ordering of careers. The third usage corresponds to the vulgar and frequent sense of the word "bureaucracy." It evokes the slowness, the ponderousness, the routine, the complication of procedures, and the maladapted responses of "bureaucratic" organizations to the needs which they should satisfy, and the frustrations which their members, clients, or subjects consequently endure.

Much of the difficulty and sterility of discussions of the problem of bureaucracy stem from this uncertainty of vocabulary. The three usages are all the more difficult to distinguish in that the three different phenomena which they evoke are not unrelated. When one speaks of the development of "bureaucratic procedures" within large modern organizations, the term is understood by reference to the tradition of state bureaucracies and to the revulsion the public feel against them. When, on the other hand, one studies bureaucracy in the political sense, one is generally affected by the perspective of the rise of "bureaucratization," which is made to seem ineluctable by the concentration of the units of production. These references would be quite natural in any case, since large private organizations have been influenced by the models elaborated by public bureaucracies, the bureaucratization of private enterprise seems to be paralleled by an extension of state administrations, and the frustrations of the public are addressed indifferently to one or the other type of organization. But the identical vocabulary seems to suggest that all these phenomena are totally interdependent, while in fact the parallelism of their evolution and the identity of their consequences have not been demonstrated.

We have chosen to base ourselves exclusively on the third usage. The subject to which we refer in speaking of the bureaucratic phenomenon is that of the maladaptations, the inadequacies, or, to use Merton's expression, the "dysfunctions," which necessarily develop within human organizations. This choice does not mean that we wish to criticize the other usages, to ignore work which has touched upon bureaucratization in Weber's sense or on bureaucracy in the political sense, or even to withdraw from the general controversies which such studies have raised. It was determined rather by the feeling that historical, predictive, and political analyses connected with these problems are merely marking time—to the extent to which they are unable to rid themselves of the implicit value judgments of the anti-bureaucratic general climate in which they indirectly participate.

In this perspective it will be better understood why a clinical approach which bears upon particular cases, and generalizes only from an intimate understanding of these cases, can serve us better than a systematic approach that seeks immediately to establish rigorous laws and thus gives the appearance of being more scientific.

Our work corresponds, in fact, to an indispensable phase of scientific development, that which could be termed the exploratory phase. At this stage, the most important thing is to elaborate the problem. The elaboration can be effected only by developing systems of hypotheses still close to the concrete, but going beyond the affirmation of banal interdependences and appearing solid and significant enough to be tested in a later phase.

Hypotheses are tested throughout the course of such elaboration; but these are descriptive hypotheses which permit only an understanding, and in part a measurement, of the diverse systems of relations constituting the phenomenon under analysis in the particular case studied. They are directly valid only for the case under investigation and the lessons they furnish do not constitute laws, but only *examples*—examples of models of systems of relations in action. These examples, however, can teach us more about the functioning of social systems of the same order and of even vaster systems than laws which a premature rigor has kept from being adequately comprehensive.

To resolve upon a clinical approach may seem regressive after certain earlier ambitions of the social sciences. However, this seems to us indispensable for all those problems which touch upon the sociology of institutions and the sociology of action. There are no shortcuts possible. General statistical relations, which can be perceived at the opinion level, are fragmentary and undifferentiated; they can testify to accomplished changes, but not to the process of change, nor to the laws of action, nor even to the general direction of the evolution. Only models of functioning at an operational level can help us progress. This is what a clinical approach can offer us. In the case under discussion, that of the "bureaucratic" aspects of the functioning of modern organizations, a clinical approach will enable us to insert a greater number of givens into the traditional schema borrowed from Weber, whose ideal type, in our opinion, corresponds to an inadequate description. The clinical approach will, above all, enable us to advance from a static fragmentary image to an integrated image of the model, all of whose elements are interdependent.

Finally, in adopting the clinical approach, we have experimented with a play of relations between empirical research and theoretical reflection that the reader may find surprising. All theory, of course, originates in a partial and insufficient contact with reality; but this origin is generally masked in the social sciences because of the separation between empirical research and theoretical problems. We have sought to bridge this gap and to use the confrontation between the two modes of thought as a stimulus for each of them. The exploratory situation which we have chosen invites this procedure and we have tried to profit from it. We believe that it is, in fact, at this modest level that the most fruitful exchanges can be established. And the contrast between rather vast theoretical ambitions and the relative narrowness of the subject of inquiry offers, along with many inconveniences, certain decisive advantages.

Our objectives have begun to emerge from these few remarks on our approach, but we shall state them more precisely. We have already specified that we wish to elaborate a theory which can be inserted both into a general theory of organizations and into a general theory of cultural systems. Let us first situate the theory of organization in relation to our own research.

As we have emphasized from the beginning of this Introduction, the development of large organizations constitutes one of the essential characteristics of modern industrial society. This is recognized by everyone. However, many have misunderstood the significance, in terms of the logic of action, of the passing of a world of small entrepreneurs, subject to the insecurities of an unpredictable human and natural universe, in favor of a world of much more stable large economic units capable of long-term prediction. It is argued, in fact, that the directors of these large units can determine their actions with the same independence as the heads of small traditional enterprises could determine theirs, without having to take any more into account than did the latter the resistance of the human means at their disposal. So schematic a view would be valid only in a mechanistic model of the complete subordination of all the rank and file to the directors of the organization—a model which has been proposed but which in no way corresponds to the practical experience of the conduct of human affairs, on either the economic or the political plane. In our modern world, the progress of standardization, of predictability, and of rationality in general paradoxically seems to be accompanied by an increasing dependence on the indispensable human means, who maintain their autonomy in regard to the goals of the organization much more easily than heretofore.

It is this intuitive experience of the resistance of the means and of their decisive importance that the sociology of organizations is seeking to ground scientifically, in order to understand the very framework of the social game and the narrow limits restraining the margin of liberty of all action. In studying the problems posed by the functioning of those large units within which most of the collective activities of industrial society will one day take place, the sociology of organizations aims to widen the basis of theories of action—of which it should increasingly constitute one of the essential foundations.

Such concentration on the means seems at first sight remote from a global analysis of society and may shock those who are used to reasoning solely in macrosociological terms. It constitutes, however, one of the elements essential to all truly comprehensive macrosociological study. It is only through scrutinizing the means that one may hope to view the mechanisms of social control and the processes of change that play such an important role in the development of social systems.

The analysis of the bureaucratic phenomenon, in the dysfunctional sense of the term which we have retained, falls quite naturally into this perspective. Ponderousness and "bureaucratic" routine can easily be interpreted as aspects of the resistance of the human means to the organizational goals. In order to understand them, one is obliged to refer to a sociology, or at least a theory, of organizations, for dysfunction can make sense only in comparison with ideally good functioning. A theory of bureaucracy thus necessarily constitutes a particular facet of a more general theory of organizations, which in turn should itself form the essential element of a sociology of action valid for a global study of society.

Our two case studies, viewed as significant examples of the bureaucratic phenomenon, not only furnish us with information especially crucial to the sociology of organizations, but are also of very great interest for the analysis of cultural systems. The resistance of the human means that is manifested in them is profoundly linked with certain primary behavior and with certain traits characteristic of the cultural system—in this case, the French cultural system. The study of these cultural aspects of the bureaucratic phenomenon will permit the introduction of a new dimension into the sociology of organizations. It seems possible to elaborate a general and universal theory of organizations, dealing with the differences between social and cultural systems only parenthetically. However, as soon as one embarks on the study of the pathology of organizations, cultural analysis becomes an indispensable tool which permits the delimitation of the global theory and its application in different cultural contexts.

At the same time—and this is our final objective—an analysis such as this might make possible a renewal of theories of cultural systems. It might be considered, in some respects at least, as more useful than traditional approaches for viewing cultural systems in terms of current reality. Until the present, cultures or cultural groups were analyzed primarily in terms of their value systems and the special psychological traits of an ideal "basic personality." They were rarely viewed in terms of the problems of action and, in particular, of the problem of the human means necessary to action in complex industrial societies.

The study of the bureaucratic phenomenon permits a new break-through at this more "operational" level. It brings to light the means of social control used, within each cultural system, to arrive at ends necessitated by techniques which have become universal. The pathology of organizations develops from the relative incompatibility between their goals, which spring from a type of utilitarian rationality, and the means of social control, which are determined by the primary behavior and values characteristic of the cultural system of which the organizations are part.

Study in this area is of great interest because it lies, for all the reasons stated above, just at the intersection of these two systems, i.e., the one area where men maintain a certain margin of liberty and where changes can be effected. One cannot directly modify values, much less the basic personality. However, the imperatives of action, the will to succeed, the advantages gained from eliminating pathological features from the system of organization on which one is dependent—these can lead to a choice of structures, to the imposition of types of relations that will ultimately have repercussions on values and the basic personality. It is only through action—i.e., by acting through institutions and by modifying these institutions themselves —that a society can transform itself. A sociology of organizations and a sociology of cultural systems are thus equally necessary to a general theory of action. The study of the bureaucratic phenomenon makes a valuable contribution to both.

One final remark seems indicated. We have spoken of systems of organization, of cultural and social systems. We have presented the elaboration of a theory as the search for a definition which accounts for the conditions of equilibrium and the development of the phenomenon in question. All these formulas connote a functionalist orientation. We do, in fact, maintain that a functionalist perspective constitutes a necessary phase of all sociological research and that it is particularly indispensable at present in a discipline the majority of whose problems are still at an exploratory stage. But this methodological necessity entails the risk of the gradual transformation of the functionalist method, the essential tool of a rational sociology, into a functionalist philosophy—the complacent approbation of uncovered interdependences. It is easy to succumb to this tendency to the extent to which it is believed that phenomena have been definitively explained that, in fact, have been merely described in their momentary state. We have sought to guard ourselves from this defect by keeping constantly foremost the problem of change, both at the level of our case studies, in our discussion of a general theory of organization, and in our essay on the models of action characteristic of the

French cultural system. The reader should not be astonished, therefore, if our conclusion consists simply of reflections on change and on the framework and limitations of action in the world of large organizations and within complex cultural systems.

Part One

THE CASE OF THE CLERICAL AGENCY

The first of the two cases which we are about to discuss concerns a large-scale Parisian administrative organization which may be described as rigid, standardized, and impersonal, and which seems unable to cope with the human and technical problems engendered by its recently accelerated growth. Its hierarchical structure, its promotional system, and its principles of organization are extremely simple. The behavior of its different categories of personnel, as actors within its social system, is therefore much easier to analyze. The actors appear to be both extremely rational and extremely predictable, as if they were playing a game that followed an experimental model. We shall use the opportunity afforded by such a situation to try to understand better one of the most fundamental problems usually associated with the concept of bureaucracy, the problem of routine.

In the introductory chapter, we shall provide some general data and descriptive comments on the tasks performed, on the actors, and on the processes of action. We shall then analyze and discuss the position of the actors within the organization, as it can be understood from the study of their first and simplest reaction, i.e., their individual satisfaction in regard to their own work situation. In the second chapter, we shall examine the more complex problems of the relationships between individuals and groups, and of the functioning of the hierarchical system. We shall then try to proceed from this starting point to discuss the processes of decision-making and to propose hypotheses which may explain why a general model of routine has developed.

Chapter One

THE OVER-ALL ORGANIZATION AND THE EMPLOYEES' INDIVIDUAL ADJUSTMENTS TO THEIR TASKS

THE OBJECTIVES OF THE CLERICAL AGENCY AND ITS OVER-ALL CHARACTERISTICS

The Parisian Clerical Agency is the Parisian branch of a large public agency, part of a government department. This branch is quite a large-scale organization by itself. At the time the data we will use were collected, it employed 4,500 people, mostly women, in a single establishment.[1] Its size—in any case huge for an administrative organization—sets it apart from the other establishments of the same public agency, since it employs four or five times more personnel than the biggest provincial establishment. Its purpose is to handle, on a daily basis, simple financial operations requested by a great many customers.[2]

It is a public service run for the public benefit and not for profit. However, since it provides the French nation with huge sums of money on a short-term basis, it has a great importance for the French treasury.

The Clerical Agency's most important present characteristic is its steady growth.[3] This growth is due not only to the general economic growth of the country, but also to the changing habits of the French public. It is not viewed with great favor by the managements of the Agency and of the Parisian branch, since it brings them many difficulties and no rewards. The managements must abide by Civil Service rules, since increase of staff and all other new expenditures are part of the National State Budget. Because of the habitual thrift of the French Ministry of Finance and the usual distrust of parliament for the executive, the necessary authorizations for budgetary expansion always lag behind. The organization must be managed in a

---

[1] At the time of writing seven years later, this number had grown to over 6,500.
[2] About one and a half million.
[3] Although there is no publicity and no sales promotion, the number of customers and the number of operations are growing regularly at a rate of about 10 per cent a year.

parsimonious way incompatible with the requirements of its development.

The main problems are the number of personnel and shortage of office space. New jobs are not created until the need for them is very great; it is thus impossible to build up reserves of personnel and to devote enough time to training. There is a heavy emphasis on productivity, but productivity tends to decrease because of the large percentage of young and ill-trained employees, and because of the poor working climate and the high rate of turnover. The working-space situation is even worse. It had been temporarily solved by introducing shift work, which made it possible for twice as many people to work in the same rooms.[4] But the Agency has now been obliged to utilize rooms formerly considered unsuitable, and this has started continuous bickering with the unions about the hygiene of working conditions.

Office installations, the internal layout, and general maintenance are equally inadequate. There are insufficient toilets, washing facilities, and locker-rooms for the increased personnel. Workrooms are extremely noisy. Tables and filing equipment are old. The whole building is cold and unattractive. The poor standard of cleaning makes it even sadder.

The technology of the Agency's work is simple and it has remained basically unchanged for thirty-five years. The employees, all female, work in production units on heavy cross-tabulating accounting machines (with six or two tabulators). A pneumatic system facilitates quick communication. Work organization is also simple. It does not involve advance planning, since everything is done on a daily basis, according to the demands of the public. The most important qualities for a successful member of management are experience of possible difficulties and a relentless drive for control. All in all, however, this system is very efficient. The Parisian branch, like all the other branches, provides extremely good service, both quick and trustworthy.

The hierarchical organization is also uncomplicated. It is a pure line organization, with no staff function at all, at least at the branch level. The basic unit is the workroom, with about one hundred employees working in two shifts of fifty each. The workroom is further divided into the regular workroom, and the special section, where half a dozen senior employees and a few members of the supervisory grades handle mistakes, special cases, and requests for information. Two inspectors—one for the special section and one for the regular workroom—and four *surveillantes* form the supervisory staff of each

---

[4] Personnel are divided into two shifts, one succeeding the other, on the same jobs; there is a weekly alternation from the morning to the afternoon shift.

shift. A section chief heads the two shifts and co-ordinates their work. There is one division head over ten such workrooms. He has about a thousand employees to care for and has two senior section chiefs and a secretary as his own personal staff. At the time of our study there were three regular divisions, with a fourth one in charge of all auxiliary work, incoming and outgoing mail, new accounts, the printing shop, maintenance, etc. Over the four divisions there was one senior division head, the formal head of the branch. He also has a very small staff—one personal secretary, a dozen clerks for handling mail, and a special office, likewise very poorly staffed, for all employment records, the delivery of pay-checks, and many odd jobs. As one would expect, this manager does not plan ahead and direct the adjustment of the organization. His function is, rather, to co-ordinate the action of the four division heads, to arbitrate among them when necessary, and to try to make them work according to the imperative rules of the Central Office.

The Agency is not autonomous, and its national management is part of the Ministry's bureaucratic structure. Executives are promoted from one section of the Ministry to another more frequently than from the field to the central office. National management has many echelons but not a very large staff. Its organization also is very rigid. Most of its bureaus theoretically have only advisory functions. In fact, however, they operate as the actual heads of the line organization and issue orders that must be applied in the field. These orders usually are presented not as special decisions but as general rules for all branches throughout France. Only the Parisian branch frequently receives special treatment because of the problems created by its size, but even this is done quite reluctantly.

The Different Categories of Personnel

Non-supervisory personnel is predominantly female. Men work only in the auxiliary services, incoming or outgoing mail, the printing shops, and the maintenance sections. In the regular production jobs there are only women, who are in one of three main categories: *contrôleurs, agents d'exécution,* and *auxiliaires.* Theoretically, only *agents* should be working on these jobs, since most of the tasks performed correspond in the official classification to the routine clerical posts for which *agents* are recruited. Yet only 70 per cent of the employees are *agents.* Twenty per cent of them are *contrôleurs,* who should have more responsible tasks while the remaining 10 per cent are either members of a complementary category or *auxiliaires*—who had not yet been ranked, and whose employment is now forbidden by law.[5]

Three-quarters of the employees come from the French provinces. They do not stay very long in the Agency; over-all turnover is around 15 per cent, and the average seniority is only three and a half years.[6] This type of recruitment from the provinces is new. Twenty years ago, almost half the personnel came from the Parisian region; but in the last ten years 85 per cent of them have come from the less developed rural regions, especially from the southwest.[7] This change in the personnel's geographical origin has involved a change in its social origin. Instead of the majority of the employees coming from families of lower-grade civil servants and urban workers, most are daughters of farmers, rural shopkeepers, and craftsmen. This tendency is stronger among the *agents,* but it can be also seen among the *contrôleurs.*

At the same time, the level of education of the new employees is much higher. Twenty-one per cent of the *agents* and 96 per cent of the *contrôleurs* recruited in the last two years had their baccalaureates,[8] while none of the older ones had such a diploma. This difference is due to the new requirements of the two *concours,* and to the general improvement of educational standards. However, the higher educational level is not compatible with the relative downgrading of this type of routine clerical job, and it is thus a source of maladjustment. Even at the simplest level, it is one of the most potent factors for the regional shift in recruitment. Parisian girls with the required schooling now very rarely accept the salaries and terms of employment of the lower grades of the Civil Service. Only girls who come

[5] The law forbids the employment of *auxiliaires* in order to maintain the standards of the Civil Service and to protect the rights of present civil servants. But how are the *auxiliaires* who are good workers but could not pass the necessary *concours* to be employed? They are kept as *auxiliaires* or in the *cadre complémentaire* (*auxiliaires* with tenure). At the time of the survey we found *auxiliaires* recruited for a few weeks in time of rush, a few *auxiliaires* with seniority, 150 members of the *cadre complémentaire,* 700 *contrôleurs,* and 2,200 *agents.*

[6] The average seniority is influenced also by the importance of the regular increase of personnel.

[7] By southwest, we mean the thirty *départements* south of a line drawn between La Rochelle and Saint Etienne, and west from a line Saint Etienne–Nîmes. These *départements,* which account for only 19 per cent of the present French population, have given 40 per cent of the present *agents* and 54 per cent of those recruited in 1953–54. In each of these, the number of the employees of the Parisian branch is at least double what it should be according to its population, although the more rural provide a far greater number than the more urban ones. For more details, see Michel Crozier, *Petits fonctionnaires au Travail* (Paris: Editions du Centre National de la Recherche Scientifique, 1956).

[8] The equivalent of the American high-school diploma, but with a higher social level because of its selective purposes. In status, it may be compared to an American college degree.

from underdeveloped areas with few employment opportunities will accept them. Therefore, the more the Ministry emphasizes educational standards the less it will be able to recruit from the Paris area. Promotion from the lower categories to the higher ones and to the supervisory grades can be achieved only by passing new *concours*. These *concours* do not have anything to do with the work at the branch; they sanction a level of education one cannot easily attain outside the schools; preparation for them requires long and strenuous efforts which very few employees are able to make. There are, therefore, very few promotions, especially at the lower level, and almost no supervisors who began their careers as *agents* in the branch.

Most supervisors, finally, are men. Women, to be sure, are *surveillantes*, but these are strawbosses', not supervisors', jobs. Male supervisors, inspectors, and section chiefs are relatively old in the job. Eighty per cent of them have worked twenty years or more in the Civil Service. Their average age is forty-five, while that of their subordinates is twenty-seven. Curiously enough, their geographical and social origins do not differ very much from those of the newer employees and do contrast with those of the older employees. This similarity and contrast suggest that the changes in the recruitment of personnel, the immediate material causes of which we have underlined, have come about within the general frame of the older network of human relationships that existed between the metropolis and an underdeveloped area. Twenty and thirty years ago, the southwest was sending its boys to Civil Service jobs in Paris. Now, when its girls seem independent and are looking for employment, they in turn are going; but the old network of relationships has not, in fact, changed very much.

THE ORGANIZATION OF WORK AND PRODUCTIVITY

The basic units of work organization are the four-girl work teams. These teams, to which more than 60 per cent of the employees belong, are in charge of the direct productive function of the Agency —i.e., the carrying out and accounting of the customer's orders. Many employees, of course, do not belong to these teams, but are doing preparatory work or handling special cases and mistakes. Among them are the people working in the special workrooms and all those employed in the fourth division. The Agency as a whole, however, remains a rather rare example of a large modern organization in which everything still revolves around a large set of autonomous and parallel productive units, working independently of one another.

The work-flow in such an organization is extremely simple. Sorting out the incoming mail in the early morning and a second mail in the late morning, processing operations, preparing the outgoing mail, and balancing the accounts of the day—these daily tasks never vary. The main characteristics of this system of work are the daily rhythm, the lack of interdependence between the teams. Every work team has to do the same thing and does not have to co-operate with other work teams to accomplish its tasks. These tasks are daily tasks, and even their quantity cannot be fixed by human decision. One principle is followed, as a sort of golden rule: All the traffic arriving on time must be handled the same day.[9]

Work, therefore, does not depend on supervisory decisions and group relationships, but on the impersonal pressure of the public at large. The only possible scapegoat for one shift is the other shift, whose alleged slowness and neglect may be seen as having made it necessary for the group to stay overtime.[10]

Within the work team, on the other hand, there are division of work and a great deal of interdependence. Two girls work at the tabulating machines and two at checking. The work process begins with a check of the customer's credentials, then the girl at the first (six-tabulator) machine types, at one time, all documents necessary for carrying out the order. The figures are then checked by the third employee; and they are finally tabulated again, for balancing the accounts, by the fourth. The girl who initiates the work process by checking the customer's demands must be the most experienced, since she has the responsibility of deciding whether or not the order can be carried out.[11] More important, in practice she sets the pace of work for her colleagues. She is considered, therefore, the team leader, although her role is not officially acknowledged and she does not receive any recognition for it.

In theory, the four girls should rotate their jobs, but this official standing order is very rarely applied, since few employees have enough experience to qualify for every job, especially for the first one. Usually there is only a partial rotation: between the first two jobs, between the second and the third, and between the third and the fourth. As it is practiced, rotation makes it possible to relieve the girls holding the machine jobs, and especially the first, which is very tiring. However, rotation does not insure equality within the work

[9] If the employees have not finished at the regular quitting time, they must work overtime.

[10] Each team of the first shift is associated with a team of the second shift, servicing the same customers. That is, each work team of the second shift will take on at midday the operations left to it by the corresponding team of the first shift. The morning shift and the afternoon shift rotate every week.

[11] Her decision will be rechecked automatically by a *surveillante* whenever the amount of the order is large enough.

team. The girls who check the customers' credentials have recognized status and prestige among their workmates, even if—as may be the case—they are only *auxiliaires* earning much less money than their colleagues.

Obviously such a system of organization de-emphasizes the role of supervision. Supervisors need not organize the work-flow; they do not have to decide about the work to be done and the people to do it. The amount of work and even its allocation are not influenced by them. Moreover, everything depends on the daily work load, so there is no possibility of planning ahead. Certainly, supervisors have some say in placing the workers when they arrive. However, once the girls have been stabilized in the work teams, they cannot be moved against their will. The supervisor's role consists only of arranging for transfers in case of quarrels, providing replacements when employees are sick, and designating the girls who are to go to another workroom when division heads ask for a new distribution.[12]

Most of the time of the *inspecteurs* is devoted to small personal tasks, especially to collecting data for statistical purposes. The functions of section chiefs are of a more supervisory nature. They handle all minor problems of discipline, take care of personnel administration, and prepare the individual ratings of their subordinates. But the division head must decide on every exception to the very strict rules, even a half-day's leave of absence. The *inspecteurs'* main worry and only important task is the technical and human co-ordination between the two shifts.

At a higher level, the main problem concerns the distribution of the work load among the different sections. Such a distribution cannot be made daily according to the requirements the organization has to meet and the resources it has at its disposal. It is made indirectly and permanently by making each section and each work team within the section responsible for all the traffic which a certain number of customers they service will eventually bring. Since the Agency is a large-scale operation, one can make adequately accurate forecasts, and the system is generally well accepted. It is made more complex by the fact that not all sections have the same working capacity, and therefore each cannot be given the same work load. Difficulties, readjustments, and some arbitrary decisions must be accepted at this level. The strength of precedent and the widespread consensus on the ranking of the sections in terms of their productivity make it much easier to make such decisions.

This kind of work organization has the great advantage of giving

[12] These requirements will be very specific and there will not be much leeway in meeting them. New repartitions of personnel correspond to the creation of new workrooms, for which it is necessary to secure a small group of senior well-qualified employees from older workrooms.

the employees a clear work load, whose amount does not depend on the arbitrary whim of a supervisor and does not lead to the petty bickering of piece-rates incentives. It has, however, more important drawbacks. All employees must be allocated to the work teams and there is no reserve staff.[13] Each team is solely responsible for handling the traffic of its own customers. But when there are traffic peaks the work load becomes too heavy; bigger units, by allowing for reserve and planning ahead, could handle them much better.

To solve this problem, the managers of the Agency put a great deal of pressure on the personnel by imposing very harsh discipline and by relying, in times of crisis, on the direct authority of the supervisors. Employees are not usually subject to arbitrary interventions, but they cannot bargain over the amount of the work load. The discipline to which they must submit is impersonal and its means of action are limited, since firing anyone is practically impossible. But it is sufficient to hold in check a woman employee whose feelings are easily manipulated by threats of public humiliation, such as official reprimands and insertions of criticism in the personal files. No kind of absenteeism is tolerated; mistakes are traced to the girls administratively responsible for them, and written excuses are demanded from each of them.

In times of crisis, the supervisor's role of watching and checking, which ordinarily does not seem to have much importance, suddenly takes precedence. The social system of the Agency itself seems to be set up for a regular alternation of long periods of routine with short periods of crisis. During the periods of routine the authoritarian structure of the organization will all but disappear behind its impersonal system of action; subordinates are left alone, and supervisors take care of their own tasks only. But when crises come, a complete transformation into a very painful climate of excitement and nervous stress occurs. A state of emergency reigns. People adjust to it, the superiors by becoming active interventionists and the girls by accepting an obedient role.

Such a system, at the same time impersonal and authoritarian—quite militaristic, in a sense—makes discussion and bargaining almost impossible and thus does not foster understanding. The Agency's productivity seems high in comparison with that of other French large-scale clerical organizations, but is achieved in a rather backward way—by keeping overhead expenses to a minimum and by imposing a heavy work load. Yet no effort is made to rationalize and

[13] The only supplementary staff in the workroom is provided by the few hours employees have to spend on the other shift. Since they spend only 36 hours at their regular shift, employees, to complete their 40 hours a week, have to come back on the other shift for four hours. This arrangement is very much disliked.

adjust organizational methods, to make them more flexible, or to plan over-all personnel policies with a view to the growth of the organization, the changing habits of the public, and the evolution of the personnel. Productivity, according to the conception prevalent in the Agency, is a matter of direct pressure and control, and not of forecasting, planning, and organizing.

The apparent results are remarkable. The Agency is very efficient both in terms of cost and in terms of service. But if one views these results in a broader perspective, one can no longer be optimistic.

Two considerations seem to be especially relevant. First, the Parisian branch has a rather low productivity compared to that of many provincial branches. The increase of size, consequently, contrary to expectations, leads to a decrease in productivity. This, in turn, points to the main drawback of this kind of work organization—the lack of integration of functions within the branch, which gives no premiums for larger units, but does make them liable to the decrease of productivity resulting from the increasing difficulty of exercising control.

The insistence on traditional means, i.e., thrift, keeping the overhead as low as possible, controls, and coercion, gives an advantage to the smaller units within which social pressure is much more efficient. This high productivity, however, appears to be achieved only through strong pressure from the top down at the expense of the employees' morale. The branch is caught in a vicious circle. Pressure for productivity will cause poor morale and consequently a large turnover of personnel. But the regular decrease in the average seniority that follows makes it more difficult to maintain the same productivity. This obliges management to increase the pressures still more, thus renouncing the possibilities of raising morale and decreasing turnover. When the limit of possible pressures has been reached, productivity itself will be affected. These are the reasons why the Parisian branch is less efficient, since it is inferior to the provincial branches on all those points.[14]

[14] Since the efficiency of the whole system depends on the ability of employees to maintain a very high speed, the organization can function satisfactorily only if there exists a large enough group of older employees who can impose the necessary rhythm as team leaders and follow it at the most painful job, the six-tabulator machine.

The link between productivity and turnover is very apparent when the sections are compared. The rank order of the sections by productivity corresponds almost exactly to their rank order according to the percentage of employees with at least five years' seniority.

One obtains almost the same ranking if one takes as a criterion the percentage of employees applying for new jobs (from 20 to 65 per cent of the employees who have the right to make such applications do it according to the sections).

The recent history of the branch shows that the number of stable, low turnover,

EMPLOYEES' WORK SATISFACTION

This preliminary analysis of the difficulties which the Agency confronts suggests the extent to which productivity—i.e., the practical results of the Agency's organizational system—can be influenced by the feelings, or "morale," of its personnel.

But this first and hasty interpretation should not be accepted as literally valid. The relationship between morale and productivity and the concept of morale itself are not so simple. Progress in research during the last twenty years has indicated: (1) that the different reactions of the members of an organization are, to a large extent, heterogeneous and cannot be explained away by referring to a common underlying factor like morale; and (2) that there is no discernible direct and permanent relationship between such a common factor or any one of its elements, on the one hand, and the results of the organization, as regards productivity, on the other.[15] Taking cues from numerous experiments, a number of modern researchers are trying now to analyze these problems in their more complex institutional and sociological settings.[16] This is the direction which we also intend to take.

We shall study the different systems of interpersonal and intergroup relationships that form these institutional and sociological settings within the organization, and condition its efficiency and the importance of its bureaucratic features. First, however, we should like to discuss the problem which much always be investigated initially in this domain, i.e., the problem of work satisfaction.

Work satisfaction is a simple and relatively clear concept, through which the individual can express well the way in which he is adjusting to his task and thus to his role within the organization.[17] The

high productivity workrooms is steadily decreasing, inasmuch as senior employees must be taken away from their original workroom in order to staff, with at least a few competent people, the new workrooms that must be opened up every year. Employees' morale, finally, appears to be decisive for understanding even the most concrete aspects of productivity.

[15] The failure of the long-range programs of the Survey Research Center of the University of Michigan to show conclusive results on this central point is, perhaps, the best example; but many other programs of the late forties and fifties ended in the same way.

[16] For example, Floyd Mann and Arnold Tannenbaum at Michigan, Leonard Sayles and Melville Dalton from the interactionist group, Chris Argyris, Norman Martin, and many others. For a bibliography, see the notes to chap. vi, below.

[17] A further, more careful analysis, however, shows that satisfaction in one's work does not equal satisfaction in one's situation within the organization and, of course, within the society. Even work satisfaction, in the narrow sense, is not a very homogeneous notion, since one can distinguish several independent dimensions, such as the interest in the task, feeling of responsibility, freedom of action, and initiative.

concept of morale has usually been elaborated from the starting point provided by answers to questions about work satisfaction. It became clear early, however, that work satisfaction does not correspond too well to attitudes toward the organization, to the way the employee appraises it, to his will to stay or to leave, and to the cooperation he is ready to give. Furthermore, work satisfaction describes only the very individual relationship of the interviewee to his environment. It does not teach us very much about the group phenomena that apparently govern his behavior at a deeper level.

A study of work satisfaction, nevertheless, should provide us with an especially interesting beginning. It will provide a preliminary description of the human climate of the Agency, and an analysis of the variables influencing work satisfaction will permit us to state the problem of the functioning of its social system.

Work in the Agency is monotonous and repetitive most of the time. In the Parisian branch, there is an atmosphere of nervous tension that makes work painful for a number of girls. Many people are thus led to believe that the paramount factor conditioning the morale of the employees and their ability to adjust to their situation is the work itself, as it is imposed on the workers by technological evolution. The journalists and politicians interested in the problem have always taken it for granted that most human problems of the Agency, like those of other large-scale modern organizations, are due to the inhuman nature of the work. Even middle-of-the-road *députés,* when speaking of the Agency, have denounced the mechanistic technology that makes people lose individuality and spirit and changes them into robots. Many senior officials in the Civil Service and even in the Agency accept such an interpretation.[18]

However, this interpretation was not validated by the results of our interviews. Work satisfaction is not especially low among the employees of the Parisian branch. It is not substantially different from what can be observed in other organizations. In their personal comments, employees tend to minimize the nature of the work, and emphasize rather those aspects of the situation that are not beyond the reach of human will.

Three main points emerge most clearly in this respect. These are: the priority the employees give to the problem of the work load rather than to the nature of the work; the range of moderate and somewhat complex opinions on work problems; and the decisive influence that

---

[18] This kind of respectable humanism can succeed, of course, only inasmuch as it gives an advantageous self-complacent position. Since mechanistic technology is here to stay and no one contemplates getting rid of progress, it can be denounced safely. Making it responsible for all human problems exonerates everybody from possible blame and excuses all from taking any action.

social status outside the organization has in shaping attitudes and adjustment within it.

THE IMPORTANCE OF THE WORK LOAD

We will not insist on the first point, which is not in the least ambiguous. The problem of the work load was mentioned spontaneously by more than two-thirds of the interviewees when answering a question about how to improve the situation of the employees, whereas only one-third talked about wages, the next item. This is all the more striking in that wages are low and protests from the unions on this point have always been loud and violent.[19] Furthermore, many interviewees pointed out that a better work organization and the building of a more stable labor force could relieve them, and they presented quite reasonable suggestions to this effect. On the other hand, only among a small minority—and only when they were answering a direct question about work—did we hear complaints about the nature of the task and its mechanical, boring quality.[20]

THE FEELINGS ABOUT WORK

The second point needs more elaboration. Let us first examine the distribution of opinions. Although employees complained bitterly about the work load, it is remarkable that their opinions about their jobs were not very different from those that other surveys have brought to light in France and in America.

This comparison is, of course, only indicative, because the same measuring instruments were not used (except for the insurance companies and the bank). It does suggest, however, that no real difference exists between the attitudes of employees who do the same kind of routine clerical work in quite different settings, and that such atti-

---

[19] When they were asked about their own salaries, our interviewees complained very bitterly.

[20] These conclusions, to be sure, are impressionistic. It is not because a problem is not spontaneously raised that it has no importance. An opinion poll gives us only a superficial view of the feelings of the public. The survey we conducted in the Agency goes further, since it enabled us to measure and to weigh different reactions. But the responsibility of the analyst in such a task remains decisive. He does not give us scientific conclusions, but an impressionistic judgment based on a wider array of facts than common-sense judgments. Only more specialized experimental studies could give us scientific proofs. One can notice, in any case, that most other research, undertaken in many different settings, tends to corroborate the point of view from which we interpret the feelings of the workers of the Clerical Agency. For an exhaustive bibliography on this point, see Frederick Herzberg *et al.*, *Job Attitudes, Review of Research and Opinion* (Pittsburgh: Psychological Service of Pittsburgh, 1957).

TABLE 1

WORK SATISFACTION IN SEVERAL LARGE-SCALE CLERICAL ORGANIZATIONS
(Four Routine Jobs Only)

	High Work Satisfaction (Per Cent)	Medium Work Satisfaction (Per Cent)	Low Work Satisfaction (Per Cent)
Clerical Agency Parisian Branch...............	12	55	33
Six Parisian insurance companies*..............	25	37	38
Major banking network's Parisian headquarters .	21	57	22
An American insurance company†.............	23	36	41

* Data still unpublished from surveys made under the direction of the author under the sponsorship of the Institut des Sciences Sociales du Travail and the Centre National de la Recherche Scientifique between 1956 and 1959.
† Data computed from a survey conducted by the Survey Research Center of the University of Michigan; see Nancy Morse, Satisfactions in the White-Collar Job (Ann Arbor: Institute for Social Research, 1953), p. 36.

tudes are not as unfavorable as one tends to imagine. This accords with the results of several recent studies on the amount of work satisfaction in different occupations.[21]

Individual comments are even more revealing, since they show better the focus of interest of the interviewees and the true nature of their grievances.[22] A few quotations from three interviewees who may be considered as especially representative will give a much more precise image of the work atmosphere and convey the flavor and human meaning of the employees' attitudes.

Let us begin with a typical interview of the average girl, one of those 55 per cent who were rated as medium in our scale of work satisfaction. Mrs. B. is a team leader with five years of seniority but only now about to be classified as a civil servant. She is from Paris, twenty-five years old, and married to a technical draftsman. Her father is an industrial worker and her mother a saleswoman. She lives in a furnished apartment.

This is what she said about her work:

I like very much having accomplished the task. . . . It was hard to get used to this kind of work. At first I didn't understand very well. I liked the ordinary typewriter much better: when one begins one finds it deadly dull, but when one is accustomed to it, it is all right . . . the only trouble is the noise.

[21] See, for example: Robert Blauner, "Work Satisfaction and Industrial Trends in Modern Society," in Walter Galenson and S. M. Lipset (eds.), Labor and Trade Unionism (New York: Wiley, 1960), pp. 340–42; Nancy Morse and Robert S. Weiss, "The Function and Meaning of Work and the Job," American Sociological Review, XX (1950), 191–98; Gladys Palmer, "Attitudes toward Work in an Industrial Community," American Journal of Sociology, LXIII (1957), 17–26; and especially Herzberg et al., op. cit., p. 3.
[22] We used free interviewing schedules, and our questions elicited many comments.

About pride in the work:

> Of course, we are all of us quite proud. And then there is the rivalry between the shifts. When I am at the checking job, especially, I like to finish early. I like very much being in charge of the team.

About conscientiousness at work:

> We have a lot of responsibility. We must do our work if we don't want to be in trouble. Whether one likes it depends very much on one's character.

About her own aptitudes:

> It suits me very well, especially the checking job; typing at the accounting machine is all right, but checking is more interesting. As a typist, one does not have to care about what one is doing.[23]

The reader will note that Mrs. B.'s grievances do not stem from the content of her work, but from the conditions under which it is done. Mrs. B. seems to be personally involved in and attracted to her work of checking customers' credentials and to her role as team leader.

The contrast between grievances bearing on the most extrinsic aspects of the task and the relative satisfaction expressed about its technical content is very widespread. The girls we have assumed to like their jobs very much are not so different in this respect from the others. They differ only in seeming to take so much interest in what they are doing that they forget, at least momentarily, all possible reservations. For example, this is true of Mrs. Axx. Mrs. Axx is forty-eight. She and her husband, a railroad worker, both come from Brittany, live in a suburban house which they have bought with their savings. Mrs. Axx works in the special workroom at one of the accounting-machine jobs similar to those in the regular workroom. This is what she told the interviewer:

> I like this kind of work very much. Before working here, I was working as a charwoman. I went back to school when I was thirty; I could not go on long enough when I was a child. . . . Friends told me to try, they did not understand why I was not trying to change work. Where there is a will, there is a way.
>
> What I do not like here: we are obliged not to care about the work although we would like to. We are not allowed to finish. It is nonsense, only the bare results count. I feel somewhat disappointed.

When asked about employees' conscientiousness at work, she says: "Being conscientious makes you feel good; this is how we hold on."

This is said with a great deal of involvement; then she goes on as if it were a sort of afterthought:

[23] This interview and the one following have been published in Crozier, *op. cit.*, pp. 68–69.

Young people are not so conscientious; they may be right after all. The superiors tell us: It's your turn, you "champs" . . . and we go.

About her own aptitudes:

This work suits me very well, it has helped me develop certain qualities: speed, carefulness, orderliness. . . . I am happy. One is working in a different milieu, one is rising up. [She shifted at that moment from "I" to the impersonal "one" form, as if she could not assume such a strong and personal affirmation.] . . . This was the dream of my life, I wanted to be a teacher, a clerk. . . . I have a temper. I could never bear being a servant.

One-third of the interviewees, however, express a completely different attitude. For them, the content of the work is as unbearable as the working conditions. It is somewhat more difficult to find a representative of this group, since it contains a much wider variety of opinions than the others. The person we have chosen, Miss X., represents the most unhappy half of the group—those who were considered as not liking their work at all—but we find in this subgroup a number of interviewees much more violent than, if not so articulate as, she is.

Miss X. is twenty, and comes from Lorraine. Her father was a well-to-do baker in a medium-sized town. She finished high school and was interested in going further in her studies. But her father died, the family was ruined by the war, and she had to go to work. She worked first in another agency of the Ministry but was transferred to the Paris branch of the Clerical Agency when classed as a civil servant. She hopes she will not stay. Like Mrs. Axx, she is a typist at the light accounting machine in the special workroom, though not in the same section.

This is what she said of her work:

It is very monotonous. . . . In the morning I have to type Series X and in the afternoon Series Y. It is quite painful. I am a sort of dreamer. . . . It is so mechanical; I am living in a different world; I never think about my work; you know it is a way of evading. . . .

Actually, it does not have the slightest interest. Sometimes I wondered. What meaning does it have? . . . One does not have the same personality here. Here in public administration, one loses one's own personality.

About pride in work:

Where I was before it was sometimes possible to be proud of one's work, but here I do not see any possibility; if it were not for the chance to daydream, one could go mad. For my colleagues, for everyone around me, it is the same. If I could have done something else—but I had to go to work right away. . . .

About conscientiousness at work:

My principle is that, whatever the work, it must be well done. I do not like making errors. But my own feeling is that the employees' zeal does not count much in running the organization. We are just like trained animals. Work has become completely mechanical, we are functioning just out of habit. . . . We do not need supervision. Once the supervisor was away, and nobody noticed it.

And about her own aptitudes:

I do not think I have learned anything here.

THE DECISIVE INFLUENCE OF SOCIAL STATUS

Our third main point, the decisive influence of social status in the employees' attitudes toward work, seems to show by far the most unexpected aspects. Work satisfaction is usually related first to the job itself, its content, and status, and, second, to a smaller extent, to the age and seniority of the employees (the elder and senior employees being, on the average, more satisfied). Among our interviewees we certainly find quite a difference between the team leaders and the other girls[24]—but no difference at all introduced by age and seniority. Actually, the social status of the employees outside the organization—a factor that is rarely conspicuous—appears to have a predominant influence here. And finally, if one combines the employee's status on the job (being a team leader or not) and her social status outside work (being middle class or not), one can predict with great accuracy the attitudes toward work.

Work satisfaction appears to be the simple result of the congruence of the expectations of the employee, corresponding to her social status, with the actuality, or at least the prestige, of her job.

We classified the girls in two rough categories, middle class and working class, according to their comments about their parents, their husbands, their friends, their education, and their way of life.[25]

[24] This difference is statistically significant at $p < 01.00$. For a review of all researches on this subject see Herzberg *et al., op. cit.*

[25] For example, the following were considered working-class:

A thirty-year-old woman, daughter of a Parisian garage mechanic, with a primary-school education, married to a skilled worker in a large suburban factory, living with their child in a two-room flat with no bath.

A young girl, daughter of a peasant miner in the southwest, with her junior-high-school diploma, living in Paris in a Salvation Army Home.

A twenty-five-year-old woman, daughter of a road-mender, with a primary-school education, married to a subway worker, living with their child in a hotel room, having entered the Branch as an *auxiliaire*.

These employees were considered middle class:

A young girl, daughter of a local postmaster, having passed the baccalaureate and the *contrôleur* examination, living in Paris in a special home for girls.

The first category corresponds to a middle-class or *petit bourgeois* orientation and the second to a working-class orientation. According to such criteria, two-thirds of the interviewees are working class and one-third are middle class. Almost all working-class girls like their work. Ninety per cent of them fall in the two first categories and none in the last (i.e., those who do not like their work at all). Among the middle class, on the contrary, 50 per cent are clearly dissatisfied. But the difference is still greater. The working-class girls like their jobs, whether they are team leaders or not: among the middle-class girls, almost only the team leaders like their jobs (80 per cent of those who have team leader status like their jobs, against only 20 per cent among their colleagues).[26]

Knowing these two status criteria—status on the job and outside the job—makes it possible to predict work satisfaction in 85 per cent of the cases. In the remaining 15 per cent, acute personal problems account for a good many of the "errors." Such clean-cut determinism can very rarely be observed. That it should appear with factors that usually do not operate is even more puzzling. Certainly it is not opposed to well-accepted hypotheses on work psychology. It is especially in accord with the discussion by Roethlisberger, Christensen, and a Zaleznik of the balance of rewards which individuals will seek in their employment,[27] and even more with George Homans' notion of congruence of the different aspects of work status.[28] Homans, of course, was referring only to congruence between the different aspects of one's work situation, and not between on-the-job and outside-the-job status elements. We could, however, extend his interpretation and state the hypothesis that, in our case, status discrepancies between the role on the job and that outside the job are so important that they obliterate all other influences.

There are many reasons for the development of such a situation. First, one can point to the very small number of roles available in the

---

A young woman, daughter of a civil servant of middle rank, having completed high school (but without a baccalaureate), married to a civil servant of the same middle rank, living in a small flat in Paris near the branch.

Finally, as a rare but not isolated example of an employee of *bourgeois* status: A young girl from a formerly well-to-do provincial family who had to find a job after her father's death and who is preparing a higher-level *concours* in a students' home, where she lives with some additional money from her family.

[26] All these differences are of course statistically significant at less than the 0.01 level ($P < .01$).

[27] A. Zaleznik, C. Christensen, and F. J. Roethlisberger, *The Motivation Productivity and Satisfaction of Workers* (Boston: Harvard Business School, 1958), *passim* and especially pp. 54–55.

[28] George C. Homans, "Status among Clerical Workers," *Human Organization,* XII, No. 1 (1953), 5–19. See also Stuart N. Adams, "Status Congruence as a Variable in Small Group Performance," *Social Forces,* XXXII, No. 1 (1953), 16–22.

Agency and to the rather great differences between them. Thus discrepancies between on-the-job status and outside-the-job status appear immediately and cannot be obscured by the complexity of the work hierarchy. Second, one can emphasize the unusually great number of employees with a higher status outside the job. Third, the employees' general youth tends to decrease involvement in the job.[29] But one can also argue that these influences converge finally with another and more decisive one, i.e., the central importance of status in a bureaucratic and stratified organization like the Clerical Agency.[30]

This last hypothesis brings us within the perspective of interpersonal and intergroup relationships. It implies that one must go beyond individual analysis of work satisfaction to try to understand the way employees participate in the social system formed by their organization. We may conclude, for the moment, that the malaise and difficulties found in the Clerical Agency do not stem from the consequences that technological givens have on the employees' psychology, since even work satisfaction cannot be explained unless more complex sociological data are utilized.

[29] This argument seems to run counter to our remark that seniority does not have influence. One can, however, very well argue that the lack of influence of seniority on the individual does not mean that the average young age and low seniority of the staff as a whole do not have decisive importance for diminishing its commitment to its task.

[30] We note that the more or less conscious policy of the Ministry, consisting of trying to recruit more and more employees of a higher level of education—i.e., for the moment at least, of a higher social status—will tend to increase the human relations strains in the Agency, since girls with such background are those who have the most difficulties in adjusting satisfactorily to their task and environment.

Chapter Two

INTERPERSONAL AND INTERGROUP
RELATIONSHIPS AND THE PROBLEM
OF ROUTINE

EMPLOYEES' SOCIAL PARTICIPATION AND INTEGRATION

There is a definite contrast between employees' attitudes toward work and their job and their attitudes and behavior in terms of social participation within the organization. The girls working in the Clerical Agency do not dislike their jobs more than the employees in other large-scale administrative organizations dislike theirs; but a general climate of apathy and social isolation such as prevails in the branch is very uncommon. The girls do not manifest any pride in belonging to the Agency or to their branch. They are not interested in participating or getting involved in any way in the branch life. Furthermore, they do not seem to interact much among themselves when on the job, nor to be able to form stable supportive clique relationships. Finally, the kind of solidarity that does develop is expressed against the higher-ups and the formal structure of the Agency.

EMPLOYEES' EVALUATIONS OF THE AGENCY

Comments on the branch were most unfavorable. We asked our interviewees the usual type of questions about their administrative organization's being a good place to work.[1] Sixty per cent of them responded negatively, while only one out of seven interviewees presented positive comments. Moreover—contrary to the usual pattern —the senior employees were much more critical than the newer ones, and the positive comments came from those with the least sen-

[1] The following questions were asked: "What do you think of the employees' situation in the branch?" "Would you advise a friend to come to work in the branch?" "If you could start all over again, would you come to work for the branch?"

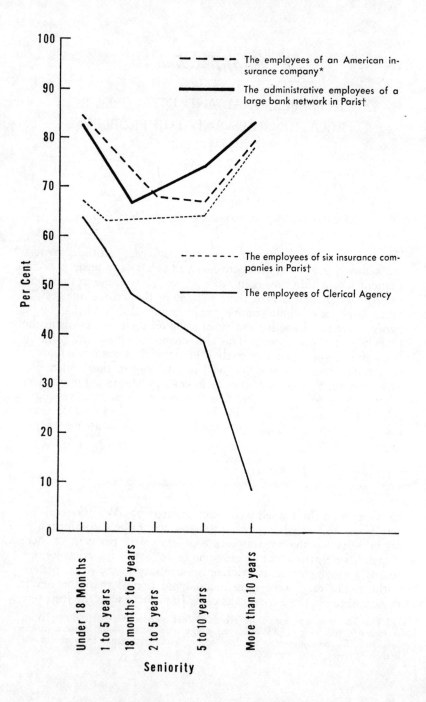

The employees of an American insurance company*

The administrative employees of a large bank network in Paris†

The employees of six insurance companies in Paris†

The employees of Clerical Agency

Per Cent

Under 18 Months

1 to 5 years

18 months to 5 years

2 to 5 years

5 to 10 years

More than 10 years

Seniority

iority. In most private companies or public administrations, the overall judgments of the employees on the organization, as well as feelings of belonging and pride in the organization, appear to follow a sort of learning curve if they are analyzed according to the employees' seniority. After a sizable drop during the first few years, corresponding to the scaling down of the first expectations, the curve gradually rises with seniority. In the Parisian branch of the Agency, however, the decline of the curve is continuous and sharp.[2]

The girls, as we have already mentioned, complain mostly about the work load, the pressure of work, and the nervous tension that pervades the whole climate of the branch. When asked more specifically about the branch, they comment about two things: the material conditions of the environment, and the behavior of the higher-ups.

Complaints about the building underline the bareness, the lack of amenities, and the poor standards of maintenance. Usually the complaints are phrased more as a sort of emotional grudge—"They do not care for us"—than as a direct grievance. Typical of these feelings is the daydreaming of one girl:

If only it were possible to have better ventilation. . . . From the outside it is modern enough, but I feel it is barren and sad. I would like to see a garden with flowers around the building, just like in modern hospitals. Now it looks like an army barracks. They do the barest minimum: there are washbasins but no towels; the closets are too small, and in the infirmary there are only three beds; when I was sick I had to keep standing; they told me I was not in a hospital. . . . They do not care for us.[3]

A feeling of animosity against the higher-ups, who are held responsible, is implicit in this interview. In other interviews such animosity is explicit and forms the core of the employees' grievances. Significantly, complaints are never directed at specific individuals, but toward "management" or toward the still vaguer "they." Prima-

[2] The questions used were not exactly the same and the height of the curves, i.e., the amount of positive comments, cannot be compared seriously; but the shape of the curves, i.e., the influence of seniority, can be.
[3] This last was said with much emphasis.

Fig. 1.—Employee approval coefficient as a function of seniority and type of organization. The questions used were not exactly the same in each factory, and the heights of the curves (i.e., the amounts of positive comments) cannot really be compared, but the shapes of the curves (i.e., the influence of seniority) can be.
* Graph established from the results of a survey made by the Survey Research Center, University of Michigan; see Nancy Morse, *Satisfactions in the White-Collar Job* (Ann Arbor: Institute for Social Research, 1953), p. 79.
† Surveys made by the author in 1957 and 1958. Results to be published.

rily, the employees of the branch feel abandoned and do not know to whom they can complain.[4]

As one of them says:

Whatever the difficulties, there is still much progress that could be made. . . . Work is very hard for the employees. They could do much more but they do not try to know about the situation; they are not interested, they are men behind their own desks; nothing can move them. We have real grievances, but they do not care. The unions complain too much and they are not listened to, but it shouldn't matter; we don't get anything settled.[5]

This general disgust is strong enough to affect even the feelings toward the Civil Service. Characteristically, the girls refuse to identify with the "fonctionnaires"; although there is not the slightest ambiguity in their status, they do not consider themselves civil servants. A civil servant, to them, is a man behind a desk who does not have too much to do. They are hard-pressed workers and have nothing to do with these people, who are so severely criticized by the public at large.

I do not feel I am a civil servant [says one of them]. People· say so many unpleasant things about them, I will never boast that I am one.

This lack of solidarity is striking for two reasons. It does not exist in public administrative organizations where employees doing comparable routine work have been studied; and at one time the Department to which the Agency belongs was well known for its *esprit de corps*. Old-timers in the branch report a different climate before World War II. It is also noticeable that a minority of employees (20 per cent of the total), usually older or of provincial origin, adhere strictly to the old pattern. In other words, they feel they are civil servants, have a high regard for public service and defend the *fonctionnaires* whenever the public criticizes them, and, finally, would like to have their children work as civil servants. For these employees this strong identification seems to be a very efficient integrative force: they consistently have much higher morale than their colleagues.[6]

[4] Nathan Leites has attributed great importance to the feeling of being abandoned which he says pervades the fabric of French social life. Whatever the truth of his contentions at a deeper level, it is significant that in a number of Parisian private organizations where we asked the same questions as in this Parisian public administration Agency, we never found it expressed, at least in such a prominent way. See Nathan Leites, "L'Obsession du Mal," mimeographed report (Paris: Ecole Pratique des Hautes Etudes, 1960).

[5] The reader will have noted the number of *they's*, and this lapidary sentence "they are men behind their own desks," which was said in an extremely bitter tone.

[6] Especially as regards work satisfaction, relationships with the supervisors, problems of discipline, and the over-all judgment on the branch.

SOCIAL ISOLATION AND THE LACK OF FRIENDSHIP TIES

The poor morale and the disintegration of the old-fashioned *esprit fonctionnaire* can easily be understood. However, the lack of friendship ties among a personnel made up of young and lively girls is curious. Nevertheless, interviews indicate that there is such a lack. Forty per cent of the interviewees say that they have no friends at all in the branch. Another 40 per cent say that while they may have friends in the branch, they prefer to have their friends outside. Only 20 per cent feel positively about their workmates as potential friends. The flavor of the comments we get are even more striking:

From a thirty-year-old working-class girl from Brittany:

I have my friends on the outside. Here in the branch one cannot get to be friends as in a small office.

From a thirty-year-old working-class girl from Paris:

I have my friends more outside. I would not like having friends here. . . . I may see some of them (my colleagues) outside work, but they are not actually friends, but acquaintances only.

From a twenty-year-old lower-middle-class girl from Paris:

We are work pals but not friends. We do not say "tu" to each other. In the work team everything is fine, although there are always jealousies, you know. . . . I have my friends outside. I would not like to have my friends here. I am not so sociable, and then most of the girls come from the country; it is not the same.

From a twenty-eight-year-old middle-class girl from the southwest:

It is only at the work team level that one can get to be friends. Anyway here I have work pals but not really friends. It is difficult to make friends.

On the other hand, the girls who make only positive comments are not so specific. A forty-year-old middle-class trade unionist is very positive.

I have most of my friends here. Sometimes we go out together. I fancy I know everybody in the branch.

But most others are not. For example, a thirty-year-old working-class team leader recently arrived in Paris:

Most girls are young. One can joke easily. The atmosphere is good. I have had to make new friends. I have made them here. Some girls go out together but I personally cannot because I live too far.

The lack of enthusiasm must be viewed in relation to the numerous social activities outside the branch that the girls report having.

Thirty per cent go to the theater at least once a month, which is a much higher percentage than has been found in general surveys or in comparable private or nationalized organizations.[7] Two-thirds of the girls said that they regularly went with friends to the movies and the theater, dancing, camping, and so on.

To understand these differences, we made a systematic comparison of the girls' comments. We used two criteria: one represented the intensity of reported interaction inside the branch; the other, the amount of reported social activities outside it. These criteria were, of course, especially rough. Their comparisons gave us, however, an interesting cue.

When working-class girls report activities outside, they also always have friends in the branch. Half of the middle-class girls, however, report having no friends at all in the branch, while having many social activities outside.

The jobs which the girls hold furnish a second cue. Almost none of the team leaders denied having friends in the branch. The middle-class girls who made positive comments about their workmates as possible friends were team leaders (half of them) and a few senior employees from the special workroom.

We find here again, in the domain of interpersonal relationships, the same kind of rigid determinism we saw operating for work satisfaction. Both variables, of course, are closely related, much more than is usual. Girls who have friends in the branch are more likely to like their work.[8]

These very suggestive findings should have been analyzed much more closely. It would have been very rewarding, for example, to probe much further into the system of interaction within the workroom by direct observation and re-interviewing. This was not possible, however; and we will present only the following hypothesis of interpretation.

The fact that interpersonal relations are confined to interactions within the small work team seems natural in such a system of work organization, considering the lack of interdependence between the teams, the pressure for productivity, the shift system, and the impor-

---

[7] According to a general unpublished survey of 1954 kindly communicated to us by the *Institut Français d'Opinion Publique*, Paris. In the Agency, regular theater was considered a significant social activity, in so far as it is perceived as one of the most important ways to participate in the middle-class culture. Girls very rarely go alone and they use the event as a center of sociability. The interest in the theater may be explained by the attraction provincial girls often feel for a specifically "Parisian" activity. Sixty per cent of them say they prefer living in Paris because of the numerous possibilities of social and cultural activities offered by the capital. Michel Crozier, "Employés et petits fonctionnaires: Note sur le loisir," *Esprit*, June, 1959.

[8] Statistically significant at less than the 0.01 level.

tance of overtime.[9] But this makes it difficult for the girls to evade the world of work. Since the rigid determinism of the work system must match the equally rigid determinism of social status—which is very strong, because of the wide differences between the girls and the general emphasis on status that we have noticed—the amount of interaction will be rather low and solid supportive cliques will be rare. This situation also makes it clear that the team leader has a decisive social role, whatever her own personal qualities, and leads to the surprising fact that only when occupying this position can middle-class girls find a reasonably good pattern of adjustment to their jobs.

THE NEGATIVE SOLIDARITY OF THE PERSONNEL AND THE EXTENT OF UNION ACTIVITIES

Employees, we have seen, do not identify themselves with the Civil Service, they are not interested in the purposes and the functioning of their organization, and they feel completely neglected. This moral isolation is not compensated by a warm atmosphere of friendship ties derived from belonging to a cohesive and diversified group. Thus individuals are left quite on their own, with the only possible support being that of their small work team. This isolation, however, forms only one side of the employees' social relationships. One must recognize the existence, at a deeper level, of a strong group solidarity —albeit a negative one. It is manifested against the branch as an institution, against management, at times even against trade unions— but never positively.

We have already quoted one sharp but representative characterization of the managers: "these men behind their desks." The branch as an institution is the main subject of the bitter yet supportive small talk of the employees. We obtained a good view of it in the interviews. Almost all interviewees, even when relatively satisfied, sooner or later made certain characteristic jokes. For example, starting to talk about the commercial success of the branch, a girl says:

> It works very well for the customers, but not for the employees. Everything customers get, they get at the expense of the employees.

A wise, placid, middle-aged woman tells the interviewer:

> It is a sort of disciplinary camp, a reformatory, it should be reserved for mischievous people.

[9] Employees do not have opportunities to know each other well enough from one shift to the other. They do not have to communicate from one work team to another. Then, because of the over-all pressure, they compete against each other to finish early. The necessity to work overtime when one is late tends to isolate each team still more.

Another girl, twenty-five years old, from Paris, tells with many details a current story about two naïve farm boys who see hundreds of girls leaving the branch. The first one insists that "it is the famous cannery X.," and the second one that it could be only the "Vaugirard packing house" (both references, of course, being very derogatory about the branch's type of white-collar employment).

A Parisian middle-aged working-class woman banters:

One must be proud of working at the branch. We have had the honor of newspaper coverage. This is just like the gallows, a really well-known place.

Unions are considered most of the time with the same angry disregard.[10] The majority of the employees (60 per cent of the interviewees) say they are necessary, but most of them say it grudgingly, making unfavorable comments.

One respectable and respected old-timer tells us, for example:

They care too much about politics and not enough about the staff.

A young Parisian supporter of Mendès-France[11] is more bitter:

I am fed up with their kind of deals. Unions are necessary—but this is one kind of exploitation against another kind.

Another old-timer expresses her distrust:

They do whatever is possible, but of course without forgetting their own interest. . . . Disinterested people—you know, I do not believe they exist.

Younger girls echo her:

They talk well and loud but they are not sincere. One finds only porkchoppers or political thrusters in the union nowadays. They mind their own business, not ours.

Solid trade unionists are not only rare—they are even quite critical. One of them, for example, after a few comments reiterating her faith in trade-union action, adds:

[10] Unionism has been very strong in the Department to which the Agency belongs for almost fifty years; although weaker in the Agency itself because of its predominantly feminine composition, it was quite successful in the twenties and thirties, when a large number of militants fought for peace and cultural promotion as well as for professional advancement. At the Liberation, the whole staff was unionized, although only a few years later the union movement was hopelessly divided into five unions—very jealous of each other, extremely competitive, and unable to co-operate.

[11] The survey was made in 1954, some time before Mendès-France came to power. We had not asked political questions, but this girl talked spontaneously about her political sympathies.

But we are defended by men[12] who do not understand the situation of women workers very well and are not able to talk the language of the average girl.

And even the most favorable talk about the way things should be and not the way they are or are going to be is rather lukewarm:

Unions should have a lot more say. We should have shop stewards with a lot of free time so that they can get in touch with everybody.

This general feeling of negative solidarity was very well expressed in the strike that took place in 1953, exactly eight months before the interviews. This strike was not the outcome of a dispute restricted to the branch, but a part—and a small part—of a successful general strike of all civil servants in France. But if the girls at the branch did not take the initiative, they certainly seized the opportunity to express with great eagerness their pent-up discontent. In that respect, it is characteristic that the girls who had struck, when interviewed eight months later, talked most of the time about the strike as if they had forgotten that it was a general strike and remembered it only as their own personal strike. At any rate, it had taken a bitter turn at the branch and had lasted almost one full month, with about half of the girls striking till the very end.

We asked the girls whether they had been strikers and whether they had struck until the end. We also asked them for their comments on the way the strike had been run and about its results.

The Agency officials in the Ministry thought of the strike as a trade-union affair and presented us with the usual stereotypes about strikers as hotheads and poor workers excited by trade-union agitators. Our interviews made it possible to check interpretations of the strike more accurately. To our own surprise, the results were extremely unambiguous. The simplest cross-tabulations showed clearly that the girls who stayed on strike until the last minute were (1) the team leaders (all of them but one), and (2) the people attached to their work who had favorable attitudes toward friendship ties in the branch.[13] All staunch trade unionists, of course, had struck; but otherwise there was no relationship between feelings toward the unions and participation in the strike. Strikers were not hotheads;

[12] At the branch level, there are no permanent shop stewards and not even one permanent union official. All union functions are carried out by voluntary service, and most of the time by the young *inspecteurs-adjoints* or eventually by *inspecteurs* whose work load is much lighter than that of the employees. But this means that in a personnel 80 per cent feminine, most union jobs are held by men, who are not likely to spend the major part of their career at the branch and who are sure to have a supervisory future. There are female union delegates in certain workrooms, but this is very informal, and no real recognition has been sought for them by the unions.

[13] All these relationships are statistically significant at less than the 0.01 level.

on the contrary, they were the most responsible and best workers. This was corroborated by a cross-tabulation with the evaluations supervisors had made of them. Seventy-seven per cent of the girls considered excellent by their supervisors struck until the end; only 33 per cent of those considered merely good workers and 20 per cent of those considered mediocre stayed out as long.[14]

Trade unions were relatively satisfied with the results of the strike, but according to their comments employees must have been extremely disappointed that this great event of branch life, to which there were still constant references the following year, had not brought them anything constructive. The strike may have been carried on within the framework of the trade unions as institutions, but in a larger perspective it seems to have been far more the expression of another and much stronger negative solidarity. The fact that it first attracted the best workers, the better-adjusted and better-integrated employees, suggests that the amount of negative feeling toward the branch is amazingly high and will sabotage all possible attempts at founding a more lively community.[15]

Authority Relationships

We have so far described the staff of the Clerical Agency merely as a huge undifferentiated mass with poor morale, very little involvement in the affairs of the organization, and no participation in its goals. We have depicted it as evincing no solidarity except in a few hostile outbursts, and as expressing generally negative feelings toward the Agency's administration.

Members of higher management are not unaware of this *malaise*, although officially they deny it. They try, however, to explain it away by blaming the immediate supervisors. They believe that the cause of the poor morale of the employees—besides the monotony of the task itself—can be found in the supervisors' poor handling of human relations at the primary level. Furthermore, they believe that

---

[14] The terms "excellent," "adequate," and "mediocre" were, of course, inflated; but their application was reviewed with the supervisors by the interviewer personally, and it may be accepted as a reasonable approximation of the supervisors' feeling, if one understands "excellent" as "good," "adequate" as "mediocre," and "mediocre" as "poor"; 60 per cent of the employees were rated "excellent," 13 per cent "adequate," and 26 per cent "mediocre."

[15] To be sure, this strike was also an attempt at another kind of action. It carried the hope or the illusion of founding a new and different order in which the positive participation of subordinates could be possible. But its actual meaning, both vis-à-vis the agency and vis-à-vis the union, did not go beyond the negative moment of this rebuilding process.

it would be almost as difficult to change this situation as to change the work process, since the Agency cannot recruit people of high enough caliber as supervisors. There remains, therefore, only the "solution" of delivering speeches and written instructions advising supervisors to pay more attention to the duties of leadership. This possibility is one of which management avails itself sporadically and with some self-consciousness.

The basic assumption behind these feelings is that there is a great deal of tension at the primary level of authority relationships. Thus, this first link of organizational activity is the weakest, although it should be the strongest.

This point of view, of course, is not original. In many widely different kinds of organizations, higher management blames all human problems arising at the shop level on the first-line supervisors. But in the present case, the gap between management's assumptions and the way the situation is viewed by supervisors and employees is especially striking.

The results of the survey did not show the pattern of tension that management expected. Relationships between employees and supervisors are, at least superficially, cordial. Moreover, these relationships do not seem to matter very much to the employees. Certainly, almost one-fourth of the employees complain about their supervisors. However, we obtained the same or a higher percentage in other, similar public and private organizations—36 per cent in a survey covering six insurance companies, 31 per cent in the administrative services of a large-scale bank, 24 per cent in another public agency.[16]

We had asked several questions: "What do you think of first-line supervisors?" "Will *your* supervisors go to bat for you?" "Are they friendly with you?" "Could you trust them?" The first question is general, the others more specific. They were never directed toward one individual, since the employees interviewed had to deal with two different supervisors. The questions elicited many comments, often rich and well balanced—but surprisingly enough, almost never emotional or even personal. Our respondents remained within the functional frame of reference they were given;[17] they took great pains to express themselves clearly and moderately; they were often sharp, but did not lose their tempers or their tolerance.

---

[16] These figures cannot be compared exactly, since the results were not obtained in the same way. Two of them come from oral interviews with closed-ended questions, and one from written questionnaires (the second public agency), while the results of the Clerical Agency were obtained, as the reader already knows, from free interviews.

[17] This is very rarely the case when one is using this kind of question, and we wanted to elicit more personal comments.

For example, one of the sharpest answers by a serious, experienced woman[18] who had a great deal to say:

> Generally, I think they [the supervisors] worry too much about their career and possibilities of promotion. They are jealous and awfully competitive. They are also sectarian. Often there is a lot of hostility between sections, and they are all responsible for it; each one of them wants to have his little kingdom. . . . They are too far above the actual work problems to understand what is actually going on. . . . I do not think they understand clearly how the work is done; they miss most of it— and most of what people feel too.
>
> They should be less numerous. The role of the *inspecteur* is not clear enough. Section chiefs have to take responsibilities, but the *inspecteur* never has to.

And when asked whether the supervisors would go to bat for employees:

> Supervisors defend us inasmuch as they think it will help them. If not, they would eventually trample on the employees. Our own section chief is very self-seeking.
>
> They are moody, very distant and cold with some employees, almost intimate with others. In the last analysis, relationships are not bad; one feels free toward them and I myself do not scruple to tell them what I think.
>
> They never talk with us about work. They say hello once in a while, convinced they will never have to learn anything, although I feel they could benefit most from contact.

It seems clear that this employee is very critical of her section chief. She is, at the same time, perceptive and rather tolerant. She analyzes the situation of a supervisor as if she were able to forget her own stake in the relationship.

Such detachment is quite common. The criticisms leveled against the supervisors by their own staff sound as though they had been made by an impartial committee. We found three major themes running through their comments:

1. The supervisors have no skill in human relations. They do not know how to deal with women.

2. They do not like to take responsibility.

3. They are not competent. They do not know how to organize or how to run a section. This last criticism is sometimes accompanied by extenuating explanations—e.g., how could they know, they have had no experience; they have just arrived and have had no training.

At any rate, a content analysis of the answers corroborates the direct results of the survey. It allows us to state that nothing in these

[18] She was classified among the 25 per cent complaining against their supervisors.

relationships reminds us of a situation of dependence and of the emotional feelings involved with one. The girls give the impression of not being embarrassed around the supervisors, who may have many shortcomings but are not awe-inspiring.

This lack of involvement is further shown in investigations of the characteristics of those who complain about their supervisors. If this relationship had much importance for them, employees unhappy about it would show a set of common traits corresponding to the unfavorable influence of this problem on their "morale" and the possibilities of a good kind of adjustment. But unexpectedly, feelings toward supervisors do not appear to be the central preoccupation of the employees. There are sharper and more significant cleavages about such an impersonal feature as discipline. Feelings toward supervisors have an important influence only on very young employees, especially those from higher social backgrounds, whose dissatisfaction is associated with poor morale.[19]

Authority relationships at the first level can therefore be considered as tolerant, reasonably cordial, and not at all tense. Against this rather moderate background, the comments made by the employees about their division heads, i.e., the second-line supervisors, appear unexpectedly personal.

We had asked only one question: "What do you think of the big bosses?"[20] Forty-four per cent of the interviewees made no comments. They stated that, having had no direct relationships with them, they could not make any fair evaluations. But 28 per cent gave sharply hostile comments, such as:

He is a no-good, he is a real skunk, they are very harsh.

Or showed some highly emotional fear:

He makes me feel helpless, paralyzed.
I have seen him only once, with a delegation, but I understood right away. He prevents people from saying anything. I could not speak one word. He did not let us explain. . . . I do not want to see him, I feel paralyzed.

Besides this group of violently hostile employees, a smaller group (9 per cent) were moderately critical, and a group of 20 per cent were favorable.

[19] Girls with some seniority have the same attitudes toward supervisors, whatever their social background. But recently arrived girls dislike their supervisors much more when they are from a higher social background, and this attitude coincides with other negative attitudes toward work ($P < .01$ level), toward discipline ($P < .01$), and toward the Civil Service ($P < .01$). This is more striking since supervisors clearly mark their preference for recruiting girls with a better social background.

[20] "Big bosses" was used by employees to mean the division heads, and this question was never ambiguous.

Favorable comments came only from girls who had been personally received by their division head in cases in which they were given satisfaction. An audience of this type, we must note, could be told with a reference to the hostile consensual background:

He was very understanding: I do not understand why all the girls are so terrified.

Such a comment is made by a trade-union girl, who is nonetheless critical of the functioning of the organization.

Finally, among the many employees who refused to answer, there were quite a number of girls who spoke again of this general consensus, but this time in an approving way.

One of them said, for example:

I have had no contact with them, but according to what one hears around I do not trust them.

Another one added:

I never saw him and I like it better that way, since one sees him only to get a scolding.

A third echoed them:

I have had no contacts with them. They come around only when they have something to complain about.[21]

The focus of hierarchical tensions, therefore, does not seem to be the face-to-face relationship with the immediate supervisors. It appears, rather, to be the more remote, indirect relationship between employees and the second-line supervisors. It seems to be no problem for the working group of one hundred employees to deal with the small supervising staff they see all day long. There are few traces of dependence and of the emotionality usually associated with it. But at the one-thousand-employee organizational level, on the contrary, workers feel that it is very difficult to approach the responsible division head, and they seem to be extremely emotional about it.

Initially, this situation may seem very puzzling. It certainly was startling for the researcher, as well as for higher management, but, like many other survey results, it seems self-evident after the survey has been analyzed. It could have been predicted from the beginning, if the very peculiar way in which the hierarchical system of organization functions had been properly placed.

We have already described the quasi-militaristic chain of command with the division head on top, the section chief and the *inspecteurs* in the middle, and almost no functional staff. The divi-

---

[21] Four other interviewees express this last idea in almost exactly the same terms.

sion head has only two senior section chiefs to help him. Yet he has to make all decisions necessary to the functioning of the division—not only the general decisions, such as fixing new goals to co-ordinate the sections' operations, and prescribing new ways of working. He also must make the specific decisions pertaining to the daily life of the employees that affect problems of work—e.g., the possibility of postponing a number of operations when the section is delayed—as well as discipline and other personnel problems.

Placed in such a situation, division heads have neither the capability nor the desire to delegate their responsibilities. Thus they have the final word on a multitude of trivial matters—e.g., whether or not to allow an employee one day off for personal convenience, or whether to blame an employee who has made errors in posting an operation. Since they themselves, even with the help of their two assistants, cannot possibly have an adequate knowledge of what is involved, they must rely heavily on the information they receive from the section chiefs. The section chiefs, however, are not in a position to provide reliable information. All ten of them are running parallel identical units that have to compete for scarce resources. Therefore, they have no relationships of interdependence and no common positive interests among themselves, and tend to view each other only as competitors. Thus they are likely, first, to bias the information they give in order to get the maximum of material resources and personal favors with which to run their sections smoothly; and, second, to put pressure on the division head to prevent him from entering into a close relationship with another colleague and to favor the latter over them.

As a result, division heads are condemned to get only unreliable information and to remain isolated from the daily problems of work. Their decisions tend to be impersonal routine decisions, i.e., decisions based on the letter of the rules and not on equity. The only possible exceptions are a few, more personal decisions resulting from chance encounters from an informal network of information—and these decisions will very likely be the cause of accusations of favoritism.

In view of the pressures arising from this kind of arrangement, one should not be surprised to discover that the employees blame the division heads, while remaining tolerant of the first-line supervisory staff. The latter are well situated to placate their subordinates by pretending to do whatever they can to defend them against the harshness of an impersonal system manifest in the division head. Indeed, it is interesting that the only really discriminating item in the comments of the employees relating to their first-line supervisors concerns this problem of defending subordinates. The girls do not trust their supervisors very much; 44 per cent of them say that it is very difficult to know, and only 12 per cent seem to trust them completely. A solid discrimination could be made, finally, on the negative side, where the decisive argument was, "My supervisor will surely not go to bat for us," and not "He is harsh."

This pattern of relationship, however, cannot be understood only through analyzing the point of view of the subordinates. We now need to broaden our perspective by entering the supervisors' world.

The Supervisors' Predicament

To understand the supervisors' behavior and feelings, one has to take into account their past careers, their expectations of the future, and the present roles—both formal and informal—that have been assigned to them within the organization. In the present case, determinism seems especially strong, inasmuch as all the pressures tend roughly in the same direction.

Supervisors are almost all men. They start, as we have already mentioned, as *inspecteurs-adjoints*. This job is considered a nonsupervisory job, and for all purposes they are treated as ordinary employees by the management. But in career terms certainly they are from the beginning members of the hierarchy, since their promotion to the first supervisory job, that of *inspecteur*, will take place automatically after they have attained a given seniority. Such a contradiction would not be very important if their term as *inspecteurs-adjoints* were short and could be viewed as a sort of training period. Since, however, it now lasts at least twelve years, one must assign a decisive formative value to it.

The main characteristics of the *inspecteurs-adjoints'* situation are the following: first, they are extremely well protected against favoritism and any justifiable or undue interference from the higher-ups, since there cannot be any exception to the seniority rules that govern their career at this stage. Then, too, their job is neither challenging nor interesting. Third, they do not have to care about their own supervisor's judgment of their performance, for this judgment cannot possibly have any effects on their career—it does not even have much relevance professionally, since their task does not prepare them in any direct way for the supervisory job. These conditions are the very best one could imagine for fostering a strong collective defensive spirit. Indeed, the *inspecteurs-adjoints* have achieved a great deal of independence within the protective framework of the rules that oppress them. Nothing can be done against them, whatever the grievances management may have against them;[22] thus they feel free to devote themselves to whatever type of hobby suits them. One can find among them sports addicts, semi-professional painters, and would-be poets and novelists—not to mention the more frequent type, the Don Juans. Many of them study hard to pass some administrative higher examinations. Others, whose prestige usually is high, are the informal leaders of the unions. This is, in a way, a very eager and resourceful group, but it does not usually participate in the achievement of the goals of the organization—and when it does, it is on very critical and non-constructive terms. Its members, when in the unions, are likely to be active more from general questions of principle than from motives of grievance. Their leadership is often inspiring, but it tends to lead people away from work problems and concrete achievements.

Inspecteurs-adjoints are promoted to *inspecteurs* when they are over thirty, sometimes at thirty-five. At that stage of their life and after such training, they are likely to have used up a great deal of their drive for action. They are now beginning to feel the pressure of the competition for promotion. Although there is now, in theory, ample scope for arbitrary choices by management, seniority still cannot easily be by-passed, and then only if the trade unions do not object too strongly. Therefore, the already very strong pattern of collective defense that had been formed early, at the *inspecteurs-adjoints* level, will continue to be as strong as ever after they are given supervisory responsibilities and are in sight of the management career ladder.

The skill he has acquired at avoiding any unnecessary involvement, at keeping out of trouble, and at putting all the blame on the higher-ups will very much help the new *inspecteur* in his job. Certainly, he will become more moderate in his opinions, at least in their expression; the skeptical aspect of his refusal to participate will take on greater importance than the idealist one. But basically his relationship with management will stay the same: he remains on the defensive; he refuses to be involved with management objectives; he relies on the group and watches his peers as jealously as they watch him to prevent any break in the solid egalitarian front they form against the interference of superiors.

This pattern will still hold ten years later, when many *inspecteurs* have been promoted to section chiefs. At that stage, the competition for a career may be more eager, but although the fight may be bitter, the stakes are not very great. It is true that only a minority will be

[22] Because of their ebullience or because of their violent trade-union and political activities.

promoted to the next step, and that very few will have the chance to become division heads. But the fundamental peer-group relationship will not be broken, because the ways of succeeding do not involve playing favorites at the work level. Certainly, being involved in trouble would prevent promotion; but successful performance in the work does not help very much. Promotion, according to the supervisors, depends on outside influences. This is very much resented, but in a way it helps to keep the system quite stable. Participating in cliques centering outside the agency[23] is not viewed as such a direct threat as a close relationship with the division head. The group prefers to ignore and criticize these outside influences, rather than to see direct competition on the job. This helps it to keep its own cohesion much better and protects every section chief against his division head.

The Ministry's behavior tends to reinforce this pattern. It resists vigorously any pretensions of the section chief to a part in managerial prerogatives. As we have already seen, it does not leave the section chiefs much initiative on either personnel or on work organization matters. Materially, it does not want to give them the status of supervisors. At the time they were interviewed, the section chiefs' main demand was to have management give them, when modernizing the workrooms, separate cubby-holes with real supervisors' desks. Management successfully resisted their request by affirming that they did not have to be isolated from their subordinates.

No wonder that the section chiefs tend to side with their employees! They have nothing to gain by assuming a managerial attitude. And defending their employees, or at least putting on a show of defending them, gives them a chance of fostering a better climate and may even please management by keeping them out of trouble. They prefer—and one easily sympathizes with them—to have cordial relationships with their subordinates at the expense of the division head than to assume, in place of their superiors, responsibilities which the latter refuse to relinquish.

It is also not surprising that the Ministry views the supervisors as apathetic and unreliable. They are, as a matter of fact, lackadaisical; they refuse stubbornly to be involved in management's plans. They feel—and it is rational enough—that they have not much to gain and a great deal to lose by giving their support to management. Management is not strong enough to reward them, and they would be vulnerable to criticism by the employees, the unions, and their peers. Section chiefs, as a matter of fact, are as critical of management and as suspicious of its motives as *inspecteurs* and *inspecteurs-adjoints*.

[23] Trade-union alignments and plain politics play an important role in these cliques.

Discussing with the researcher the problem of the *contrôleurs* who do not have a function corresponding to their status, only one of thirty-one section chiefs did not give an explanation devoid of any derogatory connotation.

To summarize the situation, we would like to propose the following hypothesis: Management's complaints come from its inability to have any influence on its supervisory staff. The supervisory staff's behavior is primarily directed by its desire to prevent management from interfering in its affairs.

Another important feature should be added. Section chiefs never criticize their division head. In their face-to-face relationships, there is the same tolerance and the same understanding we found between them and the employees. Like their employees, they focus their criticisms on the next higher echelon with which they have no direct contact. This odd kind of discrimination corresponds, we believe, to the same basic situation we have just analyzed. Here also it seems that the division head has been stripped of his power over the section chiefs by the seniority system and the general solidarity of the members of this group.

Section chiefs are not dependent on the division head and he is not threatening to them. Therefore it is better to put the blame on the higher-ups—in this case, the people at the Ministry. But this is different from the employees' case, since the Ministry is a much vaguer entity that cannot be personified in a strong authoritarian figure, and since section chiefs, while criticizing the Ministry, are quite ready themselves to play favorites with some of its members.

Two kinds of tensions are likely to arise around such a situation. Each of these tensions corresponds to one of the two kinds of double-talk supervisors are bound to develop—one, in defense of their employees, and the second, about management and promotions. The supervisors' official attitude toward their subordinates is one of active sympathy. They belong to the same unions, and quite often their voices are heard in the union councils. On the other hand, they know they cannot accomplish anything substantial. Their skepticism, which may often remain subconscious, will lead many of them to defend their subordinates only inasmuch as it helps them to keep out of trouble. At any rate, positions taken in behalf of the employees will play a role in the internal game of the organization's politics, and this will introduce much uneasiness. Furthermore, the existence of the latent pattern of militaristic authority that reappears periodically in time of crisis, and to which the section chief and the *inspecteurs* must commit themselves, contradicts the more benevolent ways of routine. Younger *inspecteurs-adjoints* play very hard on these ambiguities to embarrass their elders (who are also their superiors), and those among them who have a trade-union back-ground [24] and who are therefore the most vulnerable are likely to suffer the most.[25]

With management, double-talk is about the future and no longer over the past, but the tension is of the same kind. We have pointed out already how the group prefers to have its members take chances outside the branch rather than to compete directly within the branch. Thus the individual section chief, for the sake of a promotion, must enter into undercover relations with the people whom he professes to despise most. Many supervisors, of course, solve their dilemmas by keeping out of the competition altogether. But this does not mean that they are not also indirectly influenced by the general pervasive uneasiness that comes from the activity of those of their colleagues who are willing to do anything to succeed.

THE OVER-ALL PATTERN OF ROUTINE

We have now completed our description, which certainly does not achieve our goal in many respects. This was a pilot study which could not be checked and enlarged as we had planned in a later and more thorough study; supervisors' feelings were not systematically investigated, nor were the value systems of both employees and supervisors. A few important points, however, seem to be well established.

First, the Agency staff—whether employees or supervisors—do not participate in any way in the goals of the organization. Not only do they not feel integrated; they directly express hostile feelings and pass severe over-all judgments on the Agency and on their own condition.

Second, this lack of integration does not seem to have much influence over other aspects of the staff's behavior and attitudes. People are reasonably well adjusted to their work, to their environment, and to supervision. One should not take talk about the Agency's poor morale too literally. The staff's dissatisfaction and pessimism do not prevent a satisfactory basic pattern of adjustment. Indeed, they can be viewed as a specific way, "a grumbling way," of achieving it.[26]

---

[24] Except, of course, for those who have kept a solid union position in spite of their successive promotions.

[25] With some paradoxical results, such as the complete turnabout of some of these old-time trade unionists who find no other way to keep aloof from this unpleasant pressure than to become anti-union.

[26] One may argue, of course, that such an apathetic and grumbling way of adjusting to one's lot corresponds to what is usually called poor morale. Our remark calls for a reappraisal of the concept of "morale" within an organization.

Third, people seem to be extremely isolated. There are no stable cliques. Only the work team, which is a small and, in a way, formal group can have stability and some emotional influence. This might appear surprising in such a stratified organization, where group pressures have so major a role. But the contradiction is only an ostensible one. The groups whose pressure in the organization is so strong are not primary groups, but relatively abstract groups such as the different occupational categories. These groups are fighting primarily for equality of treatment. They are universalistic groups in the Parsonian sense; and their activity operates as a brake on the formation of stable particularistic cliques.

Fourth, supervisory relationships do not present problems at the primary group level. Whenever an opposition of interests or of points of view between two groups directly confronting each other seems likely, responsibilities for decision-making are taken away and given to a higher echelon in the hierarchy that does not have direct contact with the contending groups. There seems to be a recurrent pattern of supervisory and group relationships; tensions are allowed to develop only between groups and people who are too far apart to know each other on a realistic basis.

It is still too early to discuss the interrelationships of these four different features of organizational behavior and their meaning for a tentative theory of bureaucratic strains. But we should like, at this stage, to make the first attempt at a synthesis by trying to show how this description may help us to understand the patterns of human relationships that lead to the development and the maintenance of routine.

We have frequently pointed out the fact that responsibilities within the Agency are centralized, with no staff functions to help carry them out. This means that decisions must be made by people who have no direct knowledge of the field and of the relevant variables, and who must rely on the information given them by subordinates who may have a subjective interest in distorting the data. In this sense, one can state that the power of decision in this system tends to be located in a blind spot. Those who have the necessary information do not have the power to decide, and those who have the power to decide cannot get the necessary information.[27]

[27] The activity of the unions cannot restore communications between the rank-and-file and the decision-makers. The structure of the labor unions' *fédérations* is modeled after the pattern of the management with which they have to deal. As a consequence, it is very difficult for the employees of the Parisian branch, or even of the whole Agency, to present their personal grievances, since no bargaining committee deals exclusively or even primarily with them. Their grievances, therefore, will be discussed at a much higher level, where they will be used to obtain advantages for a whole section of the Civil Service without changing the

Now, let us analyze the case of an executive faced with the problem of making a decision which can hurt or further the feelings and interests of some of his subordinate units without being able to ascertain the value of their conflicting arguments. He is most likely to try to find some impersonal rules, or at least some precedent, on which to rely. His decision will probably be inadequate; but given his special predicament, it will be the best solution in the long run.

Our division head might make better decisions if he tried to establish for himself some special channel of information, or if he were ready to trust one or several of his subordinates. But if he did either, he would probably have to combat accusations of favoritism and to face the possibility of a serious deterioration of the climate, whatever the soundness of the end result. If he were to grant all the claims of his subordinates, he would not be able to run an organization where the constraint of scarcity remains. Routine remains the safest way for him, whatever his own feelings. One may wonder more about the (very infrequent) innovating decisions than about the reiteration of routinized behavior.

Take, for example, the case of the inadequate staffing of the Parisian branch. At the first-line supervisors' level, the difficulties created by the high turnover concomitant with the steady growth of the organization are well understood. Everyone agrees that, given at least the present arrangement of the tasks and the method of training, there is an inescapable pressure toward lower productivity and morale. People do not, of course, try to determine the sources of the malaise, but they would be ready to agree with the interpretation of the researcher. Low morale increases turnover of personnel and tends to augment the work load. This finally affects the morale—the only alleviation being a decrease of productivity. This knowledge cannot and will not be transmitted to the higher management level, the Ministry. There, the problem would be seen from the point of view of a possible discrimination among the different branches whose productivity is closely watched. Staff increases are, indeed, allocated on the basis of a ratio to the number of operations performed. Since the Parisian branch does not rank high on that account, its claim that it is inadequately staffed does not appear very serious.[28]

Its arguments may be discussed and their strength may be recognized, intellectually at least. But they cannot be made operational, cannot be carried over to the domain of action. In this domain, no

---

balance of its different parts. Even if the global advantages the unions have won seem substantial, they cannot satisfy the employees of the Agency whose specific problems are overwhelming. It seems that the staff of the Parisian branch is as weak within the unions as it is vis-à-vis the management.

[28] The official opinion on this problem is that the Parisian branch may have a lower productivity only because it is too big.

rule of productivity can be recognized other than the narrow one of a direct relationship between the number of persons and the number of operations.

We have already noticed that there is a parallel impossibility of communication on the same subject between the first-line and the second-line supervisors. The second-line supervisors are frightened at the possibility of discriminating between units in order to help them improve productivity. They refuse to allow any breach in the rules and will alleviate the work load only at the last minute, when there is no alternative. Thus both groups, first-line and second-line supervisors, evade conflict and the use of direct authority. For them, routine is a protection. The same interpretation can apply at the higher level. It also seems clear that management prefers the impersonality of rules and statistics to the risks of a more responsible course of action.

Routinism, of course, is reinforced at all levels by the special training that comes with the established career patterns. And one may even grant that some kind of self-selection may operate, that people come to work or remain at work in such an organization because it fits their personality needs or corresponds to their value system. But sources of routinism should not be sought first in the personality traits of the civil servants, but in the respective situations of the different groups to which they belong in the work organization. Patterns of behavior which have become internalized during long formative years must be considered. They must be taken into account, not as explanations of this situation—people do not refuse to take responsibility because they have been trained not to—but as an added weight to the stability of the system, as a decisive factor in understanding why change is so difficult.

Viewing the situation from another angle, we may argue that communications are biased and behavior routinized because there is too great a gap between the prescribed patterns of action and the requirements of the task. If this is so, the only solution is to add a few other impersonal rules. Since these rules will disturb some already established patterns, they will have to be imposed over the resistance of the intermediary echelons; and they will finally appear as a further step toward greater centralization. Reform will most probably take the aspect of, and appear as, a threat of centralization. It will not benefit from the good will and the experience accumulated below, and will be all the more difficult accordingly. Most people will refuse to become involved. Those who do will be accused of favoritism; the pressure for preserving equality of treatment will become irresistible.

A good example of such difficulties was provided at the branch, where a reform was being attempted at the time of our investigation. The objective was to amalgamate four sections in order to rationalize auxiliary work and therefore build up some human reserves to deal with recurrent crises. The reform was technically sound but had aroused, in a short time, the hostility of the whole supervisory force and of the unions.[29] At the first attempt, at least, it failed.[30] We can explain this failure by pointing out that the executive responsible for the reform came from the Ministry and had no contacts with the Parisian branch. His aloofness was frustrating to the people of the branch. On the other hand, his type of action—whose philosophy is openly professed at the Ministry: "There are people to think at the Ministry and others to execute at the branch level as in all field offices"—was necessitated by the impossibility of reform, i.e., adjustment to new problems from within the branch organization itself.

Social scientists are too often content to describe vicious circles, neat reinforcing feedbacks, without trying to go deeper. Description is indispensable, but it is not enough. Even if one can present only venturesome hypotheses, one should try to understand the origin and the possibilities of survival of these patterns of relationships whose unfavorable consequences have appeared, in the short run, to reinforce stability. In the present case the basic question seems to be: why did a system develop which blocks executives and supervisors in a situation of routine and produces many frustrations among employees, and how can it resist all kinds of pressure for change?

In other words, why do people build organizations where impersonal rules and routine will bind individual behavior to such an extent? Why do they build bureaucracies? Anticipating our future analysis, we should like to suggest that they are trying to evade face-to-face relationships and situations of personal dependency whose authoritarian tone they cannot bear.

In order to understand better the situation, let us examine the reactions of the branch staff to a change of structure that would give first-line supervisors all the responsibilities which have been centralized by the second-line supervisors. The latter would, of course, object, especially since the appearance of power that they have gives them prestige without risk. But the first-line supervisors are not likely to be in favor of it either. They would certainly like to have more prestige and more freedom of action, but they do not complain directly about their superiors' decisions and would not very much like to take the decision-making upon themselves. To do so would break up the solidarity of their peer group and allow higher-

[29] Employees, according to our interviews, had more moderate and less clear-cut opinions.
[30] The experiment was not stopped but was not extended, and a second attempt was not made until much later. Six years later nothing had yet been settled definitely.

ups to discriminate between them, since freedom of action would bring competition and widely different results, as compared to the status quo. It would also make them liable to direct pressure from their own subordinates, the employees, without having the possibility of putting the blame on their superiors. The employees, finally, may have immediate reasons for demanding more adequate decisions. At the same time, however, they are accustomed to the protection of the rules and of routinism. They resent any attempt on the part of the supervisors to discriminate between them. Decentralization, delegation of authority, would bring power closer to them, which would mean greater chances of redress for their grievances. But it would also involve the risk of dependence and less protection from arbitrary decisions. Their emotional reaction against authority gives the impression that such an issue would still be settled on the side of conservatism.

If we were to imagine a change in the other direction, i.e., toward still greater centralization, giving second-line supervisors enough staff help to get information directly without having to rely entirely on the line, we would find, cloaked under different arguments, almost the same reactions corresponding to the same motivations. Division heads would be afraid to give the Ministry a possible means of interfering and discriminating among them. Section heads, of course, would be violently opposed to a spy system that would leave them at the mercy of their superiors. Employees, to be sure, would be less concerned, since problems would everywhere be pushed one level higher. But basically, the opposition would be of the same sort—and strong enough from the side of the supervisors to be almost impossible to overcome.

Our argument finally relies, the reader will have noted, on the widespread reluctance of all members of the organization to accept situations where they must depend on and be controlled by the conventional hierarchy. Rules and routine, in that sense, may have a protective value. They insure that no one can interfere in the internal affairs of the immediately inferior category. They give, therefore, a certain kind of independence. People do not participate, they remain isolated and they suffer as a result. But freedom with respect to personal involvement can be viewed also as an advantage —it is, indeed, one of the main advantages of the Civil Service which our interviewees value. They complain bitterly about the price they have to pay for it, but they are, in the last analysis, ready to pay that price. They adjust to it in a grumbling way but, one way or another, they adjust.

As one very critical and skeptical girl states it: "I would not take another job and when I was younger I would not have done so either. I could not bear being at the boss's mercy."

Part Two

THE INDUSTRIAL MONOPOLY

Our second case study is that of a large-scale organization belonging to the French State, which has granted it a legal monopoly for the very simple commodity it produces. For convenience, we will term this organization the "Industrial Monopoly."

The Industrial Monopoly is a production organization only. The sale of its products is controlled by another government department, whose aims are only fiscal.[1] Since the ratio of the manufacturing cost to the selling price is extremely small,[2] and since the total amount of revenue which the Industrial Monopoly may bring in depends primarily on the fiscal decisions of the State, cutting costs and raising productivity are not central problems. Consequently, innovations requiring major investments would not be welcomed. The managers of the Monopoly themselves are in a relatively inferior position, in that they are not competent to deal with what are normally the main considerations in managerial decision-making—the fiscal considerations.

Such a situation is of great interest to the sociologist. We are dealing with an organization that has been freed from most of the pressures of the environment that usually shape the social system of an organization. Because of this freedom, this organization can develop according to its own internal requirements. We may thus consider it a kind of natural social experiment. In it, we can observe, as through a magnifying glass, those human limitations whose influence on the functioning of any organization is always decisive, but usually not so clear.

Our study of the Clerical Agency has allowed us to elaborate a general descriptive scheme within which a number of administrative practices and behavioral patterns usually associated with routinism can be explained by reference to the kind of social control used by organizations. The study of the Industrial Monopoly will enable us to go further by exploring the sources and the conditions of development of the bureaucratic phenomenon itself. Because of the special conditions we have just summarized, we shall now be able to investigate new problems whose importance will be seen to be crucial

---

[1] The Industrial Monopoly should be considered from this point of view—as a sort of giant subcontractor in a monopolistic situation vis-à-vis its unique customer, another giant and monopolistic organization. The customer is extremely tolerant, inasmuch as the selling price is very elastic and does not bear much relation to the manufacturing cost.

[2] Taxes constitute almost three-quarters of the selling price.

—the problem of power relationships and the problem of individual and group strategy within an organizational system.

Our discussion will rely on two successive studies. The first, which was specific and intensive, was made on three plants in the Paris area. The second, more superficial, involved twenty of the Monopoly's thirty plants throughout France.

The extensive study consisted of a visit to the plant and long free interviewing of the members of the managerial team and occasionally of the union leaders. The intensive study required much greater effort. The research team first devoted a month to a pilot study, largely consisting of free interviewing in a provincial plant. Then, after a rather long period of observation, systematic interviewing with closed-ended questionnaires was conducted with a sample of the production workers, half of the maintenance workers, and all the supervisors and executives of the three chosen plants. Finally, a number of group discussions were arranged so that the comments of representatives of the different categories could be obtained on the first results of the survey.

The three plants we studied intensively are located in Paris and its suburbs. They cannot be considered actually representative of the other plants of the Monopoly, because of the special characteristics of the Parisian labor force and the plant's proximity to the Central Office. But the second, extensive part of the survey showed: (1) that the differences between Paris and the provinces were not so great as we had anticipated; and (2) that they tended always in the same direction. Further, the Parisian plants appeared precisely to represent the *ideal type*, in the Weberian sense, of the organizational system of the Monopoly.[3]

In order to understand the social system of the Monopoly at the shop level, our intensive interviews were based on: (1) the attitudes and reactions of the workers and of the supervisors to the rules and to the organizational givens of the system; (2) the formal authority relationships; (3) the interrelationships between people within the various categories and from one occupational category to another; and (4) the way people adjust to their conditions and to their roles.

To understand management problems and the role of manage-

---

[3] Such a paradox results from the converging pressures of the Central Office and of the labor unions on local customs and local arrangements between a manager and his labor force, that tend to distort slightly, in most other cases, the implementation of the general rules. Rules are applied more strictly in the Parisian plants. It is almost impossible to evade them by tacit or explicit clandestine agreements. Consequently, we find somewhat more conflicts and less co-operation than in the provinces. In return, as regards the functioning of the organization, the role and behavior of the individuals and of the groups within it, the Parisian plants offer the best and the most striking example of the consequences of the organizational system of the Monopoly.

ment in the social system, we relied on the more informal interviews of the extensive study. However, comparison, checking, and new interpretations were possible in the more focused interviews and discussions we had with the members of the managerial teams of the Parisian plants, and in confronting this group with the comments of the workers and supervisors of these same plants.

We shall present, in two successive chapters, the main elements of the plant social system as they can be viewed at the shop level. First, we shall discuss the kind of plant "subculture" that has developed around the main organizational givens and the adjustment to the formal authority system that is parallel to it. In the second chapter, we shall investigate the more complex group relationships and the patterns of adjustment of the different groups. In a third chapter, we shall present human relations at the management level. This will enable us to complete our picture of the social system of the Monopoly and will furnish us with further clues for understanding the sources of bureaucratic strains.

Chapter Three

THE SOCIAL SYSTEM AT THE SHOP LEVEL

I. The Plant Subculture and the Formal Authority System

THE OVER-ALL ORGANIZATION OF THE MONOPOLY

The social system of the plants studied develops in three main dimensions: (1) the organizational givens; (2) the formal authority relationships; and (3) the relationships between the different functional and stratified groups. By "organizational givens," we mean the formal constraints of the organization that come from the interplay between the technological givens and the bureaucratic rules. The formal authority system consists of those hierarchical relationships that are another given of the organization, but, so to speak, a cultural one that is only partially determined by the instrumental goals. Group relationships, finally, bring in still more problematical elements, since they depend on the unstable and yet necessary equilibrium that must stand the struggle for power and for status to achieve the necessary co-operation between the different functional and hierarchical strata. These three dimensions determine the patterns of adjustment of the different groups and thus the nature and characteristics of the social system at the shop level.

In this chapter, we shall first analyze the organizational givens and then the formal authority system. In other words, we shall set the stage, hint at the atmosphere, and describe the actors whose performance we shall analyze in the next chapter. But, before this description is begun, a few data on the Monopoly itself, on its different categories of personnel, and on the work organization must be given.

The Industrial Monopoly operates thirty manufacturing plants, a research center, a repair plant, a large number of warehouses and storage facilities, and a few raw material conditioning shops. Most of these establishments are dispersed throughout France. It employs around ten thousand workers and more than two thousand white-collar and supervisory employees.

Most plants produce the same lines of products. Some of them, however, have traditionally been in charge of special lines. Recently, specialization has begun to increase substantially. The location of plants was determined by marketing and production conditions prevalent at the end of the nineteenth century. At that time, production was still by hand and the factories—the *manufactures*—were necessarily quite large production units averaging one thousand workers apiece. It was thus rational to locate one plant at the center of each possible regional market, since the size of such a plant was technically satisfactory and since the proximity of the consumers was a great advantage from an economical point of view. But since the coming of mechanization, forty years ago, the number of workers necessary to serve a regional market has been reduced to between 350 and 400 while the optimum size of a plant has been greatly increased and while the improvement in transportation, especially by trucks, has made regional dispersion obsolete. For many years, therefore, technical and economic factors have apparently been favorable to a general policy of mergers. There has been no attempt at geographical consolidation, however, because of the strong pressure exerted by the workers and the importance of the political forces they could rally for keeping a traditional source of employment in the smaller, and even, in some cases, bigger, towns.

The Industrial Monopoly is, on the other hand, extremely centralized. A great number of petty decisions are made at the Central Office in Paris. The Central Office is an extremely unwieldy body, with about fifty ranking engineers (half the total managerial labor force) working in thirty different autonomous bureaus.

There is more mobility between the provinces and Paris, i.e., between the field plants and the Central Office, than in the Clerical Agency, but there are still many career men in Paris who have never had any local responsibilities. Most local "directors" [1] nowadays come to Paris from time to time, but traveling allowances are far from liberal and personal contacts are not encouraged. They always meet their colleagues of the Central Office individually. No formal or informal meetings of the local directors ever take place. The prevailing mode of contact is still the circular note, the official memorandum, and the individual letter.

The Monopoly employs six different categories of personnel. Each category is recruited separately and has a special personal status. These categories are the production workers, the maintenance workers, the lower supervisors, the administrative officers, the technical engineers, and the directorial engineers.

Two-thirds of the *production workers* are female. Four-fifths of them must be recruited from among people legally entitled to em-

[1] This is the title plant managers hold in the Monopoly.

ployment by the State, according to laws passed after World War I and World War II to help war victims (war widows and war orphans among the women; disabled veterans and ex-servicemen among the men). Nor can the manager freely select people to fill the remaining positions: the unions have obtained the concession that applicants who have close relatives in the plants must be given priority. Production workers have a Civil Service tenure, which means total job security. They are protected against any kind of unfair disciplinary action and they cannot be transferred or even placed [2] by supervisory decision; job allocations must be made according to a strict seniority system. Wages are fair and equal all over France, which means a very favorable situation in low-paying areas and a much less favorable one in the more industrialized high-paying areas, especially in Paris.

The *maintenance workers*, fifty in each plant, are all highly skilled people, such as boiler-makers, electricians, and joiners. The majority of them, however, are metal-fitters who are at present working not in their traditional trade but as machine-setters and ordinary mechanics. These men are recruited through difficult competitive occupational tests that have retained some features of the masterpiece requirements of the guilds. Their wages also are fair but depend, still more than those of the production workers, on seniority increments. Thus the older men are well paid in comparison with the usual rates of private industry, but the younger ones earn much less than their peers, especially in Paris.

The same category of personnel, *chefs d'atelier* (shop foremen), staffs both the supervisory jobs in the works and the white-collar jobs in the plant offices. There may be twenty to thirty of these people in the plant; they are usually male and have been recruited through a general competitive examination. At one time most of the *chefs d'atelier* were former noncommissioned officers, but since the end of World War II an effort has been made to attract more business-minded people. Recently the baccalaureate[3] has been made a requirement for the *concours*. This requirement has tended to exclude ex-servicemen altogether, but it may also exclude the kind of men with practical industrial training who are most needed. Within this lower supervisory category, there is a second echelon called *chefs de section* (section foremen). Promotion from *chef d'atelier* to *chef de section* is made on a merit basis; but a very strong pressure is exerted for seniority appointments and this pressure is usually successful. Wages are rather poor compared to those of foremen in high-

---

[2] There are seven different categories of jobs, each one with slightly different hourly wages.

[3] Its status in France may be compared to that of a college degree in the U.S.A.

paying areas, but they may be good in comparison with those of average small plant foremen and of office workers.

Administrative jobs, i.e., purchasing, personnel, and accounting, are the preserve of a distinct administrative category with two main echelons. There are a few of these jobs in each plant, at the apex of which one finds one comptroller who is considered a member of the management team.[4]

Administrative officers are recruited in a national competitive examination. Candidates for this examination are now required to have college educations. Recruitment is difficult, since these jobs are poorly paid, especially at the beginning, and since the possibilities of promotion are known to be scarce because of the age pyramid of the group. Administrative officers move from one plant to another with each promotion. Their career is slow and almost entirely dominated by seniority. They have no other prospect than the comptroller's job, which they will reach—if indeed they do—only in the very last years of their career.

Technical engineers are still less numerous (there is only one in each plant). They are in charge of all maintenance and repair problems, whether for the regular semi-automatic machines in the shops or for general installations and heavy equipment. They are responsible for dealing with outside contractors and for preparing and carrying out all possible new works. Technical engineers usually remain for a long time, sometimes their whole career, in the same plant. They also are recruited through a national competitive examination. Recruitment has become still more difficult than for the administrative officers, and the level of the new recruits has been substantially lowered. Wages are, indeed, very low compared to what engineers of the same training earn elsewhere. In addition, there are no prospects of promotion—there are only the regular seniority increases in pay, since managerial jobs have been practically closed to the technical engineers.

Finally, there are usually two members of the high-prestige engineers corps in each plant: *the director*, who is responsible for the whole plant (production, administration, and sales),[5] and *the assistant director*, in charge of all manufacturing operations. Directorial engineers are not recruited in competitive examinations; they come from the Polytechnique, the best theoretical engineering school in

[4] There are also intermediary positions of *redacteurs principaux* and *contrôleurs principaux*, but although their importance for wages and career prospects is not to be ignored, they do not affect the functions very much. Administrative officers, finally, utilize as their staff a small number of *chefs de section* and *chefs d'atelier* who work with them as white-collar employees.

[5] Sales, as we know, are handled by another government department; but the Monopoly people also try to cover the field, even if only in an amateur way.

France.[6] After leaving school, they are given two years of additional training in the Monopoly. Then they are put in charge, as assistant directors, of the entire production of one plant under the supervision of one of their elders. They spend twelve to fifteen years as assistant directors, possibly shifting once or twice to a different plant, until they are promoted to a directorship, strictly by seniority. The next possible step, the promotion to general inspector, is not generally sought, since the rewards are not very great for most local directors.

Wages are substantially lower than in private industry, but there are compensations—a large house, a company car with a chauffeur, and some company domestic help. There is also a great deal of personal freedom, and the social status, which in the past was very high, is still an important consideration in the provinces. It might, for example, still help in making a good bourgeois marriage.

All these advantages have lost much of their importance today, and recruitment is not so easy as it once was. But the most ominous sign is the increase in turnover of the young engineers. Sizable numbers of assistant directors have always resigned, but now the rate has gone up to the point where 60 per cent leave before having been promoted to director.

The thirty plants of the Monopoly are quite similar as regards general layout, machines, and workroom arrangements. Most of them are housed in old buildings erected sixty or seventy years ago. Very few factories were built after World War I, but a few have been remodeled, or are in the process of being remodeled, since World War II. The buildings are solid structures several stories high, laid out around a central courtyard which serves as a meeting place for the workers. The plants are spacious, although not designed for convenience in ventilation, air-conditioning, or even cleaning.

The mechanical equipment is not homogeneous. Production machines are quite up-to-date everywhere. But general equipment, conveyors, sanitary devices, and air-conditioning were lagging very much at the time of the study. An attempt at modernization is being made, and there are now some new and modern installations. But progress is usually piecemeal. It is hampered by the small size of the factories whose individual production is not sufficient to pay for the best integrated equipment.

The organization of the workshops raises four different kinds of problems. The first concerns the preparation and processing of the raw material; this is simple, but apparently difficult in practice, and

---

[6] Special provisions in the rules make it possible for an engineer of another professional school to enter the corps, but in a hundred years there had been only two exceptions. The complete suppression of this anachronistic prerogative was decided on in 1961.

requires long experience to be handled correctly. The second problem, which is partially linked to the first, is the maintenance and the constant setting and resetting of machines; this matter is made difficult because of the peculiar characteristics of the raw material and the general organizational system of the Monopoly. The third problem is more common: it concerns the best utilization of machines and men in view of frequently changing production programs, the maintenance and setting problems, and, above all, the frequent transfers of workers. The fourth and last problem, which concerns the allocation of jobs, is the most difficult. It is the basic problem of the human aspect of plant organization, and it influences the solution of all other problems. Job allocations must conform to strict seniority provisions worked out in a general national code. No transfer of any worker under any circumstance can contravene this basic rule: the most senior applicant when there are volunteers, and the least senior incumbent when there are no volunteers, shall be reallocated or displaced. The provisions apply not only in the case of permanent upgrading, i.e., when there are new job openings, but also when a change in the fabrication plan necessitates stopping the production of a machine or of a shop, or when a machine breaks down, or even in a case of long absence.

Supervisors in this system act as time-keepers and accounting officers. They see to it that the workers are supplied with maintenance services and materials. They handle the rules of seniority, interpreting them on the spot—subject to the approval of the assistant director, and with the possibility of appeal by the trade-union representatives. Finally, they have no disciplinary power and very little organization leeway. As in the Clerical Agency, their supervisory role is extremely limited.

Directors and assistant directors are experts in certain problems, such as the raw material technology, the flow of work, and the utilization of machines. They have to make short-run decisions for mobilizing resources to achieve the fabrication plans and longer-run decisions for bettering productivity and financial efficiency. But their important role is ultimately that of administrator-diplomat; it is not a technical role. Their only actual success consists of inducing people and groups over whom they have no kind of control to co-operate. As regards the human aspect of management, they are, so to speak, judicial officers whose main function is to implement and interpret laws which they have not made and cannot appreciate. In technical matters, they have not much organization leeway except in certain domains, e.g., construction, or new technical installations, and in certain periods of great transformation; and they are subordinate, in any case, to the decisions of the Central Office.

Over-all productivity is difficult to assess because there is nothing with which to compare it, since the Monopoly is legally safeguarded against any possible competition in France. Work loads are heavy and immediate individual productivity may be high, but the ratio that the actual utilization of machines and equipment has to the theoretical one is very poor.[7]

Management complains bitterly all over France about the organizational difficulties that are due to seniority rules. Workers complain that "the administration" is stingy and does not care for its own employees. Both parties agree that there is waste. The problems people discuss most are machine stoppages and seniority rights. These two problems are linked, inasmuch as machine stoppages entail transfers that have to be handled according to seniority rights.

Labor relations are much more stable than in the Clerical Agency. This is due, first, to the existence of two very powerful and well-organized labor unions comprising 75 per cent of the production workers as dues-paying members—an extremely unusual situation in France. Second, there is a relatively formal and very well elaborated grievance procedure, which is also almost unique in France. This system of labor relations gives good protection to the workers and to their unions. But it is much too cumbersome and formalistic, and it has exerted a strong pressure for centralization and for curtailing the local directors' power. The frustrations which this situation fosters among managers as well as among workers tend to create a rather bitter and acrimonious climate of human and labor relations.

The Organizational Givens and the Workers' Attitudes

The constraints of technical and organizational origins that bear on the social system of a factory are numerous. We have focused our analysis, however, on three which seemed to us, during the pilot study, to be the most fundamental for the production workers and, indirectly, for the whole social system of the Monopoly. These are the work load, mechanization and the pace of machines, and, finally, the seniority rules that govern job allocations and the way they are put into practice.

It is around these three main factors that workers' reactions crystallize. These reactions, we learned from their being expressed individually in the interviews, appear to be, above all, collective reactions. Their coherence and their very constraining character have

---

[7] This is the impression we gathered after visiting similar plants, in foreign countries, utilizing the same machines.

suggested the image of a workers' subculture. Such an image goes much further than a simple analogy, since the "workers' subculture" appears to be definite and stable enough to influence the attitudes of the other occupational categories.

THE WORK LOAD

Work loads corresponding to the different jobs and the remunerations attached to them are fixed nationally by the Central Office after careful negotiations with the representatives of the trade unions. There is no collective bargaining, however, and the decisions of the Central Office are still theoretically unilateral, in order to show respect for the sovereignty of the State. But they are always, in practice at least, the results of an agreement.

Production norms, allocated delays, the basic remuneration, as well as the nature and ratio of the bonuses, are extremely precise and do not allow for local arrangements between managers and their workers. Machine-tenders, who form almost two-thirds of the labor force, are paid a flat hourly rate for producing 85 per cent of the basic standard. If they do not reach this minimum, they are penalized; if they exceed it, they get a rather simple piece-rate bonus. This system is elaborate, but it does not operate as an incentive at all. The workers have been able to control their output so well that they never exceed 100 per cent of the standard and rarely fail to achieve it. The only consequence of the system, therefore, is to prevent slowdowns by providing an automatic financial penalty whenever the worker does not produce up to the standard, and a still stronger penalty if he does not reach 85 per cent of this standard.

Workers react to this situation quite sensibly. They complain, but not very bitterly. They emphasize the general injustice of the workers' condition more than the absolute amount of the load. The majority tend to admit they can make it. However, they project their hostility to the pressure of the standard by answering much more negatively to a question bearing on the record of their workmates.[8]

[8] This is apparent, if one compares the answers obtained for the two following questions: (1) "Do you succeed in attaining 100 per cent of the standard?" (2) "Do you think the majority of your colleagues attain 100 per cent?"

The distribution of the answers is not quite the same.

INTERVIEWEE'S OWN ACHIEVEMENT	Per cent	INTERVIEWEE'S GUESS ABOUT HIS COLLEAGUES	Per cent
He makes it easily	46	They make it easily	30
He makes it but it is difficult	18	They make it but it is difficult	27
He does not make it always	20	They do not make it always	32
He cannot make it	7	They cannot make it	4
Special jobs with no standards	9	No answer	7
N = 129		N = 129	

The difference between answers to the personal question, where facts cannot be distorted easily, and the speculative question about colleagues, where a more free-playing emotional answer is possible, is in itself interesting. We obtain a very nice curve when we compare the percentage of workers who think their colleagues can make it easily (30 per cent), the judgments of trade-union delegates (36 per cent), the statements workers make about themselves (46 per cent), and the evaluations of the maintenance workers (57 per cent) and of the supervisors (67 per cent).

These differences are much more striking when tables are broken down by factory. The answers to the first question do not vary much. However, the answers to the second present striking differences between the plants and almost the opposite kind of distribution in two of them.

In the first of these two plants, the judgments of the workers on the results of their colleagues are not very different from what they say about themselves. Fifty-seven per cent of them say they make it easily and 10 per cent not always, while the figures are 49 per cent and 17 per cent respectively for their colleagues. In the second plant, on the other hand, 40 per cent of the workers say they make it easily as against 33 per cent who do not always; the figures are almost the reverse for their judgment of their colleagues, since only 17 per cent of them say that their colleagues can make it easily and 45 per cent not always.

How should we interpret such a variance? Since work standards are exactly the same in the factories, and since the manpower is equivalent in origin and composition, a strong probability exists for a comparable distribution of behavior among them.[9] Why, then, is there a different and almost opposite distribution of the guesses about colleagues?

Some cross-tabulation can provide interesting clues. Speculations about colleagues are strongly influenced by seniority, which is not the case with statements about oneself. The longer one has been in the Monopoly, the more one is likely to guess that colleagues have difficulties in meeting the standards. Cross-tabulation also shows differences according to the kind of recruitment: people whose background is more deeply rooted in the Monopoly, those who have entered through recommendations of parents or relatives, will be more pessimistic than those who became familiar with the Monopoly later in life and from different backgrounds. There is another and even more curious difference according to the kind of job people hold:

[9] This should be all the more so since, as we shall see later, we found surprisingly similar distributions of opinion in the three plants on all those items that did not concern special factory-bound circumstances.

the machine operators, for example, who have somewhat more prestige but do not suffer so much from an increase of the work load, complain more than the product receiver, for whom it may mean some physical stress.[10] We notice, finally, that the workers who present the more gloomy picture are the ones who are better integrated in the workers' group and are generally part of the responsible majority on other issues.

This suggests that guessing about colleagues is, to a certain degree at least, a group reaction compared to the individual report of one's own behavior. Its individual expressions depend on the degree of individual integration.

But why are group reactions so different from one plant to another? The small yet significant differences[11] existing in the factual reports suggest that there is a factual background for this variance; in one of the plants, it seems that workers really do have more difficulty in meeting the standards. At the same time, the comments we received, and the very strong relationship between the answers to the question on the colleagues and the working of the seniority system show that these differences are linked to the kind of deal workers feel they are able to arrange in the narrow area of the interpretation of the rules. This is a very vital domain for them, since it is the only one where there is a large enough freedom of action. In this domain, as we shall see later, one of the most important factors of the differences between shops and between plants is formed.

THE SENIORITY SYSTEM

The human relations problems to which the different occupational categories devote most of their energy at the shop level are those that develop around the permanent allocation of jobs and the temporary shifting of workers when production programs change, or where equipment is not available. These problems must be solved, as we have already indicated, according to the strict provisions of seniority statutes whose successive improvements have been transformed into a national code. The principle of these rules appears simple: For any kind of vacancy, the most senior applicant when there are volunteers, and the least senior incumbent when there are no volunteers, shall be reallocated or displaced. But this principle can be applied only by elaborating all sorts of special detailed regulations, creating a sort of legal imbroglio. One should emphasize, in order to prevent confusion, that this code, unlike most American union contracts, is not intended

---

[10] All of these relationships are statistically significant at the .01 level.

[11] They are significant, inasmuch as they go in the same direction as the judgments on colleagues.

to protect people against arbitrary lay-offs—Monopoly workers have practically full tenure on the job. It fights against discrimination on the job, and it insures complete equality among all production workers, whatever their mental or physical abilities.

These provisions were imposed by the unions more than fifty years ago after a long period of bitter fighting. Union people are proud of their past victory and still appear to be emotionally involved in its defense. Rank-and-file workers—although, of course, not so consistently militant about seniority as their leaders—seem, nevertheless, to agree overwhelmingly with the latter's basic philosophy.

We presented to them, for approval or disapproval, a battery of statements about seniority that we selected from comments workers had made to us during the pilot study.[12] The answers to three of these questions were quite consistent and allowed the building of an imperfect but solid Guttman-like scale.[13] Only 20 per cent of the production workers disapproved of the basic principle of the seniority system. At the other extreme, 20 per cent refused to admit even that it might be detrimental to young workers.

The number who are hostile to the principle is reduced to 5 per cent among the union delegates (N = 28), but it goes up to 33 per cent among maintenance people and to 70 per cent among the supervisors. These proportions are exactly the same in all three plants. The cleavage of opinion, therefore, seems clearly a group phenomenon; no influence is exerted by the individual plant's special conditions or atmosphere.

As with the attitudes toward work load, the major influence affecting attitudes toward seniority is the degree of seniority held. Production workers having less than five years' seniority are 37 per cent hostile. Among workers with five to fifteen years' seniority, the proportion declines to 15 per cent, and among those with still more, to 12 per cent. For maintenance workers the curve is even more striking—50 per cent of the people with less than five years are hostile, whereas only 10 per cent among people with more than five years are hostile.

It is understandable that the seniority system, detrimental to new workers who have to accept the more unpleasant jobs, is unpopular with them. It takes some time before they begin to benefit from, and thus become reconciled to, the system. One may wonder, however,

[12] This was our battery of statements: (1) "The seniority provisions are detrimental to young workers." (2) "The seniority provisions make it impossible for smart people to move up." (3) "The seniority provisions give equal chance to everybody." (4) "It is perfectly fair that people with more seniority should always go first."

[13] The numbers of ranks were too few for a regular Guttman scale, but the reproductivity coefficient is high (.96).

about the sharp break of the curve; seniority does not appear as a gradual influence, an aging and mellowing process. It seems to correspond much more to a group pressure that becomes overwhelming when one no longer has enough interest at stake. It is evaded only by marginal people and those young workers who cumulate frustrations and are incompletely assimilated with the environment.[14]

This group pressure explanation is further indicated by the kind of significant relationship found with cross-tabulations. Those workers who are favorable to the seniority provisions seem better integrated, more interested in the plant community, happier about their job and their status. The hostile minority, on the other hand, is composed of marginal people who are likely to criticize supervisors, management, and union leaders about attitudes and behavior. They are much less interested in the plant community and express their opinions less frequently about common problems. Finally, unlike the great majority of their colleagues, they are unhappy about their job and their status.

The attitude toward the seniority system thus seems to be central to the understanding of workers' integration into their milieu. Seniority is the principle around which they have built their image of how things should be.

People, however, do not live in Utopia, but in a practical world with many conflicting personal interests. One must ask immediately how such an ideal image can be realized. Curiously, the apparently simple and strict rules of the seniority provisions engender many controversies, discussions, charges, and counter-charges. These are settled according to a well-established pattern of appeal comparable to the American grievances procedure. The first to interpret the rule is the supervisor. He may be challenged by a union delegate. If these two cannot settle the matter, the supervisor will ask for the decision of the plant director. This decision may be challenged again by the local union. Then, if no agreement is possible, the director will refer the matter to the Central Office where the trade union's national representatives will still be able to intervene. The matters concerned are usually technicalities—delays in posting jobs, people entitled to compete, limits of the area of competition, rights of absentees and sick employees, quick transfers made on the spot without due regard to everybody's rights.

The essential feature of this problem does not come from lack of clarity and precision in the code, but from the unbearable difficulties created by trying to impose too rigorous a scheme of action on a real-

---

[14] One should not forget that, even among the younger workers, people hostile to the seniority rules are in the minority; their comments, moreover, never refer to their own personal interests.

ity that remains complex. The typical incident does not concern only one worker or only one group of workers, but two contending parties, both workers. It usually stems from some mutually convenient sidestepping of the rules that did not turn out to be so advantageous as expected for one party or that ignored the rights of a third party.[15] It is impossible to prevent arrangements of mutual convenience from being made, because of the extraordinary complications of trying to apply too strict a ruling to an industrial situation. But they are dangerous also because, in order to succeed, they require the maintenance of the original agreement. If this usually brittle kind of arrangement breaks down, each of the partners will resort to technicalities. If there were only one union, arbitration could be made within the workers' group. However, the presence of two strong competing unions provides two sets of competing lawyers to take care of the opposing points of view and tends, therefore, to exacerbate any quarrel. How do the people react to such a situation? When we take the whole of the production group, we get the following distribution of opinion. Forty per cent of the production workers are satisfied, 30 per cent moderately critical, 27 per cent violently dissatisfied (N = 192). But when we take only the workers in the manufacturing shops, where problems are more likely to arise, we find that the distribution is heavier on the negative side. Dissatisfied workers form 35 per cent, and the percentage of the satisfied has declined to 30 per cent (N = 70).

Moreover, instead of the regularity of the opinions about the principle, the three reactions vary substantially from plant to plant.

What are the complaints of the people who are dissatisfied? The comments are rarely specific. They confirm the impression, however, that dissatisfaction arises much more from temporary transfers than from more permanent reallocation in case of vacancy or new openings. But they point toward personal factors more than toward practical problems. Among the more or less dissatisfied people (60 per cent of the total), we find three approximately equal groupings. One group accuses management. For example, one woman said:

This gentleman [the director] does not want to obey the seniority code any more, he would like to suppress it, do things his own personal way.

And another:

Here what counts is whether your face pleases. Management would like to abolish the rule; unions hold on to it as strongly as they can.

[15] In fact, most of the time when mutual convenience arrangements are made, an exact equivalent cannot come from each partner, and such settlements implicitly call for reciprocity. If and when circumstances change and one of the partners refuses to honor his commitment, the other will feel cheated and will look for technicalities to defend against the letter of the law.

Those in the second group accuse the unions:

> Unions tell you one thing one day and the contrary the day after. They do what they want with the rules.
> The fault is with the unions; one always undoes what the other has done.

Finally, there is a third group, whose members do not look for a scapegoat but complain about the general disorder.

When we examine the people who are satisfied, we find a comparable division of comments. Half say that management is fair in handling problems, and the other half, that the rules are obeyed only because the union obliges management to enforce them.

This relative uncertainty is rather surprising, in view of the general loyalty to the unions. Seventy-five per cent of the workers pay dues and 85 per cent make favorable comments about union activities. A cross-tabulation with the opinions expressed about the seniority principle makes it possible to give a better analysis. There is a relationship between the two attitudes, but it is not a linear one. The people who are most satisfied are not those most in favor of the principle, but those who are moderate in their attachment. The people blindly attached to the seniority principle are almost as dissatisfied as the people who are hostile (Table 2).

TABLE 2

ATTITUDES TOWARD THE SENIORITY PRINCIPLES AND JUDGMENTS ABOUT ITS APPLICATION

	Think Rules Well Applied (Per Cent)	Moderately Critical or Clearly Dissatisfied (Per Cent)	N (Total, 129)
People hostile to the principle of seniority.......	28	72	27
People moderately attached to the principle.....	50	50	72
People very favorable........................	33	67	30

In the light of our former analyses, this unexpected relationship suggests the following interpretations: first, the application of the rules is likely at one time or another to hurt most workers, but the people who are neither marginal workers who refuse to integrate, nor so rabidly seniority conscious that they are unable to accept the real situation, will react more favorably. Second, people who have difficulties they cannot tolerate will react in either of two directions, depending on the degree of their integration into the group. They will either curse management and stick to the letter of the rule, while refusing to recognize its inconveniences; or those who are marginal will curse the general disorder and oppose the whole system.

Both explanations may be valid at the same time. A check on the background of the people who complain shows that those who are most likely to be dissatisfied have deeper roots in the Monopoly. There is a tendency for those with more prestige, more connections, and better established situations within the community to be more adamant whenever their rights are threatened. For these people, who are likely to favor the seniority principle to begin with, it seems that a personal grievance is the prime mover. But one suspects that, for the marginal people who have adopted a generalized attitude of opposition, personal grievances have an even better chance to appear, since these people's general attitudes predispose them to such grievances, rather than the reverse.

Whatever reasons people may find for their dissatisfaction with the way things in general are handled, it is striking to see that dissatisfaction with the seniority rules seems to be one of the major sources of attitude differentiation among workers. First, it is closely linked with attitudes toward production norms. The more dissatisfied a worker is with the application of the seniority rules, the more likely he is to be critical of the norms.[16]

Second, this dissatisfaction is strongly linked with feeling toward workmates. Among people who are high on the scale measuring feelings of solidarity, only 44 per cent are dissatisfied. Among people who rate low on this scale, 75 per cent are dissatisfied.

Third, this type of dissatisfaction seems to influence the rating people give to their factory as a place in which to work. Forty-eight per cent of those who say it is a good place to work also say that the seniority rules are well applied. Among those who classify their plant as a bad place to work, only 25 per cent say the rules are well applied.

Finally, there is a tendency for those who complain about machine stoppages and about the functioning of the maintenance department to be more dissatisfied with the handling of seniority rules.[17]

[16] If we use a four-point scale to rate production workers' attitudes toward the work load, and check this scale against their opinions about the application for the seniority rules, we get the following table.

	Clearly Dissatisfied or Moderately Critical (Per Cent)	Satisfied (Per Cent)
Group I. Very hostile to the production norms...	80	20
Group II. Rather hostile.....................	70	30
Group III. Neutral..........................	55	45
Group IV. Favorable........................	40	60

[17] We shall see later that maintenance problems are the other main source of dissatisfaction and attitude differentiation.

MECHANIZATION AND THE TECHNOLOGICAL ENVIRONMENT

Two-thirds of the workers are employed at semiautomatic machines whose technology has been stable for almost forty years. Of course, numerous improvements have made the machines less demanding and more rapid. But there is nothing particularly unique about this, and, if there is a difference compared to industry in general, it is that progress has been slower within the Monopoly.

The remainder of the workers work either on huge half-automatic equipment, or in transportation, packing, and shipment, or in a few non-mechanized operations of raw material preparation. In the latter, much progress could be, and has been made, but at a deliberately slow pace.

In the shops, automation will probably become feasible before very long. At the time of the survey, however, there was no likelihood of any change in the near future and no rumor of one. One plant, however, had kept most of its operations manual until only a few years ago, because hand processes seemed more appropriate to the special and costly raw material it was using. Since machines had been introduced to this plant a few years before our survey, we expected the transformation to have had its effect on the feelings of the workers. But we did not find many differences in sensitivity about the problem of technological change, whatever the plant and whatever the job held.

This sensitivity, however, was very strong. It appeared quite unexpectedly in the comments made during the free interviews of the pilot study. People complained bitterly and picturesquely about being reduced to the condition of *robots, human machines, mechanical animals, for the sole benefit of the State.* They spoke of the nervous tension to which they were submitted—tension far more exhausting than physical pain:

We live on our nerves and we lose our health; it is no use having retirement pensions, people won't live to enjoy them.

After having thus acknowledged the importance of this theme in the workers' minds, we presented our interviewees with a full battery of statements on mechanization.[18]

1. Mechanization is a necessity for modern life.
2. Mechanization makes it possible to have better work organization.
3. Mechanization makes work easier for the worker.
4. Mechanization brings unemployment.
5. Mechanization increases production for the good of the worker.

[18] We used this term only because it was most commonly used by the workers.

Responses to the last two statements were not sufficiently discriminating. Ninety-five per cent of the workers agreed that mechanization brings unemployment and disagreed with the idea that workers could benefit from mechanization.

Responses to the first three, however, were sufficiently discriminating and quite consistent. They provided a stable scale with, at one extreme, 26 per cent who did not accept mechanization as a necessity of modern life, and, at the other extreme, 16 per cent who thought it made for better organization and even made work easier for the worker. In between, there were two groupings who saw mechanization as a necessity, but did not credit it with any good consequence, or at best thought it could only improve organization.

For comparative purposes, we have generally used the break between the second and third groupings. On the one side, 63 per cent of the sample do not see any advantage to mechanization. On the other side, 38 per cent see at least some technical advantage. The reader will notice that people are more ready to recognize that mechanization makes their work easier than they are to doubt catastrophic predictions of unemployment and pauperization.

These results are quite surprising. They are not in tune with what another French investigation, made in 1956 in a steel plant, has brought to light in the only serious study bearing on the impact of modernization. There, 66 per cent of the workers said the coming of the new installation was good and 68 per cent that it was a must, as against 7 per cent who said they regretted it and 10 per cent who said it was not necessary. Only 17 per cent complained that technical progress came too fast, as against 24 per cent who complained that it was too slow.[19]

Monopoly workers are much more negative than other French workers, and the latter still more negative than their Belgian co-workers in the same plant.

How should we interpret these results?

Analysis of the cross-tabulations shows that neither the job, nor the age, nor the factory makes a great difference. Sex, however, plays a role. Women are significantly more hostile to mechanization than men. But, as with the attitudes toward the work load and toward the seniority system, the decisive difference comes with seniority. The cleavage is even sharper than in the cases of the other two attitudes, and the change of opinion appears after only two years of seniority (Table 3).

[19] Jacques Dofny, Claude Durand, Jean Daniel Reynaud, and Alain Touraine, "Attitudes des ouvriers de la sidérugie à l'égard des changements techniques" (Paris: Institut des Sciences Sociales du Travail, 1957), pp. 183, 191, and 195. (Mimeographed.)

TABLE 3

Seniority	Favorable to Mechanization (Per Cent)	Hostile to Mechanization (Per Cent)	N (Total, 129)
Less than 2 years...........................	66	33	12
More than 2 years...........................	30	70	117

This pattern strongly suggests that the opposition to mechanization is a learned attitude. People who come fresh from outside the Monopoly are very moderate about mechanization. Those who had never worked in a factory before might be expected to have more problems and to resent working at a machine. But this is not the case. On the contrary, workers become hostile little by little through a sort of learning process corresponding to their acculturation in the workers' group. The important factor seems to be the norms of the group and not the peculiarities of the situation. The lack of relationship between this attitude and variables such as the job held and the plant is a case in point.

The change is so sharp that one would predict that it would carry some rationalization with it. The answers to one of our questions fortunately provided a good example. We had asked our interviewees about the relative importance for the workers of salary problems, of the speed-up problem, and of the problem of worker redundancy. Forty-two per cent of the total named the speed-up, but in the group of workers with two to four years' seniority, 70 per cent selected this item, as contrasted to a rather stable 35 per cent in all the other seniority groups. Remembering that these special years are those following the great turning point, one may hypothesize that workers are seeking, in the speed-up situation, illustrations of, and a defense for, their newly acquired belief.

To reinforce our argument, we may point out that the naming of the speed-up as the most important problem is not otherwise linked with the belief about the evils of mechanization. It seems, rather, to be a volatile judgment varying from plant to plant, according to the general climate of opinion. More people complain about the speed-up in the plants where the work load is more resented and where the application of the seniority system is criticized. However, there is no tendency for the individuals who complain about these problems freely to specify speed-up more than their colleagues.

Like attachment to the seniority provision, hostility toward mechanization appears to be a trait of the people who are better integrated into the group. The two attitudes are closely linked. The more attached one is to the seniority principle, the more likely one is to be hostile to mechanization.

Finally, hostility to mechanization is also a group attitude that distinguishes very decisively the production workers from the supervisors and even the maintenance workers. We asked the latter two groups the same questions. Their answers could be scaled the same way, but with a distribution much more in favor of mechanization.[20] A comparison of the three groups on the discriminating questions is shown in Table 4. This variance is considerable. But it should be

TABLE 4

	Hostile to Mechanization (Per Cent)	Moderately Favorable— Better Organization but Does Not Make Work Easier for Worker (Per Cent)	Favorable (Per Cent)
Supervisors...............................	17	40	43
Maintenance..............................	20	57	23
Production workers.......................	62	22	16

noted that hostility to mechanization is a pervasive attitude. A sizable percentage within the other two groups seems to be influenced by workers' beliefs, admitting at least the contention that mechanization does not make work easier for the worker (84 per cent among production workers, 77 per cent among maintenance workers, and 57 per cent among supervisors).

Why has this opposition developed and persisted? We have no direct clues yet. However, anticipating our analysis of shop problems, we can speculate that mechanization, i.e., a change in technology, is the only significant change possible in an otherwise perfectly stable system, and that it carries, therefore, threatening implications.

The kind of solid group opposition we have measured is obvious enough to management. The will to resist which it exemplifies is an important factor in the implicit or sometimes explicit bargaining that occurs for any kind of change concerning the distribution of rewards and the evading of duties.

THE CONTENT OF THE WORKERS' SUBCULTURE

Comparison of the attitudes in the areas of the three organizational givens briefly reviewed—the work load, the seniority system, the

[20] One could notice also that it is the first statement—mechanization is a necessity of modern life—which becomes non-discriminating this time, while at the other end of the spectrum one finds a growing minority who do not fear unemployment and accept the idea of mechanization as benefiting the working class.

technological environment—discloses a number of interesting features. In all three areas, we find a solid majority presenting a rigid
ideological front. This majority is formed of the senior, better group-
integrated, and more responsible workers. Opposition to it comes
from the people who are still too new to be group-integrated, or
from the marginal people. Workers seem to pick up the majority
beliefs by a rather short learning process. Whether, and how readily,
they learn does not correspond much to their origin or to the peculiar
circumstances of their situation. It depends neither upon their working-class background and political affiliation, nor upon their personal
experiences in the shop. It develops much more according to their
kind of participation in their group. In this respect, and in a very
narrow sense, we would like to use the image of a workers' subculture. There seems to exist among workers a set of attitudes and beliefs that cannot be explained as a collection of individual responses
to a similar situation, but that suggests an autonomous group development. People accept these beliefs and develop these attitudes inasmuch as they participate in the group, and the group maintains
them insofar as necessary for its own bargaining.

The content of this subculture is in opposition to the goals of the
organization and the aims of management. It implies an idealization
of the past, some pessimism about the present, devaluation of the
future, and distrust of management. The group's demand for autonomy, and its affirmation of independence, are directed primarily
against the organization to which it belongs. This opposition is so
strong that it cuts across occupational categories and influences each
of them decisively. But paradoxically enough, the existence of this
uniform set of beliefs does not provide many cues about the problems people face in the shop and the way they handle these problems. In at least two of the three areas we have studied, the problem
of seniority and the problem of mechanization, we find a great difference between abstract principles as a defense, and practical behavior, which may be influenced by all sorts of considerations.
Around these quite fixed bureaucratic givens, finally, a rigid system
of attitudes and beliefs has developed which corresponds to the group
pressure to which the participants have to submit. This pressure,
however, has for the individuals also a very positive function, since
it safeguards for them an area of personal autonomy to which belong
most of the concrete aspects of everyday life.

THE FORMAL AUTHORITY SYSTEM

Formal authority in the Monopoly is concentrated in the hands of
the director and the assistant director. Since supervisors have to ap-

ply the rules in the narrower sense, and since the maintenance work-ers' influence is a covert one, formal and legitimate decisions are made only at the top. The power that comes with the right of inter-preting the rules and moderating them belongs almost exclusively to the managerial team.

This centralization of authority, however, seems associated with the whittling away of the content of authority; everything seems to be in the hands of the director, who is the only one whose power is legitimate. Yet, although his authority may be considered absolute, he is in most cases helpless, and the amount of actual control he can exercise is extremely small.

Directors are the only persons who can make legitimate decisions. However, this right does not give them much influence on their sub-ordinates, since the latter do not have to expect much from manage-ment. Directors may make decisions, but these are impersonal ones that must in all cases preserve all group and individual positions and privileges. Their content can be predicted, and the intentions of the decision-makers do not have to be taken into account. Thus directors cannot manipulate their subordinates and govern their behavior by using their arbitrary power to punish or to reward—since they are practically stripped of such personal power. They are the prisoners of an organizational system that decides in their place. Hiring does not depend on them. They can neither promote nor punish their subordinates seriously, and they cannot reward them. Finally, as we have already emphasized, they cannot even allocate jobs, perma-nently or temporarily.

To be sure, there are still certain things that directors can give or withhold—approve a day off, arrange for work load allowances in case of bad raw material, provide for helpful supplies, and so on. Courting management favors may help a worker to achieve his own ends, provided these ends are very narrow and do not antagonize his fellows or the union. Generally speaking, however, directors are rather helpless even in this respect because of the very centralization that gives them such power. They are somewhat too far above to be able to influence individuals by such daily give-and-take. This kind of first-line supervisory behavior does not fit either the size of the unit of which they are in charge or their own prestige situation. They cannot know their workers intimately enough, and the formal-ity of their role would make it improper for them to bargain their way through. Furthermore, all their decisions are checked and scruti-nized by the unions; and any attempt on their part to influence peo-ple is likely to bring in union delegates. Furthermore, on a collective basis their bargaining situation is not very good, since even their most minor decisions may be appealed and they are never sure of being supported. A give-and-take relationship of sorts can be established, but it will remain probably a limited and unstable one, because the unions do not have so much to gain from it as does management.

Directors command, on the other hand, a great deal of attention, and the reactions of their subordinates to their personality and behavior indicate another important aspect of the formal authority relationship. This aspect concerns managerial prestige and the indirect influence directors may acquire because of this prestige. In order to assess the attitudes of the workers and supervisors toward the managerial team, we asked a number of questions. We also analyzed the numerous spontaneous comments we obtained both in the pilot study and in the regular survey.

The first fact that struck us when reviewing the results is the importance every group seems to attach to the problem of contacts. Employees consistently complain about the existence of a gap between them and the directors. They feel that no communication is possible. The directors cannot understand, and there is no way to have them understand, *what it is really like.* These comments, of course, are neither surprising nor precise. However, their tone indicates that they are more than merely conventional. It is especially significant, in this respect, that politeness and related problems of formality in human relations constitute by far the most common item emerging from our content analysis of what people think of their director. Workers seem to be extraordinarily sensitive to the formal care and attention they receive from him.

He never says good morning. When talking he will keep his hands in his pockets.
You cannot talk to him, he does not pay attention.

These are representative of the kind of standard accusations. There are also reports of touching incidents of courtesy, gentlemanly consideration for women workers, and so forth, on a much less crowded favorable side. Generally speaking, workers have an image of their director as cold and distant and having no consideration for the status aspirations of his workers.

In fact, the results show a rather low degree of interaction with the production workers. Only 15 per cent of them have ever had the chance to exchange a few words with their director, although there are only four hundred persons in a plant and in all three of our cases the directors had been there for at least five years. Concerning the assistant directors, the results are similar in two of the plants, where only about 25 per cent of the workers stated that they had talked more than once with their respective assistant director. In the third plant, however, where an assistant director made a point of having more contacts, there is a striking difference—the percentage rises to 67.

It is interesting that there is no direct relationship between the report of having spoken with members of management and the demand for more contacts. Even in the plant where most people had talked with the assistant director, the same percentage (60 per cent) of workers wanted more contacts. The maintenance people, who report most often that they have talked with the assistant director and even with the director, are even more eager than the production workers for more contact; 75 per cent request it.

Finally, wanting more contact appears to be another mark of good integrative interest and of good participation in the plant's organized ways, especially in the unions. It is significantly associated with the tendency to make evaluations, either positive or negative, on the plant and the way it works.

The second important trait to emerge is the predominance of personality criteria over achievement criteria in the judgments production workers make about their directors.[21] Workers very rarely talk about what directors have accomplished, their technical and organizational successes or failures. On the other hand, they always have a good deal to say about the kind of men the directors are. It seems extremely important to the workers whether their director be the retiring or the impressive kind, nervous or affirmative or domineering, military or intellectual, and especially, of course, polite or rude and unpleasant. We asked a direct question on competence which did not elicit any comments. The answers themselves bear no close relation to the answers to the general question: "Would you say of your director—'He is very good,' or 'not so good,' or 'good enough'?"

This lack of relationship is all the more significant since the answers to the same pair of questions, asked about the technical engineer, were, this time, exactly parallel.

For the workers the "good director" is, above all, someone nice who pays due respect to his people and shows he is interested in them as persons. The concrete proof of his interest seems to be his often being in the plant and talking to the workers. The third important item of the content analysis is the physical presence of the director. Workers complain that he does not come, they do not see him, he is not interested in the plant, he does not care for the plant.

---

[21] We would like to suggest that such an opposition of attitudes is characteristic of the difference between an ascriptive hierarchical order and an achievement-oriented one.

We come back to the problem of contacts, but with a new connotation—the underlying suspicion that directors are retreating, avoiding their people.

The results of the more quantitative questions add a new dimension to the general picture. We have been dealing so far with over-all traits characterizing the three plants. With quantification, differences appear whose importance should be emphasized, since they suggest the existence of a sort of "affectivity" in this particular relationship. The differences are, indeed, much greater than those which appeared in the ratings workers made of their individual supervisors. They give the impression of being as unstable and variable as are direct interpersonal relationships (Table 5).

TABLE 5

JUDGMENTS OF THE WORKERS ON THEIR DIRECTOR AND ON THEIR ASSISTANT DIRECTOR

	Director Very Good (Per Cent)	Director Adequate (Per Cent)	Director Not Very Good (Per Cent)	No Answer; No Opinion (Per Cent)
Plant A............	15	65	7.5	12.5
Plant B............	32.5	42.5	7.5	17.5
Plant C............	12	37	33	18
	Assistant Director Very Good (Per Cent)	Assistant Director Adequate (Per Cent)	Assistant Director Not Very Good (Per Cent)	No Answer; No Opinion (Per Cent)
Plant A............	87.5	12.5	0	0
Plant B............	17.5	25	15	42.5*
Plant C............	14	37	24	25

* The assistant director in this case had not been there very long.

Although the percentage of the "no opinion" and the not too committed "adequate" answers is large, one can imagine how varied in themselves such evaluations may be. This is all the more striking since, as we have emphasized, directors cannot have very much influence on the workers' lot, and since in more general matters there is a regular distribution of opinion in the three plants. This display of affectivity does not, however, seem to have very deep consequences; no relationship appears between a favorable judgment of the directors and a better adjustment to life in the plant or to the worker's own situation. We can only note that favorable evaluations are likely to be associated with more conventional attitudes, and that the better integrated people are more likely to give a positive or negative answer than to stay uncommitted. Unfavorable judgments, to be sure, are associated with some bitterness about things becoming progressively worse. These negative evaluations are notably more numerous among women and among workers with more seniority, but the pattern is still not significantly consistent.

The differences among personnel categories are more interesting.

In comparison with production workers, maintenance workers are rather more aggressive, at least against the director, while the union delegates, surprisingly, are likely to be more tolerant and restrained. The pattern of distribution, however, is consistently the same in these two cases. In other words, maintenance workers and stewards will talk more or less openly, more or less aggressively, but their image of the director will remain the same as that held by the production workers. This is not the case with the supervisors. They, in addition to usually being far more restrained than all the others—which, of course, is to be expected, as they are much more dependent upon the directors—do not approve of the same people. This difference stands out when we compare results in Plant A and Plant B.

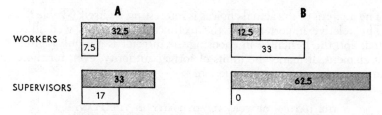

THE DIRECTOR IS VERY GOOD ☐ THE DIRECTOR IS NOT VERY GOOD

Fig. 2.—Judgments of workers and supervisors on the directors in Plant A and Plant B. For clarity, we are presenting only the really committed answers: very good, and not very good.

It is immediately noticeable that the director in Plant A, who is in less disfavor with the workers, is in greater disfavor with the supervisors. On the other hand, the director in Plant B, in high favor with the supervisors, is the very one about whom the workers complain most. This opposition points toward another important aspect of the role of the director—the arbitration aspect. Being regarded in a friendly manner by one group may easily have as its corollary the rising hostility of another.

One last finding remains to be discussed—the answers given to a relatively vague question about who has the most importance in running the plant. We expected to get only stereotyped answers, but this was not the case. There was quite a large dispersion of opinions. Some comments expressed rather well the shrewdness and the uncertainty of the interviewees, such as this humorous one:

> Here I would say it's nobody; what makes it [the plant] run is the force of habit; I am sure if everybody left it would go on running all the same.[22]

[22] One should relate this comment to the comment quoted above, on p. 28, on the Clerical Agency.

TABLE 6

The Most Important People for Running the Plant According to
Occupational Categories

	Production Workers (Per Cent)	Maintenance Workers (Per Cent)	Supervisors (Per Cent)
Director..........................	29	10	27
Assistant director................	16	3	34
Administrative officer............	4	...	3
Technical Engineer...............	10	43	13
Supervisor.......................	8	...	3
Maintenance worker..............	2	13	...
Production worker................	15	7	3
Nobody, everybody, or confused answers..	16	24	17
N................................	129	30	30

The analysis of the actual choices is interesting by itself (Table 6).
The relative importance of the technical engineer is well illus-
trated, and the hesitancy in choosing the director is a highly significant element. It marks the limits of formal authority, even for those
who are under its direct jurisdiction.

THE NATURE OF FORMAL AUTHORITY IN THE PLANT

The reaction of the employees will be better understood if one recalls
that directors have been pushed, by the pressure of the seniority system, toward occupying a quasi-judicial function. They have little
organizational leeway. The workers themselves make no mistake on
this point; they know the directors do not run the plant. But the
role of the directors remains essential, inasmuch as all formal authority is centralized. Instead of the direct attainment of measurable
production or financial goals, however, the director's primary objective is to maintain peace and order and to keep a workable equilibrium between individuals and between groups whose duties are already fixed.

It is, therefore, natural for the workers to be interested, not in the
director's achievements, but in his human qualities. This is the way
a judge might be viewed by the general public—his success will depend on his reputation, not for getting things done, but for being
fair and humane. Something more, however, is involved in the director's function that enables us to understand the importance attached
to his role and the continual focus on him. As in more ancient societies, the judicial and the administrative functions coincide. The final
judge is also the nominal head, the symbol of unity, the necessary
link that makes it possible for society to continue, since he alone can
give the ultimate sanction to its acts.

What is the meaning, in this context, of the longing for contact?

One can say, of course, that modern mores do not allow the head of a group of four hundred the aloofness of a judge and the awe and respect due a supreme administrator. More concretely, it seems that individuals and groups involved in the decisions of the person entrusted with the function of supreme arbitration strive to get closer to him in order to influence him. We hypothesized, at the end of our study of the Clerical Agency, that centralization of authority is a natural consequence of this pressure of the staff on those who have formal authority. Such a system of organization operates to the advantage of the subordinates, but it leaves the aggrieved individual with no one to whom to turn but the director. Furthermore, since this is an ascriptive society where no achievement considerations can enter, contact with the director will have a prestige value, be a reward in itself. By talking to the director, the workers get a sense of recognition, and this is their most direct way of participating in the community to which they belong.

This judicial and administrative concept of authority may well reflect the workers' ideal, but it cannot but correspond imperfectly to reality. The plant cannot be taken care of automatically through the application of the rules, and directors still have to maintain pressure for achieving production. Their influence, however, is only of the judicial administrative type, and they must use it to influence people by manipulating them into higher productivity. The pressure of the workers for more contacts can, in this respect, be viewed as an attempt to make the director conform to their own ideal conceptions, and the coldness of the directors can be seen as a tactic to keep the workers at arm's length and oblige them to compromise.

It is interesting that, in their interviews, the directors seemed to ignore completely the gap of which the workers complained. When told, during the feedback experiment, about workers' feelings, directors expressed concern about the effects of such demagoguery. They more or less consciously feared that they would become prisoners of their subordinates if they were to see them too informally. One can sense, in this reaction, some of their class-conscious feeling; having no possibility of real achievement themselves, they tend to insist more on their differences and prerogatives. But their reaction seems determined still more by the power situation. If they wish to retain a measure of their influence, that is, their possibility of bargaining, directors must keep the aloofness which is, for them, a necessary prerequisite for bargaining.

The rationale of the relationship apparently works finally as follows: the independence of the workers makes it impossible to coerce them directly; they are completely protected as long as they obey the rules. They need, however, stability and due process, i.e., peace and order; they also need some sense of purpose and recognition. Formal authority is, therefore, indispensable to them, but they would like it to be their servant and to acknowledge their status. This very demand for recognition, however, reverses the situation and the directors regain leeway. By considering their own contribution to the system, they remain able to reward and punish and therefore to influence. Retreat and distance can be a way of governing. Giving or refusing consideration, calculated coldness, will keep workers on the soliciting side and will oblige the workers to recognize the director's preserve—for the sake of "peace and order" to accept eventual compromise even in the matter of production goals.

Concern with the matter of politeness is, therefore, not an idle one. It does reflect the kind of struggle going on. The marked differences between plants show the range of bargains that can be made within this area of affective interrelations.

A completely opposite course, however, is also possible. This is demonstrated by the success of the assistant director who gets a popularity vote from his personnel as a result of abandoning formal reserve and welcoming contacts. But even in this case, one must take into account the fact that when bargaining operates this other way, it operates against the background of the other directors' reserve. It is by offering what others refuse that this assistant director is able to call for co-operation. And while his behavior provokes the hostility of his own colleagues, who feel it makes their resistance less easy, it is probably at the same time successful only insofar as the workers compare it with the more usual attitude of authority.

Chapter Four

THE SOCIAL SYSTEM AT THE SHOP LEVEL

II. *The Relationships between Groups and the Adjustment Patterns of Groups*

Our review of the kinds of adjustment people make to the organizational givens and to the formal authority system has permitted us, so far, to analyze only the more stable and undifferentiated aspects of the social system at the shop level. Now we wish to study the more contingent and specific aspects of this pecular social system, by focusing on the relationships between the most important groupings, the occupational categories. We will then be able to discuss the patterns of adjustment which bind the individuals within each of the three main groups and to propose a first interpretation of the power-relations arrangements that maintain the equilibrium of the social system.

THE GROUP RELATIONSHIPS

Three groups are represented at the shop level: the production workers, the maintenance workers, and the foremen or lower supervisors. We have already briefly described their types of recruitment and career patterns. Their roles are very distinct and clear-cut, not allowing for exchange or even co-operation. There is no intermediary buffer role. No one ever expects to be promoted (or demoted) from one role to another.

In a typical production shop there is first, one foreman, or one foreman with an assistant foreman. Their job is to keep records of individual and group production, to plan and account for all expenditures and supplies and for the utilization of raw materials, and to make day-to-day decisions regarding job reallocations necessitated by sickness, machine stoppages, or production changes. Their work is co-ordinated by four general plant foremen (second-level foremen). One of these is responsible for a quality section that regularly analyzes samples of the product. Second, there are about a dozen maintenance workers, each in charge of three specific machines for which he acts both as machine-setter and repairman. These people do not report to the foreman, but to the technical engineer responsible for the maintenance of the whole factory. Then there are from 60 to 120 production workers, machine operators, product receivers, and utility workers. This last group is composed mostly of women.

We had planned to compare results achieved by supervisors from shop to shop, but this turned out to be unrewarding; differences were small and haphazard and bore no relation to the foremen's personal characteristics. It appears that a similar comparison of the maintenance workers' records would have provided highly significant differentiation. We had, however, underestimated the individual importance of the maintenance people; and the way our sample was organized did not allow us to follow through with the comparison.[1] We shall, therefore, analyze group relationships at the group level, without discussing the possibility of differentiation introduced by individual factors.

THE RELATIONSHIP BETWEEN PRODUCTION WORKERS AND FOREMEN

The relationship between workers and first-level supervisors is generally considered to be crucial, since it provides the only direct contact between the rank-and-file and formal authority. Our study of this relationship in the Monopoly, however, yielded results similar to our findings in the Clerical Agency. They pointed to an easy kind of relationship characterized mostly by tolerance, and even indifference, on both sides.

Let us examine first the attitudes of the production workers. We had presented the workers with a number of questions on the importance and competence of their supervisors and on the way in which they got along with them.[2]

As expected, the question on competence was answered very conventionally; 70 per cent of the workers agreed that their own foreman was competent. But the questions about the importance of the supervisor's function disclosed the low regard workers have for both first-level and second-level foremen.

Answers to the other questions about the worker's own foreman

---

[1] Half of the maintenance workers in the shop and one out of six production workers were interviewed, but the two samples were independent and we could not match the production workers' answers with those of the maintenance people who worked directly with them.

[2] The questions were phrased in the following way: (1) "Are first-level foremen very important in running the plant?" (2) "And the second-level foremen?" (3) "Do you think your own first-level foreman is a competent man?" (4) "Do you think he would go to bat for his own people?" (5) "Would you call him severe?" (6). "Do you get along well with him?"

revealed a cordial relationship. These answers were closely linked (but not to the questions on importance and on competence).

Their ordering[3] shows that to express disagreement with one's foreman seems easier than to say he is a severe disciplinarian (which is a very unusual comment).[4] Also, for the two-thirds who do not see any problem in getting along with their foreman, the only attribute that counts is whether or not he will stand up for them.

This is exactly the same as the situation we described for the Clerical Agency. The problem of supervision is not a problem of authority and of contact; it is only a problem of trust. Relationships between supervisors and subordinates are good, but unimportant. And, as in the Clerical Agency, there is no relationship between the difficulties production workers may have with their supervisors and the possibilities of their adjusting to their work and to their environment. To be sure, marginal workers who criticize their union and do not agree with the seniority rules are less likely to say that they get along well with their foreman. However, this simply points in the other direction: people who have difficulties in adjusting to the special bureaucratic environment will be more reluctant to concur with any genial or hopeful statements, especially when these concern people who play a role in administering the rules. But on the more fundamental questions of satisfaction with the work and with the job, in contrast to what is usually found, the quality of the relationship with the supervisor does not make any difference.

The role of the supervisors in the Industrial Monopoly is even more devalued than in the Clerical Agency. This is apparent in the kind of answers we received to the questions about the importance of the supervisors, and especially in the noticeable lack of emotional tone and disturbance when a worker stated that he did not get along with his foreman.

If, instead of the workers' individual adjustments, we consider group reactions, the regularity of the answers suggests a number of striking differences. The similarity is almost perfect, from plant to plant and even from shop to shop, about the importance of the supervisor in general. But there are some differences in the answers regarding getting along with one's own foreman. In the three raw material conditioning shops, where the role of the foreman is more demanding, the same workers who are as contemptuous as their colleagues of the supervisor's role in general are significantly more positive about getting along with their own foreman (and about other personal questions about him). Second, in the plant where manage-

---

[3] Which is a Guttman-like scale.

[4] This is especially striking when one takes into account the fact that the question does not specify "too severe" but only "severe."

ment complains most about the poor quality of the supervisory force and where workers give supervisors the worst rating on importance and competence, quite a few comments complain about the supervisors' lack of authority. Then, in the plant where management feels it has the best supervisory force—and where the supervisors *are* younger, and most have gone through the Monopoly's special training courses—the workers are much less frequently disposed to say that supervisors are very important and are significantly less positive about them on the getting-along scale.[5]

One may characterize the feelings of the workers toward the supervisors as follows: (1) There is low personal involvement; (2) There is tolerance and cordiality, but no understanding of nor respect for the supervisory role; (3) Minimizing the importance of the role is a strong norm of the workers' group, cutting across every special situation of individual foremen; (4) Any move on the part of supervisors to enlarge their role is likely to meet a strong reaffirmation of the norm and some withholding of the usual tolerance; (5) A striking lack of achievement, on the other hand, tends to foster regrets about the supervisors' difficult situation.

Let us examine the point of view of the supervisors. All supervisors interviewed were at work in the shop—usually there were six first-level foremen and four second-level foremen in each plant. We asked them many questions about their role and the way they thought one should behave in their situation.

Their answers seem remarkable for lack of commitment. Supervisors as a group do not have a high regard for production workers, whom they consider neglectful, irresponsible, and careless. But the supervisors had no consensus about the way in which the workers should be handled. The results of the interviews on this matter were evenly divided among three recommendations: being strict, being tolerant, and deciding according to the specific issue. There is only one strong and consistent correlation in this respect, somewhat contrary to expectations. The more realistic supervisors, who admit they have problems of discipline, are more likely to choose strictness. These supervisors are younger (they have less than ten years' seniority) and most of them come from groups who have had some training and those who are hostile to the seniority principle. It seems, therefore, that as a counterpart to the cordial tolerance of the workers, there is a rather unconcerned paternalism on the part of the majority of the supervisors. A deeper involvement is likely to bring conflicts to the minority who would like to alter the situation in which they find themselves.

[5] They also say much less frequently that the supervisors are very important. In all the preceding relationships, we opposed the answers "a lot" and "enough" to the answers "little" and "not at all."

THE RELATIONSHIP BETWEEN PRODUCTION AND MAINTENANCE WORKERS

Compared to the cordiality and the lack of commitment in the relationships between workers and supervisors, the relationships between production and maintenance workers offer a sort of paradox. They contain all the tension and emotional involvement that characterize situations of dependence and that one usually expects from supervisor-subordinate relationships. This is all the more surprising in that both groups are occupationally autonomous, report to two different hierarchical lines, and are not supposed to be dependent on one another.

We became aware of the problem during the pilot study. Then, by utilizing the first comments we had obtained, we developed questions designed to elicit systematic answers. However, in the survey it proved difficult to proceed along these lines because of the resistance of the maintenance workers. We had correctly hypothesized the existence of tension, but without understanding the privileged position of the maintenance workers. Since we had had our official contacts in the local unions with representatives of the maintenance group—who were usually the actual leaders of the trade unions—we felt it would be wise to give more attention to the production workers during the two-week stage that we devoted, in the first plant, to preparing the final survey. Feeling they had been by-passed, the maintenance workers decided to boycott the study. We thus were forced to await the success of our interviews in the second plant before we could enlist their co-operation. This success was achieved by a careful presentation of the aims of the research to their group, prior to our holding any discussion with the production workers. No resentment was subsequently expressed when we asked delicate questions, since we had shown that we were duly respectful of the hierarchy.

Production workers' direct comments on the maintenance workers and on the problems of maintenance are not very abundant and seem fairly reserved. In our third plant survey, we asked special open-ended questions to elicit more comments. The workers generally answered on a technical and impersonal plane. However, a sizable minority expressed straightforward criticism.

One otherwise temperate woman said:

> My maintenance man is very unpleasant. I don't talk to him and won't talk to him any more.

Another said, in a bitter tone:

> We are dependent on them, they are the bosses.

And we got several comments like:

They do as they please.

But there are usually more complaints about the past than about present conditions. One of the interviewees expressed this attitude quite well:

They are still important people. In the old days one had to please them.

Also, many production workers suggested that the distribution of work is not fair and that the maintenance people who do not have much to do could give a hand.

We asked them the following closed-ended questions.

1. When a machine stops, how do maintenance people take care of it? [6]

2. Do you get along well with your maintenance man?

3. Do you think maintenance people have too much work, a fair amount of work, or relatively little work?

4. What do you think of the wage differential between maintenance and production workers?

5. Do you think the maintenance department is functioning well?

If we eliminate the raw material processing shops, where there is not much of a maintenance problem, the results of the first and finally more decisive question are:

Yes, they do whatever they can . . . .   33 per cent
Some are much more active than others . . . . . .   55 per cent
They usually don't do everything they should .   12 per cent
No opinion . . . .   0 per cent

The question about getting along with one's maintenance man elicited less bold answers. Even among production shops, 75 per cent of the workers said they were getting along all right. More substantial complaints were expressed in connection with the more general and impersonal questions. In answering them, 45 per cent of the interviewees said that maintenance workers did not have enough work to do; 59 per cent said that the wage differential was too great; 12 per cent said maintenance workers got too much money. On the question of the functioning of the maintenance department, we get 43 per cent favorable answers, 21 per cent dubious, and 17 per cent critical (with 19 per cent not answering).

[6] In answering, the interviewees could choose among the three following formulas: "Do you think that they do whatever they can to repair it quickly, or that some maintenance people are much more active than others, or that they usually don't do everything they should?"

General judgments on the privileges of maintenance people do not vary much from plant to plant and from shop to shop; they express a general climate of jealousy and resentment. But answers to the question concerning the way maintenance men respond to the challenge of the job are worth analyzing more closely.

There are three different patterns of organization in the shops. The first corresponds to the more difficult operations carried on in only one of the plants. In this pattern, Pattern I, one maintenance man takes care of six machines and on each of these machines two women hold similar parallel posts. Pattern II and Pattern III correspond respectively to the two main successive operations found in the two other plants. In Pattern II, one maintenance man takes care of three machines, each of which is served by one woman machine operator and by another woman who removes the finished products. In Pattern III, one maintenance man takes care of three machines. Each machine is used by one woman machine operator, two women in charge of packaging, and one man whose job is to load and unload the incoming materials and the outgoing packaged products.

In Pattern I, each maintenance man has to deal with twelve operators working in pairs, and all of them equals. In Pattern II and Pattern III, he deals only with three operators whose roles are distinct from the roles of their workmates.

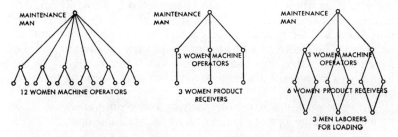

Fig. 3.—Three different shop organization patterns.

Responses to the question are significantly different in the three patterns. There are many more complaints in Pattern II and many fewer in Pattern I, with Pattern III falling in between. The specializing of a number of workers in these intermediate jobs, where one is in charge of dealing with the maintenance man, may be a main cause of these differences. The maintenance man is regarded with less suspicion when he has to deal with all the workers directly than when he deals only with a minority of them. It is in Pattern II, where workers are divided according to occupations, and are also less numerous around each machine, that grievances are the loudest, as if specialization could be more justified in a group of twelve people than in a group of six.[7]

There is another and even more significant difference in Patterns II and III between, on the one hand, the women machine operators who have direct contacts with the maintenance man, and, on the other, the women product receivers and men laborers. This is apparent in Table 7.

TABLE 7

JUDGMENTS ON THE MAINTENANCE WORKERS ACCORDING TO THE KIND OF JOB HELD

	Yes, They Do Whatever They Can (Per Cent)	Some Much More Than Others (Per Cent)	No, They Don't (Per Cent)
Machine operators...................	45	50	5
Product receivers and laborers..........	25	50	25

This opposition between machine operators and product receivers and laborers seems paradoxical until one accepts the idea of covert tension, expressed only with difficulty by the people most directly concerned. The women machine operators must deal continually with the maintenance men. In order to keep the necessary balance, they have to make an effort to adjust to the situation. If they do not want to make the effort, they can change jobs quite easily and receive a slight decrease in pay.[8] As a matter of fact, a sizable proportion of the women product receivers had been machine operators at one time. The receivers, who are not under such pressure to find the situation acceptable, are therefore in a far better position psychologically to express the antagonism that they share with the machine operators.

This interpretation is corroborated by other differences we find between machine operators and receivers. Machine operators will

[7] The importance of these organizational patterns is not limited to complaints about the role of the maintenance people; they seem to be decisive also for the climate of interaction between workmates. In Pattern III, only 46 per cent of the workers complain about not getting along well with their colleagues (a comprehensive scale rating), as against 71 per cent and 75 per cent in Patterns II and I respectively. Our sample is too small for us to analyze further the relationship between complaints about maintenance men and complaints about colleagues. One could hypothesize that Pattern III, requiring the highest degree of teamwork and at the same time giving the members of the group able to deal with the maintenance man some compensatory prominence, tends to minimize both dissatisfactions; whereas Pattern II, with the rigid two-person teamwork arrangement, makes for more difficult interactions among workmates while at the same time making the dependency relationship most conspicuous, thus tending to maximize both kinds of complaints.

[8] Such a decrease is not important enough to stop people who may be really concerned.

complain much more about the general functioning of the maintenance department than will their product receiver colleagues. Likewise, they protest more and are more pessimistic about work loads. It seems clear, therefore, that their leniency toward individual maintenance workers must not be interpreted as the sign of a more positive outlook, but as the result of a difficult effort to accept a given situation which carries at least as much tension as may be openly expressed elsewhere. Our cross-tabulations show that at the individual level the association of judgments—maintenance men are all right; production workers can't meet their work loads; the maintenance department is not functioning well—will appear among machine operators more often than chance.

This projection of complaints onto the psychologically easier theme seems characteristic of strong but covert tension. Production workers, mostly women, behave as if they were dependent on the maintenance men and resentful of it. The sex difference, of course, is probably an important element in shaping the situation. But this influence should not be exaggerated. No comments were ever made about it, and there is a complete lack of differentiation between men servants and women product receivers.[9] Whatever the sex differential component, in any case, the production workers' attitude toward maintenance men is one of resentment and guarded hostility.

On the part of the maintenance men facing this hostility, we find a tolerant paternalism and a reluctant awareness of some of the difficulties.

We presented them with the same series of questions about the way production workers do their jobs as we had the foremen. The answers were very close: 75 per cent as against 80 per cent said:

Workers do a lot of harm by refusing to work at a regular pace [trying to set up a production quota "kitty" but rushing whenever possible].

Sixty-six per cent as against 75 per cent said:

Workers do not understand anything beyond the narrow requirements of their own job.

In both cases, 66 per cent said:

Workers do not care about technical problems.

On the problem of work standards, also, the maintenance people are much closer to the supervisors' than to the workers' judgment. Furthermore, saying that production workers do not attain the work

---

[9] The only striking example of these differences concerns the influence of age. The women workers forty years old and older complain of their maintenance men at a 75 per cent ratio, as against 55 per cent among those under forty. There is no relationship of that sort among men.

standards is a criticism of their behavior—in other words, this may be more a derogatory remark than a manifestation of solidarity. We asked the maintenance people, finally, more specific questions about their relationship with the production workers.[10]

Forty-eight per cent of the maintenance men said that they often gave advice to the workers, and 29 per cent said that they did so from time to time. Sixty per cent said that when they gave advice, workers paid no attention to it. Forty per cent said that the workers did not always pay attention; or that not every worker did; or else they did not answer. Most maintenance men claimed to get along well. Initially, however, their answers were somewhat uneasy, and this response pattern intensified when they were allowed to project on their colleagues (Table 8).

TABLE 8

JUDGMENTS OF THE MAINTENANCE WORKERS ABOUT THEIR GETTING ALONG
WITH PRODUCTION WORKERS

	Maintenance Men about Themselves (Per Cent)	Maintenance Men about Colleagues (Per Cent)
Get along very well..................	41	21
Get along.........................	43	31
Don't get along always..............	11	28
No answer........................	5	20

Maintenance men seem to intervene frequently in the working behavior of "their" production workers, whom they think of as rather careless subordinates. They are usually aware of tension, even if they do not talk openly about it. It is interesting that the ones who said everything goes well appeared to be more rigid and more conformist generally. This suggests that their attitude is much more one of not admitting facts than of having found a better way of handling the situation. This, too, indicates covert tension.

THE RELATIONSHIP BETWEEN FOREMEN AND MAINTENANCE WORKERS

We come now to the third part of our three-cornered relationship. Its peculiarity, compared to the first two, consists in its being a symmetrical relationship. The two parties in it are on an equal footing, and there exists an overt relationship with people ready to express their feelings more openly. It is, nevertheless, also a very tense relationship that carries considerable personal involvement and

[10] These questions were phrased as follows: (1) "Do you often give advice to the production workers working on your machines?" (2) "Do they pay attention to you?" (3) "Do you get along well with your production workers?" (4) "Do your colleagues get along well?"

emotional overtones. Its openness makes it public, and we were warned time and again of its importance. The answers we got confirmed the general feeling.

The symmetry of the attitudes of both parties appeared in answers to a cross-question about the competence of the members of the other group. Forty-six per cent of the maintenance workers expressed doubts about the foremen, and 7 per cent refused to commit themselves by answering. A lower percentage of the foremen (33 per cent) directly attacked the maintenance workers; but if we take into account the 29 per cent who did not answer, we have a very good match.[11] The foremen's criticism can be considered all the more harsh in that management and workers alike generally acknowledge the competence of the maintenance group.

Maintenance workers were asked the same questions as the production workers about the importance of the foremen and about getting along with them. The answers were much less positive. Moreover, they showed a higher consistency,[12] as if the underlying hostility were a sufficient basis for all judgments.

We could not look for the same symmetry in the questions asked the foremen. With them, besides the question on competence, we used a question on authority. We asked them whether the maintenance men's actions jeopardized their own authority over workers. Seventeen per cent said yes; 50 per cent, no; 33 per cent refused to answer. These refusals, of course, are a sign of uneasiness. This is corroborated by the fact that the feelings they expressed are directly related to their evaluation of their own personal situation. The situations of supervisors and maintenance men may be equivalent with respect to the personal attacks made on them, but they are not equivalent as to the satisfaction the men derive from their own positions. Difficult relationships with their partners do not disturb the maintenance workers, while the supervisors seem to be deeply affected by them.

An analysis of the other attitudes of those who complain shows that on both sides aggressiveness is linked with a satisfactory kind of adjustment. Cursing the other fellow is a regular and responsible way of playing one's own role. However, the uneasiness about conflicts in authority seems to carry much more meaning for the supervisors, who have altogether very low morale. For the maintenance men, who have high morale, the uneasiness of the relationship with foremen does not cause the slightest disturbance.

[11] It seems that, in such a context, the refusal to answer can be interpreted as a negative answer.

[12] It will be remembered that, for the production workers, the answers to the question on importance and to the more affective questions could not be scaled together. They can be for the maintenance workers.

THE ADJUSTMENT PATTERNS OF EACH OCCUPATIONAL CATEGORY

We have described the norms and customs constituting the substructure of the social game and analyzed the rules of the game and the relationships between partners. We shall now try to interpret the actors' behavior. Behind individual differences and oppositions, we shall look for the general patterns to which everyone, within each occupational category, seems to conform, and try to understand the relationship of these patterns to the conditions and rules of the social game.

THE PRODUCTION WORKERS' TYPE OF ADJUSTMENT

The behavior of the production workers is characterized by a stable and consistent pattern. This pattern influences almost every one of them, and is established quite early in their work career. All the data from their interviews that we have discussed convey the impression that, on every key point, they are conforming to a kind of official norm. They are uniformly rigid and restrictive about production and complain about the work load. They are strongly attached to the seniority system, opposed to mechanization, tolerantly ignorant of the supervisors, and very demanding of management. Their conformity is the same in domains we have not yet discussed. Parallel data show that they are, for example, very critical of working conditions and of administrative practices, and that they claim that their situation is deteriorating in the same substantial way.

Great pressure on the individual by the group, or more precisely by the occupational category, is apparently involved in the way these attitudes are distributed. Seniority seems to be the chief single factor to influence them. Other determinants do not, of themselves, appear to matter so greatly. Thus almost everyone, given the time, will eventually assimilate the majority's point of view. Workers who have not been there long, and people who remain marginal and do not seem well adjusted to the environment, constitute the minority.

The chief characteristic of this pattern of adjustment can be summed up, curiously, as follows: The better-integrated worker, the good citizen of the working community, is also the member of the organization who opposes most constantly and rationally the aims of management and, in large measure, of the organization itself. This negative kind of conformity is apparently made possible by the group's complete independence of formal authority, in accordance with the seniority system. It is not surprising, therefore, that such conformity is associated with reasonably good feelings about work and a great deal of satisfaction with a job that gives security.

The findings about work satisfaction, contrary to most of the others, were very like the data for similar routine jobs in other kinds of organizations.[13] The distribution is more favorable than in the Clerical Agency. It is especially noticeable that the longer a worker has been on the job, the more likely he is to be satisfied with it. This contrasts not only with the results of the Clerical Agency study, but also with the pessimism and aggressiveness of the senior workers in the domain of norms and customs.

Answers to the questions about working for the Monopoly were still more positive. Eighty per cent of the interviewees answered "yes" to a question deliberately loaded:

"Is it *really* an advantage to work for the Monopoly?"

Seventy-four per cent said that *if they had to start all over again, they would choose to work for the Monopoly.* The primary reason for their choice was security (given by 80 per cent of the interviewees; and 75 per cent preferred security to the chance of promotion). This choice is not so traditionalistic and restrictive as it may seem. In answer to a question about their children, only 28 per cent of the same people said that *they would like their children to work for the Monopoly.* Convinced that they themselves do not have a good chance to get ahead, they are ready to settle for security —but with the understanding that their sacrifice may give their children a chance of advancement.[14]

How do the two kinds of attitude, the negative and the positive, fit together? We should like to propose a hypothesis. Production workers are apparently well adjusted, in the long run. But the privileges they enjoy, and to which they are much attached, still seem insecure to them. They feel that they must exhibit an uncompromising attitude if they wish to escape the pressure for change that is working, they believe, against them. They view mechanization, for example, as a way of continually reopening the bargain they have struck. They suspect that the managerial group are lukewarm about the formal system of which they should be the official guardians, and ready to utilize every loophole to manipulate the workers. A moderate aggressiveness may, in the final analysis, be the

[13] The exact distribution is the following: 38 per cent of the production workers said that they liked their work very much. Forty per cent said that they liked it well enough. And 22 per cent said that they did not like it much or did not like it at all.

[14] The French system of competitive examination favors this kind of rational game, since it makes promotion almost impossible without the necessary educational training. But at the same time it insures that sacrifices made for children will not be in vain.

best means of protecting the group against any encroachment. Moreover, it provides a very good rationale for enforcing discipline within the ranks and for resisting any attempt on the part of the higher-ups to divide and conquer.

However, behind this ostensibly solid façade, there is, as we have seen, a dark zone of perpetual squabbling, uneasiness, and discontent, where general rules cannot be enforced. This unease centers on the problem of the application of the rules when machines are stopped. It involves the dependence of production workers on maintenance, the vulnerability to open bargaining in an area where rules cannot easily be applied, and the effect that the impractical solutions which must be chosen may have on the achievement of work standards. It can be hypothesized that there is all the more affectivity displayed in this area, since the general conformity prevents the expression of affectivity elsewhere.

Naturally, these problems directly and substantially affect the climate of the plant. Complaints about them are directly associated with complaints about workmates, negative evaluations of friendship ties in the shop, and a poor rating of the plant as a place to work. Moreover, the plant with the most squabbling is also the one which, as a whole, is rated by the workers' consensus as the poorest.

It is most significant that, whatever their acuteness, these problems do not really interfere with the worker's over-all adjustment to the situation he confronts in the Monopoly. The hypothesis can be made, however, that all these difficulties engendered by the application of the rules and the inescapable dependence of workers on maintenance people constitute an important element in increasing the demanding attitudes toward formal authority. The more the worker feels frustrated about those personal difficulties where status is involved, the more he wishes to put pressure on the sanctioning authority to restore ascriptive privileges, and the more suspicious he is of the bargaining for which a director is likely to utilize the situation.

The adjustment of the production worker, therefore, may be summarized as follows: (1) He has a rather satisfactory over-all adjustment to the situation; (2) This is associated with a great deal of conformity in all opinions relevant to group interests (group pressures, made possible by the lack of interference from any kind of authority, may develop because of the group's insecurity and the need to present a common protective front; (3) It is also associated with many internal difficulties, which, while not affecting the over-all adjustment, may reinforce the demanding attitudes toward formal authority.

THE MAINTENANCE WORKERS' TYPE OF ADJUSTMENT

In broad outline, maintenance workers present the same kind of adjustment pattern that we have analyzed among production workers. That is, their positive over-all adjustment is associated with a great deal of group conformity, expressed especially in aggressiveness toward the official hierarchy. But this pattern is so sharply drawn that its meaning is quite different.[15]

Their happy over-all adjustment to the situation is of a different nature. Production workers are much less interested in the work than in working for the Monopoly; the reverse is true for the maintenance people. They are very proud of their skill and appear to value their work. Two-thirds of them said they liked it very much, and the other third liked it well enough. Technical engineers were the only other group in the plant to give such a strongly positive answer. In contrast, they were somewhat less enthusiastic about working for the Monopoly than were the production workers. True, the same percentage (73 per cent of the sample) said they would work for the Monopoly if they had to start all over again. However, only 65 per cent (as against 80 per cent among the production workers) said that it is *really an advantage* to work for the Monopoly. In particular, when asked whether they would prefer security or chances of promotion,[16] 55 per cent responded in favor of security and 42 per cent for chances of promotion (compared to a 75 per cent—16 per cent ratio among the production workers). One can sense a conscious regret and some kind of ambivalence here. Maintenance people realize that they have had to sacrifice something to obtain security, and they tend to feel that the price they had to pay was relatively high. This does not affect their pride in the work, but it does affect their attitude toward the organizational system. It is remarkable that those who choose chances of promotion, i.e., reject the basic principle of organization of the Monopoly, are on the whole much less aggressive and critical than their colleagues. When maintenance workers share in the values of the system, it seems that, having committed themselves to it, they are more hostile to its adverse consequences. Tolerance comes only with acceptance of personal responsibility for the situation rather than simple reliance on the system. We may

[15] Significant differences between the two groups develop in this domain, especially as regards general judgments on the directors' responsibilities and status and criticism of administrative practices.

[16] We asked them the following question: "In private employment one does not have so much job security but one has better chances of being promoted. Which do you think preferable: the system of private enterprise or the system of the Monopoly?"

thus speak of a generally happy kind of over-all adjustment. However, it can subsist, for the majority of the maintenance workers, only at the cost of a great deal of aggressiveness against the organizational system.

Maintenance workers, while adjusting differently to their work and situation, do not differ greatly in this respect from production workers. The difference is far more striking in the second trait present in the two categories, group conformity. Maintenance people showed a much higher degree of unanimity in their individual answers to the majority of the questions. They manifested generally more disciplined reaction than any other group. But their kind of conformity does not encompass the same areas as that of the production workers. They are more moderate, less committed, and, therefore, less conformist in the discussion of mechanization and of seniority. But in all questions concerning work, relationships with colleagues, with supervisors, with production workers, and in their judgments about the managerial group and administrative practices, the maintenance group rarely differed.

The pressure of the group became apparent during the feedback experiment. A group of seven maintenance men, who had all been interviewed—and most of whom had individually taken a more lukewarm attitude to their work than the rest of their colleagues— gave us collectively a completely different answer, although they were at the time confronted by a table showing detailed interview results of, among others, the group to which they belonged. They did not contest these prior results. In fact, they gave us sufficient hints that we were to understand that they accepted them as true; but they left the floor to the minority who acted as spokesmen in a sort of revised version of the original interview.

Another side of this group pressure is the image of *esprit de corps* —the feeling of solidarity and group cohesion manifested in their interviews. Sixty-two per cent protested when asked whether there might be a lack of solidarity in the plant (compared to 40 per cent of the workers; 70 per cent said that there was a lot of good feeling among workmates, compared with 45 per cent of the workers).

In considering the content of the maintenance workers' conformity, one must remember, first, the maintenance people's aggressiveness toward the supervisors and their contempt for the production workers; second, their evaluations of the directors are equally critical, especially of the assistant director—though these are still personality judgments and rather restrained; and third, when they are presented with general stereotypes, the maintenance men will, for example, give majorities of 75 to 90 per cent asserting the directors' inefficiency, stuffiness, and lack of dynamism, the inconveniences of administrative practices, and the poor way the plant seems to run. There is a consistent relationship between this kind of aggressiveness and a good adjustment. The maintenance workers who are more moderate and considerate in their judgments are likely to be the ones who have some regret about the choice they have made and who do not agree that working with the Monopoly really presents an advantage. To summarize, for the maintenance people, aggressiveness appears to be a necessary element in the pattern of adjustment to their situation.

Such a paradox will be understood better when we analyze the whole system of power relationships in the shop. At this stage, we can point to the aims of protecting the group interests, which are easier to visualize and to enforce in a small, well-knit, quasi-professional group; to the relative insecurity stemming from the threat of technological change likely to make an already obsolete kind of work organization impossible in the future; and, finally, to the frustrated aspirations of people who know they could have had chances of better jobs and promotions elsewhere.

Like the production workers, maintenance people report higher ambitions for their children. However, their desire is likely to be even greater. The general directorate of the Monopoly would like them to apply for supervisors' jobs, but they consistently refuse what they consider an unattractive offer. They would prefer to compete for the job of technical engineer. The latter, however, is a hopeless aspiration within the present organization of the Monopoly.

Very proud of their skill—which has been proved through a difficult competitive test—knowing they have capabilities for promotion, and frustrated in their ambitions, maintenance workers are likely to be adamant about their own prerogatives and very consistent in protecting them, and to explain away the criticisms of them by attacking the other groups.

THE SUPERVISORS' TYPE OF ADJUSTMENT

The supervisors' reactions, compared to those of the other two groups, seem much less aggressive, much less consistent, and much more pessimistic about their own situation. Theirs does not appear to be an aggressive and happy adjustment, but a poor, unstable, and resigned one.

Supervisors judged their plant, their superiors, and the production workers moderately. They were acrimonious about the maintenance workers. Even this built-in group reaction, however, was less unified than the reaction of their adversaries against them. They did not attack the other groups, and did not criticize management and the organization of the plant, although they did not appear to defend them, either. They clearly did not have the feeling of participating in and belonging to the official setup. They rarely said that their director or assistant director was not capable. However, they gave a majority or sizable minority endorsement to stereotypes about directors' inefficiency, stuffiness, and lack of dynamism, and about administrative practices.

Predictably, a concomitant of this passivity is a rather low morale. Only 50 per cent of the supervisors said that they liked their work very much, and 20 per cent said they did not like it. This is a high negative percentage for a supervisory activity. Their response to whether or not they would enter the Monopoly again was also characteristic. Only 47 per cent said yes (compared with 73 per cent and 74 per cent, respectively, of the maintenance and production workers). Finally, half of them stated flatly that their job was not a good one.

The third important characteristic of the supervisors' adjustment is their lack of cohesiveness. They never answer as a group, and they are generally hesitant about stating their position. Moreover, their answers seem to lack consistency even on an individual basis. There are many more contradictions in their interviews than in interviews with members of the other groups, and it is more difficult to trace group patterns of attitudes among them.

There is, however, a strange but rather solid relationship cutting across these inconsistencies that throws some light on the matter of low morale. Supervisors generally reject the workers' point of view on seniority, since the seniority system strips them of their influence and power in the shop. However, the substantial minority that accept it are likely to be much happier about their work and the interest of their job. Supervisors seem thus to adjust well only insofar as they accept the values of the workers and resign themselves to the role which workers want them to occupy. Consistent with this, younger supervisors and supervisors who have had some training are more dissatisfied. That is, those who are disposed to try to change the established relationships are more likely to be disappointed and bitter. This is further indicated by the fact that the supervisors who are not concerned with their group's lack of initiative, who do not take a stand on discipline, and who say it does not constitute any problem, are generally more satisfied than their colleagues. Supervisors' satisfaction can be only of the passive and resigned kind.

Initially, the relationship of the supervisors with the maintenance workers appears to contradict the above interpretation, in view of the finding that the supervisors with the higher morale are those who contest the competence of the maintenance workers. This group reaction shows the same sort of aggressive adjustment we have observed for the other categories, but it is not consistent with the attitudes expressed by supervisors in response to other questions. The generally combative younger supervisors are willing to recognize the competence of the other group. In this case, pessimism and realism go together. In the other instance, deprecating their adversaries' abilities fits with an otherwise happier, resigned kind of adjustment for the supervisors.

Supervisors as a rule appear to be quite close to the workers' group; they do not react as part of management, but as subordinates and simple operators. But while production workers are relatively happy and quite aggressive, supervisors are unhappy and only mildly critical. They do not care for their jobs and they complain about working conditions. Above all, their role within the social system of the shop does not fit in with the usual role expectations in modern industrial society, and it is difficult for them to limit their aspirations, both as to the nature of their work and as to rewards and promotions. They are frustrated on all these points. It is only by relinquishing such images and aspirations, or by pretending things are not what they are, that they can assimilate to the workers' group and achieve a better kind of adjustment. But such a process is an individual and difficult one. This fact makes it possible to predict not only a lack of *esprit de corps,* but even individual inconsistencies.

THE SYSTEM OF POWER RELATIONSHIPS IN THE SHOP: ITS EQUILIBRIUM AND ITS LIMITS

The behavior and attitudes of people and groups within an organization cannot be explained without reference to the power relationships existing among them. All the lessons of the past fifteen years' research in organization have brought to light more and more the importance of those problems of power and control that the first attempts at understanding leadership had neglected.[17]

The situation in the Monopoly is especially interesting seen in this perspective. A main rationale of bureaucratic development is the elimination of power relationships and personal dependencies—to administer things instead of governing men. The ideal of bureaucracy is a world where people are bound by impersonal rules and not by personal influence and arbitrary command. The organizational sys-

---

[17] This opinion has been more and more frequently expressed since the middle fifties by social psychologists and specialists in the theory of organizations. An analysis of these new conceptions can be found in chapter vi.

tem of the Monopoly has gone a long way toward realizing this ideal. It is primarily characterized by the extent of impersonal ruling. People at the posts of command do not have much leeway. Their response to most eventualities has been fixed in advance; their subordinates know this and can, therefore, act accordingly. The seniority system makes it impossible for the higher-ups to intervene in the careers of their subordinates. Of course, there are many constraints and the usual concomitant punishments; but what is important for our purpose is the impossibility of arbitrary punishment rather than the leniency of the system.

If we re-examine the functioning of the plants we have described in this new light, the system appears, on the one hand, to be very rational in this respect, yet, on the other, to yield unintended results that change the meaning completely, at least at the shop level.

The over-all extension of the rules, the stability and predictability of all occupational behavior, and the lack of interference across hierarchical echelons, all weaken the chain of command considerably. Power is weak down the line, and in its absence there is relative cordiality and lack of concern. Supervisors are passive and workers tolerant. Some provision is still necessary for giving sanctions to the system as a whole, and the roles of the director and assistant director still carry some power. However, it is important that the centralization that has occurred has caused the power of decision to be located at a level where personal influence is difficult to exercise, because of the number of people involved and the lack of immediate reliable information. Thus even the real key relationship—between the workers and the director—is stripped of its power and control function. The director, acting as a judge, remains impersonal. He cannot combine his desires for action and power with his duty as the man who interprets and applies the law.

But if power problems seem eliminated from the official line of command, there remains one group relationship with all the connotations of dependency and attendant emotional feelings. This is the relationship between the maintenance workers and the production workers. We must try to understand how it has come about and how it relates to the system as a whole.

This relationship is centered around the problem of machine stoppages. Machine stoppages, as we pointed out earlier, occur unusually often because of the difficulties in conditioning the raw material. This is a sore spot in the technological system. However, comparable problems seem to be handled better in other factories in France, and in similar factories working with the same technology in other countries. Elsewhere, at least, they are not considered the crucial events they have become in the Monopoly.

There are apparently two complementary reasons for their being crucial in the bureaucratic organizational setup of the Monopoly. First, machine stoppages are the only major happenings that cannot be predicted and to which impersonal rulings cannot apply. The rules govern the consequences of the stoppages, the reallocation of jobs, and the adjustment of the work load and of pay; but they cannot indicate when the stoppage will occur and how long it will take to repair. The contrast between the detailed rigidity of all other prescribed behavior and the complete uncertainty of mechanical functioning gives this problem disproportionate importance. Second, the people who are in charge of maintenance and repair are the only ones who can cope with machine stoppage. They cannot be overseen by anyone in the shop. No one can understand what they are doing and check on them. Furthermore, a department —a rather abstract service unit—is not responsible. Instead, men are individually responsible, each of them for a number of machines. Thus there is another contrast between impersonality and abstractness on the one side, and individual responsibility on the other.

Production workers are displeased by the consequences of a machine stoppage. It disrupts their work; it is likely to make it necessary for them to work harder to compensate for lost time; and if it lasts long enough, they will be displaced, losing friendship ties and even status.[18]

With machine stoppages, a general uncertainty about what will happen next develops in a world totally dominated by the value of security. It is not surprising, therefore, that the behavior of the maintenance man—the man who alone can handle the situation, and who by preventing these unpleasant consequences gives workers the necessary security—has a tremendous importance for production workers, and that they try to please him and he to influence them. From this state of affairs, a power relationship develops.

The contrast between the power wielded by the maintenance men and the lack of influence of the supervisors explains the advantage that the former have over the latter. Supervisors cannot check on maintenance. They may be competent in the various aspects of their work, but their competence does not extend to the only problem about which the workers care, because only its outcome is uncertain. A supervisor cannot reprimand the mechanics who work in his shop. There is likely to be a perpetual fight for control, and the supervisors will usually be the losers. It is, therefore, natural for

---

[18] They are held personally responsible for all stoppages of less than one hour and a half and must compensate for the loss of production; if the stoppage is longer, they will be displaced or may be sent around to do menial jobs if there is no possibility of bumping less senior fellow workers.

them to have low morale, and to adjust to their situation only after having resigned themselves to being the losers—using whatever rationalization they please.

Maintenance workers, on the other hand, have the best of this situation; but their power is contested. It is not an overt, legitimate power. It does not fit the usual expectations of industrial leadership. As a result, maintenance workers still feel insecure. One can understand that their aggressiveness is a way of warding off any attack, of cementing the group solidarity and making individual compromise impossible. It is a value necessary to group struggle—and effective in it. Soul-searching and moderation are qualities the group will definitely refuse to consider; and these qualities tend to make people marginal, if not outcasts.

Production workers resent their dependence, but cannot express their hostility openly, because they need the maintenance men's help and good will individually at the shop, and because, collectively, they know that they can keep their privileges only by maintaining a common front with the other workers' group. Union solidarity and working-class unity are the values in the names of which production workers accept the maintenance workers' leadership. These values are important to them, because of their feelings of insecurity. They feel that they have rights and privileges that are not customary in the usual industrial setups in France, and that they must protect themselves. They fear that they will not be able to keep these assets unless they are prepared to fight. Since the production workers are in this state of mind, the threats of abandoning them which maintenance men make are always successful.[19]

The system of organization we have described may appear quite unworkable. Groups fight endlessly. It seems that there is no way of making changes and adjusting to new conditions. The system appears completely static. Yet it works, with a low but adequate degree of efficiency, and it has incorporated, in one way or another, every stage of technological progress.

One should not, therefore, translate the burden of the opinions expressed and the attitudes revealed into too black-and-white a picture. Conflict, forces dscouraging growth, a general conservative system of human adjustment, all put a premium on conformity and conservative values. However, these tendencies cannot develop ad infinitum. There are constant checks that prevent them from going too far and threatening the permanence of the system itself. Behind

---

[19] One of these threats is for a minority of the group to start an autonomous union of maintenance workers. Such attempts are usually temporary, but they impress production workers very much.

the struggles there is also, as in any sort of organization, some kind of consensus and organizational commitment.[20]

Keeping these qualifications in mind, we can make a few final remarks about the consequences of the bureaucratic patterns we have observed.

As in the Clerical Agency, the combination of impersonal rules, the absence of promotion from one role to another, and the seniority system, tend to make the hierarchical line progressively weaker. This preserves the personal independence of each employee in respect to the higher-ups, but it produces new kinds of frustration inasmuch as it provides no way of solving immediate problems.

Second, the development of the holders of each separate role into a stratum or an estate-like group has, as its consequence, the submission of each employee to considerable group pressure. In its own way, group pressure replaces the dwindling hierarchical pressure.

In addition, there is a decline in the importance of instrumentality in all personal judgments, accompanied by an increase in the role of affectivity. Human relations, and especially group relations, are likely to be more acute in a bureaucracy than in an organization where sanction is found in relevant measurable results.

Fourth, the initiation of change is made very difficult within an organization where the only kind of leadership is an administrative judicial one. If fairness is the only legitimate value a director can advocate, then whenever there is resistance he is likely to abandon his role as an agent of change. Change will occur only when external pressure becomes impossible to withstand. The company directors will then administer such change in a very impersonal way, without paying due regard—and rightly, if they want to succeed—to the specific requirements of each plant. To counter this kind of action, subordinates will develop a very distrustful and demanding attitude, which will enable them to take full advantage of all the consequent inadequacies.

Finally, new power relationships develop around the loopholes in the regulatory system. Groups fight for control of the ultimate strategic sources of uncertainties, and their fates in the group struggle depend on their ability to control these. New power relationships will have, as a consequence, new kinds of dependencies and frustrations, which will exert pressure for more centralization and reinforce the demand aspect of the subordinate-superior relationship, creating a sort of vicious circle that, at least at this level, it will be impossible to evade.

[20] We shall analyze the theoretical problems raised by participation in and commitment to the aims of the organization in chapter vii.

Chapter Five

POWER RELATIONSHIPS AT THE
MANAGEMENT LEVEL

From the shop level, only part of the social system of the plant is apparent. No principal actor has yet come on stage—the manager or the members of the managerial team. Many questions would remain unanswered if the investigation were to stop at this point. This is especially true of the central question: "How is it possible for the formal hierarchy to be disrupted and for new parallel power relationships to develop, without provoking management into action?" and its corollary: "To what extent does the development of the plant subculture depend upon management's conscious goals or unconscious personal behavior?"

In this chapter, we shall try to combine the picture taken from the subordinates' viewpoint with the one that can be drawn after studying the patterns of conflict and co-operation at the management level —whose influence, as we shall see, cannot be neglected.

Comprehensive studies of human relations problems at the management level are usually hampered by two sets of difficulties. First, the complexity of the role structure in modern organizations causes much ambiguity and overlapping, making it impossible to match really comparable cases and to use rigorous methods meaningfully. Second, the general emphasis on status and promotions gives a crucial importance to the human relations game, thus preventing the researcher from obtaining reliable data on the central problem of power relationships.

The Monopoly, however, presents an interesting and favorable situation on both accounts. This is partly because of the unusual simplicity of the organizational setup and the clear-cut definition of roles. It is also due to the general de-emphasis of promotions and the concomitant lack of power cliques cutting across functional and hierarchical lines.

We shall discuss the career patterns of the four members of the managerial team, in order to understand better their expectations and their possible motivations. Then we shall describe their relationships with each other, emphasizing the recurrent pattern of conflict.

We shall then try to analyze the pattern of adjustment of each of these four persons and, finally, the meaning of conflict in a bureaucratic system of organization like this.

The Career Patterns of the Four Members of the Management Team

The management team, as we already know, consists of four members: one director in charge of general co-ordination, planning, and sales;[1] one assistant director responsible for production; one technical engineer responsible for both machine and building maintenance; and one comptroller in charge of supplies, accounting, and personnel administration.

The director is at least forty, usually in his late forties or early fifties. He has spent a good many years in the organization (as a rule, he entered it when between twenty-two and twenty-four). His promotion has been entirely due to seniority. In fact, the process of his selection may be seen as working against the interests of the organization, since at least half of the assistant directors in the past have left before being promoted, and the ones who stayed are likely to be those who were afraid they could not succeed elsewhere. On the other hand, the intellectual abilities and the early training of the director make him fit, or make him think he is fit, for a much more important job. He is a man, therefore, who tends to feel superior to his functions but has usually renounced looking for another position. He is not well paid by ordinary business standards, but he receives some tangible fringe benefits—among others, the free use of a large house and of a car and chauffeur. To these material perquisites, one should add the amount of independence he enjoys and the prestige of his way of life. He can employ his time very much as he sees fit—some of the directors pursue their own scientific or scholarly research; some have permission to assume other administrative duties beside their own, usually as consulting experts; some teach part time in higher institutions. In the past, at least some of the members of the "engineer" corps have made minor but distinguished contributions in the field of the arts and sciences. Generally the freedom of action and the gentlemanly status that such a position brings its occupant remind one of the liberal professions in the late nineteenth century.

By contrast, the director's role in the plant is small. Production

[1] Sales is a not very important function since the organization does not deal with private dealers directly but with another public agency; sales problems involve only the planning of deliveries, stock, and warehouse organization.

goals are narrowly fixed by the central office. Processes are stable, and change is extremely difficult. The director does not have the right either to hire or to fire; he does not even have the right to assign workers to various jobs. The only people who are really dependent on him are those in the extremely weak supervisors' group. His only chance of making his influence felt is to administer the rules in such a way as to diminish the constant squabbling their application brings, and, in that way, to inspire people with more positive attitudes toward production. The great majority of the directors interviewed considered, in any case, that production was mere routine and not at all interesting. Since sales are not a challenge either, the only problem which remains is that of new construction—remodeling of plant facilities and general equipment and the general planning of future development. Three-quarters of the directors interviewed gave priority to this aspect of their activity: no wonder that some of their critics accuse directors of "building mania"!

The assistant director is a younger man, twenty-five to forty, who generally has had to choose a state career because of lack of business connections or because of personal shyness. In the past, graduates of the Polytechnique were eager to seek employment in state organizations. Now they tend to choose state careers only as a last recourse.[2]

As an inexperienced young man fresh from college, the assistant director is eager to learn the job of industrial organization. He feels, moreover, that being put immediately in charge of the whole production of a plant is a splendid opportunity to get the experience he seeks —and to get it quickly and without risks. Usually he is shifted from plant to plant two or three times, if not more, during his years as assistant director, and this gives him some challenges and some new experiences. However, once he feels he has learned everything that can be learned from such a situation—a stage which comes more quickly than he had expected—he becomes progressively more interested in finding another job. The rate of departure has always been high, but it seems to be increasing as the spread of economic development provides more opportunities for highly trained engineers. At present the rate is well over 60 per cent.

The comptroller is usually a man considerably past fifty, who has been promoted to the top rank of his own profession after a long wait. As a rule, he has not been working long in any particular plant, and is not expected to remain long. He has with him younger ad-

[2] Since the Polytechnique is a military school, board and tuition are free; but students have to reimburse all the fees to the state if they do not serve in the Army or in the Civil Service for at least ten years. Many private business firms will lend the man they hire the money necessary to repay the state, but this in itself can still raise problems.

ministrative colleagues of the same "corps" who are impatient for turnover and over whom he has limited influence. Officially, he has important responsibilities. As financial officer, he has to post bond; but his job, in reality, is quite routine. With one or two exceptions, the comptroller does not strike one as having the opportunity to make his personality count.

The technical engineer is the only one of his category in the plant.[3] He has no other man of the same "corps" to talk to—an isolation which is far from a trivial matter in such a small community. Maintenance of all general equipment, supervision of machines, maintenance and repair, discussion with outside contractors, and supervision of their work keep him constantly busy and at times overworked. He feels his job is a challenging one, but he knows he will always remain a subordinate and he resents this. There is a good chance of his being considerably older than the assistant director, with more seniority in the plant than all the other members of the management team. He has no status compensation. Recruiting technical engineers is, therefore, apparently becoming very difficult.

The relationship of these four men to one another is governed by a number of detailed rules, but some ambiguity still remains. The director, of course, is clearly the number one man, but he is obliged to call a "council" at least once a week and to listen to the advice of the other members of the team. This provision of an old statute is not really enforced now; a few directors make it a point never to hold such meetings, while others hold them as a matter of sound business practice rather than to comply with the rule. There is, however, still a technicality involved in this institution: The technical engineers can participate only if they are especially appointed by the Central Office to be members of the council; all senior technical engineers are so appointed, but the younger ones are not.

The comptroller reports to the director. Because of his financial accountability, however, he has to countersign the most important business transactions of the director and has, therefore, the ostensible function of checking on him. Practically, there is no question about the comptroller's being a subordinate, and the checking is perfunctory. The only consequence of this ambiguity is the uneasiness and frustration felt by those comptrollers who think they are entitled to more authority. The assistant director has no direct relationship with the comptroller, so there is no problem about who has superior status. But there are some overlapping of functions and some difficulties in assessing the reciprocal situation of the assistant director and the technical engineer. Theoretically, the technical engineer re-

[3] Except for the few plants where a junior technical engineer is made assistant to a senior one.

ports to the assistant director. However, this subordinate relation, which is emphasized in the status difference, does not hold consistently in practice. The two men usually argue on an equal and relatively free basis. Most assistant directors hold a supervisors' conference in their own office two or three times a week. They always ask the technical engineers to attend. However, when technical engineers do come, they tend to act as observers and to avoid behaving like committed participants—feeling that such behavior would mark their subordination.

Respective age and respective seniority are important aspects in the equilibrium of the team. Usually there is the following combination: the comptroller is the older man, rather aloof in his administrative department, where he deals with his own kind of people, and not much involved in the problems of the plant, where he is rather new and where he does not expect to stay long. The director is somewhat younger, but already a seasoned civil servant, likely to have more seniority in the plant than the comptroller but much less than the technical engineer. The director is expected to stay for some time and has the final responsibility for what is going on, which means that he has a direct and important commitment to the organization and to its people. The technical engineer's seniority varies considerably, but normally, he has more seniority than any of the others, and, because of his kind of patch-up job, he knows more and is more competent about plant problems. The assistant director, in contrast, appears new and inexperienced, and is not likely to have a great commitment either to the people or to the organization.

Our brief description has demonstrated that such a situation presents certain aspects of a laboratory experiment for observing conflict within organizations. We are dealing with a clearly defined group, in the experimental sense. There is no ambiguity about who belongs and who does not. The group's members are isolated—one might even say, cut off—from the outside environment. They have no other persons to talk to among the rest of the staff, since there is an impassable gap between them and their subordinates.[4] They are also removed from people playing the same role, that of industrial manager, in private organizations, as well as from people having comparable status in the Civil Service. Executives in private business view them as people with a kind of experience which is not relevant and cannot even be understood, and with whom, therefore, they have no common professional ground. Other civil servants of the

---

[4] This is only partially true for the comptroller, whose three or four subordinates hope eventually to be promoted to his rank and therefore act on more equal terms with him. We shall see later that this is of some consequence for the comptroller's kind of adjustment.

same rank may have the same primary interests to defend against their common employer, the national state, and before the same suspicious general public; but the management group of the Industrial Monopoly is composed of technicians with organizational responsibilities, a combination whose problems are apparently peculiar.[5] One can safely assume, therefore, that if they are not quite in the laboratory vacuum, they are nevertheless much better insulated from outside influence than most people in normal contemporary professional situations. Finally, this setup is duplicated thirty times, in identical terms, all over France.

To summarize these background elements: we have four players, separated from the rest of the world and obliged to play together. These players have very different cards to play. Their powers, their abilities to impose their views, are unequal. Moreover—and this makes the game more complex—they do not have the same interests, since some expect to quit the game (the assistant director) or can achieve professional satisfaction outside it (the director).

If our four players had the same stakes and commitments, and no differences in roles, we could predict the formation of coalitions according to their respective powers.[6] However, the problem is not so simple, because of the interplay of many more factors and the interference of another variable, the type of participation or commitment of the players to the game. This difficulty focuses our attention on a very fundamental given which is too often forgotten but which throws light on the functioning of an organization.

In the co-operative game, the individual does not play with power only. He can also agree or refuse to commit himself and can measure out his own participation. This kind of game is more individualistic and secret, and it is extremely difficult to understand without some depth psychology analysis. The situation that has been created in the Monopoly is interesting from this point of view. Even this most intimate aspect of the relationship between the individual and the organization has been at least partly institutionalized, so that one can understand and predict individual commitment and withdrawal as well as success and failure in the realm of action.

Before proceeding to the necessary theoretical analysis, however,

---

[5] Technicians in the Civil Service are professionals in a staff capacity; personal responsibilities are never given to them, and industrial organization has not developed yet as a recognized technique, although some progress had been made during the last ten years.

[6] See, for example, the studies made on coalitions in a triad. Th. Caplow, "Theory of Coalitions in the Triad," *American Sociological Review*, XXI (1956), 489–93; W. E. Vinacke and A. Ackoff, "Experimental Study of Coalitions in the Triad," *Am. Soc. Rev.*, XXII (1957), 406–15; William Garrison, "A Theory of Coalition Formations," *Am. Soc. Rev.*, XXII (1957), 373–82.

we shall follow the exploratory and empirical course of the research itself. We shall begin with a description of the conflicts actually observed and a discussion of one very curious fact: one major type of conflict appears consistently in almost all the situations observed. An explanation of this phenomenon will furnish us with an analysis of the depth structure of these situations. We shall then study the interplay of personalities within situations so structured: how people adjust to the role they have been given, and how they are molded by the kind of game they are obliged to play. Finally, we shall discuss the real meaning of conflict in an organization like the Monopoly, and what limits to its development are set by social control.

THE EXISTING PATTERNS OF CONFLICT

In the twenty cases we were able to study, we found sixteen clear cases of conflict between the technical engineer on the one hand, and the assistant director and/or the director on the other. Besides this dominant pattern of opposition, there were six or seven cases of assistant director versus director, and two or three of comptroller versus director. The latter types of conflict were not only less numerous but also more diffuse and less demanding than the former. The dice, we may assume, are loaded for one kind of outcome. Whatever the character of the people who happen to staff the different roles, and whatever the peculiar types of combination which may occur in their distribution throughout the thirty different plants, clashes of personality will almost never occur outside these quite narrow patterns.

THE COMPTROLLER-VERSUS-DIRECTOR CONFLICT

We have already mentioned the kind of problems raised by the relationship between the director and the comptroller. Interviews showed us that comptrollers may be frustrated by their lack of promotional opportunities and somewhat jealous of their Polytechnique colleagues. We occasionally obtained comments like the following from a mild-mannered comptroller:

It is not necessary to have a training in advanced math to be in charge of a factory. . . . I do not understand why a good, serious, and efficient comptroller could not be a successful director.

From a more aggressive and unpopular one:

There are far too many graduates from the Polytechnique. They poke their noses into everything. They claim they are administrators with a mathematical training whereas their role should be primarily a technical one.

But it is usually only a casual remark or a way of speaking which marks the uneasiness. In this context the comptrollers view their financial responsibility, which theoretically entitles them to check on the director, as a very important function. Since they will be held accountable for any commercial decision they countersign, they may claim the right to discuss its appropriateness and aspire to utilize their signatures as a sort of veto power. But withholding a signature would be considered an abuse of position by the Central Office. Their duty is to check the legality, not the appropriateness, of the decision; they have no leeway—and, furthermore, the decisions of the director are themselves likely to be merely routine. The comptrollers' bargaining power, therefore, is clearly low. Since they are not very strongly committed to the job, they are likely to retreat and diminish their stakes, since they know they cannot succeed. Some wishful thinking, however, will remain, along with the chance of conflict whenever a poor handling of the prestige problem makes it impossible for a more aggressive comptroller to settle for some kind of special consideration. But this is exceptional.

THE ASSISTANT DIRECTOR-VERSUS-DIRECTOR CONFLICT

The conflict between assistant director and director is much more commonly expressed and is somewhat deeper. It is also a rather natural and acceptable one, since it revolves mostly around those permanent problems of human society, the training of the younger generation and the stepping aside of the older. Director and assistant director must work closely together—first, because plant production, the domain of the assistant director, represents the core of the directorship responsibilities; second, because the assistant director must be trained on the job (it is his first job) both for the role of assistant director and for the role of director, since he will in due time become a director himself. The director is supposed to train his assistant director and gradually give him a greater part of the work load. However, since this work load is not very heavy, and since the first assignment given to the assistant director (the problems of personnel and of plant organization) happens to be the most difficult and dangerous one, there is a strong likelihood that conflict will develop around the division of work. Assistant directors will complain that they are kept in tutelage, and directors will complain that assistant directors are unable to assume any responsibility.

This is more or less what we found in the interviews. But, though there are some traces of opposition in the majority of the cases, direct conflict is rather rare, and there are even a few cases of solid partnership.

The following excerpts, matching comments of directors and assistant directors about each other, will indicate the tenor of the relationship.

First, the usual allusive statements. One director said:

I now have an assistant, but I don't know for how long. Since I have been here, I have had four of them. The first one remained three years, which means that I had some help during the last two years, but none of the later ones lasted a year. Not only did they not provide any help —they took a lot of my time and even the time of the technical engineer.

And his assistant director commented:

The director is quite aloof. I have very little contact with him and no possibility of being trained by learning from him.

Another director said:

My assistant director has been here two years. For us it is quite a problem: as soon as they are trained, they quit.

His assistant director had this comment:

My director is a good old man, awfully conservative.

A third director was quite happy:

My assistant director is very smart; he is a really wonderful guy.

But his assistant director did not follow suit:

My director always has sweeping ideas and keeps changing them constantly; I have to agree without being able to suggest anything to him.

Then there are the more conflicting comments. In these cases, the assistant director is usually more aggressive. For example, one said:

My director is just hopeless. He does not accept the possibility of any solution that he has not himself seen before. One has to have his approval for the slightest detail.

And the director, for his part, said:

My assistant director has neither the technical nor the administrative training required; I am obliged to take care of everything.

Another assistant director complained:

My director is very opinionated. He is authoritarian—at least when he can get his way.

And his director echoed:

As regards the assistant director, I will give you my opinion. He has the engineering-school disease, theory. He has no training at all and has a lot of trouble getting along.

Third, as an example of a better kind of relationship, this characteristically shorter duet. The director:

I let him try and muddle through; I will only interfere when he needs help.

And the assistant director:

My director is very liberal.

It is noticeable that the director tends to remain impersonal and to avoid judging directly the behavior of his subordinate, while the assistant director is consistently and outspokenly personal; thus the conflict between generations makes itself felt in style as well. It is also apparent that the same problem exists in all groups: the junior man does not want control but needs backing; the senior man does not understand backing without control. In addition, the general feeling in the organization is that a successful adjustment is the exception. The most exuberant assistant director, after having said:

Here I have been able to achieve a lot because the director has given me a really free hand and at the same time has backed me whenever I needed it.

adds immediately:

I have had extraordinarily good luck.

The word "extraordinarily" is also used by two of the three other satisfied directors.

The opposition may be aggravated, too, by the change of outlook of the present generation. It has shifted considerably from the more traditional gentlemanly behavior. Young assistant directors seem interested chiefly in efficiency and technique.

The main factor, nevertheless, remains the amount of responsibility. The cases of successful teamwork are also the cases where an important program of rebuilding and technical transformation of the plant has given enough interesting work and responsibility to both the assistant director and the director.

It is important that the conflict, although diffuse and well argued, is not really very deep. Assistant directors are able to identify with their directors; their anger is the anger of people who have been disappointed. Moreover, the temporary nature of the relationship provides some relief. Assistant directors come and go, and directors can evade responsibility for them easily. In turn, the assistant directors know that their situation will change in the not too distant future. There is a definite structure to the situation, but much leeway is allowed to the protagonists within it.

THE CONFLICT BETWEEN TECHNICAL ENGINEER
AND ASSISTANT DIRECTOR

By contrast to the foregoing pattern, the conflict pattern seems difficult, and the involvement great in the relations between the technical engineers and the members of the "engineers" corps (director and assistant director). Throughout France, our interviewees reported the same problems and almost the same feelings.

This is especially true for the responses of the technical engineers, who consistently express their irritation with and even their hatred of the *Polytechniciens*. However, the assistant directors are also quite committed. Most of them, when asked about getting along with other members of the team, will refer to the technical engineer—often in a violent and passionate way which shows how central is their preoccupation with the problem.

What strikes us first in the interviews is the directors' constant emphasis on the subordinate position of the technical engineer. They will say:

He is my subordinate—he must report directly to the assistant director.
He is responsible for the maintenance of machines and equipment according to my planning of the organization.
He is a subordinate.

At the same time, they know that these assertions do not fit the reality, and they worry about it:

The problem is that the technical engineer has a very special situation. He is a member of the team as well as my subordinate.

Some assistant directors try to explain this difficulty away by complaining about the right of the technical engineer to attend the council, or by deploring the fact that they are given older men as subordinates. Others locate the trouble at the training and professional level and admit their helplessness in facing the technical engineer. One says, for example:

The school did not prepare us very well for the practical technical problems of the plant. I constantly have to ask the technical engineer for advice. This makes me lose face.

Another, after explaining the inadequacy of his school preparation, adds:

> We are not self-confident. This may be the source of our difficulties with the technical engineer.

A third admits bluntly:

> The assistant director can discuss technical problems only if he can get along well enough with the technical engineer.

The majority of the assistant directors conclude moderately that they do not get along too badly with the technical engineers. Nevertheless, the discrepancy between expectations and reality frequently fosters more violent reactions. For example, the three following comments are typical of the tone of the discussion and of the arguments presented:

> We [assistant directors] think that the plants are becoming too much a sort of Mexican army with everyone wanting to be a colonel. . . . We do not need technical engineers; a good storeroom manager and a good technical foreman would be quite enough . . . And to run the whole thing, we are here; the Central Office seems to forget.
>
> One must confess that the technical engineers constitute the most impossible group. . . . One cannot trust a technical engineer . . . and the mere existence of such a job is absurd; the service would be better with a good foreman. When somebody comes from an engineering school he cannot be reduced to a foreman's job. I personally think the post should be abolished.
>
> The technical engineer supports the rebellion of the maintenance workers against me. If he could have his way, I would not be able to interfere in the slightest in what [he feels] is his own business, i.e., everything in the plant. . . . Technical engineers should be suppressed; there is not room for two men. They do not have the tactfulness, the human relations skill to be in charge of the personnel.

Technical engineers may be somewhat less violent than the assistant directors in these last examples, but they are consistently critical and aggressive. All but three directly or indirectly criticized the members of the "engineers' corps," and the only one who was positive added to his comments this significant understatement:

> The temper of the young *Polytechniciens* has changed very much. They do not think they know everything in advance. Some of them are even modest.

His colleagues, for the most part, complained of the haughtiness and the incompetence of their assistant directors and of *Polytechniciens* in general:

The depressing thing is the lack of technical experience on the part of people whose job it is to be industrial leaders. . . . We have no voice and they just don't know.

Some of them related, with allusive details, what one skilful story-teller called "[their] unbelievable, terrible mistakes."

But the most widespread frustration concerns the monopoly that the engineer corps has on the possibilities of promotion. This is re-sented as a general conspiracy of the *Polytechniciens.* Only some older and better-established technical engineers refrain from what they tend to consider to be begging for promotion. These say they would like only to strengthen the position of the technical engineer versus the assistant director.

It is not surprising that comments on the over-all relationship are rather sour:

There is no teamwork possible between the *Polytechniciens* and our-selves. The gap cannot be bridged.

Our bosses are all *Polytechniciens;* it is a feudal system. . . . There is not enough work for them. . . . One should cut through the services, democratize and suppress the monopoly; it is a sort of Mafia.

The directors, for their part, try to avoid making this kind of per-sonal remark. They, of course, benefit from the existence of the as-sistant director, who acts as a buffer between them and the technical engineer. The directors tend to respond in more general terms, dis-cussing the problems involved instead of passing judgment. Their comments are of the following type:

The difficulty we have with technical engineers comes from the fact that, in our system, no role is clearly defined. The role of the technical engineer is poorly defined. A lot of problems stem from this inadequacy.[7]

A few directors, however—usually those who have been at some time, or are still, without an assistant director—will present, in more reserved terms, a picture similar to that presented by the assistant director.

My technical engineer is very competent. Unfortunately, the Central Office did not give him satisfaction and he thinks I am responsible in-stead; he is very aggressive and bitter.

My technical engineer is very good, but he is also hypersensitive. We are at odds with each other. . . . He has no ability to synthesize.

From this brief report, the feelings of the players emerge rather clearly, and some of their motivations appear. We can now turn to

---

[7] This desire for defining roles better is especially significant, as perhaps nowhere in French industry are roles so clear-cut as in the Monopoly.

an analysis of the conditions and the rules of the game they are playing.

Theoretically, the technical engineer reports to the assistant director, who is in charge of production, all his duties, maintenance, repairs, and work contracted for outside, which must be subordinate to the over-all imperative of production. But this arrangement inevitably hurts the feelings of the technical engineer. It is a permanently subordinate situation from which he himself has no chance to rise by eventually occupying the top position. At the same time, it is a situation which does not fit our society's regular expectations about necessary training and competence, and which may even contradict some of these expectations, such as those concerning age and seniority.

A permanent "non-legitimate" state of subordination will usually produce either revolt or retreat. This particular situation, however, is peculiar in that it does not leave the technical engineer helpless. It provides him with so many possibilities for retaliation that he can practically invalidate his official subordination by making it impossible for his superior to initiate action without his approval.

The process works more or less in the following way:

First, production has become completely routine, and only maintenance raises problems. As a consequence, the trouble-shooter, the man who can find solutions, is the technical engineer. He will defend his position of strength (the impossibility of his superiors' getting along without him) by keeping his own domain free from any rationalization.

Second, the assistant director will not be able to control the technical engineer. The domain of maintenance is that of the rule of thumb, and the assistant director lacks the necessary practical training to learn the tricks of a trade that the technical engineer jealously preserves. Moreover, the official hierarchical decorum which surrounds the "engineers' corps" will protect the technical engineer by making it impossible for the assistant director to undertake a trial-and-error learning process and thus lose face. As a result, the assistant director can give formal orders to the technical engineer but cannot control their execution. The technical engineer—who, of course, cannot give orders to his assistant director—can control his behavior, since he is able to set the limits of what is possible and what is not possible for him to do.

Third, the assistant director has a weak chain of command. The foremen who relay his orders are not very efficient, and he distrusts them. The technical engineer, on the other hand, can rely on a strong group of journeymen who are competent and active. At the shop level, these journeymen, the maintenance workers, are in a position of strength vis-à-vis the foremen, and, for all practical purposes, they are the real bosses. This last element of the situation is, naturally, vital. The technical engineer protects the privileges of the maintenance workers, who cannot be controlled by anyone but him. The maintenance workers, in turn, make the position of the technical engineer very secure, allowing him to develop and maintain the advantages described in the preceding paragraphs. As one of the technical engineers summarized quite frankly:

I personally have my journeymen well in hand, and because of that, what I want to do I can do and the director is obliged to go along with what I want.

Finally, any change in the organization of production itself, any move of the assistant director in his own domain, will be subject— because of the position of the maintenance workers as natural leaders in the shop—to the interference of the maintenance department and its all-powerful chief. Another technical engineer explains this in dry terms:

On top of our duties, we are often obliged to take up the work of the assistant director.

The practical success of the technical engineers is bound to have repercussions in the formal setup. It was through this that they won the right to sit at the Council. This right means that even formally there is an ambiguous situation where, on the one hand, the technical engineer is the subordinate of the assistant director, and, on the other, as a member of the Council and usually a senior member, he cannot be brushed off easily. As a consequence, the director has become a rather weak arbitrator between a senior and a junior executive. As one assistant director put it, very angrily: "The Council is becoming a soviet."

The reactions of the assistant directors to this situation are likely to be bitter. They have as many reasons to feel frustrated as the technical engineers. They are invested with formal authority but are constantly prevented from exercising it. And they have no alternative. Personnel administration is taboo. They cannot initiate any action in the rigid bargaining relationship between the unions and the Central Office. Training, reallocation of jobs, the use of morale and promotional incentives are all made impossible by the strictness of the seniority system. The daily problems of running the plant are completely boring. The only possibility of action, the only challenge, for the young assistant director is the kind of progress which comes from technical improvement and the concomitant reorganization. Here, to, he must encounter the technical engineer's knowledgeable comments. The assistant director may settle for a moderate course, choose the diplomat's way, and concede much to get a few limited results. This kind of choice is all the more rational in that his situation is a temporary one and he can regard himself as being in a learning position. More frequently, however, because he is young and self-conscious, he will fight back and try to keep the technical engineer in line. In this case, the stage is set for one of those perennial petty wars where the antagonists are not able to decide any case on its merits, because each of these struggles can be used to weaken the position of the other fellow.

A typical example illustrates the possibilities of this situation very well, at least as regards the behavior of the technical engineer. The potential opponent in this case is the director, in the temporary absence of an assistant director in the plant.

A new foreman had been brought to the plant a few weeks before the incident. Unlike his colleagues, he had had, through previous industrial employment, some good technical training. An important piece of equipment happened to break down in his shop. The maintenance worker responsible for its repair was called in, fumbled around, and reported that it was serious and that production would have to stop until further notice. The foreman resented his arrogance and an argument started immediately. The foreman told the maintenance worker that he was lazy and incompetent. He proceeded to work on the equipment himself, and soon discovered that the problem was not serious and that the breakdown was the result of the poor maintenance of one of the parts. Furious, he approached the second-line foreman to enlist his support in asking for drastic punishment. This man told him to quiet down and to see the technical engineer first. When approached, the technical engineer did not want to listen. Another argument began, and finally the foreman was told that he had no right to interfere with a problem which was not his own responsibility in the first place, and with which he was surely incompetent to deal—as all foremen are. Still more furious, the foreman immediately burst into the director's office. The director listened to him quietly and carefully and congratulated him for his zeal, but told him, with all the tact he could muster, that he would have to inquire into the matter further and that he did not think he would be able to impose a sanction because there was not enough proof; then he dropped the whole matter.

Relating the incident later, the director explained that his decision was the only rational one possible. Had he punished the maintenance worker, the whole maintenance group would have struck immediately, with the covert support of the technical engineer. They would have been able to shut down the plant, and the Central Office would never have supported him on such a trivial and ambiguous matter. His acting in the case, therefore, would have made him lose face completely. A corollary, of course, was the unpleasant consequence of discouraging a rare foreman who could have been a decisive influence in the plant but who instead quit in disgust. But, although it was a painful decision, the director still felt that it was the right one. In retrospect, he was happy that he had not had an assistant director at the time; he felt that one would surely have capitalized on the case—only to make matters worse.

The kind of conflict-filled situation described above appears to be very well structured. The four exceptions (20 per cent of the cases) and the differences among the rest of the cases raise interesting problems, whose analysis can teach us a great deal about the possible range of deviance.

The rebuilding and remodeling of a plant, with all the reorganization thus made possible, present the only material factor that can upset the regular pattern. As we have already seen, renovation gives both the director and the assistant director enough responsibility and scope for initiative to make the relationship between them easier. In addition to this, however, it also gives them a clear lead over the technical engineer. The uncertainty in planning ahead no longer comes from maintenance and repair problems, but from decisions which the director and assistant director will make about the new layout and the carrying out of the plans. Two of the exceptions to the regular pattern coincide with the two most important remodeling projects; and in a few other less important cases of transformation, we can observe things that are clearly repercussions in the relative bargaining powers of the antagonists.

The personality and the ability of the technical engineer make for a second type of difference. Generally, a successful senior technical engineer is more cautious and less aggressive, which entails a more peaceful relationship. At one extreme of the range of possibilities, there is a technical engineer who has succeeded so well under a weak director and constantly changing assistant directors that he is the covertly recognized master of the house. This makes him very tolerant of and friendly to the *Polytechniciens*.[8] At the other extreme, there is a technical engineer who could not stand the strain of his role and seems to have broken down, neglecting his own work and taking refuge in a hands-off policy.

The personality of the assistant director has some relevance, but it never accounts for such extreme differences. It may change the

[8] Contrary to what one would expect, this does not make for less trouble in the plant, since the maintenance workers, who have lost their natural protector because of the truce in the daily war, feel more insecure and will fight more bitterly to keep their privileges at the shop level.

general tone of the relationship, but it will not alter its balance. No assistant director will break down over the situation, nor will one succeed in brushing off the technical engineer except in cases of plant transformation. One gets the impression that players here play such a tight game, and are so anxious to get the maximum out of it, that, provided there are no special circumstances, one can accurately predict the general outcome. Since no one is ready to give up, and all the variables are known in advance, there is very little left for individual initiative; and the interplay of personalities cannot transform the situation except in truly exceptional cases.

The Patterns of Adjustment of Each Occupational Category

THE TECHNICAL ENGINEER'S PATTERN OF ADJUSTMENT

The technical engineer's relationship with the assistant director seems to be well structured. In addition, his whole pattern of adjustment, and even the salient points of his attitudes toward the job, can be quite accurately predicted.

The close conformity of the interviews of most technical engineers throughout France is indeed surprising, since these people rarely see each other and thus surely cannot be influenced by personal interaction.

First and foremost, the technical engineers love their job. They are very proud to list the whole series of their duties. They glory in being busy, and at least one-third of them complain of being overworked, of not having the time to look after everything. But even when they claim they are exhausted, they seem no less enthusiastic[9] about their "diversified and challenging job"—that job so essential to the functioning of the plant that

if there is something that does not work in the maintenance department, the whole plant will be directly affected.

Jack-of-all-trades, competent and active, the technical engineer thinks of himself as the man on whose shoulders the whole plant rests.

Then, too, the technical engineers appear to be authoritarian and paternalistic with their subordinates. They alone in the system take exception to the seniority principle, claiming that they would like personally to have the responsibility of rewarding and punishing. They talk of their subordinates, and of the workers generally, without observing the usual precautions. In the two cases we have been able to analyze most closely, the workers complained of their author-

[9] They may be even more enthusiastic.

itarianism, although giving them the most whole-hearted support otherwise. The relative harshness of the technical engineer, however, does not mean that he does not communicate. On the contrary, he seems to be more perceptive of the feelings of the workers than the other members of the management team are, and more realistic in his appraisal of them.

Third, while they are overly paternalistic with their subordinates, the technical engineers are extremely critical of their superiors. They are ready to pounce on their superiors' mistakes with unfailing jealousy, and they are extremely intolerant of any kind of control. They complain bitterly about the incompetence of the "engineers' corps" and the lack of courage of the people at the Central Office. They disapprove of the way the system works and seem to hold the *Polytechniciens* responsible for "the whole mess"—especially for the poor wages and absence of promotion.

Moreover, the technical engineers are quite pragmatic. Their interviews are more precise than those of the others; their arguments always revolve around practical problems. They appear to want to present an image of themselves as senior, responsible, overworked people who are constantly on the run to repair the mistakes of intelligent but irresponsible playboys. This self-image jibes well enough with the comments made about them by the other members of the team, who see them as intolerant and unpleasant, but nevertheless most competent, fellows. It also coincides with the comments of their workers, who see them as paternalistically inclined, but also efficient, leaders.

Finally, this lonely, austere, and bad-tempered man is apparently very happy—and all the more happy when he has some gripes to express. However paradoxical it may seem, there is a definite tendency for technical engineers to express much less fondness for the job when they cease to be aggressive with other people. To be sure, the relation is not linear, but the association between griping and fondness for the job is more positive than negative.

What about the four technical engineers who did not fit the usual conflict pattern? Their attitudes, of course, are also exceptions to the individual adjustment pattern; but their deviations from this pattern are smaller than might appear at first glance.

If we take, first, the cases of the three technical engineers who were dominated by the assistant director, we find that these people still said that they liked their job and still made some of the usual complaints. The missing factors are their pride, their activism, and their aggressiveness. They are passive and grieve silently. They even seem to have lost their authority over their own subordinates when they became unable to fight their superiors. This may help in understanding the situation which the technical engineer has to face. His is a rewarding situation, but a situation of great strain because of the responsibility and overwork, the loneliness of the job, and the constant fight it requires. Some people are bound to break down and become misfits.

At the other extreme, in the one clear case, as well as in the one or two more dubious cases, of success—where conflict seems to recede because of the dominance of the technical engineer—gripes become less frequent, and the austere technical engineer will mellow a little, without, however, losing his caution.

The fight for power seems, in the last analysis, to be the major determinant in the technical engineer's adjustment. And power, in his situation, can be gained only by following a very narrow path. There is no alternative; either he adopts the required behavior of his own social role, or he gives up and loses his self-respect. It is, of course, impossible to ascertain to what extent the situation molds the personality traits and to what extent a self-selection process is operating. Since there is relatively little turnover, it seems, however, that the constraint of the situation is the dominant force.

A last consequence is worth mentioning. As the technical engineer's success in the fight for power comes from the lack of rationalization of his field of action, so it is this lack which gives him the strategic advantage of controlling the only source of uncertainty in an otherwise routinized setup. He will, therefore, try very hard to keep it that way. Thus he is likely to adopt a generally conservative attitude on all matters of organization, and he will devote his innovating abilities to sideline problems—never trying to make progress in the control and predictability of his own field, but, rather, holding to the individual rule-of-thumb way.[10]

THE DIRECTOR'S ADJUSTMENT PATTERN

There is as much variation in the reactions of directors as there are similarities in the responses of technical engineers. Such a contrast may seem surprising, since both groups exist in the same bureaucratic climate and both must adjust to a constrained situation where they cannot deviate much from the usual pattern of behavior. But the contrast fits in well with our hypothesis about the importance of power relationships for individual adjustment. The director's situation in this respect is very different from that of the technical engineer. He does not have to adopt a definite pattern of action in order to assert his position. He is given prestige and influence without having to fight for them. However, he is, at the same time, frustrated

[10] This is clearly expressed in the interviews.

in his enjoyment of them, because he cannot institute change. Unlike the technical engineer, the director has no other group to hold directly responsible for his frustration. The differences found in the directors' reactions correspond to the feelings of uncertainty and of relative helplessness of a group in a situation of inferiority.

We have already described how the director does not have the right to hire and fire, nor even to place workers where he thinks best; no one depends on him except the weak group of foremen or supervisors. Production and sales problems are routine. Maintenance is in the skilful hands of the technical engineer. Only new works and general reorganization may present a challenge. The director's kind of leadership is, therefore, more a judicial-administrative than a managerial one.

Of course, a judicial-administrative function can be very rewarding, and many people will adjust successfully to it. But, in the present case, such a function contradicts the training and the prior expectations of the directors, and also, at least in part, their present values and frame of reference. They are constantly called upon to act as administrators—but they are also reminded that they are industrial managers and therefore responsible for progress and efficiency. They even have, within their own organization, a few men who are examples of success in this industrial sense, and whose prestige is the highest in the organization.

The director, therefore, does not get much satisfaction from his professional career. Certainly the prestige of being a member of the "engineers' corps" still has some value; but, in France's competitive modern economy, it no longer carries much weight. Rewards tend to be purely formal, and there is little likelihood of their inspiring a real sense of achievement. In his relationships with his staff, the director can keep the distance to which he is entitled, but he cannot help being unpleasantly affected by the climate.

These difficulties of adjustment, however, cannot lead to a unique pattern of behavior, since in contrast to the technical engineers' group, the directors' group is a dominant one and can rebel only against the whole bureaucratic system. The Central Office, of which they complain a great deal, is staffed by members of the "engineers' corps" like themselves, from whom they consequently cannot completely dissociate themselves. They have no common objective for which to fight; and, because of their personal freedom, they can find an easy retreat in personal achievement outside the job.

Directors adjust to such a situation in three different and even opposing patterns which correspond to three distinct ways of life, and in a fourth, intermediate one.

The first pattern, that of happy, successful adjustment, is very rare. It corresponds to the two or three cases of complete and success-ful plant reorganization. The directors who have been able to achieve this, in the organizational climate which we have described, must have had rather special qualities. But they also must have had good luck, since, under the actual conditions, the Central Office can allow the necessary allocation of funds for reorganization to only a few directors. Each director can attempt to attract the attention of the Central Office to his "sound" project. However, since most plants are in need of change, he must have special and solid ground to win out over his competitors. Regardless of the directors and the intrinsic value of their plans, certain factories will be considered first simply because of practical material arguments, and certain others because of a long history of precedents. Of course, a director is not appointed to a factory without there having been some consideration of his personal qualities; he must fit into the possibilities of the situation, although the hazard of seniority may interfere with rational place-ment.[11] Moreover, it is difficult for assistant directors and directors to furnish proof of their qualities of leadership. As a result, except for special cases for which particular people have to be chosen, the choices are not made on the basis of accomplishments but rather on the more chancy factors of personality: diplomacy, skill at patching up, at smoothing down, at compromising—these qualities tend, in the long run, to be better appreciated, while the more independent personalities, who could have succeeded well in another environ-ment, are often set aside.

Seen through his colleague's eyes, the successful director's happy adjustment looks like a matter of luck and favoritism. At the same time, its rarity gives it a brilliant aura. For the man himself, it is extremely rewarding—it allows him the satisfaction of two contra-dictory demands, the demand for security and the demand for achievement. For the organization, this kind of adjustment, rare as it is, has a tremendous importance—it offers an embodiment of perfec-tion as a yardstick for measuring other performances. Directors them-selves, although they usually profess to reject such a standard, are greatly influenced by its existence.

At the other extreme, in the usual routine plant situations, there are two contrasting types of reactions corresponding to two different ways of life.

Directors who choose the first of these claim that they have the entire responsibility for everything which might ever happen in the plant. They justify their claim by taking their formal power seri-

[11] One man who, because of his special qualities, was well qualified to lead the necessary reorganization of a certain plant was not available when an appointment was to be made there.

ously. When giving the stamp of their authority, they pretend that they are perfectly free. They happen, of course, consistently to choose certain kinds of solutions; but they explain this by emphasizing their concern for the general interest. They are careful and cautious people who believe that they have to sacrifice short-run advantages for the long-run benefit of the institutions of which they are in charge. This constant denial of reality makes for a rather dramatic public character, who can play (sometimes with great sophistication) the part of an elder statesman, carrying with him the impressive majesty of the public service—however weak his actual decisions. His own private person seems itself to be influenced. The aura of glory one sees surrounding him will not leave him at the factory gate. A poised and dignified person in and around the plant, he shows all the external marks of happy and successful activity.

Those of his colleagues who have chosen a second kind of adjustment appear, on the other hand, to be extremely unhappy. Their solution of their difficulties is not to deny or to sublimate reality, but to exaggerate its unpleasant aspects. The elder-statesman type pretends that he is free to do everything he would like to do, that nothing has ever been imposed on him that he himself had not previously required. These others claim that they do not have the slightest leeway, that they are just transmission cogs with no initiative, and, finally, that their job is completely useless. But their pessimism is more sophisticated than it appears at first glance. By minimizing their professional role, they are preserving the self-respect of their own private lives. If a director does not have any possibility of achievement at all, one cannot accuse him of not having succeeded professionally. He can, therefore, still claim to be a brilliant and distinguished citizen, however poor his work achievements are in his own eyes. While their colleagues identify with the successful director, the directors of this second sort deny the possibility of success.

These two opposite patterns of behavior are, of course, not often so clear-cut as in this description. But a sizable group of directors have reactions surprisingly close to these models. One out of four directors claims that he is perfectly free and responsible. One out of three claims that he does not have anything to decide upon.

In between these two so-called unsuccessful groups, there are a variety of different personal adjustments wherein one can recognize traits of both patterns. Usually, however, people in this intermediate group are more realistic and sensible about their own possibilities. A number of directors among them may be considered as somewhat closer to the successful pattern which we first described. In certain other cases, however, we find more incoherence than realism, some people claiming at the same time that they are all-powerful and unable to take independent decisions.

Assistant directors seem able to stand realistic appraisal of their own situation better than directors. But, although their individual re-actions do not conflict so sharply among themselves as do those of their elders, they are still quite diversified and their reactions are far from being as structured as those of their natural antagonists, the technical engineers.

This type of adjustment, i.e., a realistic appraisal of their position, is well in line with the peculiarities of the assistant directors' situ-ation. Theirs is simultaneously a learning job and a very secure job, so that they do not have too much to worry about. They have less at stake than either the directors or the technical engineers; being lucid about their problems will not endanger their self-esteem.

Their relatively inferior situation in the power relationship is, naturally, a strain, and it does involve them affectively. However, it does not affect their entire outlook. Assistant directors can find scape-goats in the old generation, curse the organization, and believe that it will eventually change. Whether they wait patiently for their turn to come, or fight back bitterly, or prepare for their departure from the organization, criticism still remains, for most of them, a healthy, enjoyable activity which does not have to become self-derogatory. Thus, one senses in their interviews, and coloring most of their attitudes, a feeling of detachment, a certain freedom from commit-ment, that makes it easier to adjust temporarily, and reasonably well, to a situation, without ceasing to criticize it. Intellectual aggressive-ness can still coincide with a rather well-balanced affectivity.

Regarding the job itself, however, the conditions for a happy kind of adjustment are few. Three different factors about which the assist-ant director himself has little, if any, influence, are decisive. The first is the existence of a program of reorganization, or at least of considerable non-routine activities in the plant. Second is the will-ingness of the director to give the assistant director a free hand. The third factor is the relative helplessness of the technical engineer. Usually, all these givens exist at the same time. When there is a program of reorganization, the director is likely to be more broad-minded and co-operative, and the technical engineer will lose his decisive veto power. In this kind of situation, the assistant directors are enthusiastic about their jobs and generally far better adjusted. Such an adjustment, which can be recognized in three or four of our cases, is apparently conducive to more tolerance of Central Office policy, and to more moderation and realism in the discussion of problems. Happy assistant directors, however, still criticize the system of organization and the behavior of their elders. They still think that they may eventually quit the organization. However, they seem to have a much greater sense of their own responsibilities and more interest in practical problems. Beyond this, they do not appear to share similar personality characteristics.

The difficulties most of the other assistant directors (at least three-quarters of the cases studied) encounter do not produce a consistent pattern either. In a general climate of moderate frustration, there are all sorts of individual adjustments—with, however, some common characteristics. These are: (1) the generalized hostility to the system of the organization and to the older generation which we have already mentioned; (2) sharp comments on the technical engineer, with, at the extreme, a demand that his job be eliminated or suppressed; and (3) a general emphasis on technical and organizational problems as opposed to human problems.

These common traits seem to constitute an ideological orientation more than a pattern of adjustment, and surely they are perceived by the assistant directors themselves as coherent reform propositions. But, if they are analyzed as steps in the process of adjustment to the organization on the part of future directors, a different logical thread is discernible in them.

When they enter the organization as students, at the so-called preparatory school, the assistant directors say almost unanimously[12] that they have been attracted to public service, and especially to the Monopoly, by its liberal tradition. They wanted a job which could give them broad human responsibilities rather than narrow technical ones. When asked how they imagined their role as assistant directors, all of them answered that they wanted to give more weight to their human responsibilities than to their technical ones. In their observations about factory life, they always emphasized the importance of being a leader, of assuming a leader's responsibilities toward the workers and toward the community. They saw themselves as members of a generation conscious of the human problems of industry and impatient to introduce change in that domain. They felt themselves to be as much opposed to their elders' timorousness and conservatism as to the engineers' paradise where human beings have no place—for which they feel that some of their peers, fascinated with technology, seem to yearn.

[12] We were able to interview the twelve engineers who were studying at the school at the time of the survey.

Their colleagues with just a few years' seniority—and they themselves a few years later—find such opinions quite childish. The assistant directors with more than one or two years' seniority do not have the slightest regard for their role as chiefs of personnel. For them, human problems are not to be taken seriously. Their only concern is for *technique* and for the possibilities of achievement through the use of *technique*. When asked about problems of leadership and about the training in "industrial psychology" they were given at school, they are generally very bitter. Such training does not seem, to them, to have any bearing on the realities of factory life.

We cannot prove that such a reversal does not correspond to a change in the mood of two successive generations. However, it seems reasonable to assume, in view of the relatively small age difference of the individuals concerned (five to six years, on the average), that this reversal is the outcome of a psychological crisis which the young assistant director has to surmount in order to adjust to his role.

Having held the belief that those of the older generation were inefficient, weak, and uncaring because they were conservative and old-fashioned, he has not yet come to realize that the situation does not allow one to be active and efficient. He understands, also, that his human leadership role is only formal and that he cannot, even with the best of intentions, influence the workers' behavior. There is no give-and-take possible, because there is no freedom to compromise on either side. Whatever his own earlier orientation, he must recognize that the only way to effect change is through technological progress. Technology is his only chance, and he is likely, after some bitter disappointments over problems of personnel, to change his own views to fit the situation. Even here, of course, he will not have a great deal of success, because of the opposition of the technical engineer. But such a struggle in its more personalized form will be more exciting and eventually more rewarding than the fight against bureaucratic rules. Then too, there are the examples of those factories where important innovations have been successfully introduced, and with whose staff assistant directors are much more ready to identify than are the more envious directors.

The assistant directors' ideology, therefore, is not an idle one. Under the mask of rationalizing industry, it presents a powerful argument for giving their group a chance to get things done. The obsession with *technique* may be narrow-minded, but it is producing change; and change has become the assistant directors' first goal.

What still seems puzzling, however, is the second reversal, which will occur when the assistant director becomes a director. How is it that the same people who once were active and aggressive in promoting technological arguments, and in setting aside all other problems, are not cautious and consistently give the lead to human considerations? To understand it, we must qualify what we have said about the assistant directors' ideology. It is, to be sure, not an idle philosophy; it is a philosophy intended for action. But it is not the rationale for actual action. Assistant directors cannot and do not introduce significant change outside the few cases of over-all reorganization; they fight for change but do not succeed, and do not even completely believe that they can succeed. Their lack of responsibility and of actual commitment makes it possible for them to state their point lucidly, without assuming the burden of the consequences. But when an assistant director becomes director, he must assume, in one way or another, responsibility for the system as it exists. This means giving priority to human relations, since, in a bureaucratic egalitarian organization, these considerations become preponderant. Yet his view of human relations has now become rather skeptical and conservative, and will become increasingly so as the possibilities of his own achievement narrow down. Things do not change easily, he feels, and perhaps they ought not to change easily. Human problems are the key to everything, but a key rather for locking than for unlocking. Humanism in this contest will mean recognition of the other fellow's right to oppose change, i.e., acceptance of the status quo.

The entire career development of the members of the "engineers' corps" can be interpreted as a gradual adjustment to the organization as it stands—with its principles of seniority and its impersonality, with its rigidity of behavior and its resistance to change. In making this adjustment, the directors will resign themselves to the further narrowing of their expectations. But they will not really abandon their former ideology. They will still view change as a positive value which only special circumstances oblige them to discard.

Their kind of adjustment contrasts sharply with the aggressive type of adjustment of the technical engineers. The latter can adjust successfully only when they deny the formal order of the organization, and, indirectly at least, some of its main principles. One may well wonder, however, at this paradox: the leaders of a stabilized, conservative, bureaucratic system profess a philosophy of change in organization patterns, while the group of "coming men" opposing them are consistently conservative in that respect.[13]

[13] This paradox is only ostensible. As we shall see later, such opposition is a necessary condition of the equilibrium of the social system.

The Meaning of Conflict
in a Bureaucratic System of Organization

At the root of all the conflicts we have analyzed, there is clearly some kind of fight for power. Our findings are well in line with the results of most recent researches in organizational behavior, and these have shown how central the notion of control and power may be for understanding human relations in large-scale organizations.[14] We shall investigate these findings more extensively in the next chapter. For the moment, we can bear in mind that there are no organizations without power problems and conflicts arising from them, and, moreover, that there are none where these conflicts are not checked by some kind of social control. We shall now try to discuss on a more general basis, in terms of the forces operating in all bureaucratic systems of organization, the meaning of the special traits which make these conflicts so acute in the case we have studied, and the nature of the social control which still holds the organization together.

Two striking facts emerge when we compare the situation of our management team with the situation of the most common type of organizational hierarchy. First, many forces which usually prevent the development, or at least the expression, of conflict are absent. In addition, there is a peculiar balance of power, of prestige, and of involvement in the job that makes it necessary and even rewarding for the protagonists to engage in conflict.

In the absence of the traditional forces which prevent conflict, three main observations can be made. First, our four group members have perfect security, not only in regard to tenure but even in regard to promotion. They do not depend upon one another or upon higher-ups with whom they could ally themselves. They have, in this respect, nothing to fear and can be as independent as they please. Second, they have no chance of being materially rewarded or even of gaining in status by their personal achievements. Personal achievements are not even measurable. It is almost a private affair for each individual concerned, so that they are delivered not only from fear, but also from hope. Third, the differentiation of their roles and their specification are such that teamwork is not necessary to keep the system going; teamwork certainly may help morally and materially in achieving the required goals, but the absence of co-operation does not cause much strain. Our four individuals, therefore, may be

[14] We shall discuss, in the next chapter, the abundant literature on the subject.

considered as completely autonomous, in the sense that there is nothing in the system to which they belong, that requires them to co-operate, to adjust to each other, or to compromise on their conflicting interests. They have little to gain in the long run by teamwork and compromise—since successful performance does not require them, and their future is already set up in advance and will not be changed by the kind of relationship which they have with their colleagues.

In the presence of a balance of power peculiar to this organization, the opposition between maintenance and production—which is found in all industrial setups but does not usually cause much trouble—is at the root of our main conflict. A rough comparison of Monopoly factories with factories producing the same product with the same technology in other countries shows that some of the technical difficulties with which people in France are so concerned do not even come to mind in different systems of organization—the human relations and power relations arrangement of the Monopoly seems to be solely responsible. According to our findings, we can explain the acuteness of the conflict as being due to an unusual distribution of the power of initiating action in the plant, of the official prestige, and of the commitment to the job. The person whose official prestige is lowest and whose commitment to the job, because of his lifetime involvement with it, is highest, is in a position—because of his control of the major source of uncertainty in the routine of factory life—to control also the initiating of action within the usual range of behavior. His antagonists have no way of retaliating effectively, except in special circumstances. However, they can adjust to their situation because their lesser degree of commitment to the job makes retreat easier.

At a more abstract level, the major elements of the conflict situation appear to be the rigidity of the social roles the organization presents to the individuals, their isolation from one another, and the lack of congruence of these roles with the actors' expectations. There are only a few roles, and they are all well structured and do not allow for individual experimentation and innovation. People do not expect to shift from one role to another and do not depend much upon one another for the attainment of their goals. They can, therefore, take up the cause of their group without having either mental reservations or provisions for an eventual change of circumstances. Where there is a possibility of an equal fight, an otherwise trivial opposition of roles will develop into a basic conflict which will permit the actors to express their own frustrations about their professional situation.

Such an arrangement reminds one of earlier role differentiations in Western societies. Modern professional role systems, compared to, say, those of the eighteenth century, appear to be characterized by a tremendous diversification of the professional roles and a constant shifting of individuals from one role to another. As a consequence, lifelong intergroup conflicts have receded considerably. One can argue that the tensions they generated have been at least partially replaced by the tension of interpersonal competition and by the personal anxieties of individuals who have been obliged to internalize some of these earlier role conflicts. But, in any case, people who could conflict on a more permanent basis tend now to be too far apart; and people who are in constant contact are much too dependent on each other and know too much of each other's viewpoint to be able to develop such basic conflict.[15]

This is not the case, we know, in the Monopoly. There, the groups closest to each other are also those that engage most violently in permanent conflicts of a traditional kind, reminiscent of the disputes of the brotherhoods and guilds of the *ancien régime* over their rights and privileges.

Such a comparison provides a perspective which enables us to consider the organizational system of the Monopoly in the series of all possible systems. But in order to go further, we must still try to understand the logic and rationale of such a pattern.

Three related principles govern the social system of the factories we have studied: (1) complete quality between people who are in the same hierarchical ranking and who have roughly the same role, with seniority alone accounting for differences and promotions; (2) separate recruitment from the outside for each of these major roles, with abstract competitive examinations as criteria of selection; and (3) impersonal and detailed rules applying to all possible happenings, so that most uncertainty and concomitant human intervention can be eliminated. There may be some theoretical opposition between the principle of equality-seniority and the principle of outside recruitment. However, if one views them both as a way to concur with the common goal of eliminating all human intervention from the organizational machine, they are mutually reinforcing.

From these principles, one can see very well how isolation and rigidity of roles develop. Strict application of equality and seniority make interpersonal fights within the group impossible. Outside recruitment separates the groups and prevents communication. The elimination of uncertainty and human intervention, however, should act as check insofar as it is intended to suppress power relationship.

[15] It goes without saying that this description exaggerates certain tendencies of our Western societies. The tendencies are, furthermore, perceptibly less developed in France than in America.

But our example has demonstrated that there are always weak spots and that power dependencies and conflicts will grow around them. We shall see later that these three principles of action are the core of the bureaucratic system of organization and that they are present as tendencies in all large-scale organizations. In private organizations, however, they are checked by the powerful unifying force provided by the control of the promotional ladder. However, the lower we go on the hierarchical scale, the weaker this control becomes—with the result that intergroup fights tend to develop in the lower echelons. In public administrations, this control also becomes more difficult at higher levels, especially in the older and more "bureaucratic" ones, of which our case is an extreme example. Rigidity of roles and lack of communication between them make conflict likely in all weak spots of the system.

But even in the case under examination, social control sets limits. Other people's privileges cannot be infringed upon; minimum production standards, order and decorum, status pre-eminence of the director must be observed. In this respect, two sets of forces seem to be at work. The first is the feeling, in members of all groups, that their privileges depend at a very high level upon the other groups' privileges. This means that the authority of the director as a final arbitrator for keeping peace and order must be recognized. Second, there is the feeling that the standards of the organization's achievements and practices should be comparable to general expectations in the larger society. The first kind of pressure keeps the system working on a routine basis; the second accounts for change and progress that come from the top down impersonally, with the members of the "engineers' corps" as agents of change. Occupational or professional roles, however, remain frozen into a very ancient pattern with no likelihood of internal motivation for change. This alone invites us to foresee some kind of crisis when the acceleration of progress will make it impossible for such a system to adjust to modern society.[16]

---

[16] The Monopoly seems to be entering, at this time, such a period of crisis.

Part Three

BUREAUCRACY AS AN ORGANIZATIONAL SYSTEM

Until now, this report has been mainly descriptive. We have tried to present all the data necessary for understanding the relevant aspects of our two case studies and to propose an interpretation of their interrelations. But we have not yet referred to the theories of organization and of bureaucracy that can be applied and discussed in this context.

We should like to broaden our perspective and to discuss our own observations and conclusions in relation to other experiences and other interpretations. We hope in this way to throw more light on the problems already discussed and to make a new contribution to the theoretical controversy.

Chapter vi will be devoted to a discussion of the general meaning of those problems of power which were central to our analysis of the two case studies, and especially of the Industrial Monopoly. Chapter vii will attempt to extrapolate an analysis of bureaucracy as a general system of organization.

Chapter Six

POWER AND UNCERTAINTY

Our analyses of the two cases we have discussed have clearly demonstrated the central nature of problems of power in the development of the bureaucratic phenomenon. The paralyzing structures and virtually irresistible mechanisms of routine that we have described seem closely associated with the fears, hesitations, and conduct of all the participants in the matters of power and of relations of dependency. But we cannot remain satisfied with these empirical evidences; we are going to try to propose a more theoretical interpretation of them that will permit us to explain them and to generalize about them.

We are going to begin by examining the resources, in this regard, that are provided for us by the successive theories that have been proposed as explanations of the functioning of organizations.

POWER AS THE NEW CENTRAL PROBLEM OF THE THEORY OF ORGANIZATION

Power is a very difficult problem with which to deal in the theory of organization. It refers to a kind of relationship that is neither unidimensional nor predictable like the kind of stimulus-response relationship which social psychologists found so rewarding to study when they began to use scientific methods for understanding organizational behavior. Moreover, the use of power carries a distinct value connotation, so that ideological, as well as methodological, reasons have been working simultaneously to cause researchers to avoid facing the issue.

The consequences of this kind of approach have been serious. Communication problems, problems of work motivation, and problems of morale had been widely discussed and seriously studied in theory, empirically, and even through experiments. However, only a few years ago, the positive analysis of power relations did not seem to have progressed much since the days of Machiavelli and Marx. A brief review of the place that power problems have had in the development of modern organizational theory will give us a clearer perspective of their implications for the present and enable us to understand better the general framework within which our data must be discussed.

The early rationalistic theory of organization tended to ignore the problem of power altogether. Its mechanistic model did not allow for relationships as complex as those which power fosters. Its promoters, on the other hand, were fighting for a radical departure from the remnants of an aristocratic past too much concerned with the methods of ruling and controlling subordinate groups. They believed mankind had to shift from the government of men to the administration of things, as their precursor Saint-Simon had claimed; and they felt they were achieving their aims by emphasizing financial stimuli and technical controls instead of human leadership. The delusion that they had suppressed power relationships prevented them from understanding the true nature of their own actions, which nevertheless had direct consequences on the power structure of modern organizations.

Early twentieth-century Marxists, although they viewed all contemporary problems of the capitalist world through the spectacles of power dialectics, also found themselves in the same predicament when dealing with the future. They felt that, when ownership relationships had been eliminated, an administration of things similar to the one Western industrialists were proposing would take care of all power problems. Lenin's famous definition of socialism, "Soviets plus electrification," was a terse statement characteristic of the same desire to escape the power problems of modern bureaucracies that was driving organizers and industrialists of the West.

Power problems were not squarely faced by the sociologists, social psychologists, and philosophers of the thirties and forties, whose "human relations approach" nevertheless made it possible to challenge more fundamentally the rationale of the classical theory.[1] This was true for the *interactionists*[2] as well as for the early *Lewinians*.[3]

To be sure, by directing devastating attacks against the mechanistic model of behavior upon which the classical theory rested, and by making it obvious to everyone that the human factor was a de-

---

[1] Borrowing their arguments against Taylorism from the anticapitalist reformers of the time, they kept the same naïve approach as the Taylorians about their own constructive propositions.

[2] We use the term "interactionist" to designate the Harvard School of the thirties (Elton Mayo, T. N. Whitehead, Fritz Roethlisberger, Elliot Chapple, Conrad Arensberg, William Foote Whyte). See W. F. Whyte, "An Interaction Approach to the Theory of Organization," in Mason Haire, *Modern Organization Theory* (New York: Wiley, 1959), pp. 154–82.

[3] At least before 1955.

terminant, the *interactionists* were preparing the way for an understanding of power relationships. If one accepts the concept that human behavior cannot be directed by simple financial stimuli alone, that *sentiments* have an impact on *activities,* one must soon also admit that the allocation of power and the system of power arrangements have a decisive influence over the kind of adjustment people are able to make within an organization, and over the practical results and the efficiency of that organization.

Most interactionists, however, have tended to shy away from discussing such matters. They have preferred to study interactions in their most physical aspect, without taking into account the hierarchical system of domination.[4] They can explain the emergence of spontaneous leadership,[5] but not the impact of an authority imposed from the top down and of the concomitant struggle for power. Finally, one can view their attempts at understanding sentiments and activities by measuring interactions as another stimulus-response approach, as simplicistic in several aspects as the mechanistic model they had rightly criticized.[6] Moreover, the very imperfection of the instrument prevents analysis of the extent to which technical rationality may be shaped and determined by the human factor. It thus tends to reinforce the hold of mechanistic factors in decision-making.

At a deeper level, their avoidance of power problems seems to be linked with a conservative philosophy. According to this, as Clark Kerr has pointed out, human relations problems can be understood and solved without accepting dissatisfaction, antagonisms, and group conflicts as the price an open society has to pay for progress.[7]

Lewinians have not escaped power problems so simply. Their long-continued ignorance of the sociological and organizational aspects of leadership, however, has made it difficult for them to understand the struggles, the peculiar alignments, and the kind of bargaining engendered by the impact of power. They wanted to understand what makes an organization efficient, but at first they did not anticipate going beyond their demonstration of the superiority of permissive leadership and their rather naïve search for the best way of converting people to it. Research results, however, while contributing in a decisive way to our knowledge of the way organizations operate,

---

[4] This is what can be deduced from the classical restatement of George Homans in his book, *The Human Group* (New York: Harcourt, Brace, 1950).

[5] The most illuminating piece of research on that account is still W. F. Whyte, *Street Corner Society* (Chicago: University of Chicago Press, 1943).

[6] This is still the impression one gets after reading the 1960 presentation of W. F. Whyte in Mason Haire, *loc. cit.*

[7] Clark Kerr and Lloyd Fisher, "Plant Society, The Elite and the Aborigines," in *Common Frontiers in the Social Sciences* (Glencoe, Ill.: The Free Press, 1957).

have not validated their assumptions.[8] It was demonstrated, for example, that it was the supervisors who enjoyed more popularity with their subordinates who were apt to be those who had more influence within the organization—not the most permissive ones.[9] The main experimental project conducted by the Michigan Survey Research Center in an insurance company had mixed results; the authoritarian system of leadership appeared to be as successful as the "permissive" one.[10] Careful investigations, by Floyd Mann at the University of Michigan[11] and by Fleishman, Harris, and Burtt at Ohio State,[12] of the net results of human relations training, then demonstrated conclusively that it had been a conspicuous failure. As many people had suspected, it was useless for changing people's attitudes outside of their own work and power structure surroundings. Floyd Mann and his associates devised new ways of intervention, taking into account the organizational structure. But even their feedback techniques fell short of integrating the problems of power—to whose importance their own researches testified.

The logic of those cumulative experiences and the critical discussion they caused were not without results. During the last five years especially, power problems have come to the forefront of the study of organizational behavior. Social psychologists such as Robert Kahn and Arnold Tannenbaum, small group psychologists such as Dorwin Cartwright, J. P. R. French, and associates, sociologists with a more anthropological bias such as Melville Dalton and Norman Martin, are conducting researches on the problems of control and power.[13]

Approaches to this new field, however, still seem to be awkward and groping, as if the factors which prevent people from dealing

[8] For a discussion of these results with a very convincing reassertion of the permissiveness philosophy see Rensis Likert, *New Patterns of Management* (New York: McGraw-Hill, 1961).

[9] Donald Pelz, "Influence, a Key to Effective Leadership," *Personnel,* III (1952), 3.

[10] See Nancy C. Morse and Everett C. Reimer, "Experimental Change of a Major Organizational Variable," *Journal of Abnormal and Social Psychology,* Vol. LII (1955); and Rensis Likert, "Measuring Organizational Performance," *Harvard Business Review,* March, 1958, pp. 41–50.

[11] Floyd Mann, "Studying and Creating Change: A Means of Understanding Social Organization," in *Human Relations in the Industrial Setting* (New York: Harper, 1957), pp. 146–67.

[12] E. A. Fleishman, E. F. Harris, and H. E. Burtt, *Leadership and Supervision in Industry: An Evaluation of a Supervisory Training Program* (Columbus: Ohio State University, 1955).

[13] See, e.g., Arnold Tannenbaum and Robert Kahn in Dorwin Cartwright (ed.), *Participation in Local Unions* (Evanston: Row Peterson, 1958); W. Lloyd Warner and Norman Martin, *Industrial Man* (New York: Harper, 1959); Melville Dalton, *Men Who Manage* (New York: Wiley, 1960); Michel Crozier, "De l'étude des relations humaines à l'étude des relations de pouvoir," *Sociologie du Travail,* I (1961), 80–83.

with power problems were still active when the investigators finally chose to study them.

The shyness and escapism we have described seem to be associated with the rejection of the human relations approach by the strict rationalist, and, at the opposite pole, by ignorance about all rational problems on the part of the strict "human relations" proponents. If one believes that co-ordination, conformity to orders, and the will to produce can be brought about with only economic and financial incentives—i.e., if the world of human relations is ignored altogether —then power problems need not be taken seriously. But the exact reverse is operating within the human relations approach. If one believes that a perfect equation between satisfaction and productivity can be achieved under permissive leadership, one does not have to study power; one has only to fight to accelerate its withering away.

A realistic appraisal of power relationships and power problems, however, can be made only when one has realized that there are no shortcuts. One must face at the same time the problem of the rational achievement of goals and that of the human means.[14] But even if one accepts both approaches as necessary, one can still see them as completely separate, pretending, implicitly at least, that they do not interfere. This is more or less the conventional contemporary view of two independent worlds which must be studied independently—the rational and technical world, under the primacy of goal-setting and goal-achieving; and the world of personnel, morale, and human organization.

Only with the recent developments of neo-rationalism and of the decision-making approach has it been possible to go beyond this lip-service integration and to understand how each set of determinants establishes the limits of the other sets' possibilities of application. The classic rationalists did not consider the members of an organization as human beings, but just as other cogs in the machine. For them, workers were only hands. The human relations approach has shown how incomplete such a rationale was. It has also made it possible to consider workers as creatures of feeling, who are moved by the impact of the so-called rational decisions taken above them, and will react to them. A human being, however, does not have only a hand and a heart. He has also a head, which means that he is free to decide and to play his own game. This is what almost all proponents of the human relations theories, as well as their early rationalist opponents, tend to forget. This explains their failure and

[14] Talcott Parsons has pointed out that power, as the development of the decision process, must become the central problem of organization theory. Talcott Parsons, *Structure and Process in Modern Societies* (Glencoe, Ill.: The Free Press, 1960), pp. 41–43.

the hostility they have met among workers, in spite of their positive contributions and their most excellent intentions. By ignoring the subordinates' claims to freedom, they immediately created among them fears of being manipulated.[15]

Neo-rationalist or strategic analysis methods have been used, until now, mostly for understanding decision-making at the managerial level. But they can have an even greater impact if they are used for understanding subordinates' behavior. Subordinates can be considered as free agents who can discuss their own problems and bargain about them, who do not only submit to a power structure but also participate in that structure. Of course, their degree of freedom is not very great, and their conduct, when viewed from outside, may seem to a large extent to be determined by non-rational motivations. But one must never forget that to them it is rational, i.e., adaptive.

March and Simon, among others, have put the problem in the proper light, with their concept of bounded rationality and their analysis of the different sets of factors that limit rationality. Such an approach allows us to deal with the problems of power in a more realistic fashion. It enables us to consider, at the same time, the rationality of each agent or of each group of agents, and the influence of the human relations factors that limit their rationality.[16]

In such a light, we shall try to analyze again the data of our case studies—and first, the Industrial Monopoly case study—with a view to understanding the interrelations of both worlds within an integrated theory of organization.

THE EXAMPLE OF THE INDUSTRIAL MONOPOLY

The Industrial Monopoly offers us the great advantage of being a very simple social system with only a small number of personnel categories which are well separated and clearly defined. Such a system tends to simplify the strategy of each member, thus making it easier to analyze it and to test the neo-rationalist method we are proposing.

Let us focus on the strategy of each occupational category in turn, trying to understand what it means for the individuals.

---

[15] We personally participated in the diffusion of these fears ten years ago. See Michel Crozier, "Human Engineering," *Les Temps Modernes*, July, 1951.

[16] James March and Herbert A. Simon, *Organizations* (New York: Wiley, 1958). We shall use, quite often in this section, the contribution of these authors, which we believe will stand as decisive. Let us say, however, that their attempt at integrating the two approaches (human relations and neo-rationalism) does not seem very satisfactory to us.

THE PRODUCTION WORKERS

Production workers are the only actually dependent people in a system where each group is well protected against any kind of interference from members of another group. This dependence, however partially, causes them some frustration and some aggressiveness. But these reactions remain covert; only operatives who are not directly dependent on the maintenance workers express the aggressiveness of the production group against them. Those who have more to suffer from the relationship will transfer their aggressiveness to the domain of the norms and of the work load.

This is a good example of the necessity of the human relations approach for understanding the basic relations of dependence. The usual psycho-analytical schemes—dependence, frustration, aggression, transfer—apply exactly but they fill in only part of the picture. One should also ask why production workers retreat before the maintenance people, why they cover up, why we do not find an overt superior-subordinate conflict.

In this kind of analysis, we must resort again to rational arguments. Our first question should be what the production workers' behavior means to the group relationships within the Monopoly. If production workers keep up a good front toward the maintenance people, if operatives who have to deal with them take it upon themselves not to complain, we must conclude that good relationships with maintenance men are highly valued in the production workers' group and that it is an important element of the latter's strategy to keep their alliance with the maintenance crew. At the same time, this alliance must be viewed as a dangerous one. It must not go too far and lead to certain consequences. Maintenance people must be warned about possible limits. They have to be pressured and blackmailed. This cannot be done overtly under the direction of the leaders of the group, because the leaders are the ones who have to keep up a good front. It will be done with guerrilla tactics, covertly in face-to-face contacts with the maintenance workers, more overtly behind their backs. Such tactics can be viewed as the results of frustrations; but they are also rational, at least at the group level. Maintenance people sense the hostility around them, as their interviews show significantly. Thus this pressure is a very efficient sort of social control, and one may hypothesize that it keeps maintenance people well within the limits of what is culturally acceptable in present-day France.[17]

Why maintain an alliance that may seem, at the shop level, to be

[17] Many stories were told to the interviewer about the maintenance people's oppressive behavior, but they were all taken from a rather remote past. No present case of direct abuse was ever reported.

rather a one-way relationship? Would it not be more rational to break up, side with the supervisors and the formal hierarchy, and get rid of this cumbersome dependence? Such a calculation is not completely absent from the minds of the production workers, but is merely an alternative, to be considered in extreme cases only. This is easy to understand, since the whole system of labor relations depends on the close alliance of the two groups. Workers feel that they have achieved a great deal from the hierarchy as regards independence, as well as working conditions and wages, and that they can wrest a very good bargain from the *Direction Générale* within the existing system. They fear—and with reason—that both materially and organizationally this system, and especially the seniority provisions, would be completely disrupted should the maintenance people break away.[18] In a way, the production workers feel that they have to choose between a limited dependence on the maintenance men and a return to the usual hierarchical system.

Of course, this alliance is placed under the banner of working-class solidarity, and it arouses many strong sentiments among workers. In that sense, it is a natural alliance, and one should not ignore the limits which such sentiments set to rational behavior. Nevertheless, the alliance has a good, cold rationale. Maintenance people are in a strategic situation in case of a strike; with them success is sure, without them it is doubtful.[19]

Production workers as a group, therefore, make a rational choice when submitting to the maintenance workers' leadership. The expression of the machine operatives' frustrations in relation to maintenance workers through complaints against the work load, furthermore, is not so arbitrary as it appears at first. This ambiguity is at the center of the production workers' choice, since their bargain is in fact to accept their dependence upon the maintenance people in order to wrest concessions about the work load from their fight with management. Translating this strategy into a gross psychological equivalence is not bad tactics, since resentment, even when transferred, can be a good weapon.

Finally, besides belonging to a separate group, many maintenance workers act individually as social leaders of the whole worker group. Production workers need them, not only because of their strategic situation, but also because they can provide the talents necessary for organizing social life.[20]

---

[18] Maintenance people are very skilful at reminding their partners of their vulnerability by presenting a recurrent threat of forming a separate craft union.

[19] In a certain way, class feelings may be considered as the crystallization of earlier strategic calculations.

[20] They are male and therefore the natural aristocracy of the working class among a predominantly female working-class group.

These leadership qualities are also important within each small group dependent upon a maintenance worker in the shop. The machine operator who is in close contact with her maintenance man can play the role of second to him and identify with his leadership, which means that, for the individual, keeping up a good front, besides being demanded by her role, can also provide some psychological rewards.[21] One indication of this is the much greater satisfaction of the machine operators in Pattern III, where, because of the greater size of the group they have a more interesting role as seconds to the maintenance men.

THE MAINTENANCE WORKERS

The behavior of the maintenance workers is not so ambiguous, since they are not dependent and cannot contemplate a reversal of their policy. Their strategy is a very simple and rigorous one. It aims, first, to keep the area under their own control free from outside interference. For this purpose, they prevent both production workers and supervisors from dealing in any way with machine maintenance. We have mentioned the case of the failure of a supervisor who used an otherwise excellent opportunity to enter the field.[22] The same barrier exists for the workers; the one unforgivable sin of a machine operator is to "fool around" with her machine. Maintenance and repair problems must be kept secret. No explanation is ever given. Production workers must not understand.[23] Maintenance workers keep their skill itself as a rule-of-thumb skill. They completely disregard all blueprints and maintenance directions, and have been able to make them disappear from the plants.[24] They believe in individual settings exclusively, and they are the only ones to know these settings. These and all the other tricks of the trade are learned through companionship on the job. Every job is done individually, but there is a great deal of solidarity for learning purposes and whenever there is a difficult problem. However, no explanations are ever given, and the learning process is therefore painful. It is an old handicraft apprenticeship, the harshness of which explains the impatient reactions of the newly arrived men. But these practices are necessary for preserving the group's absolute control over machine stoppages.

[21] Such an argument can be valid only in a social system where ascriptive values predominate over achievement values.

[22] Cf. above, p. 127.

[23] This may be the main reason why they are viewed as incompetent and unable to understand technical matter; see above, p. 97.

[24] It was impossible for the researcher to find, in the plants, any written instructions about the setting and the maintenance of the different kinds of machines. Such instructions, however, were easily available at the *Direction Générale*.

Discipline, complete submission to the official creed of the group, and a sort of idealization of the technical engineer, are other important elements of the maintenance workers' collective behavior. Such patterns of attitudes make sense only, we believe, if one accepts the existence of the strategy we have described. Not the slightest weakness can be allowed to develop on the maintenance department front line.

In this perspective, the importance that the maintenance workers attribute to their overt antagonism to the lower supervisor is also quite rational. The lower supervisor is in a position to be the only agent of the formal hierarchy against the maintenance system. The aims of the maintenance people about them must, therefore, be to weaken them in their authority and to keep them at arms' length from the machine problems and from the relationship between the production workers and the maintenance workers. By constantly attacking them and depreciating their efforts, by making it impossible for them to assert their authority, the maintenance men succeed in demoralizing the lower supervisors. In so doing, they are merely pushing to the extreme their initial advantage—their control over the last source of uncertainty remaining in a completely routinized organizational system.

THE LOWER SUPERVISORS

Since it is impossible for them to enter the maintenance field, lower supervisors should try to assert their organizational decisions in other fields, where they retain more leeway, in order to maintain adequate authority over the production workers—if not over the maintenance men. But they are unable to follow this strategy, except in a few isolated cases—such as the raw product conditioning shops—where the setup of work within the unit and the regularity of the process afterward depend, partially at least, on their own decision. They generally back down, their claim to authority not being a well-founded one, since theirs is the simple responsibility of repartition and accountability. This does not allow for much leeway and would not earn them adequate support from management if they incurred the hostility of the union.

The best strategy of the lower supervisors in these circumstances is to refuse to get involved either in the production workers' problems with management or in their fight with the maintenance men. Minimizing their contribution to the system, and discharging their duties with a minimum of involvement and participation, insure the lower supervisors a more satisfactory adjustment than trying to fight back. But this is an individualistic kind of adjustment and very difficult to achieve. This is the explanation of why this group is the least successful and therefore the most frustrated one, with much retreatism and individual incoherence.

THE MANAGEMENT TEAM

The same kind of analysis can be applied to the management level. The strategy of the plant director and his assistant is determined, first, by their lack of freedom of action. Their ability to initiate action has been much curtailed by rationalization. Their decisions are usually about purely routine matters. The only exception to this, for the director, is the planning and carrying out of the construction of new buildings and new physical layouts for the shops. They cannot even permit a breach of the rules easily; thus they have no bargaining power in the most trivial affairs. On the other hand, they derive a certain leeway from their role of adjudicating conflicting claims between groups. By virtue of his conspicuous position and his duties as impartial arbitrator and as permanent representative of the plant community, the director can still exercise a great deal of influence over his subordinates. He is a sort of fashion leader in human relations. By punishing with a show of reprobation or even through calculated coldness, and by rewarding with the gift of his attention, he can even consolidate his influence into a capital that gives him some freedom of action with which to bargain.

However great the directors' skill may be in making full use of these minor advantages of their position, they find pretty close limits. They will become masters of the game only if there are large-scale transformations of the plant. In such circumstances, the possibility that they will have to initiate new arrangements to face new problems will transform completely the nature of the game.

The directors' strategy, therefore, is to fight for change. This is because, in the event of change, the function of their competitors, the technical engineers, is devaluated and their own much enhanced. If large-scale transformation is not possible, they will try to undertake some construction and remodeling as less satisfying alternatives. Whatever their own feelings at the beginning, they adopt the strategy of technological change. They come to understand that the only possible way to increase their own power and put the technical engineers back in their subordinate place is to impose large-scale changes within the plant. They are in favor of technical progress not for ideological reasons, but for strategic ones. When they become older and realize that they cannot win, or that their only chance to win is to play safe on the human relations side, they become more mellow. Then they rely more on their capital as administrators and judges, and what is likely to remain of their fighting for change is what we have called the "builder's complex." This does not mean that their basic strategy has really changed. It means that they are not so confident as they were before and feel they must retreat, according to circumstances, for temporary tactical periods or as a more permanent overt or covert avowal of defeat.

Technical engineers, on the contrary, are on the defensive, and their strategy is a conservative one. Like their subordinates, the maintenance men, their main preoccupation is to keep, free from anyone's interference, the area they have under control, which is the source of their power. For this reason, they support the maintenance men in instituting disregard of any formal written instructions for maintenance and make it possible for them to lay down the law in the workshop.

The paradox is striking. Directors and assistant directors, socially conservative, fight with great passion for technical change and modernization. At the same time, technical engineers, who would like to transform the present social order, are very conservative about technical matters; they do whatever they can to keep their skill a rule-of-thumb one and to prevent efforts to rationalize it. This is the reason that they like to act as trouble-shooters, even if it means always running to patch things up, and that they oppose any kind of progress which could free them from certain of their difficulties. Their only solution has always been to ask for an assistant, and they are quite ready to remain overworked if this demand cannot be met.

What is the common thread among these diverse strategies? Each group fights to preserve and enlarge the area upon which it has some discretion, attempts to limit its dependence upon other groups and to accept such dependence only insofar as it is a safeguard against another and more feared one, and finally prefers retreatism if there is no other choice but submission. The group's freedom of action and the power structure appear clearly to be at the core of all these strategies.

THE ROLE OF POWER WITHIN AN ORGANIZATIONAL SYSTEM

We shall now utilize these sketches of group strategy in discussing the nature of power within an organization. But before trying to generalize from the example of the Industrial Monopoly, we should like to attempt to understand in more formal terms how power is likely to appear in a rational system of organization.

Let us take, to begin, Robert Dahl's[25] definition of power: *the*

[25] Robert Dahl, "The Concept of Power," *Behavioral Science*, II (July, 1957), 201–15.

*power of a person A over a person B is the ability of A to obtain that
B do something he would not have done otherwise.* It seems clear
that a perfect rational system, such as was imagined by the exponent
of the classical or of the Marxist theory, does not allow power relationships to develop in the normal course of the functioning of an
organization. In such a system, we believe, there is only one rational
choice to be made by each protagonist in a collective endeavor. Provided the goals are given, there is only *one best way* at each level to
achieve the assigned task, and one best way also to arrange the hierarchical levels and to assign the necessary tasks. If there were actually only one best way to do things, individuals could not maintain
any leeway in accomplishing their tasks and in making decisions
about other people's tasks. Their behavior, therefore, would be entirely predictable, and they could, in turn, predict and rely on the
behavior of all the other protagonists. One can say that they would
simultaneously be bound as regards their own possibilities of action
and free from any kind of personal dependence. Someone who has
only one course of action available cannot ingratiate himself with
the organization or with any individual within the organization. He
does not have any possibility of bargaining. Power relationships
could not develop in a context where no one could change the behavior of anyone else.

But contrary to the hopes of the industrialists and progressivists
of the twenties, the very progress of rationality in the field of organization has shown how deceptive such beliefs in the *one best way*
were. Power relationships and discretion in human interaction cannot be suppressed with rationalization; and the failure of classical
rationalists does not stem from the resistance of an earlier power-
ridden social order.[26]

Against this background, let us now consider the functioning of
the Monopoly. Two contrasting sets of facts are clear. First, there is
a very strong tendency along the hierarchical line to reproduce the
power-free situation of the perfect rational system. Extremely limiting rules prescribe behavior in every event, and no one has kept, at
least in theory, any real discretion in appraising the situation he
must face and in choosing the course he will have to follow. As a
result, as we have pointed out, relationships of dependence cannot

[26] In practice, the *one best way* philosophy was used to provide the managers,
whose job it was to discover and elaborate this sole rational solution, with the kind
of absolute power that was necessary to break down the habits and privileges of
all other groups. And this is one of the most striking paradoxes of recent social
history: the fight of the pioneers of scientific work organization, as well as the
fight of the Bolsheviks for substituting the administration of things for the government of men, ended very often with an increase of the dichotomy between managers and managed.

form along the hierarchical line. Second, a whole system of bargaining and power relationships has developed around those areas where the actors' behavior is rather unpredictable, especially in the maintenance system.

It seems clear, therefore, that within the Monopoly, people have power over other people insofar as the latter's behavior is narrowly limited by rules whereas their own behavior is not. This unintended consequence of rationalization must be indicated: in the bargaining relationships we have analyzed, the predictability of one's behavior is the sure test of one's own inferiority.

Reality, in fact, appears extremely different from the perfect administration of things. Even in such a privileged case as the Monopoly, where it would be possible to simplify and rationalize to the extreme by cutting ties with the environment, strategical analysis makes it possible to discover that power can neither be suppressed nor ignored. It stems from the impossibility of eliminating uncertainty in the context of bounded rationality which is ours.[27]

In such a context, the power of A over B depends on A's ability to predict B's behavior and on the uncertainty of B about A's behavior. As long as the requirements of action create situations of uncertainty, the individuals who have to face them have power over those who are affected by the results of their choice.[28]

At present, a complete reversal of earlier conceptions about ration-

[27] There may be many examples to confirm this analysis of power relationships. We have analyzed, for example, the case of a few experts in a public agency, whose job has been rationalized in such a way that it has become pretty much routine, in contrast with a much simpler but more exposed job where the unpredictable reactions of the public might endanger the reputation of the whole department. The holder of this last job, who can partially control this variable and whose influence is preponderant for his colleagues' success, has much more bargaining power than they have and they are subject to his influence, whereas he is not to theirs.

[28] One should be precise and specify *relevant* uncertainty, although the notion of relevance is vague and subject to change according to the objectives of the organization and to the progress of knowledge. People and organizations will care only about what they can recognize as affecting them and, in turn, what is possibly within their control. When there are no possibilities of control, power can be claimed by no one—although it may be argued that, in a more diffuse way, the necessity of submitting to leadership will be greater in a situation of true uncertainty, as certain experiments on the advantages, under conditions of duress, of the centrality system over more democratic circular systems and the role of the leader among small primitive groups on the verge of starvation seem to have proved. See for example Harold J. Leavitt, "Some Effects of Certain Communication Patterns of Group Performance," *Journal of Abnormal and Social Psychology,* XLVI (1951), 28–50; and Claude Levi-Strauss, *Tristes Tropiques* (Paris: Plon, 1958), pp. 325–339. This notion of uncertainty has been also used recently by an American political scientist, Herbert Kaufmann, in an interdisciplinary report on administrative theory ("Why Organizations Behave As They Do: An Outline of a Theory"). Kaufmann analyzed only organizations' global behavior, but his conclusions are similar to ours.

ality can be discerned. The greater confidence effected by the progress of knowledge, the possibilities of mastering the environment that it implies, have not tended to reinforce the rigidity of the decision-making process. They seem, on the contrary, to have obliged organizations to discard completely the very notion of *one best way*. The most advanced organizations, because they now feel capable of integrating areas of uncertainty in their economic calculus, are beginning to understand that the illusion of perfect rationality has too long persisted, weakening the possibilities of action by insisting on rigorous logic and immediate coherence. Substituting the notion of program for the notion of operational process, introducing the theory of probability at lower and lower levels, reasoning on global systems, and integrating more and more variables without separating ends and means, they are experiencing a deep and irreversible change. The crucial point of this change consists, for us, in recognizing—first, implicitly, then more and more consciously—that man cannot look for the one best way and has not actually even searched for it. The philosophy of the one best way has been only a way of protecting oneself against the difficulty of having to choose, a scientist's substitute for the traditional ideologies upon which rested the legitimacy of the rulers' decision.[29] Man has never been able to search for the *optimum* solution. He has always had to be content with solutions merely *satisfactory* in regard to a few particularistic criteria of which he was aware.[30]

The reasoning on uncertainty that makes it possible to use the theory of probability in decision-making opens, at the same time, new ways to take into account all the affective reactions that are brought about by the power and dependence relationships around areas of uncertainty. Research in this domain, we feel, will be decisive for all future progress in the field, since it is there and there only that the world of rationality and the world of affectivity will be integrated.

Let us now abandon the theoretical discussion for a while. We shall try to apply our new method of analysis and the scheme of interpretation we have just described to two kinds of general and abstract problems, the superior-subordinate relationship and the workers' reactions to the work standards imposed on them by management.

[29] The collapse of the illusions that formed the rationale of scientific work organization, and still form that of the present Soviet organizational system, makes it possible to transform the role and situation of the managers that can now be more easily stripped of any mystic connotation. Indeed, the taboos that once surrounded power relationships are beginning to disappear, and one will be more and more able to analyze them rationally without having to question the whole organizational system.

[30] See March and Simon's pertinent demonstration, *op. cit.*

THE PROBLEM OF THE SUPERVISOR-SUBORDINATE RELATIONSHIP

Let us take, as an example, an organization that has been completely rationalized in the classical sense that it has undergone scientific work organization. If the task assignment is such that neither the superior nor the subordinate has any kind of initiative, in relation not only to the processing of the task, but also to its amount and quality, which are rewarded independently on an automatic basis— i.e., if the supervisor does not personally control any important variable affecting his subordinates' behavior, he cannot obtain from them increases of their output or better the quality of their production. But if the supervisor has some leeway, if he can tolerate a breach of the rules, a distortion of the work process that might make it easier to accomplish the task, his subordinates who want or need such tolerance will be dependent on him on that account. Supervisors will thus have at their disposal some kind of influence which is ultimately power that they will be able to utilize to attain their own personal ends.

We can thus envisage two complementary sorts of discretion within an organization. The first one comes from the uncertainty of the task itself, and the second from the rules that have been devised to make it more rational and more predictable. As long as some uncertainty remains about carrying out the task, the most menial subordinate retains some slight discretion. And, in a way, as long as a human being is preferred to an automatic machine there will be some uncertainty. On the other hand, the rules that limit the discretion of the subordinate to a minimum can and will be used by the supervisor for preserving an area of discretion and the possibility of bargaining.[31]

To the impossibility of suppressing completely the discretion of the subordinate, therefore, there corresponds the persistence of personal discretion in the interpretation and application of the rules. Thus pressure can be applied to force the subordinates to use their discretion for the benefit of the organization.

The battle between subordinates and supervisors involves a permanent basic strategy. Subordinates try to increase their amount of discretion and utilize it to oblige higher-ups to pay more for their co-operation.[32] Conversely, they exert pressure for new rules limiting

---

[31] This can be seen in Alvin Gouldner description of the way supervisors use disciplinary rules in their relationships with their subordinates. Alvin Gouldner, *Patterns of Industrial Bureaucracy* (Glencoe, Ill.: The Free Press, 1954), especially pp. 172–74.

[32] In so doing, they must be very careful not to expose themselves to the risk of furthering rationalization; this is why their pressure is usually indirect.

the power of the supervisors; but they try, at the same time, to profit, whenever possible, from whatever discretion the supervisors have kept. Supervisors apply pressure symmetrically on both fronts, rationalization and bargaining, to gain as much co-operation as they can for what cannot be rationalized. Both sides must use double-talk. Officially, each supports the rules, and puts as much pressure as possible on the other side to oblige the latter to obey these rules, while it is fighting to preserve its own area of freedom and making covert deals in defiance of the same rules it is promoting.[33]

THE PROBLEM OF THE WORK STANDARDS

Let us now turn to the typical production workers' behavior in terms of work standards. The well-known phenomenon of the fight of machine operatives for "making out" or accumulating a "kitty" that has been studied in so many different contexts, and can be observed in the Monopoly as well as in the plant where Donald Roy made his famous study, can be viewed along the same line.[34]

According to the classical theory, it is an irrational act *par excellence*. Workers will take great pains, will even work at a breakneck pace, for no other reason than to accumulate pieces in advance and be able to loaf at a later time. Such behavior used to seem, and often still does seem, incredible to industrial engineers. Workers will not gain financially from this practice; it is tiring; and they have to fight pressure from supervision. This is one of the domains where the interactionist approach brought us extremely good descriptions of a hitherto forgotten world and a forgotten worker.

The human relations analysis, however, is not entirely satisfactory. It tells us of the security needs of the worker, of his desire to break the monotony of the task, to play a game against the clock, and to take revenge upon the foreman.[35] These wants are certainly present, but one should not assume that such behavior is irrational. By building up "kitties," workers also achieve rational ends, and their behavior is not different from that which can be observed among executives. "Making out" gives them a greater freedom of action to cover

[33] There is an important distinction to be made between rules prescribing the ways in which the task must be performed and rules prescribing the way people should be chosen, trained, and promoted for various jobs. Subordinates fight rationalization in the first area and want it in the second, and supervisory personnel do just the reverse; but there is such a great link between both sets of rules that, by and large, ambiguity remains.

[34] See Donald Roy, "Work Satisfaction and Social Rewards in Quota Achievement," *American Sociological Review*, XVIII (October, 1953), and the discussion of W. F. Whyte, *Money and Motivation* (New York: Harper, 1955), pp. 31–38.

[35] See Whyte, *Money and Motivation*, pp. 31–38.

up any personal activities in which they want to engage. It protects them by showing their supervisors that they have more resources than engineers or time-keepers believe. This is very rough planning indeed, but it does increase the amount of discretion a worker may have for dealing with a task, as simple as it may be, and it is a sort of invitation to bargaining.

To be sure, this behavior is also quite symbolic, since its affective side—showing off one's independence—is very important. But one may well argue that it is absolutely necessary to manifest one's independence if one wants to keep it and eventually use it for bargaining purposes. The risk, of course, is that by disclosing too much the know-how necessary for "making out," the workers give weapons to help further rationalization. This is another reason for keeping such practices at least half secret.

We would like to uphold the view, finally, that workers who have been restricted by scientific work-organization to a completely stereotyped task use every available means to regain enough unpredictability in their behavior to enhance their low bargaining power. Also, their struggle for making out is one of the essential elements of their strategy.[36]

The Influence of Power Relationships on Organizational Structure

If we admit, according to our hypothesis, the importance of the link between the predictability of behavior and bargaining power, we must consider the impact of such relationships within an organization and the way that the necessity of handling them shapes organizational structure.

The possibility of prediction stems not only from the objective conditions of the task, but also, sometimes to a major extent, from the way information is distributed. The whole system of roles is so arranged that people are given information, the possibility of prediction, and therefore control, precisely because of their position within the hierarchical pattern.

This situation, in which certain individuals control variables unpredictable to other people, has an only partially objective foundation. It is man made and socially created, but it is nevertheless not arbitrary. It is the indirect result of the power struggle within the organization.

---

[36] We do not tackle here the problem of wage bargaining, which is, of course, the core of the strategy of each side, but we believe it is merely the most convenient battlefield and not the rationale of these strategies.

Were it to take place without any check, the power struggle would bring paralyzing conflicts and unbearable situations. It is thus necessary that a hierarchical order and an institutional structure impose discipline on the different individuals and groups, and arbitrate between their claims. But this power—which, of course, cannot be absolute—must bargain and compromise with all the people whose co-operation is indispensable at each level. It must, therefore, also dispose of an independent bargaining power. To be sure, it can use the influence of ideology, the ideas of the "common good" and of the "general interest," and it will do this. But this is insufficient, as the managers of socialistic communities have experienced time and again.[37] Its major means of action, finally, can only be the manipulation of information or at least the strict regulation of access to information.

Two kinds of power will develop out of these situations. First will evolve the power of the expert, i.e., the power an individual will have over the people affected by his actions, through his ability to cope with a source of relevant uncertainty. Second, there will emerge the power necessary to check the power of the expert. As we have stated earlier, every member of an organization is an expert in his own way, though his expertise might be extremely humble. He will, therefore, exercise some power upon other persons whose success depends, to a certain extent, on his own decision.[38]

As a matter of fact, one could thus generalize to the whole structure of an organization, the peculiar strategy of the supervisor-subordinate relationships analyzed earlier. We should like to suggest that studies be made on the repartition of roles and on formal regulations within an organization on the basis of such assumptions.

No organization can function, indeed, without imposing some check on the bargaining power of its own members. Thus certain individuals must be given enough freedom of action to be able to adjust conflicting claims and to impose decisions about general development—in other words, to improve the game they are playing against their environment. In order to obtain this necessary freedom of action, the *manager* will have to have power over his subordinates, formal power to make decisions as a last recourse, and informal power to bargain with each individual and each group to persuade them to accept his decisions.

To achieve his aims, the manager has two sets of conflicting weap-

---

[37] See, for example, a long series of articles by Robert Valette in *Communauté*, the magazine of the French federation of "Communautés de Travail," during 1957 and 1958.

[38] Workers affected to the most routine jobs have some power over their supervisors, inasmuch as they jeopardize supervisors' plans and imperil their careers, by slowing down, loafing, and just being careless.

ons: rationalization and rule-making on one side; and the power to make exceptions and to ignore the rules on the other. His own strategy will be to find the best combination of both weapons, according to the objectives of the unit of which he is in charge and to the degree to which members of the unit are interested in these objectives. Proliferation of the rules curtails his own power. Too many exceptions to the rules reduce his ability to check other people's power. Formal structure and informal relationships should not be opposed. They interpenetrate and complete each other. If one wants to understand them, one must study them together, along with the system of power relationships that helps integrate them.

THE EVOLUTION OF POWER RELATIONSHIPS SYSTEMS

Comparing the competing claims of the different individuals and groups within an organization, one can state that, in the long run, power will tend to be closely related to the kind of uncertainty upon which depends the life of the organization. Even the managerial role is often associated with this kind of power—witness the successive rise to managerial control by financial experts, production specialists, or budget analysts, according to the most important kind of difficulties organizations have had to solve to survive. As soon as the progress of scientific management or of economic stabilization has made one kind of difficulty liable, at least to a certain degree, to rational prediction, the power of the group whose role it is to cope with this kind of difficulty, and of the people who represent it, will tend to decrease. It should be rewarding to analyze such recurrent trends in order to throw more light on a problem that is often discussed, but very rarely on the basis of power relationships—the problem of the power of the expert in those societies in which accelerated change has become a permanent feature of life.

Technocracy is still a constant cause of fear, at least in Europe, as well as a sort of fascination. Many intelligent observers[39] feel that

---

[39] See for example of course, James Burnham, *The Managerial Revolution* (Bloomington, Ind.: Indiana University Press, 1960) and among a very abundant French literature, the discussions of the symposium organized by Georges Gurvitch, *Industrialisation et technocratie: Travaux de la première semaine sociologique"* (Paris: Armand Colin, 1949); Jacques Ellul, *La Technique ou l'enjeu du siècle* (Paris, Armand Colin, 1954); Nora Mitrani, "Attitudes et symboles techno-bureaucratiques," *Cahiers internationaux de sociologie*, XXIV, 148. For a more realistic discussion, see Jean Meynaud, *Technocratie et politique* (Lausanne, 1960), and the discussions of the Fifth Congress of the International Political Science Association around the report of Roger Gregoire, "Les Problèmes de la technocratie et le rôle des experts" (Paris, 1961).

because of the complexities of our technical age, certain groups of people, technical experts or managers, through their role as technicians of organizational life, are coming to hold more and more power in society as a whole, and that these technocrats will form the new ruling class or the new feudal order of our era.

Such a belief is not validated by a careful analysis of modern decision-making. It derives from a misunderstanding of the situation created by technical and scientific progress. The invasion of all domains by rationality, of course, gives power to the expert who is an agent of this progress. But the expert's success is constantly self-defeating. The rationalization process gives him power, but the end results of rationalization curtail this power. As soon as a field is well covered, as soon as the first intuitions and innovations can be translated into rules and programs, the expert's power disappears.

As a matter of fact, experts have power only on the front line of progress—which means they have a constantly shifting and fragile power. We should like to argue even that it can be less and less consolidated in modern times, inasmuch as more and more rationalized processes can be operated by non-experts. Of course, experts will fight to prevent the rationalization of their own tricks of the trade. But contrary to the common belief, the accelerated rate of change that characterizes our period makes it more difficult for them to resist rationalization. Their bargaining power as individuals is constantly diminishing.[40]

The Primacy of Organizational Goals and the Limits of the Power Struggle

We started with the mechanistic model of a rational system of organization and tried to show that such a model did not make it possible to understand and to place properly the kind of power relationships people are directly experiencing everywhere. To this model, we have opposed a "strategic" model relying solely on these same power relationships which it seems impossible to ignore. With this new model we can understand, at the same time, the power of the experts and pseudo-experts and the necessity of imposing a managerial authority to check their powers.

But even if we accept the usefulness of such a model, we must

[40] The medical profession, which may be considered as one of the best examples of a group of experts whose role and influence within modern society have remained extremely strong, still does not offer to modern physicians the comparative remunerations and authority their predecessors enjoyed. Yet the public is much more resentful of its privileges and much more critical of its income than before.

now ask ourselves to what extent it is sufficient. In order to achieve its own goals, an organization must elaborate a hierarchical structure to prevent the power struggle from becoming an intolerable burden. Can it do so only through a process of blackmail and bargaining and a pyramid of dependence relationships? Is such a conceptual system not so much a caricature of reality as the perfect rational system of classical theory? Are there other ways and other kinds of influence to control and limit the power struggle?

If we took into account only power relationships in the narrow sense, it would be difficult to understand how modern organizations could reasonably function. Melville Dalton, in the otherwise remarkable book we have already quoted, has fallen into such an error.[41] He is so haunted by the fear of being misled by the formal structure and the formal definitions of the roles that, in his analysis of the ways managers really behave, he reports only irregularities, back-door deals, and subtle blackmail. Dalton's description is extremely suggestive and should be welcomed as a real landmark in our understanding of the managers' role, but he forgets the rational side of the organization and the series of social controls that prevent people from taking too much advantage of their own strategic situation. No organization could survive if it were run solely by individual and clique back-door deals. For example, let us examine his analysis of the meeting as a façade necessary for presenting several partners with the opportunity of communicating informally, for starting the two-way funnel, and for preparing and carrying out private undercover deals. This may appear to be true in extreme cases; but even then, people must play the game of co-operation in order to maintain a good strategic position. They therefore have to pay a price which is a not inconsistent check on their bargaining possibilities. Finally, one may also conclude that, even in such extreme cases, the undercover relationships of the formal meeting are manipulated in a constructive way by the organization, since the participants are forced to express themselves in the language, and through a formal setup, of co-operation.[42]

The same problem appears, although in a simpler context, in the Industrial Monopoly. If one were to follow to its extreme the logic of our analysis of the dependence relationships in the Monopoly, one could easily conclude that the maintenance men can do exactly as they please in the shop, and that the director and assistant directors are completely paralyzed except in case of large-scale transformations. Yet maintenance men observe certain aspects of discipline, al-

[41] Dalton, *op. cit.*
[42] *Ibid.*, pp. 220–40.

ways keep decorum as regards work, and, finally, care competently for the machines. They introduce certain whims in their way of giving service to the people in the shop, but nevertheless, they do provide the service. Directors may be severely restricted in their possibilities of taking initiative, but they are not totally paralyzed. They have, as we have already seen, indirect kinds of influence; and a change of director can bring substantial differences to a plant.

One should not translate, therefore, the logic of the struggle into an overly black-and-white picture. Even so simple a strategy as the one of the production workers, or of the maintenance men, or of the lower supervisors at the shop level cannot be reduced to win-or-lose considerations. Other forces are operating which insure the minimum of consensus and organizational commitment that prevent people from extracting too much from, or from being too much exploited in, their reciprocal deals.

What are these forces? Let us analyze them in the simple case of the Monopoly before trying to raise the problem of more complex systems. Four main factors apparently must be reckoned with in the Monopoly: the necessity for the members of the different groups to live together; the fact that the existence of each group's privileges depends to quite a large extent on the existence of other groups' privileges; the general consensus among all groups about keeping certain minimum standards of efficiency; and, finally, the very stability of group relationships.

The existence of the first factor is obvious. But it does not receive all the attention it merits. If all the participants in the power game know that they will have to live with each other, whatever the results of their quarrels, a minimum of harmony and good fellowship must be maintained, whatever the opposition of roles. And this harmony can be achieved only if the other fellow's feelings are not too much hurt, according to the conventions of the culture of which they are members.[43] This is a very powerful, although usually ignored, cultural restraint. Because of this restraint, feelings and the expression of feeling may be used as a weapon in the power struggle. We have pointed out already that the dependence of the production workers upon the maintenance men cannot exceed what is considered acceptable in present-day France, and that production workers are very skilful at using the pressure of cultural norms to put their maintenance men on the defensive. We can generalize very well from

[43] The capacity of individuals and groups to tolerate conflicts and overt or covert expressions of hostility constitutes, as we shall see later, a very important element for understanding power relationships and the kind of bureaucratic system that can develop within a given culture.

this example. The members of an organization who can complain of some unfairness in regard to current norms will never fail to utilize their feelings of frustration for very rational goals. They know that their partners are vulnerable and cannot bear difficult interpersonal relationships for very long. Expressing true or half-simulated feelings will thus have a direct impact in bargaining. Certainly, if the roles of the protagonists permit avoidance techniques, some cold and guarded relationships are possible. This can be observed between lower supervisors and maintenance men. But the necessity to play the avoidance game is also a check upon the exaction of too heavy a price from the situation.

The second powerful force at work, the awareness of the interdependence of all privileges, is widely diffused among the different groups. No one would say it openly, but it is quite clear that every member of each of the participant groups, is convinced that their privileges depend to quite an extent on the privileges of the other groups and that an attack upon another group can endanger the whole system and, indirectly, the special interests of the attacking group. We have discussed the alliance of the production and maintenance workers and the mutual restraints resulting from this alliance. But this is only part of the picture. There is solidarity, not only between allied groups, but also between enemies. This was almost openly acknowledged during our experiment when the results of the survey were communicated to the different groups. Comments by the attacking groups, to our surprise, were directed at minimizing the sharpness of the attack. Far from capitalizing on the weaknesses of the attacked group as revealed by the survey, they tried to ignore them, as if fearful of upsetting the status quo.

One has to take into account, of course, the fact that the employees of the Monopoly feel, at least to a certain extent, that they occupy an especially advantageous position.[44] Because of this position, they may consider that they have something in common to defend, for which they must sacrifice some of their own claims against their partners. But what about organizations that do not enjoy special privileges? We may hypothesize, of course, that conflicts will go much further and that they will be less manageable. We must, however, take care to re-examine the definition of privileges. The sheer violence of a competitive world may transform survival into a common privilege and an acceptable goal, at least within certain limits. One may even argue that the privileges obtained in the non-com-

[44] There are, of course, differences. For certain groups, though not for others, this is a very advantageous position. The latter, however, are those whose role is to identify more with the whole organization, and those whose stock-in-trade in the ' argaining relationship is in reference to the common whole (i.e., the supervisors nd director).

petitive world of public administration are necessary to offset the absence of such a unifying force.[45] The third factor, the general agreement of all groups about what constitutes a reasonable degree of efficiency, operates along the same lines. Maintenance men are definitely featherbedding. However, they are on the defensive, because of what is considered, generally and in the Monopoly, as a fair day's work. Certainly such a notion is elastic. However, one should not neglect the pressures that can be put on a group because their contribution does not fit the general pattern of our industrial civilization. This pressure is well utilized by management, with the backing of other groups, to set limits to such a group's special claims.

Within the Monopoly, the *Direction Générale* was able to induce the maintenance men to service three machines instead of two. Maintenance men resisted for a long time, but their position was relatively weak because it was too well known that they had very little work to do. Generally, one may say that the norms concerning interpersonal relationships, the aims of an organization, and the contribution to be expected from its members are very powerful forces, shaping the field of bargaining and restraining the full use of its own power by each group.

At the same time, the organization can manipulate the need of each individual to realize and to actualize himself. All the members of an organization are influenced by and attracted to the kind of collective and constructive achievement it is capable of offering them. These feelings expressing the individual's subjection to the norms of efficiency of his society, upon which these norms in turn are founded, give a great deal of power to the people who can mobilize them within the organization—especially, of course, to management.

The last factor, the stability of intergroup relationships, is peculiar to the Monopoly, although its actual implications may be wide. In the Monopoly, as we have shown, the general position of all the groups is relatively frozen and the individuals themselves cannot pass from one group to another. This long-time commitment reinforces group solidarity and the power struggle. However, viewed from another angle, it is a powerful stabilizer which tends to regulate the equilibrium of conflict.

Let us try to be more precise. It could be concluded, from a too

[45] One must notice, however, that the moderating pressure that comes from the different groups' awareness of the interdependence of their privileges is only a very imperfect force of integration. It is "conservative" and its regulating functions operate within extremely wide limits. Reinhard Bendix has underlined this force in his comparison of Western and Soviet kinds of organizations (*Work and Authority*, p. 247).

rapid reading of our analysis of the power relationships, that such a situation cannot last forever, that it is in the process of deteriorating. This is not the case. The equilibrium we have described is a conflictive equilibrium, but a very stable one. Groups bargain to defend their own privileges in a changing world, and they are fearful that their partners will gain some points over them if they are put off guard. But as a matter of fact, they know their risk is not too great; they are not by any means engaged in a life-and-death struggle; theirs is a war of position. This is another decisive factor in the power struggle and in bargaining. Groups know they cannot get rid of their partners, that they will have to live with them and compromise with them—if not forever, then at least for the foreseeable future. This stability has direct and important consequences on individual motivations and behavior. No one in any group expects to change affiliation or could be lured away from his basic group solidarity—not only for personal egalitarian purposes, but even for bettering the functioning of the whole. Let us imagine, for example, what the outcome of the game would be if the Monopoly were a private organization and people could transfer from one category and one occupation to another without difficulties. Certain technical engineers would use the temporary strength of their group to succeed personally in becoming managers. But they would be appointed only insofar as they could be expected to rationalize at least the maintenance field; and they would do this, thus curtailing the power of their own group and putting an end to the struggle we have analyzed.

The Monopoly situation can, therefore, be characterized as an unusually stable equilibrium—a special case within the general context of dynamic relationships characteristic of our industrial civilization. It is extremely interesting from a methodological point of view, because the elimination of all sources of uncertainty but one makes it a sort of laboratory medium in which to explore the mechanism of power relationships. The stable equilibrium we were able to describe may be considered as a useful slow-motion process of group bargaining.

Let us now try to state more clearly the differences from this case that are brought about by the usual context of dynamic relationships. Two main features of organization seem significant to us in this respect. First, there are usually several competing sources of uncertainty within the same organization. Second, groups are not normally permanent. They may disappear or change substantially in the near future; still more frequently, for a number of individuals, membership in a group is likely to be temporary.

The outcome of such influences is the development of much more complex bargaining systems where several groups are competing, each one with its own possibilities of applying pressure, and where fights between groups are held in check by the consideration, by individual group members, of their own selfish interests. The power of management is likely, of course, to benefit from this double complication of the simple pattern, since its function of adjusting conflicting claims will have more importance and since it will be able to influence key individuals within the groups. A most important angle to consider is the role which the sheer survival of the organization will often play as a paramount source of uncertainty; this will still further reinforce the position of management.[46]

What are the possible consequences of the existence of such traits? In conclusion, the three following hypotheses are presented about the sort of power relationships and the sort of social controls that will accompany them in the usual context of dynamic equilibria:

1. The more complex and dynamic the system of power relationships and of bargaining, the more likely are social controls to be directly and consciously enforced by management instead of being left to the operation of the indirect forces of the milieu (although the existence of these same forces remains essential for management's ability to operate).

2. The limits that management consciously fixes for the development of the power struggle are usually much narrower than the natural limits set by the pressures of the milieu. Factional quarrels and group bargaining are not allowed overt expression so easily as in organizations where power relationships are stable and simple.

3. The dynamic equilibrium system is much more favorable to change, since the pressure to eliminate uncertainty, in the instrumental domain, will not be held in check by the resistance of well-entrenched groups.

Anticipating the discussion in the next chapter, we now turn to the external conditions of such processes. It seems perfectly clear, at first glance, that public administration, being less under pressure

---

[46] The history of the Industrial Monopoly provides a good illustration of this. Much of the rationalization process that decisively curtailed the power of the managers and of the supervisors was achieved when workers were able, after a ten-year struggle, to impose the adoption of a carefully written seniority code. Their success, it may be argued with good reason, may have been due to the fact that the supervisors' power of intervention in the allocation of jobs was nothing more than a man-made source of uncertainty. This power, wielded by the supervisors and, through them, by the director, was not in any respect necessary to allow them to cope with other sources of uncertainty in the production, the selling, or the personnel problems of the organization, since all other elements of their activity were stable and easily predictable.

for survival, stands a much better chance of eliminating the over-all source of uncertainty, and thus more difficulties, to maintain the managerial power. It will give, therefore, undue importance to the remaining areas of uncertainty, protect the experts who are in charge of them, and allow them to stabilize the power struggle and develop stationary equilibria that favor them.

Such an opposition between public administration and private organization, however, is not so clear-cut as it may seem. In many cases private organizations are as well protected as public agencies. Under conditions of stable technology and stable markets, the private ones may have to face less uncertainty than a public agency, which exists under the pressure of an active political system. If it were possible to make a precise comparison of the French nationalized railroads organization (SNCF) with the American private railroad companies, one would most probably find a greater number of pro-tected sectors for the workers, the supervisors, and the executives in the average American private company than in the French bureau-cratic nationalized corporation.

Then, within otherwise dynamic systems of organization, one may often find stationary equilibriums in one or more protected sectors that have grown, at least temporarily, apart from the main bargain-ing system.

Gouldner's study, *Patterns of Industrial Bureaucracy*[47] and Selz-nick's *TVA and the Grass Roots*,[48] present two cases paradox-ically opposed in this respect. Stationary equilibrium is the principal feature of a sector of a private organization, while a much more fluid system of relationships is characteristic of the public agency.

In Gouldner's case, miners control all sources of uncertainty at the work level in the mine.[49] Not only do they alone have to face the material risks involved in this activity, but the amount of work and the results of production depend directly on their decisions. Decisions must be made on the spot by the individual miner or by the team of coworkers. They do not depend on the foremen and on the maintenance men; but the whole of the organization depends on the miners' work, which cannot be controlled under present circumstances. They have been able, therefore, to maintain the stationary equilibrium they are enjoying because of the position of strength they occupy, since it has become extremely difficult to re-

[47] Gouldner, *op. cit.*

[48] Philip Selznick, *TVA and the Grass Roots* (Berkeley: University of California Press, 1949).

[49] The organization described by Gouldner is dominated by the opposition be-tween the mine and the surface plant. In the mine, men are their own bosses, while the surface workers face a completely rationalized organizational system.

cruit people for this hazardous lower-class occupation.[50] As a result, they hold in check the power of all other groups and enjoy a very rewarding situation in a context otherwise completely rationalized, where their own behavior is the major source of uncertainty.[51]

The case of the TVA, as analyzed by Selznick, presents a much more complex relationship. Although this is a public corporation, several sources of uncertainty are competing, and management uses this complexity to increase its freedom of action. It has slowly elaborated a complex process of co-optation that allows it to pick up people in the different pressure groups and to have them participate in managerial problems. The fight for survival, finally, although appearing only covertly, is extremely important. It accounts for the development of a special kind of social control, the ideological allegiance of the members of the organization.[52] These two examples will make it possible for us to understand better the case of the Clerical Agency, a curious mixture where we find at the same time traits of stationary equilibrium and other traits more characteristic of organizations under the impact of the struggle for survival. There is no actual fear about survival, of course, but the only source of uncertainty—instead of being, as in the Monopoly, within the production system—comes from the outside. The amount of work and the possibility of achieving the aims of the organization according to the rules depend on the behavior of the customers. The success of the organization itself, if it does not depend on the fluctuations of the free market, is still subject to the sanctions of government and Parliament. Management, finally, as we have shown, has been able to shift directly to the employees' shoulders the pressure of the public in a completely impersonal way. One finds, therefore, at the same time in the Agency, the bureaucratic protection that stems from centralization and from the distance central power has created around itself, and, second, a very strong hierarchical pressure that is exerted without the usual recourse to humiliating personal dependencies. In this respect, the Clerical Agency appears to offer the paradoxical example of an impersonal system of organization which has been

[50] A much higher degree of rationalization has been in operation for a long time in most coal mines in the Western world, but social and economic conditions are quite different from this small gypsum plant in the U.S. See the discussion about the system of organization in the English mines, Eric Trist and E. L. Bamforth, "Some Social and Psychological Consequences of the Longwall Method of Coal Getting," *Human Relations*, IV (1951), 3–38.

[51] Miners enjoy a particularly favorable position, inasmuch as their freedom of action contrasts directly with the complete predictability of behavior of the surface workers, who have not been able to oppose rationalization.

[52] We shall come back to both cases in chapter vii, and analyze them in greater detail.

able to eliminate the usual power dependencies but must rely instead on a rigid and authoritarian system of hierarchical social relations. Such a system can survive only because of the very deep and anachronistic dichotomy between managers and managed and the acceptance, partial at least, of their inferior social position by the subordinates. It is reproducing, forty years later, the paradox and contradictions of scientific work organization.

Chapter Seven

THE BUREAUCRATIC SYSTEM OF ORGANIZATION

THE PROBLEM

Study of the way power is allocated and an analysis of the bargaining strategies between individuals and groups within an organization are unusual starting points from which to try to reach an understanding of the function of an organization. We have taken this course because of its provocative and challenging properties in a domain that often seems paralyzed by formalism. Our effort appears to have been worth-while. For example, the distinction between organizations characterized by a stationary power equilibrium and organizations with constantly shifting systems of bargaining is apparently useful for the theory of organization. However, as we have also shown, the world of power is only one aspect of the complex relationship between the individual and the organization. The world of consensus and the world of the co-operative game are other important aspects of this basic relationship.

We shall approach our subject in another, broader way. We shall attempt to analyze these two complementary aspects of the functioning of the organizations we have studied and we shall interpret our data in the light of the theory of bureaucracy—that theory in terms of which sociologists since Max Weber have been considering the processes of organization.

There is a paradox, however, in the long series of discussions over the theory of bureaucracy. During the last fifty years, many first-rate social scientists have thought of bureaucracy as one of the key questions of both modern sociology and modern political science. Max Weber had furnished a very brilliant description of the "ideal type" of a bureaucratic organization, and a suggestive analysis of its historical development, that apparently paved the way for a positive value-free sociological analysis. Yet the discussion about bureaucracy is still, to a large extent, the domain of the myths and pathos of ideology.

The paradox, indeed, exists already in Weber's work. In his studies on law and on Prussian bureaucracy, it is true, Weber presents a view which is richer and more sophisticated than the rationalist model of the famous chapter of *Wirtschaft und Gesellschaft*. But when he claims the superiority of modern bureaucracies that embody the "ideal type," one may wonder whether he does not think that these organizations succeed only inasmuch as they can impose a substantial and dangerous amount of standardization on their members. Some of his statements show how much he was worried by such a trend.[1]

Among Weber's successors and contemporaries who used similar models more rigidly, contradictions are still deeper. On the one hand, most authors consider the bureaucratic organization to be the embodiment of rationality in the modern world, and, as such, to be intrinsically superior to all other possible forms of organization. On the other hand, many authors—often the same ones—consider it a sort of Leviathan, preparing the enslavement of the human race. Optimism and pessimism are mixed in various ways. Whatever their proportions, there is always a double belief in the superiority of bureaucratic rationality—in the domain of efficiency, and in its threatening implications in the domain of human values.

This was well exemplified by Robert Michels' syllogism of the "iron law." Michels, after cruelly "disenchanting" the "charismatic" enthusiasm of the Socialist movement, pointed to the dilemma of all democratic social action, reformist or revolutionary: democratic social action is possible only through bureaucratic organization, and bureaucratic organization is destructive of democratic values.[2]

This paradoxical view of bureaucracy in Western thought has paralyzed positive thinking on the problem and has favored the making of catastrophic prognostications. This has been most clearly perceptible in the great stream of revolutionary pessimism which has so pervaded Western political and social thought from Rosa Luxemburg and Trotsky to Bruno Rizzi, Simone Weil, and C. Wright Mills—to cite only the most famous names. A desperate gamble is the only hope. The picture is blackened, and the attack against what is felt to be inevitable if human beings accept their fate is exaggerated. Thus, by a pointing up of the paradox, only one alternative is left—the dialectical overstepping of revolutionary belief.

The same paradox is also perceptible in more conservative circles. For example, it may be discerned in Burnham's simplifications, and in the great number of attacks, such as those of William H. Whyte,

[1] See, for example Max Weber's remarks at the 1909 convention of the *Verein fur Sozialpolitik*, as quoted by J. P. Mayer, *Max Weber and German Politics* (London: Faber & Faber, 1943), pp. 127–28; and by Reinhard Bendix, *Max Weber: An Intellectual Portrait* (New York: Doubleday, 1960), pp. 455–56.
[2] Robert Michels, *Zur Soziologie des Parteiwesens in der modernen Demokratie* (Leipzig, 1912).

Jr., against bigness and the bureaucratization of modern life. As Alvin Gouldner quite sensibly said:

> Wrapping themselves in the shrouds of nineteenth century political economy, some social scientists appear to be bent on resurrecting the dismal science. Instead of telling men how bureaucracy might be mitigated, they insist that it is inevitable.[3]

March and Simon have argued that Max Weber's thinking about bureaucracy corresponds to the early rationalist theory about human behavior in organizations. This statement may be exaggerated as regards Weber himself,[4] but it is quite accurate for Michels and all the revolutionary analysts of bureaucracy. We go even farther and suggest that the modern "dismal school" delusion, whatever its intellectual sophistication, results from its relying on the same crude theory of human motivation as the scientific engineers. It is only because its exponents accept, at their face value, the Taylorian arguments, that they can believe that modern organizations are succeeding because of their evil features.

The first decisive progress in resolving this contradiction was made when Robert K. Merton, and after him other American sociologists like Gouldner and Selznick, began to question the perfection of the "ideal type," and to discuss, in a positive and empirical way, whether the opposition between organizational efficiency and the freedom of the individual was actually possible. Beginning with the theory of unintended consequences successive research by the sociologists of bureaucracy has suggested that the routine and oppressive aspects of bureaucracy are so many elements of what may be described as a "vicious circle"[5] that develops from the resistance of the human factor to the mechanistic rationalist theory of behavior which is being imposed on it. This very resistance, paradoxically, tends to reinforce the use of the theory. Research has demonstrated that the ideal type of bureaucracy is far from being completely efficient.

[3] Alvin Gouldner, "Metaphysical Pathos and the Theory of Bureaucracy," in Amitai Etzioni, *Complex Organizations* (New York: Holt, Rinehart, 1961), p. 82.

[4] One can argue that Weber is more interested in the problem of social control than in the problem of rationality, and that he never forgets to take into account the fact that a bureaucracy must have some kind of legitimacy and thus rely ultimately on consensus. Yet one can notice that, in his analysis of bureaucratic rationality, he emphasizes above all the predictability requirements and the standardization of behavior that provides the only way to meet them. There we can understand how his ideas can converge with those of promoters of scientific work-organization. If the latter do not want to see anything but the simplest economic motivations in human behavior, this is because such a simplified approach makes it possible for them to consider each human being as an interchangeable instrument whose response to organizational stimuli is entirely predictable.

[5] March and Simon were the first to point out these logical implications of Merton's analysis; the image of the "vicious circle" is ours.

This demonstration, however, has so far been more negative than positive. It does not enable us to answer Weber's question about the evolution of industrial society. It suggests that the link between the rational and successful features of a bureaucratic organization and its dysfunctional ones is much more complex than the Taylorian engineers and their contemporary critics thought. It has not, as yet, explored to any extent their interrelations and the conditions of their symbiosis. In order to avoid the paradox, one should analyze more precisely the general etiology of the dysfunctional features of bureaucracy, their limits, and the extent to which the development of modern organization is influenced by such features.

In this chapter, we should like, through a re-reading of our data, to examine the possibilities of going beyond this first stage of understanding by considering bureaucratic[6] traits of behavior, not as dysfunctions, nor even as necessary dysfunctions of the modern system of organization, but as rational parts of the "bureaucratic. systems of organization." This will enable us to answer, in completely different terms, the question Weber raised about evolution. We shall try to show that a bureaucratic system is restricted in its possible rate of development, and that evolution toward large-scale organizations is not so unrelenting as Weber thought—it depends, to a large extent, on the ability of men to break out of the bureaucratic "vicious circle."

Before attempting such an exploration, however, we must consider more seriously the decisive contributions made by the sociologists who have used, directly or indirectly, the theory of dysfunctions to analyze bureaucratic phenomena.

The Theory of Bureaucratic Dysfunctions: The "Human Relations" Approach to Bureaucracy

Interest in the dysfunctions of bureaucracy evolved with the discovery of the human factor and the wide development of the human relations approach in industry. This is not fortuitous. As March and Simon have shown, there is a logical link between the rationale of human relations theories, whatever their kind, and the theory of bureaucratic dysfunctions.[7]

If we accept the conclusions of the interactionist school or of the

---

[6] "Bureaucratic" is used here in the popular, pejorative sense.

[7] James March and Herbert Simon, *Organizations* (New York: Wiley, 1958), pp. 36–47. We will rely heavily throughout this section on the extremely penetrating analyses of these authors.

Lewinian school, or of both, it is as difficult to uphold Max Weber's thesis as to believe in the credo of scientific work organization. When one believes that human activities depend on the feelings and sentiments of the people involved, and on the interpersonal and group relationships that influence them, one cannot expect that imposing economic rationality on them will bring constant and predictable results. The functioning of a bureaucracy can never henceforth be totally explained by the combination of impersonality, expertness, and hierarchy of the "ideal type." If, in addition, one thinks that the most efficient leader of a group is a permissive leader, one must also believe that the best results will not be achieved by the most rational organization in the Weberian sense. They will be attained by the organization in which subordinates participate most in the decision-making process.

Sociologists, however, did not break with the Weberian model in the way that "human relations" analysts did with the classical Taylorian model. When Merton pointed the way with his two famous pioneering articles of 1936 and 1940,[8] he did not contest directly the validity of the "ideal type." He simply indicated that such a system of action entails secondary consequences that run counter to its objectives and principles of action; and he did even this indirectly. Little by little, however, a new scheme was suggested, the rationale of which is more clear today. Merton contends that the discipline necessary for obtaining the standardized behavior required in a bureaucratic organization will bring about a displacement of goals. Bureaucrats will show "ritualist" attitudes that will make them unable to adjust adequately to the problems they must solve. This will entail the development of a strong *esprit de corps* at a group level and create a gap between the public and the bureaucracy.

Such an analysis is implicitly based upon the following argument. The behavioral rigidity, difficulties of adjustment to the task, and conflicts with the public that exist in a bureaucracy reinforce the need for control and regulation. Thus, finally, the unintended and dysfunctional results of the bureaucratic model tend to reinforce their hold. In human relations terms, dysfunction appears to be the consequence of the resistance of the human factor to standardized behavior that is imposed upon it mechanically. Immediately, however, naive questions emerge: Why do people stick to the mechanical model if it does not bring the desired results? And if they do stick to

[8] Robert K. Merton, "The Unanticipated Consequences of Purposive Social Action," *American Sociological Review*, I (1936), 894–904, and "Bureaucratic Structure and Personality," *Social Forces*, XVIII (1940), 560–68.

it, why is the model a static one, why does it not deteriorate? After all, if the dysfunctional consequences of the model entail the use of more control and more regulation, one should gradually find more and more dysfunction. Merton does not discuss such questions, which is the reason one can say that he remains within Weber's frame of analysis. His aim at the time of writing was only to show that the "ideal type" includes a fair amount of inefficiency and to understand the reason for such a discrepancy between Weber's model and the reality.

Many American authors—e.g., Reinhard Bendix, Philip Selznick, Alvin Gouldner, Peter Blau, and Robert Dubin—have followed in Merton's footsteps. Their empirical studies have confirmed Merton's views. Their considerations have made possible the elaboration of a much clearer and richer scheme for the understanding of what we should like to call the "vicious circle" of bureaucracy. We will examine here only the works of Selznick and Gouldner, the two best-elaborated studies. Their theses demonstrate well both the progress realized by, and the inherent limits of, the "dysfunctional school."

Selznick's 1949 study[9] deals with the TVA, at that time at the height of its prestige as a model of democratic organization and as the symbol of the yearnings of the New Deal. In a way, Selznick's book is similar to the Michels' study; it shows the development of bureaucratic oligarchy behind the veil of democratic procedure. Selznick's aims, however, are different from, if not the opposite of, those of Michels. Selznick starts with the assumption that bureaucratic pressures must be taken for granted and that the problem is to understand how people manage to control them partially—thus answering the second of our questions about Merton's scheme.

Selznick's domain, however, is not the same as Merton's. Selznick uses similar reasoning about unintended results, but applies it to a different part of Weber's ideal type, expertness. He shows how the same kind of vicious circle can develop with expertness and specialization as with hierarchical control and standardization. Specialization grows because decisions have to be made on neutral technical grounds. However, specialization makes the experts more narrow-minded and caste conscious at the same time that outside economic interests and pressures converge with their caste policies. These dysfunctions naturally call for more specialization, and a new vicious circle develops.[10]

---

[9] Philip Selznick, *TVA and the Grass Roots* (Berkeley: University of California Press, 1949).
[10] We are borrowing this scheme of analysis from March and Simon, *op. cit.*, pp. 40–43.

Selznick's most original thinking, however, deals with the problem of the regulation of dysfunction. How does an organization limit the cumulative influence of its dysfunctions? Selznick observed two mechanisms widely used in the TVA. The first concerns the power situation: this is the mechanism of co-optation, through which outside sectional interests and internal, narrow, expert points of view are given a share in the decision-making process—opponents are co-opted to policy-making bodies. The second is the diffusion of a special TVA ideology that secures, by its pervasive influence on people in every echelon, the necessary minimum of conformity and loyalty to the organization.[11]

In this new perspective, bureaucratic dysfunctions are perceived as more diffuse than in the scheme of Merton. They correspond to the rigidity of the organization that may manifest itself in the logic of specialization as well as in the logic of centralization. Moreover, Selznick deals not only with the problem of the resistance of the human factor to the mechanistic model, but also with the problem of power and participation. This second—and, in our opinion, central—problem, however, is analyzed only as regards the possibilities of controlling the development of dysfunctions, rather than as the source of them. Thus Selznick still remains within the Weberian scheme.

Gouldner's study is, in a way, more limited since it does not raise questions outside the hierarchical control pattern delimited by Merton. Nevertheless, it goes one step further in this direction, by showing better the inherent contradiction of the ideal type.

Gouldner makes a primary distinction between bureaucracy centered about expertness and bureaucracy centered about punition. He deals (much too rapidly for our taste) with bureaucracy founded on expertness—accepting, on inadequate evidence, that it can escape dysfunction, since the values on which it rests can be accepted by everyone, and the rules that regulate it can be elaborated with enough participation by those who must submit to them. Gouldner's actual subject is punitive bureaucracy. He sees it from three different angles: (1) as a vicious circle around problems of subordination and control; (2) as a behavioral pattern with some latent functions; and (3) as a rational response to an accidental but ineluctable event, succession.

The central bureaucratic vicious circle, in Gouldner's view, concerns the problem of close supervision. Impersonal bureaucratic rules evolve because they alleviate the tensions created by subordination

---

[11] This analysis was first presented in Selznick, "Foundations of the Theory of Organization," *American Sociological Review*, XIII (1948), 25–35.

and control; but at the same time they perpetuate the very tensions that bring them into being.[12] They especially reinforce the low motivation of the workers that makes close supervision necessary.[13]

The latent function of bureaucratic rules is to reduce the tensions that are due, in part, to the differences of values among groups, to the impossibility of elaborating norms acceptable to everyone, and to the steady decrease of friendly informal interactions.[14]

Gouldner's analysis, at this stage, is not completely satisfactory. At first, it is not easily perceived why values of different groups have to be different, why friendly interactions must decrease, and why acceptable norms cannot be developed. One must seek another underlying factor; and this Gouldner does with his theory of succession. In his final view, the impersonality of bureaucracy is a global organizational response to the problem of succession. This summoning of an external, accidental cause is not very satisfactory, although the case study is an extremely perceptive one. All modern organizations must face the problems of succession, but they nevertheless have very different and disproportionate kinds of dysfunctions.

Gouldner's decisive contribution, however, does not lie in his last and somewhat confused explanatory stage. It is in his earlier and more suggestive interpretation of the role of punitive bureaucratic rules. He has shown how such rules may be used in an organization by supervisors and subordinates alike. Both groups take advantage of them for punitive purposes and as a bargaining tool, inasmuch as each can suspend their application or insist upon it.[15] Unfortunately, Gouldner does not use this insight to broaden his functional analysis. His functional analysis remains partial insofar as it does not integrate the problems of power relationships and the bargaining processes between groups.

This time, nevertheless, the Weberian model is at least partially overstepped. Gouldner does not understand bureaucratic features as merely a means for achieving efficiency; he views them, rather, as a way to reduce tensions within an organization.

These three examples, the most striking of human relations researches on bureaucracy, demonstrate a substantial moving away from the original Weberian model. These three authors give more and more place to the routine and oppressive aspects of bureaucracy that finally become an autonomous parallel system of human causation. But all three—with the partial exception of Selznick—tend to neglect the aspect of rationality and efficiency that is central to any

[12] Gouldner, *Patterns of Industrial Bureaucracy*, p. 177.
[13] *Ibid.*, p. 178.
[14] *Ibid.*, p. 240.
[15] *Ibid.*, pp. 172–74.

kind of organization. Moreover, they do not try to analyze the possible interdependence between rationality and dysfunction. This makes it impossible for them to question the dynamic part of the Weberian model, its analysis of the unrelenting evolution toward large-scale bureaucratic organization. Their contribution is inadequate for a discussion of whether or not the resistance of the human factor to the rationalistic push toward more and more efficiency can be successful, or whether or not it can have indirect consequences on organizational rationality itself. Even Gouldner's analysis remains static. At best, it can be described as viewing bureaucratic evolution as a cyclical process with alternate bureaucratization and debureaucratization phases according to the accidents of succession.[16]

Finally, as March and Simon have pointed out, all these contributions, while setting the stage for further progress, are limited by the human relations theories on human behavior upon which they rest. To go one step further, one must accept the fact that members of an organization are not governed solely by affective motivations but operate as autonomous actors, each one with his own personal strategy; this means giving a central place to the power problems we have analyzed in the last chapter. To do this, we shall first examine the problems of government raised by the functioning of an organization. Power relationships can be considered as the operational consequences of these.

THE PROBLEM OF THE ACHIEVEMENT OF CONFORMITY

Let us accept the main weakness of the sociological theories of bureaucracy as their difficulty in integrating change and development and their reliance on exterior factors to explain the emergence of bureaucratic patterns. Then, in order to go beyond their process-centered analysis, we must raise, in political science terms, the more general question of an organization's government and its minimum requirements.

Planned co-operative action is possible only if one can rely on a great deal of regularity of behavior on the part of all the participants. In other words, any organization must obtain from its members a variable but always substantial amount of conformity. Members will conform partly voluntarily, partly because of coercion. Whatever the

---

[16] In their recent book, *Formal Organizations* (San Francisco: Chandler, 1961), Peter Blau and W. Richard Scott present a more sophisticated point of view on change, which they tend to see as a much more natural and complex process. This excellent contribution, which I was able to read only after my book had gone to the printer, seems to converge on many points with mine.

proportions, the achievement of the necessary conformity will be the central problem of an organization's government.

When we review more analytically the means used to influence people to conform, we can observe very striking changes in modern times. Only two centuries ago, conformity within an organization was obtained through very harsh and direct means, with a great deal of open coercion. No regular army could function without the painful and unavoidable experience of drilling that we have all but forgotten today. Supervision by overseers in the eighteenth-century mills was almost equivalent to brutal coercion, and, after all, the galleys were one of the great organizations of their time. Religious or religious-like ideologies partly helped people to internalize organizational aims, but these ideologies themselves were of a fanatic type and terror-ridden. Moreover, conformity could not be obtained in a specialized and limited way; rather, it required a life-long total commitment. As a consequence, people were molded in a way that would deeply mark their whole personalities for life. Whether they were employees of the Fugger House, members of the Jesuit order, or Prussian grenadiers, they had to devote themselves completely to the organization. Leaving it was equivalent to treason; no large-scale organization could be efficient without such drastic conditions.[17]

Comparisons with modern organizations may seem overdrawn. Yet they must be made, to bring some perspective into the traditional debate on the standardization and the threatening enslavement of modern man. Modern organizations, in contrast to their predecessors, use a much more liberal set of pressures. They deal with people who, through their education, have already internalized a number of basic conformities and a general ability to conform easily to an organization's way. Then, too, there has been a great deal of progress in the field of training, and no one feels obliged any longer to make people spend months trying to master the exact observance of petty details. Most important of all, human behavior is now better understood and therefore more predictable. Because of this, a modern organization does not need the same amount of conformity to get as good results as did earlier organizations. The modern organization can tolerate more deviance, restrict its requirements to a more specialized field, and demand only temporary commitments. For all these reasons, it can and does rely more on indirect and intellectual means to obtain conformity: communication structure and work

[17] Sociologists have so far neglected the very important and in some ways crucial body of knowledge to be gained by examining the records of the first large-scale commercial organizations, integrated armies, and religious orders. The theory of organizations could well be enriched by a renewal of such studies.

flow, the technical setting of jobs, economic incentives, and also, perhaps, rational calculus of a higher sort. The punitive aspect of the conformity achievement process has declined. Direct coercion is still in reserve as a last resort, but it is very rarely used, and people apparently no longer have to see it operate often to retain it in their calculations.

The contrast is further demonstrated by comparing the quasi-monarchal type that seemingly was necessary for maintaining large-scale organizations at the beginning of the capitalist era with the relatively easy-going and tolerant corporation of the affluent society.[18] But even during the last thirty years, there has been a not insignificant change throughout the Western world. Compare, for example, the discipline and conformity of dress and behavior imposed on the sales force of a large department store today with the standards of thirty years ago—a great deal more was required then, and in a much harsher way.

Such a reminder makes it possible to understand that, contrary to some easy generalizations, certain "bureaucratic" traits were more likely to appear in earlier organizations than in those of today. Displacement of goals is a case in point. People trained to a rigid conformity, entailing consequences for their whole personalities during their whole lives, are much more likely to indulge in "goal displacement" and "ritualism" than people who are only temporarily specialized—even, as is most often the case, if this specialization is a far narrower one.

Rigidity, however, is not engendered only by pressures coming from above. Conformity is not a one-sided process. Subordinates will bargain with their own conformity and use it as a tool with which to bind management. This is just another aspect of the fight for control. Subordinates tacitly agree to play the management game, but they try to turn it to their own advantage and to prevent management from interfering with their independence. When this double pressure is stabilized and leaves very little freedom for adjusting difficulties, then an organization has become deeply rigid. This was the case with the earlier ritualistic clerk who made a point of following his instructions to the letter and ignored the reality with which he had to deal, not only because of his "trained incapacity," but because he needed protection against too harsh treatment in case of error. His "bureaucratic" behavior was not the consequence of the weakness of his own human nature. It resulted from the way conformity and rationality had to be observed at that time, when there were so few possibilities of intellectually understanding and

---

[18] Notwithstanding William H. Whyte's and many others' criticism. For a full discussion of their stand see below, pp. 297–98.

foreseeing complex situations, and thus of devising in advance flexible programs to adjust to them.[19]

There are comparable modern patterns—e.g., in the Clerical Agency. Supervisors prefer taking routine, inadequate decisions to facing hostile relationships and possible risks of failure. This modern bureaucratic behavior originates in more complex organizational processes; but these processes, too, are the outcome of bargaining among various groups, and between the organization and these groups, about the way to impose conformity and rationality.

Every organization, however, must continually adjust to some kind of change. It must be flexible. To achieve this vague but primary end, it must rely on individual and group ingenuity and cannot discourage it too much.[20] The organization must consider this goal when devising ways to impose conformity, since it is counter to the other primary goal, predictability. What will be the outcome of these two conflicting aims? Its environment, its goals, the kind of fluctuating reality to which an organization must adjust, will be the most important factors to be taken into consideration in this perspective. But market uncertainty, as such, is not an omnipotent deterrent to rigidity. Extreme conditions of uncertainty will tend to result in more conformity and rigidity, since trying to adjust to completely unpredictable situations will not be rewarding enough. Too little uncertainty, on the other hand, will make it feasible to prescribe in great detail all possible forms of behavior, thus achieving a high degree of rigidity. There will be a tendency to escape from reality at the two extremes, when reality is too difficult to cope with and when it is no longer a challenge.

It is clear, in any event, that in any kind of organization there is a constant pressure to escape from reality. This tendency corresponds to what popular sentiment calls "bureaucratic tendencies." Centralization is one of the ways to achieve it; completely impersonal rules are another. Both permit escape from otherwise necessary adjustments.

But in a normal case, evasion cannot go too far. There is a constant feedback of information that permits and even obliges the organization to take account of its errors and to correct them. We shall describe as a "bureaucratic system of organization" any system

---

[19] Even not so long ago, at the beginning of mass production, the product was imposed on the consumer without any possible adjustment. Motorists had to like their Fords black until it was deemed possible to predict well enough the probable variation of tastes.

[20] In the traditional framework of the nineteenth century, it is the entrepreneur who monopolizes the organization's capacity of adjustment. But such a system was feasible only because production units remained small.

of organization where the feedback process, error-information-correction, does not function well, and where consequently there cannot be any quick readjustment of the programs of action in view of the errors committed. In other words, *a bureaucratic organization is an organization that cannot correct its behavior by learning from its errors.* Bureaucratic patterns of action, such as the impersonality of the rules and the centralization of decision-making, have been so stabilized that they have become part of the organization's self-reinforcing equilibria. Finally, when one rule prevents adequate dealing with one case, its failure will not generate pressure to abandon the rule, but, on the contrary, will engender pressure to make it more complete, more precise, and more binding.

THE BASIC ELEMENTS OF A BUREAUCRATIC VICIOUS CIRCLE

Let us now try to build a model of such a self-reinforcing "bureaucratic system" by using the characteristic traits that emerge from our two case studies. In doing so, we shall, of course, be limited by the specifically French nature of our data. But we shall at least have a starting point, from which we can see whether other models can be imagined and whether there are some traits, some underlying patterns, common to all possible "bureaucratic systems."

We shall begin with the basic elements of the bureaucratic "vicious circle" as we observed them in the daily operations of the Clerical Agency and of the Industrial Monopoly. This will give us a static model comparable, in many respects, to the models of Merton and Gouldner. But this first model's main achievement will be to enable us to discuss the system's reactions to change and its own pattern of change. This last step will make it possible to present a general assessment of the self-reinforcing equilibrium.

Four basic elements seem to be necessary for the stability of the vicious circle we have observed: the extent of the development of impersonal rules; the centralization of decisions; strata isolation and concomitant group pressure on the individual; and the development of parallel power relationships around remaining areas of uncertainty. We shall analyze them successively.

THE EXTENT OF THE DEVELOPMENT OF IMPERSONAL RULES

Impersonal rules delimit, in great detail, all the functions of every individual within the organization. They prescribe the behavior to be followed in all possible events. Equally impersonal rules determine who shall be chosen for each job and the career patterns that can be followed. In our two cases, as well as in most sectors of French public administration outside the higher executive class, two basic rules dominate the field. The first rule is that open competitive examinations (*concours*) govern promotion from one main category to another. The second rule is that seniority determines job allocation, transfer, and promotions within each main category. Candidates' personalities and past work achievements must be ignored when these examinations are evaluated, as well as when the seniority rules are applied. Judgment must be made only on their most abstract abilities or their most impersonal characteristics.

This system, of course, always affords some loopholes, but viewed from a certain distance it looks extremely tight. In the Clerical Agency, the work behavior of the people occupying all routine and lower supervisory jobs is minutely prescribed. All operations to be performed, the way to proceed, and even their sequential succession, are specified. As regards promotions, exceptions were made to the rule of competitive examinations as determining career patterns at the time of the Liberation, when many people were "integrated" into the next higher category during the great reshuffle of the organization. Since then, no exceptions to this rule have been possible. The seniority rule does not apply absolutely to the supervisory jobs, but exceptions are made only at the end of an individual's career— i.e., after twenty years of seniority promotions. Rules are even more strictly enforced at the Industrial Monopoly, where for many years there have been only a very few promotions[21] from one to another of the six categories, and where seniority prevails even for the executive jobs.

As a consequence of the combination of these two sets of rules about job specification and job allocations, nothing seems to be left of the arbitrary whim and individual initiative of an organization member. The daily behavior of everyone, as well as his chances of having to perform a different routine later, can be predicted exactly. In such a system, as we have established, hierarchical dependence relationships tend to disappear or at least to decline considerably. If no difference can be introduced in the treatment given to subordinates, either in the present definition of the job or in the fulfilment of their career expectations, hierarchical superiors cannot keep power over them. Superiors' roles will be limited to controlling the application of rules. As a counterpart, subordinates also have at their disposal no possibility of pressure, no bargaining power over

---

[21] And only from production worker to lower supervisor after many years as temporary supervisor.

supervisors, inasmuch as their own behavior is entirely set by rules. Every member of the organization, therefore, is protected both from his superiors and from his subordinates. He is, on the one hand, totally deprived of initiative and completely controlled by rules imposed on him from the outside. On the other hand, he is completely free from personal interference by any other individual—as independent, in a sense, as if he were a non-salaried worker. Such a system of human relations devaluates superior-subordinate relations. Data have shown, both in the Clerical Agency and in the Industrial Monopoly, that such rapports have lost their affective significance for the supervisor as well as for the subordinates, and that they exist only on a conventional basis, with little emotional commitment from either side.

Practically, of course, the system can never be so tight as it can theoretically. There is always some possibility of play within the framework delimited by the rules, and therefore dependence relations and bargaining are never completely suppressed. The curious practice of the *grève du zèle*—striking by slowing down the work flow and paralyzing the functioning of the organization just by observing, to the letter, all the required prescriptions—has been repeatedly used in many sectors of French public administration, precisely as a way of expressing the fact that rules cannot take care of everything and that management must rely on workers' support and must therefore bargain for it.

THE CENTRALIZATION OF DECISIONS

The power of decision-making within a bureaucratic system of organization is located exactly at the points where the stability of the internal "political" system is preferred to the achievement of the functional goals of the organization. This trait can be considered as strongly complementary to the first one. If one wants to keep strictly to the climate of impersonality, it is essential that all decisions that have not been eliminated by the system of rules be made at a level where those who make them are protected against personal pressures from those who are affected by them.

Therefore, the power to make decisions and to interpret and complete the rules, as well as the power to change the rules or to institute new ones, will tend to grow farther and farther away from the field where those rules will be carried out. If the pressure for impersonality is strong, such a tendency toward centralization cannot be resisted. As a consequence, constant priority will be given to internal political problems—the struggle to get rid of favoritism and discrimination and to maintain the equilibrium between the different parts and subsections of the system over the problems of adjusting to the environment. The pressure of the latter suggests locating the power of decision-making where all the relevant facts will be best known at first hand. This is not possible if one gives precedence to internal considerations. The power of initiating decisions, given at one arbitrary level, cannot but introduce differences among individuals at this level, and, as a secondary consequence, introduce dependence relationships above and below. Such dangerous power can be placed only very carefully, and due account must be taken of all groups' and subgroups' particular claims. Centralization is thus the second means of eliminating discretionary personal power within an organization. The price the organization has to pay for it is still greater rigidity. People who make decisions cannot have direct firsthand knowledge of the problems they are called upon to solve. On the other hand, the field officers who know these problems can never have the power necessary to adjust, to experiment, and to innovate.

The Clerical Agency was the best example of such centralization. We have dwelt at length upon the reciprocal relationships between lower and higher supervisors. These embodied perfectly the dilemma of a bureaucratic organization and the choice it is bound to make. But the same pressures operate and the same solutions are taken above that level, in the Department to which the Clerical Agency belongs. The same is true, as noted, in the Industrial Monopoly, where the director and the assistant director have to decide on all shop problems, about which they are not in a position to know firsthand. By and large, patterns of this sort, if not always so easily perceptible, exist throughout all French public administration.

THE ISOLATION OF THE DIFFERENT STRATA AND THE CONCOMITANT
GROUP PRESSURE ON THE INDIVIDUAL

The suppression of most possibilities of discretion on the part of superiors and of most possibilities of bargaining interference on the part of subordinates, through the system of impersonality and centralization, has another important consequence. Each hierarchical category, each stratum, will be completely isolated from all other strata, above and below. A bureaucratic organization, therefore, is composed of a series of superimposed strata that do not communicate very much with each other. Barriers between strata are such that there is very little room for the development of cliques cutting across several categories.

This strata isolation is associated with a pressure of the peer group on the individual that is much stronger than usual. Where hierarchical pressure dwindles and where there can be no cliques that unite people of different strata, the peer group—i.e., the group of equal members of the same stratum—becomes the only force that stands between the individual and the organization. Since there must always be complete equality among the members of one stratum, the only possible discrimination is that of seniority; competition and bargaining occur between strata, and the pressure of the peer group on the individual is inescapable, at least in all matters that are subject to bargaining. Deviant impulses will be severely sanctioned, and the discipline imposed by the peer group will be one of the main forces, apart from the rules, which regulate behavior. Since supervisors may not interfere, and since there cannot be much sanction by comparison of individual work results, individuals must conform only to impersonal rules and to the group norms that support, interpret, and complete these. The importance of the peer group was marked in our two case studies, and especially in the Industrial Monopoly, by the remarkable concordance of answers among members of the same group for all relevant matters, and also by the discrepancy between private opinion, which could be deviant, and publicly expressed opinion, which had to follow the official line.[22]

This pressure of the peer group is one of the most relevant factors for understanding the bureaucrats' *esprit de corps* and ritualism. The displacement of goals that is basic to them could not take place if it were not enforced by the peer group as a way of protecting itself against other groups and against the organization. Task impersonality and petty regulation are, in fact, very well developed in many private large-scale modern organizations, without important effects on ritualism. The same forces have a direct impact in a bureaucratic system of organization because the isolation of each stratum allows it to control its own domain and to ignore the organization's wider goals. We should further like to argue that, in order to get the best bargain for its own members, the peer group must pretend that their partial objective is an end in itself. The members' ritualism provides good means to achieve such an end. It enables the group to assert its own differences and uniqueness, to pretend its own functions are the most crucial for the success of the whole organization. Then, finally, it helps develop and reinforce group solidarity among the group's own members.

There is a great difference of attitude, at the same level of task prescription, between an employee controlled by the kind of bureaucratic system of organization we are elaborating here and an em-

[22] See chapter 4, p. 104.

ployee of another, less bureaucratic system of organization. Ritualism is an asset for the former, since the possibilities for betterment depend on the success of his group and on his status within his group. It is a liability for the latter employee, whose chances depend on his ability to join other groups and to show that he is able to understand larger goals.[23]

THE DEVELOPMENT OF PARALLEL POWER RELATIONSHIPS

We devoted space in the preceding chapter to the problem of parallel power relationships; we shall summarize our conclusions here. Since it is impossible, whatever the effort, to eliminate all sources of uncertainty within an organization by multiplying impersonal rules and developing centralization, a few areas of uncertainty will remain. Around these areas, parallel power relationships will develop, with the concomitant phenomena of dependence and conflict. Individuals or groups who control a source of uncertainty, in a system of action where nearly everything is predictable, have at their disposal a significant amount of power over those whose situations are affected by this uncertainty. Moreover, their strategic position is all the stronger because sources of uncertainty are very few. Paradoxically, in a bureaucratic system of organization, parallel power increases in direct ratio to its rarity. In many French public agencies, for example, there are cases of low-ranking employees whose opinions may be decisive in important affairs, simply because of their fortuitous occupation of a strategic position in an otherwise over-regulated system. There are similar examples of groups that maintain exorbitant privileges in the face of over-all egalitarian custom.

Parallel power relationships can develop within the hierarchical line. However, as a rule—and in the Industrial Monopoly especially —they develop outside it. This has as a consequence a complete reorganization of the organization's human relations.

Strata of experts are often privileged groups from this point of view, inasmuch as their task cannot be prescribed and regulated in a detailed way. Decentralization of the type described by Selznick will be the consequence of their successful pressure. Such decentralization is not so inconsistent with administrative centralization as it may seem to be. It is within the general framework of the impersonal and centralized "bureaucratic system," and because of the rigidity of such a framework, that experts' privileges can be maintained and developed.

---

[23] This is often, of course, only partially true, since in many instances the peer group in a non-bureaucratic organization can also control its members very strictly.

We have learned, in studying the Monopoly, that the position of the experts is much stronger in an organization where everything is controlled and regulated—i.e., as long as their own task cannot be rationalized. Paradoxically, the more narrowly the organization is regulated, the greater the independence of the experts.

THE VICIOUS CIRCLE

The difficulties, the poor work, and the frustrations that are the consequence of these four basic elements tend to develop new pressures in favor of the climate of impersonality and of centralization that has produced them. In other words, the "bureaucratic system of organization" is primarily characterized by the existence of a series of relatively stable vicious circles that stem from centralization and impersonality. The schemes suggested by Merton and Gouldner are good examples of such vicious circles. But it is possible to elaborate new ones and to integrate them within a still broader scheme.

We have already discussed the vicious circle of the displacement of goals. In our view, it could be explained not only by the rigidity of the human personality, which maintains itself within the mold to which it has been submitted, but by the isolation of competitive strata, which use the displacement of goals to assert their influence against one another. The dysfunctional consequences of displacement of goals—i.e., difficulties with the customers, poor communication with the environment, and unsatisfactory adjustment to it, difficulties in achieving the task, a lower productivity, etc.—cannot and will not lead to greater flexibility within the system. The only weapon that can be used by the people who must make decisions is a greater elaboration of the rules and further centralization. Also, individuals and groups who directly face these difficulties and poorer results at the field level do not apply pressure to obtain more autonomy. On the contrary, they attempt to use the dysfunctions to reinforce their position vis-à-vis the public and within the organization. Their struggle against centralization is not directed toward helping the organization to adapt better to the challenge of the environment, but rather toward safeguarding and developing the kind of rigidity that is protecting them.

The vicious circle of control and supervision that has been analyzed by Gouldner can also be extended. He argues that the proliferation of impersonal bureaucratic rules reduces the tensions created by too close supervision, while, at the same time, the frustrations and the poor performances that develop in an impersonal bureaucratic world reinforce the need for close supervision. One can go further and argue that inasmuch as the bargaining power of the supervisor dwindles—the natural tendency in all bureaucratic systems of organization—the vicious circle goes further the foreman-worker level and tends to include the whole set of hierarchical relationships within the organization.

The Clerical Agency provided the perfect example of such a generalized vicious circle of close supervision, impersonal rules, and centralization. The frustrations of the different groups, which cannot discuss the decisions that will affect them and must submit to the close supervision of their activities, build up so much that higher-ups do not feel solid enough to face the problem, and the whole process of decision-making tends to move one rung higher. If people who make decisions do not have to confront those who will be affected by these decisions, tensions are reduced; but frustrations go on, and so does the pressure for centralization. Of course, efforts to change the whole system, to open it up are possible; but such attempts would run counter to the general fear of dependence relationships that is a contingent cultural trait of great relevance for the understanding of the development of bureaucratic systems of organization. This fear, in turn, is fed upon and reinforced by the frustrations emerging from the parallel power relationships that are likely to arise in such regulated organizations. The existence of those privileged relationships is the indirect consequence, as we have seen, of the development of impersonality and centralization; it tends to generate a very powerful secondary drive for more centralization and impersonality.

By and large, the common underlying pattern of all the vicious circles that characterize bureaucratic systems is this: the rigidity of task definition, task arrangements, and the human relations network results in a lack of communication with the environment and a lack of communication among the groups. The resulting difficulties, instead of imposing a readjustment of the model, are utilized by individuals and groups for improving their position in the power struggle within the organization. Thus a new pressure is generated for impersonality and centralization, the only solution to the problem of personal privileges.

Such a scheme of interpretation is no longer founded on the passive reaction of the human factor, offering resistance to certain kinds of interference and manipulation. It is based on the recognition of the active tendency of the human agent to take advantage, in any circumstances, of all available means to further his own privileges.

THE PROBLEM OF CHANGE
IN A BUREAUCRATIC SYSTEM OF ORGANIZATION

Our model of a bureaucratic system of organization as one unable to correct its own errors, whose dysfunctions, therefore, are part of its self-reinforcing equilibrium, meets certain criticisms made earlier of the human relations theories of bureaucracy. It is general and systematic; it emphasizes rational patterns instead of the logic of sentiments; and, finally, it provides us with a good operational definition. But it still falls short of making it possible to understand the development and the limits of bureaucratic phenomena, which it still presents to us in a static and descriptive way.

To go one step further, we must consider the problem of change for such a bureaucratic system. Any organization, whatever its functions, goals, and environment, has to face change from within and from without. And if it is first necessary to study the steady state of day-to-day operations to discover regular patterns of action, then the way the organization reacts to change and tries to control it raises questions basic to the understanding of the real meaning of the regular routines, of which functional analysis could make only the internal mechanism understood.

The first, and quite obvious, point to make here concerns rigidity. A system of organization whose main characteristic is its rigidity will not adjust easily to change and will tend to resist change as much as possible. Constant transformations affect a modern organization. They concern the services it provides the customers and the public with whom it has to deal, the techniques of performance, and even the attitudes and capacities of the personnel it employs. Adjustment to these transformations can be gradual and more or less constant, if the agents of the organization who are at the level where the necessity of these changes is more obvious can introduce the wanted innovations or obtain such innovations from the competent authorities. But, as we have already pointed out, a bureaucratic organization does not allow for such initiative at the lower echelons;[24] decisions must be made where power is located, i.e., on top. However, this concentration and the concomitant strata isolation make it impossible to expect a permanent adjustment policy from the higher echelons. For one thing, they will be spared any advance warnings and predictions, because of the failures of the communication system. Then, when

---

[24] Especially as regards human problems.

they do learn of it, they have difficulties making decisions, because of the weight of the impersonal rules that may be affected by change. One may validly argue that, as a result, a bureaucratic system will resist change as long as it can; it will move only when serious dysfunctions develop and no other alternatives remain.

However, while a bureaucratic system of organization resists change longer than a non-bureaucratic system, it must nevertheless resort to change quite often in our adaptive modern society. Rigidity can obtain only within certain limits, and dysfunctions will reinforce the bureaucratic vicious circle only within a certain margin. Resistance to change, therefore, is only one part of the picture. Another important part—one that there is a tendency to forget—is the very peculiar way a bureaucratic organization adjusts to change.

From the above analysis, it emerges that change in a bureaucratic organization must come from the top down and must be universalistic, i.e., encompass the whole organization *en bloc*. Change will not come gradually on a piecemeal basis. It will wait until a serious question pertaining to an important dysfunction can be raised. Then it will be argued about and decided upon at the higher level and applied to the whole organization, even to the areas where dysfunctions are not seriously felt. Only in this way can the impersonality system be safeguarded. One may even contend that very often change will lead to further centralization, by providing a way to get rid of local privileges that have developed around the rules.

Because of the necessarily long delays, because of the amplitude of the scope it must attain, and because of the resistance it must overcome, change in bureaucratic organizations is a deeply felt crisis. The essential rhythm prevalent in such organizations is, therefore, an alternation of long periods of stability with very short periods of crisis and change. Most analyses of the bureaucratic phenomenon refer only to the periods of routine, and this is the image that emerges from our description of the bureaucratic vicious circles. But it is a partial image. Crisis is a distinctive and necessary element of the bureaucratic system. It provides the only means of making the necessary adjustments, and it therefore plays a role in enabling the organization to develop and, indirectly, for centralization and impersonality to grow.

Crises are important in another way. They exemplify other patterns of action, other types of group relationships—temporary, but of decisive importance. During crises, individual initiative prevails and people eventually come to depend on some strategic individual's arbitrary whim. Forgotten, strained dependence relationships reappear. Personal authority at times supersedes the rules. Such exceptions, made possible by the loopholes of the routine setup, will be tolerated because they can last only as long as the problem to be solved remains unsolved. They are the short periods of a war of movement necessary to permit more rational realignment of the war of positions. Their role, however, remains important. First, they perpetuate the fear of direct authority and arbitrariness among the members of the organization. Second, they continually create a new demand for authoritarian reformer figures in the midst of the bureaucratic routine. Such figures are just the opposite of Merton's "bureaucratic personalities," but they are also characteristic and play an indirect but powerful role in shaping the values and countervalues of the organization.

Crises, finally, can develop at different levels. In the Clerical Agency and in the Industrial Monopoly, we analyzed minor but recurrent crises that played a significant role in the strategy of the different groups. In the Industrial Monopoly, possible plant reorganizations were an important element in the strategy of the different groups. In the Clerical Agency, the periodic overwork crises that stemmed from the discrepancy between the routine, stable allocation of work and the periodic traffic jams caused by seasonal influences provided an example. These crises perpetuated older authority patterns and increased a concomitant deep-seated distrust of face-to-face relationships. However, other, more remote crises still had weight— the crisis over seniority in the Monopoly; the introduction of the accounting machines and the personnel reorganization in the Clerical Agency after the Liberation. Crises can come from within or they can be accidents imposed from without. Wars and social and political crises that upset the customary power equilibrium provide very good opportunities for effecting changes that have long been overdue.

More sophisticated and older bureaucracies have made special efforts to deal with the problem of change on a more rational basis. The older departments of French public administration, for example, have tried to domesticate and control the difficult and dangerous roles of change agents in order to regulate, and eventually eliminate, crisis. To achieve this, they have tended to create separate castes of higher civil servants. These are isolated from the bulk of the Civil Service by their recruitment, training, and career expectations, and are therefore protected from possible pressures from within. These *Grands Corps* provide, whenever needed, the personalities capable of imposing the necessary reforms on the administrative units that need them. At the same time they maintain as much as possible the rules of these units and minimize the authoritarian aspects of their own role by their impartiality and the prestige they enjoy because of their elite situation.[25] However, such a way of dealing with the problem of change is cumbersome; and it may be argued that it provides a decisive element of instability at the higher levels of the political system.[26]

Such patterns, of course, are peculiar to French culture. But it is significant that cultural differences are most striking in the problem of dealing with change. We shall discuss the problem more thoroughly when we try to analyze a bureaucratic system from a cultural point of view. For the moment, it is sufficient to conclude that a bureaucratic system of organization is not only a system that does not correct its behavior in view of its errors; it is also *too rigid to adjust without crisis to the transformations that the accelerated evolution of industrial society makes more and more imperative.*

THE BUREAUCRATIC PERSONALITY

Traditionally, the bureaucratic personality has been viewed as developing around ritualistic behavior. This especially is implied in Merton's call for a study of the relationship between bureaucratic structure and personality.[27] In Merton's categories, ritualism is characterized by emphasizing the institutionalized means while ignoring or rejecting the over-all goals.[28] It is thus opposed to the three other possibilities of the famous paradigm—conformity, retreatism, and rebellion—as if bureaucracy were the embodiment of one special category of social action, that of giving prominence to means over ends.

Such a view is highly suggestive and stimulating. However, it remains too one-sided, and, as we have pointed out, it overlooks the complexity of individual and group strategies in modern organization. Merton stresses only the impact of specialization and training; he cites the famous formula, "People may be unfitted by being fit to an unfit fitness." For the bureaucrat, "Training has become an incapacity."[29] This interpretation, of course, still remains partly true

[25] On the role of the *Grands Corps* and their gradual transformation from a function of stabilization and unification of administrative action to a function of reform, little has been written as yet. See, on the *Inspections des Finances,* François Pietri, *Le Financier* (Paris: Hachette, 1931), a good literary account; and Philippe Lalumière, *L'inspection des Finances* (Paris: P.U.F., 1959), a less good presentation of more recent facts.

[26] Cf. below, pp. 255–56.

[27] Robert K. Merton, "Bureaucratic Structure and Personality," *Social Forces,* XVIII (1940), 560–68, republished in *Social Theory and Social Structure* (rev. ed.; Glencoe, Ill.: The Free Press, 1957), p. 206.

[28] *Ibid.,* p. 140.

[29] *Ibid.,* p. 198.

for any large-scale organization. But it is much more suited to old-line bureaucracies, which relied on gross, inadequate drilling of their agents and imposed lifelong commitments on them, without any prospect of change. In modern organizations, even bureaucratic ones, even the lowest group is able to devise its own strategy, and change, even if it is resisted stubbornly, remains a basic element in the game to be played. We have already argued that, in this perspective, ritualism is not the simple result of training, but is also a very useful instrument in the struggle for power and control and in the protection of a group's area of action. Ritualism in such a context, if one considers the actor's frame of reference and not the whole organization, must be viewed as conformity to what is expected from him and no longer as over-conformity. It is the rational response and not a "professional deformation."

At the same time, however, as it becomes less clear-cut and more diffuse, ritualism appears to form a lesser part of the general picture. Other possible alternatives of behavior emerge within a bureaucratic system of organization, according to the constraints of a wider variety of roles than is usually thought. In our analysis, for instance, numerous examples of retreatism and rebellion appeared; and, even though it is partly mythical, the role of innovator retains a great deal of importance. Finally, outside the paradigm, an important category of social action remains that of submissiveness to and identification with the power of other groups.

Retreatism at first seems to be a very central category of behavior in a bureaucratic system of organization. One may even argue that it is as decisive as ritualism. Confronted with an over-demanding situation, with no expectation of significant reward, individuals will choose to reduce their involvement and to commit themselves as little as possible to the organization. The pattern of impersonality and centralization brings great pressure in this direction. On the one hand, it deprives people of the possibility of personally influencing decision-making, and thus precludes any hope of recognition. On the other hand, it does not demand anything but formal compliance from individuals. People are not invited to participate, and, if they retreat, they risk little punishment. However, such a response is not so free as we may think, because of the decisive influence of the peer group, whose powers of coercion are much greater than in a less rigid organization. Our case studies show that groups allow full retreatism only inasmuch as they are weak and discouraged. Successful groups prohibit retreatism completely. Intermediary groups are characterized by a mixture of different attitudes and behavior.

The purest example of retreatism is provided by the lower supervisors in the Industrial Monopoly. Their involvement is extremely slight, they rarely hold strong opinions, and their answers are often not even coherent. They do not take pride in any part of their work. One would imagine that they would emphasize those bureaucratic functions that they can accomplish without any interference from the maintenance men, but they do not—at least, most of them do not. As a group, they are not ritualists. They might have been in earlier times, according to legend, when they still had some power. But they ceased to be so long ago, except for a handful of old-timers who have kept a number of ritualistic patterns within the general framework of retreatism. A few of them, however, as we have noted, try to fight back. Those "rebels" are much more dissastisfied than their colleagues, but they are the only ones really involved in the affairs of the Monopoly.

The supervisors of the Clerical Agency present some of the same traits, but in a very different mixture. They certainly reduce their commitment to the Agency, but they still expect promotions and know they are likely to be transferred to another agency. They are, therefore, generally quite involved in the affairs of the over-all department to which they belong, and they often act at least partially as rebels within the Agency. Trade unionism is, for many of them, a good expression of their hostility. As regards their work, they fight to preserve the status quo and to keep problems and entanglements to a minimum. From this point of view, they are, above all, retreatists. They have a few very "bureaucratic" duties to perform, but they do not emphasize them in a ritualistic way. A very small group of zealous over-conformist individuals are found on top, among those who can expect a higher promotion. But their emphasis is not on ritual but on the specific achievements measured within the Agency —productivity and quality per head, i.e., that which is considered a goal by management. Theirs is submissive, more than ritualistic behavior.

The directors of the Industrial Monopoly are also strongly retreatist, but they present a different combination. The "dignified elder statesman" we have described may be considered a ritualist. His emphasis constantly bears on the forms and on the decorum of his role. He tends to ignore the productive goals of the organization. When talking with the interviewers, one of them used to repeat this, for him, characteristic joke: "We are here to write reports and process papers . . . [the service given to the public] is only a by-product." [30] But this ritualism appears much more as a way to preserve

---

[30] This joke, to be sure, is ambiguous; but we can ignore the reversal of roles that makes the organization responsible to focus only on the way this director seems to be fascinated by bureaucratic practices. The rest of the interview, as a matter of fact, shows what exaggerated importance he himself gives to written documents and to formalism.

a façade and to hide from oneself and others the futility of one's role, than as an occupational deformity. And only a minority of directors adopt such behavior. At the other extreme are the directors who exaggerate their helplessness; these are pure retreatists who try to preserve their self-respect as individuals by separating themselves from their job and deprecating it. They simply refuse to be involved and choose to concentrate on possible achievements outside their job. Most directors present a combination of both patterns of behavior. This contradiction, as one can discern from the incoherent comments of a few individuals, is quite characteristic of the group as a whole. But one can understand it only if one refers to the role of innovator played by two or three of them.

Innovation, Merton's supplementary category, is not absent from a bureaucratic system. Curiously, the innovator seems to be the polar figure of the whole system and innovation the most envied achievement, the one for which people are most ready to fight. The innovator in a bureaucratic system, however, shows certain special characteristics. He is a legislator, a Solon type, rather than a discoverer. He is someone who will once again put everyone in his own place, who will reorder the world in a better way, rather than someone who will launch new patterns, new ways, of doing things.

People try to prepare for this role. The changing strategy of the members of the Monopoly's engineers' corps, as their age and seniority increase, can be viewed as dominated to quite an extent by their hopes and realistic expectations as regards this glorious role.

The role of innovator can interest, in fact, only a small minority of civil servants, since innovation appears only on the top and people must compete for it. But its importance reaches far beyond the immediate group it affects directly. In the Monopoly, success is more a myth than a reality; but its mere possibility arouses fears and resistances which would otherwise slowly disappear. Change and a fresh meting out of justice will return some day, like a long-forgotten specter, and one had better have one's defense prepared.

In other contexts, however, where the innovation-legislation function is given more importance, the whole strategy of the system depends on it and we have a completely different setup. One typical example is provided by the role of the prefect in French provincial administration.[31] Among French bureaucrats, the prefect is probably the one whose innovation-legislation function is most developed. He has discretion and is supposed to use it. The staff around him show a characteristic pattern of adjustment. Intermediate officials are extremely cautious, timid, and submissive. They pretend that they

---

[31] The prefect is a sort of appointed governor in charge of all administrative affairs for an area of a size intermediate between a county and a state.

have no responsibilities whatever in making decisions. They feel that they are merely anonymous helpers of the great innovator figure with whom they identify. Petty officials, on the other hand, appear to be extremely ritualistic and, at the same time, rebellious. They are attached to the status quo and resent possible innovations as so many violations of the order which they must impose on the public. They feel themselves to be betrayed, and their position undermined, by the prefect's initiative. Their strategy is a strategy of opposition and rebellion; they try to impose their ritualism on the prefect and to obtain some compensation for his trespassing on their jobs. We see here the importance of the gap created by centralization. Petty officials cannot make the necessary adjustments. Power to innovate is reserved for superior figures with prestige. As a result, petty officials behave as extremely jealous ritualists for all practical purposes, and try to use to the utmost advantage the parcel of power involved in the rites imposed on them. At the same time, they question the whole system and pose as rebels. Sentiments are more complex than one would expect from reading Merton. There is a sort of paradox in this respect: when a petty official obtains promotion to a middle rank that permits him to escape the chicanery of petty regulations, he foregoes this theoretical rebellion and becomes humble and submissive.

I should like to argue that the freedom and discretion of the innovator figure require the strict ritualism of the petty officials and the submissiveness of the middle officials if they are to develop fully. Petty officials are given the unpleasant role of enforcing the rules without the slightest leeway; they must refrain from anything personal for fear of arbitrariness. This is a protection for the public and, although indirectly, for the official as well. But the dysfunctions thus created make it necessary to resort to an innovator. This figure can make the wanted adjustments, and his prestige will be all the greater, since he is entrusted with the only discretionary power within the system. Intermediate officials will act as transmission links. They are too involved in the discussion of arbitrary exceptions to the rules and in the resetting of the rules to adopt the ritualist and rebellious attitudes of their subordinates, but too helpless themselves to assume responsibilities. Power of discretion, finally, is so exceptional that it must be far removed from face-to-face relationships and surrounded by an aura of awe and submissiveness.

We now confront new images of the bureaucrat, the self-satisfied glorious innovator, the submissive assistant, and the rebellious and ritualist subaltern. This set of roles corresponds to a regular hierarchical arrangement within a very active and powerful agency. Significantly, there is little retreatism in such an arrangement. Retreatism seems associated with an increase of rigidity and the disappearance of the innovator function. Whenever change and power are present, we find more and greater involvement and deeper feeling.

Finally, the last roles still presenting a problem among those we have studied are those of the maintenance man and of the technical engineer in the Industrial Monopoly. The people who assume these roles are very much committed to their jobs. Still, they are precisely the opposite of the innovator. In a way, they are staunch conservatives—they guard the status quo to protect their own privileges and are natural enemies of the potential innovators. But maintenance men and technical engineers are not ritualists by any ordinary standards. Their privileges do not stem from the rules but, on the contrary, from the impossibility of introducing a rule. They are ritualists only as regards the system as a whole, giving priority to the technical and human relations arrangements over the functional goals. For the rest, they seem more practical, more instrumental, more goal-minded than anyone else. They exemplify still another dimension of the bureaucratic personality: practical conservatism. The other pole in this respect might be bureaucratic idealism—reliance on the power of the rules to make change. This last attitude is much more diffuse and it is often associated with retreatism. Lucidity and the emphasis on intellectual understanding are the usual compensation of the retreatist idealist. They constitute another very important dimension of the bureaucratic personality. It was especially prominent among directors and supervisors of the Industrial Monopoly and among higher and lower supervisors of the Clerical Agency. This polarity is a good counterpart of the submissiveness-rebellion couple we have seen surrounding power and innovation. A bureaucratic system will revolve around one of these axes, inclining completely in the direction of retreatism-conservatism in the sectors and periods of routine, and admitting a large dose of power, and therefore of submissiveness-rebellion, in the sectors and periods of crisis.

THE INDIVIDUAL'S STAKE IN BUREAUCRACY

We have now described the typical processes of a bureaucratic system of organization and analyzed its ways of adjusting to change. In so doing, we have shown how its gross inadequacies and "dysfunctionality" follow from its rigidity and from its tendency to escape from reality. At the same time, we have suggested that these traits are not only unintended consequences but also necessary elements of a system whose rational aim is to obtain a minimum of conformity from the members of the organization. This bureaucratic phenomenon has thus appeared to be a function of the equilibrium between the kind of social control used to maintain the organization as an ongoing system and the reactions of the human group that is submitted to it. Both depend on the state of the larger society's cultural norms and on the technical possibilities of diminishing the uncertainty of social action.

But it can be argued—and repeatedly has been—that, whatever the requirements of organization, individuals suffer from the kind of social control always imposed by social action, and that co-operative forms of action are possible and would appear more rewarding than our present power-ridden forms. We should ask, therefore, why men still consistently choose conflicting types of games instead of more co-operative ones. Why is it that they make it necessary to resort to bureaucratic rigidity, imposing on themselves the roles of "ritualists" or "retreatists"? We have seen the problem from the organization's point of view; we must now consider it from that of the individual. We must ascertain the individual's stakes in bureaucracy.

Co-operation means participation in decision-making. The possibility of more co-operative forms of action depends on the attitude of people toward such participation. Human relations theoreticians, especially those of the Lewinian school, have long assumed that people want to participate, and are ready to participate, under all and any conditions.[32] They have always argued as if the reasons for lack of participation were to be found only in the contingencies of organized activities and in the misgivings and apprehensions of managements—if only superiors could be converted to more permissive leadership, subordinates would be glad to participate. We certainly do not defend the contrary view: progress can always be made in the area of participation. However, the limits are narrower than one usually thinks they are, and it is necessary, if one wants to determine them to inquire into the actors' motivations.

It is a partial view indeed which expects people to be always eager for participation. People are very ambivalent toward participation. It is difficult to have a clear and well-argued position in an area which is only beginning to be explored. We shall merely present a few remarks that are suggested by these new developments. On the one hand, people would like very much to participate in order to control their own environment. On the other hand, they fear that if and when they participate, their own behavior will be controlled by their coparticipants. It is far easier to preserve one's independence and integrity if one does not participate in decision-making. By refusing to be involved in policy determination, one remains much

---

[32] See, for example, Erich Fromm, *Escape from Freedom* (New York: Rinehart, 1941).

more free from outside pressure. Recent research has shown that members of an organization are not always enthusiastic when invited to participate more in its functioning. The relative ambivalence of subordinates' attitudes toward participation emerges from the results of scientific controls on the consequences of experiences in human relatons training,[33] as well as from the results of the ambitious program of decentralization tried in a large insurance company by the Survey Research Center of the Unversity of Michigan.[34] Chris Argyris, among other researchers, has shown that, within the framework of the usual psychological contract into which individuals have entered with their organizations, every change that implies greater participation is viewed unfavorably.[35] Arnold Tannenbaum, in a series of studies on the problems of control within different kinds of organizations, voluntary as well as business, has found most challenging contradictions to the usual hypotheses.[36]

If one accepts participation, one is bound to co-operate, i.e., to bear one's coparticipants' pressure whether they are one's equals or one's superiors. People therefore rarely agree to participate without some substantial counterpart. They try to negotiate about their participation, and give it only if they feel that they will be adequately rewarded. This is true even at the lowest level, where participation means only being committed to one's own job's goals; it is very markedly so when participation concerns leadership problems of allocating resources and delineating duties. Retreatism can be a very rational form of behavior whenever the individual concerned has good reason to believe that the rewards he is offered are not commensurate with his efforts, and feels that there is a good chance that he will be manipulated. The will to participate, finally, depends to a large extent on the degree of trust and openness in interpersonal relations

[33] See, for example, E. A. Fleishman, E. F. Harris, and H. E. Burtt, *Leadership and Supervision in Industry: An Evaluation of a Supervisory Training Program* (Columbus: Ohio State University, 1955); Floyd Mann, "Studying and Creating Change: A Means to Understanding Social Organization," *Human Relations in the Industrial Setting* (New York: Harper, 1957); Rensis Likert, *New Patterns of Management* (New York, McGraw-Hill, 1961).

[34] The famous experiment at Prudential has shown that the "democratic" program of increasing the employees' possibilities of participation has entailed serious problems of interpersonal relations at the group level. See Nancy Morse and Everett Reimer, "Experimental Change of a Major Organizational Variable," *Journal of Abnormal and Social Psychology*, LII (1955), 120–29.

[35] Unpublished data we have gathered in a systematic comparison of forty groups in six insurance companies show concomitantly that people working in self-administered groups are afflicted by interpersonal difficulties.

[36] Arnold Tannenbaum and B. S. Georgopoulos, "The Distribution of Control in Formal Organizations," *Social Forces*, XXXVI (1957), 44–50; Arnold Tannenbaum and Robert L. Kahn, in Dorwin Cartwright (ed.), *Participation in Local Unions* (Evanston: Row, Peterson, 1958).

characteristic of the cultural norms to which people adhere.[37] In a society where proving one's own independence is considered to be a value in itself, retreatism is the most satisfactory mode of adjustment as long as the proposed participation does not adequately insure full rights of control.

Another basic cultural datum, the norms of attitudes toward authority relationships, is still of much importance. The possibilities of participation must, in actuality, remain limited. Participation is likely to be viewed as only partially satisfactory, since some constraint must be imposed from the top down to meet the remaining uncertainty within and without. If the inescapable authority relationships are not accepted easily, pressure for centralization will be strong, and a certain type of rigidity, comparable to the vicious circles we have analyzed in our two case studies, will tend to develop within all organizations. But other possible types of rigidity can develop. For example, if authority relationships are accepted submissively, with passive resistance as the outcome, one can hypothesize vicious circles of successive controls.[38]

In any case, the system's general equilibrium relies on the bargains which individuals can make. These bargains depend on individual expectations and values, on the one side, and on the requirements of organized activities, on the other. These requirements are themselves determined by the technical means employed by man to control his universe and by the same cultural data that shape individual reactions.

Within this general framework, bureaucratic systems of organization such as the ones we have studied offer individuals a fairly good combination of independence and security. The modern observer is especially struck by their dysfunctional aspect: he emphasizes the heavy price that people must pay for such results. But one should not forget that, if one takes due account of people's values and expectations and of the boundaries of social action, the bargain is usually quite a good one.

Rules protect the people who submit to them. Within the area delimited by the rules, they are free to make their own contribution according to their arbitrary whim. They can participate or take refuge in retreatist behavior, commit themselves to the organization's aims, or reserve their moral forces for some personal endeavor. Of course, they have very little chance of making a success of their activities within the organization. They will not obtain distinction among

---

[37] It depends also of course on their position in the hierarchical order and on the model of social relationships between social strata characteristic of their culture.

[38] This is the case in Russian and Soviet bureaucracy. See below, pp. 227–31.

their colleagues, but, on the other hand, they do not have to fear failure or face hostile reactions from competitors.

We shall go even further and argue that a bureaucratic system of organization always relies on a certain amount of compulsory participation which appears to be, under the present conditions, more gratifying for the individual than the voluntary participation for which— as is, perhaps, too readily believed—he is fighting. We do think that, even in those cases in which we have diagnosed retreatism, ritualism, and rebellion, there is much commitment and participation that should not be neglected. Their importance can be appreciated when one compares the attitudes and performances of members of such "bureaucratic" organizations in Western industrial societies, with those of any kind of modern organizations in underdeveloped societies, where people are unable to give the necessary attention and commitment to their task, whatever their apparent willingness.[39]

Compulsory participation of that sort implies no avowed responsibility.[40] It is clandestine, and people do not feel that they may become involved. Individuals who participate in this way remain completely free vis-à-vis the organization. Such an arrangement makes it possible to solve contradictions that would otherwise remain insoluble. On the one hand, members of a modern organization must participate, and they know that the organization cannot get along without their participation. On the other hand, they know that the organization cannot reciprocate in the way that would be requisite if they were to commit themselves to it seriously and thus renounce part of their freedom. If the organization imposes on them, through its official system of rules, a kind of compulsory participation without responsibility, they will be able to achieve two contradictory aims at the same time. They can give meaning to their work by participating in the common enterprise, and they can safeguard their independence in a situation where an avowed responsible commitment would mean a risk of alienation. Furthermore, such retreatism puts the organization in an unfavorable bargaining position; it obliges the organization to remain on the soliciting side, to beg for support.

The latent function of bureaucratic rigidity can be understood in this perspective as primarily a protective function. It provides the

[39] As we have already noted, the grève du zèle offers a good means for subordinates to remind management that they cannot dispense with the former's intelligent participation.

[40] We do not distinguish here between participation in decision-making and participation in the application of decisions. For we are interested in what is common to both kinds of participation, i.e., the feeling of responsibility and commitment the actors may have, whatever their place in the hierarchy.

individual with the minimum of security necessary to him for dealing with his fellows in the pursuit of the necessary co-operative activities. This kind of security is valuable, especially in a world where
the individual feels he is extremely vulnerable. One can anticipate,
perhaps, that, as our industrialized societies become more flexible
and can give all their members due protection against failure, the
lure of the protected status of the bureaucrat will diminish, and people will be progressively less ready to pay the price of rigidity.

Finally, the bureaucratic model we have analyzed seemingly has
still another limited but important function. It may be viewed as a
very good way of maintaining some of the individualist values of a
pre-industrial world within our modern societies. One may argue
that its development in France is associated with the resistance of
older ways of life which was brought to a special perfection before
the Industrial Revolution. Resistance to participation, and preference
for centralized authority and the stability and rigidity of a bureaucratic system of organization, by preserving for each member a minimum of autonomy and individual discretion, proceed from the same
values which peasants, craftsmen, and noblemen embodied in the
delicate balance of human relations that characterized the *art de
vivre* of traditional France. In a certain way, a bureaucratic system
of organization provides a combination of the values of a traditional
ascriptive society and those of a modern *achievement-oriented* society.[41] People can compete for any position; no formal barriers prevent them from doing so. But competition has been institutionalized
and separated from the daily life of the work environment; and its
formalism has, at least partially, the same protective value as the
older ascriptive rules.

Such arrangements, however, present substantial drawbacks for
the individual. The bureaucratic world is an arbitrary world. People
are protected, but at the price of being partially cut off from reality.
They have security and are protected from the sanction of facts; but
they have no way of taking the measure of their own endeavor. This
engenders a secondary kind of anxiety and explains the paramount
importance of human relations within a bureaucratic system. What
people gain in security they lose in realism. They must rely on human relations sanctions instead of on the usual achievement sanctions. Theirs is a world of petty bickering and the endless battles of
the war of position. People escape the lower-middle-class status
panic; instead, they develop the skimpy outlook of the petty power
struggles of a tight social system.

---

[41] For a new discussion of the Parsonian distinction between ascriptive values
and achievement values and its relevance for national characteristics, see S. M.
Lipset, "Democracy and the Social System," in *The First New Nation* (New York:
Basic Books, 1963).

Part Four

BUREAUCRACY AS A
CULTURAL PHENOMENON

THE FRENCH CASE

In the preceding chapters, we have presented an analysis of bureaucracy in terms of organizational theory. The behavioral regularities, the patterns of interdependence, and vicious circles we uncovered, enabled us to comprehend the workings of a system of action, its rules, and their meaning. In the following pages, the same data will be analyzed. This time, however, it will not be analyzed within the internal logic of the system, but in terms of its relations with the social and cultural system of the society of which it is part.

Curiously, no such study has ever been seriously carried out by sociologists. Intuitively, however, people have always assumed that bureaucratic structures and patterns of action differ in the different countries of the Western world and even more markedly between East and West. Men of action know it and never fail to take it into account. But contemporary social scientists, perhaps because of the unpleasant experiences associated with the *Völkerpsychologie* of another epoch, have not been concerned with such comparisons.

In an earlier period, De Tocqueville presented some brilliant suggestions in that direction. He tried, in *La démocratie en Amérique* as well as in *L'Ancien régime et la révolution,* to combine several approaches: institutional analysis, the study of social and political "rules of the game," and the study of what we now call the primary group.[1] His pioneering lead, however, was not followed. Many distinguished people in France took cues from his works, but only in a narrow sense. Taine used comparisons between France and England for his fight against centralization—more, however, in a perspective of social conservatism than as a scientific endeavor. Since then, in the cases of Le Play's followers, who tackled the problem in the 1890's,[2] regionalist reformers of the 1910's, the Vichy people in 1940–42, and Michel Debré in 1947,[3] comparative thinking has remained dogmatic and narrowly political. It has not again been invigorated by the kind of general and comprehensive sociological analysis that De Tocqueville used.

This problem has become fashionable again among American

[1] See his very modern analyses of American primary group relationships and his discussions of the relationships between different social categories within the French *ancien régime.*

[2] For example, Edmond Demolins, *La Supériorité des Anglo-Saxons* (Paris: Firmin Didot, 1897); Charles Mourre, *D'où vient la décadence économique de la France* (Paris: Plon, 1899).

[3] Michel Debré, *La Mort de l'Etat Republicain* (Paris: Gallimard, 1947).

social scientists, who are beginning to understand the errors of appreciation that were engendered by their believing too easily in the universalistic value of American experiences. But the efforts, made first by anthropologists,[4] then by social psychologists and sociologists, have been too exclusively devoted to the study of values and value orientations. Here, differences may be very striking. However, they are not so easy to measure, or even to understand, because they are much distorted by semantic complexities. We personally feel that the institutional level, and especially the organizational field, will be more rewarding. It is through the medium of complex organizations that modern man can express himself realistically, and it is through this same medium that a society can learn by being confronted with the problems of action. Then, and then only, it will elaborate new patterns of human relationships, or at least transform the old ones. The study of such mutations—a study which is not possible at the level of value orientation—will completely change the meaning and the scope of comparative analysis and sever it from the immanentist tradition of *Völkerpsychologie*.[5]

We shall not be able to go far in this direction, since we do not have the necessary data. We should like, however, to emphasize how decisive the study of this domain could become by showing the suggestive hypotheses that can be launched even with our insufficient results.

Our first objective, however, is even more modest. We wish to round out our theory with a wider perspective and to suggest the extent to which certain basic national traits can emerge from behind our abstract and over-rational image of organizational behavior. By discussing those traits, we shall be able to criticize our model from another viewpoint and thus to assess its meaning and its limitations more accurately.

[4] See, for example, the series of the research group on contemporary cultures led by Margaret Mead (and especially, for the French case, Rhoda Métraux and Margaret Mead, *Themes in French Culture* [Stanford, Calif.: Stanford University Press, 1954]) and the long series of the Harvard University Russian Research Center. A suggestive experience of a more psychological and experimental bent, recently reported by Stanley Milgram, should also be taken into account; it showed a greater amount of resistance to conformism among Frenchmen than among Norwegians (Stanley Milgram, "Nationality and Conformity," *Scientific American*, December, 1961, pp. 45–51.

[5] As noted earlier the new progress of neo-rationalism makes possible a new and wider understanding of social action, thus eliminating the fiction of the *one best way*, upon which management philosophy has so long relied. It has begun to be realized that several different organizational models can be used to achieve the same results, and comparative analyses of organizational structures and dysfunctions are beginning to be accepted as a rational endeavor. It will now become possible to integrate intuitive hunches on cultural differences in a general theory of action, without having to oppose some immanent features of the different industrialized nations to scientific rationalism.

The second point is concerned with what we shall call "the over-tones" of our bureaucratic model. In many walks of French life, there are a number of patterns that may be closely compared to those we have analyzed. From these patterns, similar models of vicious circles can be elaborated—the educational system, the industrial relations system, the politico-administrative system, the bourgeois business system, and the processes of innovation and change. These similarities, we believe, conceal deeper correspondences associated with two different kinds of factors. On the one side, the human interaction patterns that form the rough material of those systems of action are deeply conditioned by the same cultural traits which condition the equilibrium of power relationships and the increase of bureaucratic patterns within organizations. On the other side, all the systems of action that constitute these bureaucratic organizations are interdependent and reinforce each other.

Through these overtones of our first model, we shall grapple with a last problem, namely, the scope and the role of bureaucracy and of the bureaucratic phenomenon within an entire society—in this case, the French society. At the simpler level, the usual connection drawn, especially in France, between public administration and bureaucracy is much too rash. We have shown that bureaucratic rigidities will appear in all sorts of organizations and that the reason that public administrations are even more liable to this than other organizations is in no way mysterious. Can the following question, however, be raised at a far higher level of abstraction? Do the role played and the place taken by public administration organization as privileged means of social action within a society express the existence of bureaucratic dysfunctions and bureaucratic vicious circles at the level of the whole society?

A study able to answer this question, dealing globally with society as an organizational system, must remain highly speculative for a long time. This orientation, however, makes it possible for us to view bureaucracy in a wider perspective and to suggest a broader analysis of the way a given society uses social control to maintain the necessary equilibrium and to introduce equally necessary changes and innovations.

Chapter Eight

THE FRENCH BUREAUCRATIC SYSTEM
OF ORGANIZATION

The model of a bureaucratic vicious circle and its four basic elements
—the impersonality of the rules, the centralization of decisions, the
strata isolation, and the development of parallel power relationships
—may appear to have a universal application. And we have tried to
work out the most general and abstract schemes from our case
studies.

However, could not another interpretation be made that would
explain what we observed and described? The many parallels that
can be drawn enable us to think that the behavioral traits and the
patterns of human relations that we have relied upon to elaborate
our bureaucratic model correspond to a number of traits typical of
French society.

If this is so, we shall have to ask to what extent our model is
exclusively a French model, and whether other kinds of models can
be worked out for different cultural systems. In any case, it will be
necessary to have a new and broader perspective in order to judge
the relevance and the limits of usefulness of one model.

We have already shown the importance of the cultural dimension
in analyzing the specific advantages that members of an organization
derive from the existence of a bureaucratic system of organization.
The cultural dimension seems almost impossible to avoid when one
passes from an explanation in terms of dysfunction to an explanation
in terms of latent function.[1] We had then, however, only recognized
the problem. It is now time to deal with it.

In order to discuss it in more rational and empirical terms, we
shall set the terms of this problem differently. Instead of starting with

---

[1] Gouldner, for example, may try to remain on a universalistic plane when he
presents as the basic latent function of bureaucratic rules the need to reduce
tensions due to the decline of friendly and informal interactions and to the difference and opposition between the values of the different groups. But these new
notions he puts forward are universalistic only in appearance. When one discusses
dysfunctions in terms of interactions and of values, cultural differences are as
important as differences in time periods. This confusion he makes between the two
kinds of influence, it seems to me, is the reason why he can still equate the growth
of bureaucratic dysfunctions to the growth of bureaucratization in the Weberian
sense. See the discussion of his thesis, pp. 181–83, above.

the model of dysfunctions that we have already elaborated, we shall return to our original data and try to assess the extent to which they may be considered to express specifically French traits. We shall thus first examine interpersonal and intergroup relationships, since it is in this area that cultural determinants are apparently easiest to discover. Then we shall discuss authority relationships and the general fear of face-to-face relationships, and eventually present a first general hypothesis covering the French features of our model. We shall finally come to the problem of change, and try to understand, in cultural terms, the paradox which we have already emphasized: the weakness of the omnipotent power at the top of the bureaucratic pyramid. We shall then be ready to work out other comparable models for the different dysfunctions and rigidities that can develop in different cultural environments.

The Problem of Interpersonal and Intergroup Relationships

Interpersonal and intergroup relationships present some characteristic, and rather similar, traits in the Clerical Agency and in the Industrial Monopoly. These traits—the isolation of the individual, the predominance of formal over informal activities, the isolation of the strata, and their struggles for privileges—play an important role in our model of a bureaucratic system of organization. Strata isolation, especially, is a key point for the development of the vicious circle which is the basis of our scheme of interpretation. Yet all these traits may also be considered as permanent French cultural traits.

Let us examine our data carefully. We noticed how few informal relationships there were among the employees of the Clerical Agency. Girls remained isolated, although this entailed hardship for many of them who were strangers in the city and had been abruptly severed from families and friendship ties. They reported that they very rarely had friends in the agency. They reiterated that they preferred having their friends outside. Even among those who had friends, the friendships seemed never to develop into articulate groups. There were very few associations of any sort—no cultural, educational, or leisure joint activities worth mentioning. Trade unions were more active; but for the average girl, whether or not she belonged to one, they remained rather formal affairs in which she did not participate. On the whole, we were left with the impression of a significant lack of informal groups. No clans or cliques of any sort were able to exist for long, and none of them was ever able to cut across different categories.

More friendships were reported in the Industrial Monopoly, but they did not develop into cliques or even into stable informal groups. Cliques were viewed with great disfavor, and groups that could cut across several categories were inconceivable.

These patterns contrast strongly with the usual picture of the American industrial shop climate as it has been portrayed since the first experiences of the Hawthorne testroom. They contrast also with reports on American public agencies,[2] such as those of Peter Blau, and of Roy Francis and R. C. Stone.[3]

These pecularities fit very well with the rationale of the strata system that we have analyzed. In a bureaucratic system of organization, the individual is adequately protected by the abstract formal group[4]—i.e., the stratum or ranking category—to which he belongs. The rules of seniority prevent interference by outside authorities and impose a strict equality among all the members of the group. As a consequence, the individual does not need the protection of an informal group. In addition, he knows that separate informal activities are likely to threaten the cohesion of the formal category to which he is bound, and he is vulnerable to the pressure of this whole formal category against such activities. Cliques that cut across categories are especially objectionable, since they inevitably foster *favoritism,* the system's cardinal sin.

Thus, in a world where conformity is achieved through the joint influence of impersonal rules that apply to all, and of group pressure that polices behavior within each category, the formal group takes precedence over the informal, and the individual remains isolated. This mechanism, which was especially obvious in the Industrial Monopoly,[5] is directly linked with the disappearance of formal and informal hierarchical pressure. Instead of the usual pattern of subordinates' developing informal groups to resist the pressure of the superordinate system, we have a very different pattern. Here, the superordinate system has been stripped of its potential of dis-

---

[2] Peter Blau, *The Dynamics of Bureaucracy* (Chicago: University of Chicago Press, 1955); Roy G. Francis and Robert C. Stone, *Service and Procedure in Bureaucracy* (Minneapolis: University of Minnesota Press, 1956).

[3] One can contend that the French industrial shop climate is also characterized by many informal group activities, but the evidence for this is not so conclusive as it at first appears. We have shied away from such discussion for lack of relevant empirical data. See Jacques Barbichon, "Etats d'insatisfaction, la vie parallèle dans l'entreprise et dans les loisirs," *Peuple et Culture, XIIème Congrès National,* 1956.

[4] It is abstract, in the true sense, for the technical engineer who never sees his own colleagues.

[5] It will be remembered that production workers and maintenance men conformed rigorously to the norms of their group in all strategic areas and that the official line took precedence in a public encounter over individual personal opinions. See above, p. 104.

crimination by being too well formalized, and isolated individuals control and check each other in order to maintain the formalism that protects them.

The precedence of the formal group over the informal, the tight control of each stratum over its members—these are associated with the isolation of the strata, the difficulty of promotion from one stratum to another, the difficulty of communicating across strata, and the development of ritualism. We have analyzed the importance of the formal peer group as a direct consequence of strata isolation and an indirect consequence of the pressure to impose impersonal rules, in order to eliminate the discretionary will of any individual.

But it can also work the other way around. If they already exist as distinct cultural patterns, such traits as the isolation of the individual and the lack of informal activities may act as powerful incentives for the development of this kind of bureaucratic system of organization. In any case, they will be important elements for understanding the success of certain patterns of organization within a given cultural context.

These traits indeed appear, to a large extent at least, to be rather well-established French cultural traits. We cannot rely, unfortunately, upon neat comparative tests, since empirical comparative studies remain to be made. But most observers have pointed out the low state of free group activities in France and the difficulty that Frenchmen experience in co-operating on a formal basis.

The few serious anthropological studies made provide significant and concordant details in the same direction. Lucien Bernot and René Blancard, in their thorough study of a village near Paris, note, for example: "Already, among children, one discovers one of the characteristic features of Nouville's life, the absence of groups. One does not find among the children any gang or clique within the village." [6] The same thing, they tell us, prevails among adults, and even among the industrial workers of the nearby factory, who do not develop lasting ties although, or perhaps because, they live in the same close community. The only group that exists in the village is a group of youngsters who have a significantly higher status than the rest of their peers; but their group, which has no leader, is not very successful. If the Catholic priest and the schoolteachers were to leave, "the very small amount of collective life or organized leisure would disappear because of the apathy of a youth group that does not dare to take the risks of responsibility." [7] The political field is the

---

[6] *Nouville, un village français* (Paris: Institut d'Ethnologie, 1953), p. 148.
[7] *Ibid.*, p. 169.

exact image of this apathy, although a good part of the votes will go to the extreme left in a general election. There is rather more activity in the sunny village in the Vaucluse that Lawrence Wylie discusses.[8] However, the insightful remarks of the author indicate that the situation is basically the same. People tend to remain aloof; they have the same difficulties in co-operating. No organized activities are allowed to disrupt the theoretical equality between the villagers. Anyone who shows initiative is likely to be accused of trying to boss the others.

In a study of a rural community under the impact of drastic change (flooding of the area for the erection of a big dam), Jean Dubost[9] documents the same amazing lack of constructive organized activities. Leadership emerged only in the last extremity—and then on a temporary basis and for a negative purpose.

In the past history of France, there is abundant testimony to the persistence of these patterns over long periods of time. None is more eloquent than this short statement of Turgot, the most famous reform minister of the late Monarchy, as quoted by De Tocqueville: "A French parish is a congeries of huts and countryfolk as inert as their huts." [10]

The most penetrating analyst of these traits is De Tocqueville himself. He explains at length how the municipal policy, and especially the fiscal policy, of the kings in the seventeenth and eighteenth centuries had quelled all possibility of spontaneous organized activities, especially at the lower levels:

> Such was the system of taxation that every taxpayer had an urgent and unfailing motive for spying on his neighbours and promptly notifying the Collector of any increase in their means.[11]

He sees clearly the link between the isolation of the individual and the lack of collective spirit, on the one side, and the isolation of the different strata and their perennial fight for rank and status, on the other:

> Each group was differentiated from the rest by its right to petty privileges of one kind or another, even the least of which was regarded as a token of its exalted status. Thus they were constantly wrangling over questions of precedence, so much so that the Intendant and the courts

---

[8] *Village in the Vaucluse* (Cambridge, Mass.: Harvard University Press, 1958).
[9] Jean Dubost, "Commissariat General du Plan, Paris" (unpublished paper).
[10] Alexis de Tocqueville, *The Old Régime and the French Revolution* (New York: Doubleday, 1955), Book II, chap. 3, p. 121.
[11] *Ibid.*, Book II, chap. 12, p. 183.

were often at a loss for a solution of their differences. "At last an order has been passed that the holy water is to be given to the judges of the presidial court before being given to members of the town corporation. The parlement had been unable to come to a decision, so the King took the matter up in Council and had decided it himself. It was high time, too, as the whole town was in a ferment." When a group was not given the precedence it claimed in the general assembly of notables, it ceased to attend, preferring to withdraw from public affairs altogether rather than to stomach such an affront to its dignity.[12]

Leadership and constructive activities could have merged only if groups cutting across ranks had developed. However, their development was prevented by the continuous policy of the royal administration, which preferred failure to the risk of competition:

> Any independent group, however small, which seemed desirous of taking action otherwise than under the aegis of the administration filled it with alarm, and the tiniest free association of citizens, however harmless its aims, was regarded as a nuisance. The only corporate bodies tolerated were those whose members had been hand-picked by the administration and which were under its control. Even big industrial concerns were frowned upon. In a word, our administration resented the idea of private citizens' having any say in the control of their own enterprises, and preferred sterility to competition.

The privileges and particularisms of the *ancien régime* have gone. But the same patterns—individual isolation and lack of constructive co-operative activities on the one side, strata isolation and lack of communication between people of different rank on the other—have persisted.

The persistence of strata isolation was especially well analyzed in the 1920's by a shrewd observer of the French bourgeois pattern of living, the philosopher Edmond Goblot. According to Goblot, bourgeois society in France was ruled by two great principles, which he called "the barrier" and "levelling."[13a] "The barrier" refers to all the kinds of obstacles raised by the bourgeoisie to prevent people from achieving bourgeois status. "Levelling" refers to the theoretical equality conferred to each person once he has crossed over. Goblot's study consists mainly of analyses of all the different and indirect kinds of obstacles and the rationalizations used to justify them. Classical cul-

---

[12] *Ibid.*, Book II, chap. 9, p. 157.

[13] *Ibid.*, Book II, chap. 6, p. 132. For an analysis of the persistence of this spirit in contemporary France see Arnold Rose, "Voluntary Associations in France," in *Theory and Method in the Social Sciences* (Minneapolis, Minn.: University of Minnesota Press, 1954).

[13a] Edmond Goblot, *La Barrière et le Niveau, étude sociologique de la bourgeoisie française moderne* (Paris: Alcan, 1925), pp. 126–27.

ture as sanctioned by the baccalaureate, professional ethics, fashion, and art have provided ways of isolating the bourgeoisie from the common man. But whatever the obstacles, they are conceived as restrictive for those who are outside and in an equalitarian way for those inside. Here again, we see the link, emphasized several times already, between equalitarianism and stratification.

Finally, echoing De Tocqueville, Goblot insists on the social and collective aspect of the barrier. It does not vanish because individuals can cross it. On the contrary, it becomes even more humiliating.[14]

Individual isolation and lack of constructive activities have been studied more recently by an American sociologist, Jesse R. Pitts. Pitts has presented a new and interesting interpretation of this pattern of action.

According to Pitts, informal activities are not absent in the French way of life. However, they are negative, instable, and never expressed openly. To characterize them, Pitts has coined the suggestive term, the "delinquent community," which he used first in an analysis of the children's activties at school.[15] It suggests a kind of implicit solidarity among all members of the same rank, which can be tapped when necessary but can never appear in the open. This is a negative kind of solidarity, directed against superiors and against other groups. It is extremely successful in preventing any attempt at leadership within the group. For Frenchmen, the delinquent community is the model of all collective activities in which they participate.[16] In a recent paper, Pitts summarizes its importance as follows:

> The school peer group is the prototype of the solidarity groups which exist in France beyond the nuclear family and the extended family. They are characterized by jealous equalitarianism among the members . . . conspiracy of silence against superior authority, incapacity to take any initiative outside of the interpretations and accommodations with the directives of superior authority, in an effort to create for each member a zone of autonomy, of caprice, of creativity.[17]

This analysis of the "finishing school of the French citizen" fits

[14] De Tocqueville himself said about the French nobility: "But the barriers between the French nobility and the other classes, though quite easily traversed, were always fixed and plain to see; so conspicuous, indeed, as to exasperate those against whom they were erected. For once a man had crossed them he was cut off from all outside the pale by privileges injurious both to their pockets and their pride." (De Tocqueville, *op. cit.*, Book II, chap. 9, p. 152).

[15] Jesse R. Pitts, "The Bourgeois Family and French Economic Retardation" (Ph.D. diss., Harvard University, 1957), pp. 329–31.

[16] *Ibid.*, pp. 338–43.

[17] Jesse R. Pitts, in *In Search of France* (Cambridge, Mass.: Harvard University Press, 1963).

very well with our own observations of the girls and their supervisors in the Clerical Agency, and of the production and maintenance workers in the Industrial Monopoly. The delinquent community, in those cases, is the implicit pact of defense of all the members of the formal group, and its meaning is narrow but clear. If and when a member asks for help from another member of his formal peer group, for the protection of his zone of independence and free activity, any other member is required to assist him, whatever the former's feelings toward him may be.

THE PROBLEMS OF AUTHORITY AND THE AVOIDANCE OF FACE-TO-FACE RELATIONSHIPS

The specific patterns of action of the French peer group as described by Pitts, the isolation and lack of initiative of the individual as described in the remarks of Bernot, Blancard, and Wylie, the protective role of the strata which Goblot analyzed, and the long tradition of apathy in public affairs that De Tocqueville and Taine emphasized, correspond to the patterns of interpersonal and intergroup relations that we observed in our case studies. At the same time, it seems quite clear that all these traits finally revolve around the basic difficulty of facing conflict and developing acceptable leadership at the level of the primary group. They directly raise the problem of the cultural aspect of basic authority relationships.

This is apparent in each case. The "delinquent community" is a protective device against external authority—whether that of the teacher, that of the state, or that of the boss—and at the same time an indirect but extremely efficient way of making it impossible for an individual member of the group to become its leader. Groups described by Bernot, Blancard, and Wylie are extremely anxious to prevent any one of their members from raising himself above the others. If a group member shows initiative, he risks being deserted by his fellows and being deeply humiliated. Apathy, the refusal to participate, as we have argued in the preceding chapter, is a rational response if people want, above all, to evade conflict situations and to escape dependence relationships. Strata isolation, focusing on rank and status, and the impossibility of informal grouping across strata, all stem from the same difficulties. All these traits ultimately refer to the basic cultural conditions predetermining the possible scope of authority relationships.

We should like, at this point, to review the data, remarks, and analyses of other social scientists and writers who have studied this central relationship. Unfortunately, authority has been a neglected field—at least, authority as a modern cultural pattern. We have little reliable information about it, and nothing comparable to the greater amount of material on interpersonal and intergroup relationships. The works of philosophers and essayists who have studied the peculiarities of French rationalism and Cartesianism as a basis of French culture cannot be too helpful.[18] The work of the study group on contemporary cultures inspired by Margaret Mead,[19] and the cultural analyses of the characteristic plays and movies of a period as performed by Wolfenstein and Leites,[20] may be more interesting, but much consists of anecdotes and is often debatable. We can point out, however, that the descriptions of the classroom by Wylie, and to some extent by Bernot and Blancard, confirm the scheme Rhoda Métraux and Margaret Mead propose in *Themes in French Culture*.[21] Furthermore, there is no contradiction between this scheme and our model. But the field is still so unexplored that one cannot make too much of these correspondences.

We shall thus have to be content with a more modest endeavor. We shall elaborate a working hypothesis, starting with our observations in our two case studies, and discuss the extent to which it fits with the recorded experiences of the functioning of other organizations.[22]

In both cases we analyzed, there is a central and recurrent pattern. Direct face-to-face authority relationships are avoided as much as possible. Open conflicts appear only between groups that do not directly confront each other. Partners appear just like the children described by Wylie, or the famous characters of the Pagnol folk plays, who shout insults at each other only in situations where they

[18] One may, however, propose some subtle indirect analogies in the works of such astute observers as Ernst Robert Curtius, *Essai sur la France* (Paris: Grasset, 1941); Paul Distelbarth, *La personne France* (Paris: Alsatia, 1942); and Salvador de Madariaga, *Anglais, Français, Espagnols* (Paris: Gallimard, 1930).

[19] Rhoda Métraux and Margaret Mead, *Themes in French Culture* (Stanford, Calif.: Stanford University Press, 1954); Margaret Mead and Martha Wolfenstein (eds.), *Childhood in Contemporary Cultures* (Chicago: University of Chicago Press, 1955); see also the valuable study of Erik Erikson on Germany, in his *Childhood and Society* (New York: Norton, 1950).

[20] Martha Wolfenstein and Nathan Leites, *Movies: A Psychological Study* (Glencoe, Ill.: Free Press, 1950). Recently, Nathan Leites has moved forward again in that direction, discussing, in a very brilliant although still anecdotal manner, the basic cultural traits of French society and of its elite. See Nathan Leites, "La Règle de jeu" and "L'Obsession du mal" (mimeographed reports; Paris: Ecole Pratique des Hautes Etudes, 1960 and 1961).

[21] According to these authors, it will be remembered, French education "is characterized by a tight control and a repression of movement and physical aggression, a great pressure of the outside world with socialization achieved by shaming and nagging and á reliance on oral aggression as a way of relief."

[22] In the next chapter we shall use this hypothesis as a scheme for analyzing a number of characteristic patterns of action in other walks of life—thus putting the model to a kind of test.

do not run any physical risk. Authority is converted, as much as possible, into impersonal rules. The whole structure is so devised that whatever authority cannot be eliminated is allocated so that it is at a safe distance from the people who are affected.

We wish to suggest the following hypothesis. This pattern of human relations may provide an adequate answer to the problems raised by the functioning of modern organizations. It is its "bureaucratic," or one of its "bureaucratic," answers. But at the same time it is also specifically French. Face-to-face dependence relationships are, indeed, perceived as difficult to bear in the French cultural setting. Yet the prevailing view of authority is still that of universalism and absolutism; it continues to retain something of the seventeenth century's political theory, with its mixture of rationality and *bon plaisir*.[23] The two attitudes are contradictory. However, they can be reconciled within a bureaucratic system, since impersonal rules and centralization make it possible to reconcile an absolutist conception of authority and the elimination of most direct dependence relationships. In other words, the French bureaucratic system of organization is the perfect solution to the basic dilemma of Frenchmen about authority. They cannot bear the omnipotent authority which they feel is indispensable if any kind of co-operative activity is to succeed. It can even be argued that this dilemma has been perpetuated by the long tradition of the French bureaucratic patterns, whose strength comes from their meeting two contradictory and equally potent aims, preserving the independence of the individual and insuring the rationality of collective action.

Bon plaisir is the law of formal apparatus. Authority at each echelon is conceived of as absolute. There are no checks and balances. There is not so much respect for due process as in Anglo-Saxon countries.[24] But although subordinates are not protected by law and are thus more vulnerable to arbitrary procedures, they benefit from another and equally strong protection—the counter-pressure of the

---

[23] *Bon plaisir* ("good pleasure," i.e., the arbitrary will of the ruler) was the official term for legitimating the king's order at the time of absolutism. In Parsonian categories, the French conception of authority should be considered as diffuse, in contrast to a more modern "specific" conception. In this perspective, the main contradiction of French society, made possible by the permanence of a bureaucratic system of organization, is the coexistence of universalistic traits with diffuse, non-specific ones.

[24] This analysis, of course, would have to be qualified in many ways. Good observers have contended that in no other country were subordinates as well protected against arbitrary action as in the French public service. Yet the government public administration theoretically disposes of a great number of discretionary powers and only administrative courts can review their acts. See Brian Chapman, *The Prefects and Provincial France* (London: Allen & Unwin, 1955).

peer group.[25] *Bon plaisir,* however, is not completely imaginary. It is expressed in the symbols and paraphernalia of the ranking system. It bears on the status rewards received from membership in each of the strata. Finally, it may become operative during a crisis, when people must overcome their *amour-propre* and co-operate to achieve common ends.[26]

Individual isolation and strata isolation, on the other hand, allow some part of *bon plaisir* to everyone, although largely in a negative sense. People are protected against interference from above. They do not have to yield to someone's pressure; what they do, they do of their own accord. Work tends to be done without any obligation or pressure. People do not work because they have to, but because they want to.[27] This freedom from interference—this independence—is, therefore, another form of the absolutist conception of authority. To compromise, to make deals, to adjust to other people's claims is frowned upon; it is considered better to restrict oneself and to remain free within the narrower limits one has fixed or even those one has had to accept.

This insistence on personal autonomy and this pattern of restriction are old in France. They were, and to some extent remain, one of the main elements of the value system of traditional French peasantry. The terms in which De Tocqueville, among others, has characterized these feelings are meaningful: "On the other hand the small landowner's motive for action comes from himself alone; within his narrow sphere he moves freely." This is to be understood in contrast to "la petite fortune moblière" despised by the French, with which "one is dependent almost always, more or less, on the whims and fancies of someone else. One must bow before the rules of an association or the will of another man." [28]

A bureaucratic system of organization of the French type makes it possible to retain something of the independence of another time within the framework of modern organization. One always obeys the rules, but one need not submit to other men's whims. This is, how-

[25] This relative helplessness of central authority enables us to understand why it is so desperately attached to maintaining arbitrariness when applying the rules. This is the only way for it to retain some influence over subordinates otherwise impossible to cope with.

[26] This may be one of the reasons why people are so fascinated by crises and why crises are so frequent.

[27] This is, of course, in many cases a figure of speech; yet there are frequent instances of careers completely divorced from achievement at work, and situations in which people are rather free to choose whether to give or to refuse their personal co-operation at work.

[28] Freely translated from De Tocqueville, *L'ancien régime et la Révolution* (Paris: Gallimard, 1952), p. 52.

ever, a negative advantage; on the positive side, one does not gain so much. Each member of a superordinate group is given a judicial function over some members of the subordinate strata. It is still an absolute and awe-inspiring function, and he may enjoy it if he does not care too much for actual power.

Privileges, strategic individual and group influences working everywhere within the organization, only reflect the impossibility of isolation from the outside world. They are the dark spots in an otherwise perfect rationalistic system of organization. But they, as we noted earlier, actually reinforce it. They give the system its short-run dynamism. The issue of equality and resistance to favoritism is kept alive by the persistence and constant reappearance of privileges. From this viewpoint, French public administration must not be considered as a static organization. It is always in the process of rationalizing, eliminating abnormal situations, undue interference, and undue competition, and, above all, it is constantly chasing privileges.[29]

To conclude: To the French, a bureaucratic system of organization seems the best way to afford some participation in *bon plaisir* to the greatest number of persons. Its development may be analyzed as a process of granting new strata adequate status and the concomitant guarantees of participation in the game. Certain of the lowest subordinate groups do not participate very much as yet, as, e.g., the girls of the Clerical Agency. But even these employees have some leeway, and, in any case, they are supposed to be there only for a few years and may accept their lot because they have the prospect of future rewards.

THE PROBLEM OF CHANGE
AND THE PARADOXICAL WEAKNESS OF POWER

In the preceding chapter, we analyzed the problem of change in a bureaucratic system of organization from a rather formal point of view, for the sake of the mechanism. There was some universal validity in the general model of change we presented, since the main problem of such a system of organization is its lack of flexibility in the face of a constantly changing environment. But the specific mechanism of the alternation of routine and crisis that we have shown operating must be considered as a distinctively French fea-

---

[29] One can see a paradox in the contrast between the relentless egalitarian claims one always hears in all French bureaucratic organizations, and the relative lack of favoritism that really occurs compared to other countries' patterns of action. From this point of view, the difference between private and public organization may be smaller than is usually expected.

ture, inasmuch as it relies on the complex model of individual isolation, lack of communication between strata, and avoidance of face-to-face relationships that we have described. We have shown that, if authority is conceived of as diffuse and absolute, if it cannot be shared or compromised, and if dependence relationships, at the same time, are not easily accepted, then impersonal rules and centralization offer the only way out of the inevitable contradictions. As a consequence, however, power will tend to recede further and further away, and the kind of rigidity that will develop will make it impossible to adjust gradually to the transformations of the environment. No real change will be accepted without a formal rewriting of the rules, and this will be considered a great crisis by all the people who may be affected.

One can now understand the paradox of the weakness of the ostensibly omnipotent central power that has been frequently emphasized by many observers of French administrative practices, as well as French traditional political life.

People on top theoretically have a great deal of power and often much more power than they would have in other, more authoritarian societies. But these powers are not very useful, since people on top can act only in an impersonal way and can in no way interfere with the subordinate strata. They cannot, therefore, provide real leadership on a daily basis. If they want to introduce change, they must go through the long and difficult ordeal of a crisis. Thus, although they are all-powerful because they are at the apex of the whole centralized system, they are made so weak by the pattern of resistance of the different isolated strata that they can use their power only in truly exceptional circumstances.

This is what we observed in both the Clerical Agency and the Industrial Monopoly. In the Clerical Agency, the whole militaristic structure converged on a weak and divided management whose only function was to maintain the system in its present stable steady state. This management, unable to discriminate between its supervisors, could not even try to propose change. Change could come only from further up, i.e., from the all-powerful Ministry. However, the Ministry's services were so far removed that their possibilities of action were extremely reduced and their grand schemes very rarely put into practice.

In the Industrial Monopoly, only the director and his assistant were able to make changes in the factory. But their power, which was theoretically great, was held completely in check by the inadequacy of the communications system that was the consequence of the power structure we have analyzed. The general management, which had always been careful to preserve all its rights and privileges of absolute power, was completely the prisoner of the tight impersonal system it had built to maintain these prerogatives.

Such stalemates can be broken only through crises. Indeed, serious crises attended the source of the main developments of the two organizations. These situations are, of course, characteristic of well-protected areas, where bureaucratic tendencies can develop easily. But similar patterns are recurrent in France's organizational life in the political as well as in the economic field. This is well known in the over-centralized polity, where, as we shall see later, there has been a regular rhythm of small crises, whose problem-solving functions were preponderant, deeply felt regime crises, and revolutions corresponding to major readjustments.[30] Even in the social and economic field the resistance to change of a rigid structure seems to have led also to successive crises of readjustment.

A Parsonian interpretation of the whole system may easily be made by emphasizing this extremely important end product. Or one may simply say that, basically, French society did not accept change as a value or did not accept it so much as Anglo-Saxon societies, especially American society. Upon careful study, however, it does not seem that the French record is too bad, compared to its neighbors'. In terms of the rate of increase of the whole national product, France has lagged behind at certain periods but made up for it later. In the long run, all Western European countries have ended up with 2 or 3 per cent annual increases,[31] and the slight differences which can be observed cannot rationally be considered to correspond to such deep differences in values.

In our view, the pattern of change, and not the amount of change itself, must be considered as the basic variable. Certain values condition the prevailing patterns—the values of harmony, security, and independence, the difficulty of assuming face-to-face conflicts and face-to-face dependence relationships and of tolerating ambiguous situations; ultimately, the value of *bon plaisir*, the primacy given to rational well-ordered mastery over the environment. Frenchmen do not dislike change; they dislike disorder, conflict, everything that may bring uncontrolled relationships; they cannot move in ambiguous, potentially disruptive situations. Like players in stalemate (or adversaries in a war of position), they wait for an opening; and when it comes, most probably from the outside, they move in, all at once, thus reconstructing a new stalemate. What they fear is not change itself, but the risks they may encounter if the stalemate that protects them (and restricts them at the same time) were to disappear.

---

[30] Wars have often performed the function of revolutions.

[31] See e.g., Charles Kindleberger, "The Postwar Resurgence of the French Economy," in *In Search of France* (Cambridge Mass.: Harvard University Press, 1963), pp. 118–58.

One may argue that the prevalence of these values in a given society is certain to prevent progress, but this is only partially true. The French model of change also presents certain advantages. It does not prevent, and may even stimulate, individual pioneering; and it is especially successful in establishing rational and coherent impersonal systems.[32] As we shall see later, French successes have always been most conspicuous at the two ends of the scale—individual explorations in science and adventures where man is complete master of his own endeavor; and large-scale routine operations where a bureaucratic system of organization that protects the individual completely from human interference is more efficient than more flexible competitive systems.[33]

OTHER POSSIBLE MODELS OF
BUREAUCRATIC SYSTEMS OF ORGANIZATION

By emphasizing French bureaucratic patterns, we have risked confusing bureaucracy with the French type of centralization. Similar tendencies, however, seem to exist everywhere in industrialized countries, and their consequences are similar to those in France. The fact that they are more prevalent in France does not necessarily mean that French organizations are more bureaucratic, since bureaucratic patterns may develop out of other tendencies. Adhering to our definition of a bureaucratic system of organization as a system where the feedback process does not function well—i.e., where errors cannot be taken into account to correct the system—we may easily conceive of other models of complex organizational behavior that may be considered bureaucratic.[34]

Only systematic, empirical, international comparisons that bear on the different patterns of interpersonal and intergroup relationships within complex organizations could enable us to propose a truly general theory. But we can broaden our first hypothesis by discussing

[32] Frenchmen have been known throughout modern history both for adventurous explorations and for bureaucratic achievements. The comparison of French and British colonization in the New World is a good example. On the one side, a centralized and well-controlled society and a multitude of lone adventurers, the *coureurs de bois*; on the other, more diversified and richer self-governing communities, but much fewer daring explorations by lone adventurers. See below, pp. 263–69.

[33] The railroads and the postal services are two conspicuous cases of such outstanding successes.

[34] Such a definition is broad enough to accommodate to the common language in which the complexity of American corporations or trade-union organizational patterns, the totalitarian rule of the Soviet bureau, and the unpleasant approach of France's petty bureaucrats will all be called "bureaucratic."

two other possible models of bureaucratic dysfunctions. The first corresponds to the Russian system of organization, the second, to the American one.

THE RUSSIAN SYSTEM

It is rather difficult to compare the Russian system of organization with the French, since we do not have much direct sociological information about the patterns of interpersonal and intergroup relationships in the state organizations of Soviet Russia. Most observers, however, agree that there is a tremendous difference between, on the one side, an oppressively authoritarian system, and, on the other, a rather mild democratic rule where the right of individual resistance to the state has been developed, both theoretically and practically, as much as possible. Yet both systems have been called bureaucratic, and there is some common ground in the French and the Russian absolutist conceptions of authority. Militaristic centralization has been essential to both systems, and some echoes of the French equalitarian pressure can be discerned also in the Russian system.

There are several remote causes for this paradox. We shall not discuss them but shall focus on a more immediate difference between the two systems that is directly relevant for an understanding of the wide possible range of modern organizational patterns. In the French pattern, authority is helpless against subordinates because it cannot discriminate among them. Authority in Russia disposes, on the contrary, of all the necessary tools with which to interfere in subordinates' affairs. This is well accepted by the subordinates themselves, who do not object much to such arbitrary discretion.[35]

To understand the way that this works in practice, let us take the example of the Clerical Agency and consider how the difficulties we have noted could be solved in an organizational system of the Soviet type. We have suggested two ways of ending the stalemate of routine—either decentralization that would give more power to those who have the necessary information; or, while leaving the power of decision to the top echelon, giving them all the staff help of controllers and informers necessary to check accurately on the subordinates' claims and the exact situation at the primary group level. The latter solution to the dilemma is not unusual in the Western world. How-

---

[35] There are several significant comments on this point in the interviews analyzed by the Harvard University Russian Research Center. See Raymond A. Bauer *et al.*, *How the Soviet System Works: Cultural, Psychological, and Social Themes* (Cambridge, Mass.: Harvard University Press, 1956), pp. 75–81 and 53–73; see also Margaret Mead, *Soviet Attitudes toward Authority* (New York: McGraw-Hill, 1951).

ever, it encounters many obstacles because of the general climate of suspicion it fosters, and it does not work very well at present outside the lower echelons of an organizational hierarchy. But let us suppose that the measuring instruments are of doubtful value and that we want to break the vicious circle of routine and inefficiency, not only at the lower levels, but at all levels. Instead of checking the facts, we shall go on to investigate the persons and develop a whole set of checking and counter-checking relationships in which all members of the organization will participate. This is the Russian system.

Such a system escapes the French type of bureaucratic vicious circle but results in others. Let us ask first of all whether it can be really efficient. Its central problem, of course, arises from the resistance of the subordinates. Subordinates have had to internalize the autocratic rule to the point where they accept favor and arbitrariness as givens one does not discuss. But they cannot help protecting themselves. They do so in two ways: on the one hand, they remain passive, slow, apathetic in a way that is different from, for example, the French lack of participation (the French lack of participation does not mean chronic slowdown); on the other hand, they constantly build informal groups that traditionally have served as protective networks. The Russian primary group has always been warm and protective, and these qualities have persisted through the most tremendous changes. Modern observers continue to testify to the persistence of these traditional primary group ties, and the qualities of human relationships which one finds as a consequence, in the Russian people.

The present regime may be characterized as an attempt to integrate primary groups more and more within the sphere of influence of the central power and within the domain of rationality and efficiency. Because of its special mode of action, however, this attempt has succeeded only partially; and it apparently has not disrupted the Russian pattern of human relations. Many Western analysts think that the Russian informal network of complicity, the *blat,* is indispensable to the functioning of the productive system.[36] Only because, at the middle and lower levels, people trust each other and are ready to enter into all the necessary deals and semi-legal or illegal arrangements can the most glaring discrepancies between the announced objectives and the means provided to achieve them be glossed over and the orders of the sacrosanct "Plan" respected.

Thus the resistance of the primary group entails contradictory yet logical consequences. Central power is invited to exert pressures more and more disproportionate to its objectives. At the same time,

[36] Joseph Berliner, "A Problem in Soviet Business Administration," *Administrative Science Quarterly,* I (June, 1956), 86–101.

it is able to achieve some minimal degree of success only because primary groups take it upon themselves to evade its orders and even to disobey them.

The mechanism of the information network necessary for checking and controlling is the crucial point of the whole system. Its operation entails another series of limits. In the Clerical Agency, the lower supervisors' claims could be checked simply by giving more means to their superiors. But we maintain that this is possible only because the problem is limited and that it would be easy to get information whose accuracy no one could question. If the whole hierarchical system were put on trial, and if, instead of facing the open resistance of abstract hierarchical categories, the central power had to deal with informal and hidden networks of solidarity, the problem would be much more difficult. One would have doubts about the people doing the checking. There are, indeed, many instances where good sense, and even a sense of the general interest, should lead a controller to bias his reports to allow the primary group to achieve the necessary results. There are also many more times when the average controller naturally tends to weight them in order to please his superiors. It seems, therefore, necessary to check on the controllers. People in this type of system, where no consensus independent of the power structure can develop, cannot, however, be trusted. There is no way of ending suspicion, and on this point, the all-powerful state remains helpless.

Every police system in the Western world must meet this problem, and no one has solved it satisfactorily. Suspicion, however, can be kept within manageable limits because of the influence of the outside world. But when the whole productive apparatus has been pervaded by this pattern of suspicion, bureaucratic vicious circles of a type more rigid than those we have analyzed will develop.

At this most general level, the functioning of the system can be visualized as follows. People must engage in illegal activities to meet their obligations toward the state. This makes them more dependent by making them also feel morally guilty. The rulers are thus in a good position, since they have complete discretion over all the subordinates, who depend on them both materially and morally. At the same time, the rulers are unable to trust anyone, since there is no way to achieve the goals they set except by flouting their orders. The rulers must, therefore, resort to checks and counter-checks. This endless chain of suspicion tends to reinforce the need for the protection of the informal primary group and for illegal *blat* activities, finally calling for more checks. The source of this set of patterns is in the strong discrepancy between the goals set by the rulers and the real possibilities of the subordinates. Its first inevitable results are the reinforcement of this discrepancy and extraordinary difficulties in exposing and identifying errors, no feedback of information, and all the characteristics of bureaucratic rigidity.

A bureaucratic system of organization thus develops from premises entirely different from those we have analyzed. Instead of evolving from individual isolation, it seems to be the consequence of warm primary group relationships; instead of relying on the avoidance of face-to-face relationships, it goes with the acceptance of the most arbitrary discretion. It is founded on the dilemma of trust and suspicion, and not on the predicament over authority. Some patterns of centralization similar to the French ones may exist in Russia, but they have been developed, not in order to escape conflicts, but to apply the pressure necessary to make the system work in spite of the impossibility of trusting people.[37]

THE AMERICAN SYSTEM

The American system of organization may be considered as another extreme model whose analysis will help us properly to place the

[37] The Japanese bureaucratic system of organization presents many interesting similarities to the Russian, but also some striking differences, and it should be very rewarding to study it in a cross-cultural comparison. At first glance, the Japanese primary group seems to provide as warm a protective network as the Russian, and there may be even less individual isolation. A strong authoritarian pattern of hierarchy has been internalized, and conflicts are handled more by subservience than by avoidance. But although the Japanese system of organization has at times shown many recognizable features of the vicious circles of suspicion, and still retains some marks of it, its own distinct solution to the problem of controlling the behavior of subordinates is centered on a model of stratification which presents some similarities to the French system. One finds, indeed, in Japanese society the same pattern of strata isolation with the same difficulties of communication across strata and the same egalitarian pressure within each stratum. Japanese society is more class-conscious and more attached to symbolic details than the French bourgeois society of Goblot's time. At the same time, and in contrast to the French patterns, the prevailing pattern of participation is collective and not individual, founded upon the fact of belonging to a class and the predominance of the primary group. Thus the Japanese system of centralization presents some similarities both to the French system and to the Russian. Unlike French bureaucracy, whose main function is to maintain law and order in a rebellious society, Japanese bureaucratic power has a decisive role as prime mover. It is the only way out for an over-controlled society that cannot find other sources of initiative.

On Japanese bureaucratic features see Rudolf Steiner, "The Japanese Village and Its Government," *Far Eastern Quarterly*, XV, No. 2 (1956). On Japanese class society see R. P. Dore, *City Life· in Japan* (Berkeley: University of California Press, 1958), especially pp. 208–9. On the Japanese primary group see William Caudill, "Tsu Kisoi in Japanese Psychiatric Hospitals," *American Sociological Review*, XXVI, No. 2 (April, 1961). Some interesting hints may be found also in Ruth Benedict, *The Chrysanthemum and the Sword* (Boston: Houghton Mifflin Co., 1946) and Jean Stoetzel, *Jeunesse sans chrysanthème ni sabre* (Paris: Plon, 1954).

French system. While the Soviet system relies on hierarchy, suspicion, and control, the American system emphasizes functional specialization and due process. The dysfunctions developing from it are of an entirely different nature from those engendered by the Russian and even the French systems. Foreigners, Frenchmen especially, often wonder at the complexity of American administrative organizations, whether public or private; yet they do not recognize, when dealing with them, the same bureaucratic traits which they criticize in their own countries. Some of them, unable to conceive of mores different from their own, cannot understand how American organizations can possibly function and imagine that Americans must submit to the most unbearable Leviathan.[38] Others, fascinated by the absence of the dysfunctions to which they are accustomed, tend to believe that bureaucracy belongs only to the Old World. Few observers have understood that the American type of organizational rigidity, although it is quite different from anything known before, does actually exist and is not more oppressive—is, perhaps, less so—than other and earlier types.

The model that governs power relationships, and thus the evolution of organizational dysfunctions within the American system, corresponds to a large extent to the general evolution of industrial society. However, it is also closely linked with a number of decisive cultural givens. It may also be argued that the organizational and economic advances of American society are due to the better adaptation of these givens to the problems that have had to be solved.

A century ago, De Tocqueville had shown that the English-speaking tradition allows greater individual leeway in the use of power and more active participation by subordinates. Strata isolation is not very apparent. Leadership can be provided and accepted as the need for it arises, since nobles and bourgeois do not shy away from contacts with social inferiors. People are, therefore, less independent and participate more in common decisions. It is thus less necessary to resort to a central bureaucracy. Power is less universal but stronger within its own limited domain. The rights of individuals also are not so universal; but they are better protected, since they are protected by due process of law more than by peer-group resistance. This system provides better feedback with reality. It is more responsive to change and can tap human resources better.

De Tocqueville's scheme still retains some truth a hundred years later, when both societies have undergone many changes. His analy-

---

[38] See, e.g., Jacques Ellul, *La technique ou l'enjeu du siècle* (Paris: Armand Colin, 1954); L. L. Mathias, *Die Entdeckung Amerikas anno 1953 oder das geordnete Chaos* (Hamburg: Rohwolt, 1953); and Cyrille Arnavon, *L'Americanisme et nous* (Paris: Del Duca, 1958).

sis, however, remains insufficient, in so far as it ignores the dysfunctions that have developed from the weaknesses of the English-speaking type of social control.

In order to understand better the how and why of those dysfunctions within a system over-idealized by De Tocqueville, we must try to examine more closely the routine functioning of specific organizations. Important differences between British and American society immediately become apparent. British organizations maintain their effectiveness by relying on the old pattern of deference that binds inferiors and superiors within the limits of the necessary cohesion. American organizations, on the other hand, must use many more impersonal rules in order to achieve the same results.

These differences emerge in a spectacular way in the study made by an English social psychologist, Stephen Richardson, on the organization of work and the pattern of human relations and of authority relationships on two merchant-marine cargo ships, one British and one American.[39] British sailors take it for granted that they are in a position of inferiority vis-à-vis the petty officers and the officers; their respect for traditional deference patterns makes it possible to maintain simpler organizational patterns. There are fewer impersonal rules; the leaders' authority, since it is well accepted, makes up for this. The system operates at a lower cost and without conflict. In the social system of the American cargo ship, the situation is quite different—the authority of the superiors is not easily accepted. Subordinates are not prepared to accept their inferior position and to show deference to their superiors. Their individualism and their resistance to authority cause many more difficulties and conflicts. In order to handle these problems, American ship organization has developed in two directions. First, like the French organizations we have studied, it has elaborated a great number of impersonal rules which take the sting out of authority relationships no longer protected by deferential habits. At the same time, and in contrast to the French patterns, it has proceeded to divide authority, which has become much more specialized and functional.

S. M. Lipset, in a seminal article devoted to the comparative analysis of the values and social systems of the major Western democracies, has given a great deal of emphasis to this opposition between English and American values. Reviving De Tocqueville's and Bagehot's arguments, he shows how

American Society can be characterised as emphasising achievement, equalitarianism, universalism and specificity while English society, though accepting the values of achievement in its economic and educa-

[39] Stephen Richardson, "Organizational Contrasts in British and American Ships," *Administrative Science Quarterly*, I (1956), 206.

tional system, retains generally the assumption inherent in elitism that those who hold high position be given generalized deference and in ascription, that those born to high places should retain it.[40]

The converging results of these different works enable us to propose a more elaborated and differentiated model than the early model of De Tocqueville. But these studies are still very scanty and rely on too little actual empirical work. Furthermore, they do not devote enough attention to the specific dysfunctions of each system, and this may blur the differences. If one reads Richardson superficially, for example, one may be led to think that the differences between the French and American patterns are not very great, while both of them are in contrast to the British. Yet the differences pointed out by De Tocqueville remain basic. In an American organization, individuals do not remain isolated as they do in a French one. It is easier for them to co-operate, and they do not try to avoid face-to-face relationships. Centralization, therefore, is not necessary to smooth over human relations. If it develops, it does so for technical reasons only.

This is exemplified in the comparison between the American and English cargo ships, if one examines it more extensively. Aboard the American ship, personal authority has not dwindled so much as it would in a French bureaucratic organization. Its scope has been limited and it has become merely functional, but it has retained more of its former leeway. At the same time, the impersonal rules that have developed assume a different meaning. In contrast to the French type of rules, they cover procedures more than substantive issues. This corresponds to different types of dysfunctions. American bureaucratic dysfunctions do not revolve around the routine of a centralized power that has become paralyzed because of its omnipotence and its concomitant isolation. They emerge from the innumerable conflicts that develop between the different centers of decision-making. They consist of the procedural complications and rigidities necessary for handling them, and not of the routine of executives who are in a situation where assuming one's responsibilities seems to be the less rational choice. The main problems of French organizational systems concern the difficulty of communication between isolated hierarchical strata; those of American systems concern the strictness and the arbitrariness of jurisdictional delimitation of competence. The great development of the judicial function which Lipset has noted is a case in point; nowhere in the world do lawyers have such importance as in America.

Even voluntary organizations, like the labor unions, suffer from the same dysfunctions as business and public organizations. American labor unions are plagued by raiding practices and jurisdictional conflicts. They must devote much time and energy to finding judicial solutions for the endless cases of conflict that develop naturally from the multiplicity of their functional decision centers. These practices are a wonder to European trade unionists—especially to the French, since such conflicts are clearly impossible in a country where each centralized labor federation has complete control over its affiliated branches and where due process is not a central concern.[41]

Let us now compare the administrative system of both countries at the operational level of the county. Differences are even more striking. On the one hand, in France a representative of the central power, the *prefect,* is theoretically in charge of all the administrative activities for which he has been delegated power by the government. A number of civil servants do not report to him, and many others report only in a formal way; but he has some degree of indirect control over them all, and the scope of his influence is still exceptionally wide. He exerts his influence through the numerous committees that have sprung up to handle the multiple decisions which may affect several different groups in the *département;* this is easy, since he is ex officio chairman of all those committees. He is the necessary co-ordinator of all co-operative activities and the natural arbiter of all conflicts. Moreover, the mayors and the municipal councils must operate under his guidance. This is stated officially and asserted in practice because of the very peculiar financial situation that makes towns and cities powerless, since they can raise only 10 to 20 per cent of their expenditures through local taxes. Whatever his own personal inclinations, the *prefect* must govern through distance, aloofness, decorum, and skilful manipulation of his central position in regard to all possible information in every field and the weight of hierarchical routine. In the long run, his role cannot be but conservative, with law and order as his central concern.

In the United States, on the other hand, in a comparable unit of administration there are multiple decision centers. Each of them has autonomous legal prerogatives and extremely confused and intricate duties: school boards, tax assessors, municipal councils, county officials, sheriffs, etc.—altogether dozens of autonomous decision units, without even mentioning the local offices of state and federal au-

[41] We shall analyze the pattern of development in the French trade-union movement more closely in the following chapter.

thorities. The complexity of relationships between all these units is tremendous, and jurisdictional problems are numerous. This system has great advantages. It makes it possible to tap many kinds of human resources which would otherwise remain indifferent or hostile. Very diverse kinds of initiatives flourish, and citizens participate at all levels of the decision-making machinery. No one is kept at a distance by central authorities because there is no other way of preserving their working efficiency. The whole system is more open; vicious circles of routine and apathy do not last so long and one cannot imagine the development of the peculiar pattern of forced participation that we have described. On the other hand, the detours imposed by the mere existence of all these different authorities, the difficulty of co-ordinating them and of harmonizing possibly conflicting decisions, call for an extremely complex strategy of procedures that is the focal point of American administrative dysfunctions. Wilful individuals can block the intentions of whole communities for a long time; numerous routines develop around local positions of influence; the feeble are not protected so well against the strong; and generally, a large number of vicious circles will protect and reinforce local conservatism.[42] The American system may also be viewed as a system that cannot correct its errors easily. One must conclude that, on the whole, it seems somewhat less entrenched and somewhat more open to change than the French.[43]

[42] This is, in a way, the situation described by Selznick when he analyzes what we have called a "vicious circle of decentralization" (see above, pp. 180–81). We may note, at the same time, that Merton's analysis of ritualism fits the American pattern much better than the French.

[43] We have excluded the dysfunctions of the British system from our comparison, in order to simplify it. But the reader should not get the impression that British organizations escape bureaucratic dysfunctions because of the persistence of deferential patterns. Although they are less apparent and less bureaucratic in the usual impersonal sense, British dysfunctions are more stifling than American ones. In order to maintain the "deferential patterns" of social control, a number of symbols, privileges, and institutional arrangements must be maintained that foster unnecessary detours and constraining forms of discipline and submissiveness. In England, as well as in France, the individual may be paralyzed by these pressures, his will to succeed broken, and his creativity damped. The over-all power of "the establishment" weighs very heavily on the possibilities of renewal in British society. Centralization and state intervention, on the other hand, have become more and more the indispensable way to preserve the system as a whole in an otherwise too rapidly moving world. We may at times, therefore, find the cumulation of hierarchical bureaucratic patterns and of the complexity of deference, with an over-all result that might be even less prone to change than the French system.

Chapter Nine

THE IMPORTANCE OF
BUREAUCRATIC PATTERNS OF ACTION
IN THE FRENCH SOCIAL SYSTEM

BUREAUCRATIC PATTERNS OF BEHAVIOR AND SOCIAL INSTITUTIONS

The processes by which organizational control is achieved are central to modern societies. Through examining bureaucracy as an organizational system, we have analyzed the abstract mechanisms which modern large-scale organizations require and the rationale of the bureaucratic patterns which develop from them. Through studying bureaucracy as a cultural phenomenon, we are trying to show that, contrary to what ethnocentric tendencies lead one to believe, these processes are not uniform, and that, in any given society, they are closely linked with basic personality traits, social values, and patterns of social relationships.

Our first attempt at broadening our interpretation, made in the preceding chapter, centered around personality traits and social values. We emphasized the extent to which bureaucratic processes depend on the way authority relationships and conflict situations are handled in a given society. We showed that these relationships and situations are determined by basic cultural traits and, at the same time, feed back on them. This gives a new meaning to our French model of bureaucratic control of organizational activities. By comparing this model with other national models, we tried to ascertain the singularity of this peculiar system of interrelationships. We have been able to show the range of other possible types of development within equally industrialized societies; and this has provided ample proof of how distinctively French the apparently universal patterns we had analyzed were.[1]

[1] We have discussed social values only incidentally. This is mostly because it seems as difficult to ascertain value difference as to ascertain basic personality traits. Parsons' categories do not yet appear to be useful at the operational level. It cannot easily be decided whether French culture in general, and even French cultural subsystems, are more particularistic than universalistic. On the contrary, it is easier to admit, according to the available evidence, that Frenchmen are not so prone to co-operate and to accept a leader as English-speaking peoples. This evidence could be tested experimentally.

Organizational patterns, however, do not correspond only to simple primary traits, whether social values or basic personality traits. They are equally closely linked with more elaborated institutional patterns, such as class relationships and the educational system. These institutions, of course, are themselves interrelated with the same basic personality traits and social values. But the interest of studying this other network of relationships is in the fact that organizational patterns form the decisive link between the institutional level and the basic personality or social value level. To understand them better, we believe, one must analyze them simultaneously from these two directions, trying to discover the rationale of their interrelations with institutions as well as with the value system.

In doing so, one may throw new light on a number of interrelations between values and institutions which are taken for granted but which have remained indistinct.

Our objective in this chapter, however, is more limited. By outlining a few central and specific institutions of the French way of life—the educational system, the industrial relations system, the politico-administrative system, and the colonial system—we shall try first to indicate some similarities to our model. Thus we may buttress our original argument by showing that our model can fit both our rather scanty knowledge of French basic personality traits and social values and the more precise understanding we have of the functioning institutions. Second, we shall use this general review of some of the main areas of French life to try better to assess the role of the bureaucratic system of organization within the whole complex of French institutions, and the importance of bureaucratic patterns in general for the French social system.

THE FRENCH EDUCATIONAL SYSTEM

The educational system of a given society reflects that society's social system, and at the same time it is the main force perpetuating it. It may be perceived as the most powerful means of social control to which individuals must submit, and as one of the most universal models of social relationships to which they will refer later. If our French model of organizational control is applicable, we should find, in the French educational system, the main characteristic patterns of the bureaucratic system of organization which we have analyzed, since they all revolve around the problem of social control and could not remain in existence without being handed down and reinforced by education.

As a matter of fact, the French educational system may be called bureaucratic. It is bureaucratic, first, in its organizational structure, which is highly centralized and impersonal. Second, it is bureaucratic in its pedagogy, since the act itself of teaching and the human relationships which it involves imply an unusually wide gap between the teacher and the student that corresponds to and prepares the strata isolation of the bureaucratic system. It is also bureaucratic in the content of the teaching, which is rather more abstract and divorced from actual life requirements than instruction in other industrial countries, and, finally, because it generally aims as much, or even more, at selecting people for entering definite social strata than at training them for their future productive functions.

The centralized nature of the French educational system is well known. Seventy years ago, Hippolyte Taine gave a vivid description whose main traits are still valid today, in spite of numerous reforms:

> Nowhere does a rule applied from above bind and direct the whole life by such precise and multiplied injunctions as under the University regime.
> School life is circumscribed and marked out according to a rigid, unique system, the same for all the colleges and lycées of the Empire according to an imperative and detailed plan which foresees and prescribes everything even to the minutest point, labor and rest of mind and of body, material and method of instruction, class books, passages to translate or to recite, a list of fifteen hundred volumes for each library with a prohibition against introducing another volume into it without the Grand Master's permission, hours, duration, application and sessions of classes, of studies, of recreations and of promenades, that is to say, the premeditated stifling of native curiosity with the masters and still more, with the scholars, of spontaneous inquiry, of inventive and personal originality.[2]

It took years for this rigidity to soften. For a long time, the secondary school system, which was and still is to some extent the cornerstone of the whole educational establishment, maintained the militaristic methods imposed by its imperial creator. As late as the Second Empire, the Minister of Education could pride himself on being able to announce, just by consulting his watch, which page of Virgil all schoolboys of the Empire were annotating at that exact moment.[3]

The monopoly of the Imperial University was suppressed in 1850,[4] but the competition of conservative and usually inferior re-

[2] H. A. Taine, *The Modern Régime*, trans. John Durand (London: Sampson Low, Marston & Co., 1894), II, 162 (*Les origines de la France contemporaine*).
[3] Taine, *Les origines de la France contemporaine* (Paris: Hachette), II, 163.
[4] With the passing of the controversial *Loi Falloux* which started the century-long political quarrel over the freedom of teaching and laicization in schools.

ligious schools did not bring much fresh air to the *lycées* and *collèges*. The centralized system was extended to the primary schools, which developed, after the fight for free schooling was won in the first years of the Third Republic, along the same lines as the secondary schools. The state monopoly has persisted, for all practical purposes, for the universities, which have not since been granted much autonomy and can all be considered as detached units of one huge state university.

To be sure, there has been much change in the course of a hundred years. Programs have become less ritualistic, teachers have won a great deal of personal independence, and the schools have gained some autonomy. But by and large, the French educational establishment has remained an extremely ponderous bureaucratic machine with all the traits of our model of the bureaucratic vicious circles. The centralized authority of Napoleon's *Grand Maître* and the accompanying political pressures disappeared. However, what has taken their place corresponds closely to our bureaucratic model of the seemingly omnipotent central power, made powerless by the development of the impersonal rules it has fostered and the perfection of the machine it has created. Especially important in maintaining conservatism and routine has been the lack of ties with local authorities, the parents, and the public in general.[5]

It should not be forgotten, however, that the French type of centralization has brought many advantages to education. It has allowed the maintenance and development of very high educational standards. It has helped poor communities to eliminate poor schools and has thus brought a greater degree of educational equality, at least geographically. But today it suffers some unintended consequences; the overcrowding of programs, among other problems, seems to be the inevitable result of the natural play of experts' vested interests within the bureaucratic system.[6]

Finally, this organizational setup, which can be taken as a good illustration of our French bureaucratic model, protects its members very well. French teachers received good tenure very early—they were probably the first in the world to do so. They have been able

---

[5] Many efforts have been made, most of them at the primary school level, to bring together teachers and parents to discuss the development of the schools. For every school there must be a school fund raised and administered by a local association. But the range of decisions left to these associations is so narrow that they do not attract much attention and do not furnish any leadership. At a higher national level, parents' associations may be more active, but they act as pressure groups and do not permit much training and participation of the public in school problems.

[6] Each group of experts defends its own field of interests, which is the source of its influence, and there is no power arbitrating in favor of the students.

gradually to secure for themselves the most perfect independence, as long, of course, as they keep within the limits set by the rules.[7]

The second specific trait of the French educational system concerns the atmosphere of human relations at the primary group level, the human aspect of the act of teaching. No psycho-sociological study of the interpersonal and intergroup relationships in the French classroom has ever been made. However, the many reports and observations of laymen tend to confirm the insights of sociologists like Pitts and Wylie,[8] the first elements of which can be found in Taine's eloquent protest against nineteenth-century French educational methods.[9] There is, on the one side, an intense rivalry between the children, who are led to compete fiercely against each other with the teacher acting as an impartial judge. On the other side, there is a very strong pattern of opposition between the teacher, who soars well above his pupils and delivers the truth in an unquestioned, uninterrupted way, and the "delinquent community" of the children, who can resist the strong pressure of the system only by resorting to an implicit negative solidarity and occasional anarchistic revolts, the famous *chahuts* ("uproars").

This climate and this system of relations could well be reinterpreted in the terms of our own bureaucratic model, to which they correspond exactly. We find there the isolated individuals unable to unite for constructive activities, and the absence of face-to-face relationships between the subordinates (the children) and a distant authority (the teacher), while impersonal rules give the only standard measurement of achievement. The bureaucratic climate is reinforced by the abstract content of the curriculum, which does not make communication easy between the teacher and the students, by the special status and high aspirations of the teachers, who feel at least (at the secondary school level) well above the requirements of their role, and, finally, by the methods of teaching that stress perfect achievement, the elegant mastery of a problem and of a subject matter, and tend to ignore, if not to depreciate, the long and painful learning process.[10]

This analysis best fits the secondary schools, which still remain

---

[7] Their situation has always been, and is still in this respect, much better than that of the American teachers under the guidance of the school boards.

[8] Jesse R. Pitts, "The Bourgeois Family and French Economic Retardation" (Ph.D. diss., Harvard University, 1957), pp. 329–31; Laurence Wylie, *Village in the Vaucluse* (Cambridge, Mass.: Harvard University Press, 1957), pp. 55–97.

[9] Taine, *op. cit. passim*, especially pp. 181–83.

[10] The greatest prestige in the school community goes to students who can pride themselves on knowing without learning, with a concomitant emphasis on learning tricks and on the artifices of presentation.

the backbone of the French educational system,[11] but the same elements exist at the primary school level.[12] At the university level, the organizational setup itself widens the gap between professors and students. The number of professors is very small and there are no intermediary roles such as instructors, assistants, or tutors.[13] The university climate, therefore, is—even more than that at the secondary level—a climate of isolation and anonymity, with no face-to-face relationships and a completely impersonal system of rewards and sanctions. Students receive little help from a narrow-minded bureaucratic administration or from the overworked and busy professors who seem like bright inaccessible stars.[14]

However, since discipline and direct pressure have gone, students also dispose of the independence that goes with their being a recognized stratum within the system, and the system becomes a protection for them as well. Many students, it is true, can maintain a dichotomy between the world of examinations and competitions and the free realm of their own intellectual pursuits. Their education, however, then tends at best to be a solitary preparation for mastery instead of a gradual acculturation to the world of arts and sciences.[15] It fits perfectly well with the alternation of routine and crisis required by a bureaucratic system of organization and with the persistance of the authoritarian reformer model.

The abstract character of the curriculum constitutes the third distinctive trait of the French educational system. The emphasis of French education on principles, and on the deductive aspects of science, the place it gives to subject matters requiring precision and clarity, and the reluctance it shows for controversial or ambiguous problems, have been noticed by many French and foreign observers. We may discuss here the advantages and disadvantages of specific school curricula, but we should like to note that the French type of curriculum is well in tune with bureaucratic values of order, precision, and clarity, and that its persistence is due largely to the centralized nature of the educational bureaucracy that must prefer, for

---

[11] See the remarks of Edmond Goblot, *La Barrière et le Niveau* (Paris: Alcan, 1925), *passim*.

[12] See Lucien Bernot and René Blancard, *Nouville, un village français* (Paris: Institut d'Ethnologie, 1953), pp. 128–53.

[13] Recent reforms tend to introduce these roles, but this is only a beginning.

[14] On all these points see the very suggestive article of Raymond Aron, "Quelques problèmes des universités françaises," *European Journal of Sociology*, III, No. 1 (1962), 102–22.

[15] For the consequences of such a system on research activities, see Joseph Ben David, "Scientific Productivity and Academic Organization in Nineteenth Century Medicine," *American Sociological Review*, XXVI (December, 1960), 828–43; and Joseph Ben David and Awraham Zloczower, "Universities and Academic Systems in Modern Societies," *European Journal of Sociology*, III (1962), 45–84.

its own standardizing and controlling purposes, a general, abstract, and non-controversial curriculum. And we may point out that this kind of substantive content will reinforce the aloofness of the teaching corps by preventing outside groups from finding opportunities to interfere in educational problems.

The last distinctive trait we should like to consider is the priority given to selection purposes over functional training purposes. The place taken by examinations throughout the school years, the prestige given to such a simple examination as the grade school graduation certificate, with the social cleavage it brings among the most modest people, and the decisive and often even irreversible importance of the *grands concours* for the upper classes—all these independent features testify to the obsessive passion for selection that characterizes the French educational system. This obsessiveness is nowhere more apparent than in the competitive examinations for entering the top professional schools. Their graduates have a *de facto* monopoly on the top bracket of the Civil Service, the universities, and medicine, and decisive advantages in entering most professions and many industrial organizations. For the majority of the best French students, these examinations are the sole objective; learning will be viewed much more as a way to achieve success at the *concours* than as the necessary training for a career or as the mastering of a scientific discipline.

All these traits of the French educational system may be analyzed as being in functional interdependence with the French model of a bureaucratic system of organization. We can summarize the interrelationships between the two systems in the following way. The French bureaucratic model requires high educational standards because it must meet three somewhat contradictory aims. It must train young people for the different and difficult roles of a complex industrial society, select them for entering the higher strata by completely impersonal methods, and yet prevent the social status quo from being upset by an overly rapid social mobility. Abstract standards and early selections according to these standards[16] make it possible to meet, at the same time, the requirements both of impersonality and of the class bias.

This solution, however, entails unpleasant consequences. It makes for much inefficiency in terms of training, because of the inadequacy of a curriculum thus thoroughly divorced from life experiences and of methods of education that emphasize competition more than the

[16] Early selection according to an abstract curriculum makes it extremely difficult for children from lower strata to enter universities. Only this fact can explain the paradox of the small number of students of working-class origin (8 per cent) in a country where there are no university fees worth mentioning and where the workers are not badly off.

learning process. To overcome this handicap, educational standards must be raised much higher than they would otherwise be. As a result, the French system of education is extremely heavy for the student. It is reasonably efficient, however, at least for the elite, because of the possibilities it provides, for the teacher, for manipulating the students with the help of intense competition. But it condemns the student to isolation and fosters a great deal of aggression against the teacher. The teachers themselves, who have been molded by the centralized organizational setup, meet this conflict-filled situation by evading face-to-face relationships and by relying on the impersonal rules of the system. Separation of teachers from students will thus finally arise, and with it, the model of the delinquent community, which all future citizens will have internalized and which, therefore, will help perpetuate the model of the centralized stratified society it reproduces.[17]

The French Labor Movement and the French Pattern of Industrial Relations

If the educational system of a given society reflects and perpetuates its social system, the labor movement and the pattern of industrial relations form one of the few key spots where the society's class relationships and most basic authority relationships can be studied *in vivo*. This is what makes these institutions especially relevant for discussion from the point of view of our model.[18]

[17] We have ignored, for the sake of clarity, one of the other most fundamental characteristics of the French educational system: the dualism between the great professional schools and the university. This dualism has important consequences for the equilibrium of the French social system. It has been, up to now, one of the main sources of the complex pattern of relationships traditionally found between the bourgeoisie and the state administration. Studying this feature, however, would have led us still further away from our main line of thinking. We will find some echo of it in the next chapter.

[18] This explains the renewal of interest of modern sociologists in a field that their predecessors had long neglected. See e.g., among abundant literature, Leonard Sayles and George Strauss, *The Local Union: Its Place in the Industrial Plant* (New York: Harper, 1953); Seymour Martin Lipset, Martin A. Trow, and James S. Coleman, *Union Democracy: The Internal Politics of the International Typographical Union* (Glencoe, Ill.: Free Press, 1956), and especially the mushrooming discussion about the role of labor movements and of the different possible patterns of social controls in the process of industrialization. To cite a few works: Reinhard Bendix, *Work and Authority* (New York: Wiley, 1956); Wilbert Moore, "A Reconsideration of Theories of Social Change," *American Sociological Review*, XXV (1960), 810–18; Clark Kerr et al., *Industrialism and Industrial Man* (Cambridge, Mass.: Harvard University Press, 1960); and a recent paper by Lipset, "Trade Unions and Social Structure; A Comparative Analysis," *Industrial Relations*, 1961. In Europe, the field is still mostly considered from a legal or from a practitioner's point of view. For a sociological point

If this model really expresses the patterns of action and of interpersonal relations of French society adequately, it must also be apparent in the industrial relations system of contemporary France. At first glance, however, the organizational system of the French labor movement does not seem to be in accord with our analysis of French bureaucratic patterns. French workers have always been fiercely opposed to "bureaucratization" and have usually preferred to remain relatively helpless rather than to allow rigid "union bureaucracies" to develop. Compared with American and even other European movements, the French labor movement is still highly fluctuating and brittle; it is much more a collection of ideological associations than a solid bureaucratic establishment. Industrial relations are not very well institutionalized. They are still haphazard, and may at times become explosive.

At a deeper level, however—if we agree to consider the whole setup of employer-employee relations in the perspective of the social control necessary for the operation of the production apparatus of an industrial society—we can recognize some of the characteristic patterns of our model. Indeed, the basic problem that seems to plague French industrial relations concerns the difficulties of direct communication between workers and their unions, on the one side, and between workers and management, on the other. This problem seems to be the exact parallel of all those problems created by the fear of face-to-face relationships in our model. If this is true, the rigidity of French industrial relations may have some features almost opposite to those of intra-organizational rigidity. It has, however, the same source and some of the same meaning.

To understand the importance of this paradox, let us analyze all the different possible models of worker-management relationships and see how specific the French solution is in comparison to the others.[19] Three main models can be distinguished in the course of history. In the first, there is complete separation between both partners. Management, of course, pays attention to workers' reactions, and workers react to management's decisions. But this happens without contact or discussion, in an indirect way which is extremely easy to distort. Employers retain all the prerogatives of absolutist rulers, and the

---

of view see Michel Collinet, *Esprit du Syndicalisme* (Paris: Les Editions Ouvrières, 1952); Michel Crozier, "La Participation des ouvriers à la gestion des entreprises," *Preuves*, XCIII (November, 1959), 50–58; Alain Touraine, "Contribution à la Sociologie du mouvement ouvrier, le syndicalisme de contrôle," *Cahiers Intern. Soc.*, XXVIII (1960).

[19] We have developed a fuller theoretical analysis of these models in an earlier paper. See Crozier, "La Participation des travailleurs à la gestion des entreprises," *loc. cit.*

labor movement, when it develops, contests radically all of management's rights.

In the second model, which corresponds to institutionalized collective bargaining, each partner recognizes the right of the other to discuss at least some of its decisions, and direct communications develop within the framework of a contractual system of mutual obligations.

In the third model, which constitutes a further elaboration of the second, discussions, instead of being restricted to the top level of management's and workers' organizations and occurring only once a year, at the time of the renewal of the collective contract (or, more often, once every two or three years), tend to become permanent and to involve lower echelons—the shop stewards and the plant supervisors. The emphasis shifts from formal negotiations to grievance procedure which make possible, for the workers, a more limited but also more effective kind of participation in many short-range decisions.[20]

The second model prevails generally in Western Europe, while the third model is developing in America with the institutionalization of the grievances procedure system. France, from this point of view, must be considered as a very special case. It remains, to a large extent, within the framework of the first model, while most problems discussed in an American plant are also settled through discussion in a French plant. But instead of being handled directly between the concerned parties, these problems, in France, are discussed and settled in a different context, through the intervention of a third party, the state and its field representatives. To be very precise, one should add a fourth to the three classical models: the French model.

Centralization and state intervention have comprised the standard French solution to the problem of communication between workers and management—or, to use the term current in English-speaking countries, the problem of industrial relations. This has made for much misunderstanding. The power of the French working class is not negligible. French workers are as well off as the workers of the neighboring countries; and their weight in the socio-political game is considerable. It is not so easy to assess properly as in England, but one can measure it indirectly by the kind of protection which workers have obtained, the precautions all governments feel obliged to take when dealing with them, and the ideological deference paid to them by all rival political groups. Instead of bargaining directly with

[20] On the meaning of the grievances procedure system see Larry Cohen, "Workers and Decision-making in Production," in *Proceedings of the Eighth Annual Meeting, IRRA* (New York, 1956), pp. 298–312; see also Crozier, *Usines et syndicats d'Amérique* (Paris: Les Éditions Ouvrières, 1951).

the employers, however, the French working class directs all the pressure it can muster at the state. It is the state that later will impose on the employers the necessary reforms, by way of impersonal mandatory rules. Reforms will thus come from the political world and not through compromises directly negotiated by the interested parties.

The existence of these patterns of action makes it possible to understand why French labor unions always give precedence to political and national considerations over economic and local ones, to centralized patterns of action over local bargaining. The domination of trade unions by political parties in France is thus neither an accident nor the result of an ideological choice, but is a necessity in a system of relationships where the central state holds the key to most problems.

The consequences of this situation can be observed directly at the plant level. First, there are problems, such as social security and family allowances, that are now as completely out of the range of workers' and employers' possibilities of control as national taxes.[21] Second, most problems of discipline and working conditions are left entirely to the employer, subject to the ultimate review of a specialized Civil Service organization, the *Inspection du Travail*[22] (part of the Ministry of Labor). The most crucial problem of lay-off, for example, will never be discussed directly between union and employers. It will immediately involve the national state as a decisive partner; even at the local level, where the *inspecteur du travail* will be in charge from the beginning, the game which unions will play for public opinion will tend to influence the state much more than to influence the employers. Only basic wages are left for collective bargaining. Even in this last domain, collective bargaining has not yet taken solid root in France; it was officially superseded by the state from 1939 to 1950, and since then the margin of freedom of the partners has been extremely narrow. The state can manipulate the field by fixing the minimum wage, which is its duty—and the psychological consequences of this are often decisive—and by itself taking many influential decisions as France's biggest employer. Finally, its role is dominant principally because of the reluctance of both partners to commit themselves. Wage negotiations are concerned practically with minimal conditions on a regional industrial basis. They affect real wages only indirectly. Moreover, employers will often have discussions only with the minority trade unions, while the pressure for action will come from the uncommitted, more

---

[21] The fact that such an important part of the French workers' income—about one-third of all their earnings—is already removed from the possible scope of the partners' discussion should never be neglected.

[22] Their authorization is sometimes necessary to take a final decision.

populous CGT, which will refuse to be part of the settlement. Communication admittedly is indirect. The only field where discussion and co-operation are easy is the one involving social welfare activities that have been taken over by the *comités d'entreprise*;[23] but even there, one has the impression that often it has been left to these committees more than it has been discussed with them.

Such a system of action could not last if it did not correspond to workers' and employers' usual patterns of behavior and to their social values. As a matter of fact, it has substantial advantages for both. Because of the system, employers do not have to yield to their subordinates. They can retain all their prerogatives over their subordinates and are not limited in any way by any kind of personal interference on the part of the unions. This may be considered as a perfunctory satisfaction, since they must, on the other hand, submit to the impersonal rules decreed by the state,[24] but it is rewarding enough, if one considers that they prefer impersonal binding rules to the risk of face-to-face relationships. Workers, in turn, have a still more vicarious kind of *bon plaisir*, inasmuch as they can enjoy it only in the realm of fantasy, by indulging in the radical philosophy of revolution. But, if our earlier interpretation of the problem of participation is correct,[25] they prefer this solution. It gives them a kind of negative independence, while safeguarding their own material interests and protects them against the emotional difficulties of the face-to-face relationship with their own employer.

This system is self-reinforcing on both sides. The employers' frustrations and resentments against the state—the natural outcome of the necessary inadequacies of the impersonal rules the state indicts against them—nourish their reactionary attitudes and reinforce their attachment to anachronistic and inefficient prerogatives. This makes it more difficult for them to negotiate with their working-class partners, and more necessary for the state to intervene, if only to prevent explosions.

On the workers' side, the whole process is even more cumbersome and frustrating. It is impossible for the common working man to understand the link between his own grievances, his own action, and the bureaucratic measures that will one day result.[26] People do not participate, to any degree, in the decisions that affect their own direct

---

[23] The *comités d'entreprise*, which were established in order to impose copartnership on the employers by the Reform majority of 1945, were a complete failure except for social welfare activities.

[24] French employers are more limited in many respects than American employers in their possible action. But they have to care much less about the reactions of the workers and the unions.

[25] See above, pp. 204–7.

[26] Such frustrations exist in any system of industrial relations, but the third model we have analyzed engenders a striking improvement.

environment. Their pent-up frustrations about the inadequate application of the impersonal rules in the daily life of the plant, and the
impression they have that *their own* personal grievances will never
really be settled, reinforce their radical beliefs, and thus provide more
support for the revolutionary philosophy that gives them vicarious
omnipotence and makes actual participation more difficult.

The trade-union leaders, in turn, know that their own successes
and the only advances they have made have come through the mediation of politics, and that the real power with which to deal is the
power of the state. In short-range terms, their most rational strategy
must give priority to influencing and blackmailing the state by
political action, manifestations, and strikes which can upset the
delicate balance of the political game.[27]

A comparative analysis of the two deep social crises that shook
social relations in France and in the United States in 1936–37 provides the best illustration of this peculiar system. The French and
the American sit-down strikes present many similarities. They appeared in a comparable political climate and raised the same passions
among the same groups. In both countries, the strikers won with
great popular enthusiasm against a very powerful and numerous
opposition; the alignment of forces was comparable, and the methods
were similar. Yet the consequences in the two countries were extremely different.

In America, the labor movement succeeded in imposing the general spread and the institutionalization of the collective bargaining
system which has never been called into question since. It prepared,
with the introduction of the shop stewards, the further development
of the third model of industrial relations.

In France, the success of the sit-down strikes failed to impose a
recognition of the unions on a permanent basis. It led, finally, to a
further bureaucratization of industrial relations and to the ascend-
ancy of the Communist party as the preponderant influence on the
French workers. The socialist ministers who governed France at the
time, although very new in this role, had the same cautious and
bureaucratic reaction that any other French government would have
had. In order to control the possible consequences of the movement,
they established a state system of compulsory arbitration and imposed
the extension of the provisions of already signed collective contracts
on all other enterprises of the same type in the same region.[28] At the
time, this procedure increased the gains of the workers. However, it

---

[27] This pattern has not changed under the Fifth Republic, although, during the
first two years, the trade unions' possibilities of putting pressure on the state had
been, temporarily, sharply curtailed.

[28] This procedure, which has not been widely studied, is still one of the great
innovations of the French system of industrial relations.

transformed the results of these first attempts at bargaining into a sort of first draft of legislative action, and gave the state a decisive influence over the whole field. Their decisions may have been influenced by their fear of the Communist threat, but they finally helped the Communists to consolidate their influence. The Communist party may have benefited in any case, through being the only organization capable of providing leadership on a large scale for the sit-down strikes and for the hundreds of new locals and committees mushrooming everywhere afterwards.[29] Still, the intervention of the state gave the Communists the crucial argument by preventing the new rank-and-file leaders from participating on a serious basis in any decisive discussions. The new labor leadership at that time all experienced personally the fact that the only important struggle was at the national level, and realized that to be serious and responsible leaders they would have to use their own local grievances to further the revolutionary cause. No wonder they became ready to trust blindly the party which most consistently upheld a point of view both radical and responsible. It corresponded exactly to their situation and to their wants.[30]

The present apparent helplessness of the labor movement is the direct consequence of this recent history. It stems from the predominance of this "bureaucratic" pattern of action which it has helped to reinforce and to extend to this new field. The French labor movement is both weak in numbers and quality of participation, and deeply political and radical in orientation. It must be politically oriented because of the importance of the state in the strategy of the social struggle; but this political orientation makes for weakness, because it imposes bureaucratic centralization and prevents the rank-and-file from participating directly and consciously. To fill the gap, it is necessary to resort to a radical ideology which is the only way to maintain the coherence of the movement and to give some rationale to the cumbersome tactics and the many manipulations of the local groups. Radical ideology, however, frightens the bulk of the working class; in France, it inevitably brought and maintained a state of division. There is no way out of this vicious circle other than a profound crisis. Trade unions are weak because of their political orientation. But since they are weak, and since their only possibilities of influence develop through political maneuvering, they must continue and cannot diverge on a new course, for fear of losing whatever influence they have. The divisions of the labor movement

---

[29] This was true, also, although to a lesser extent, in America.
[30] For an analysis of this period, see Jacques Danos and Marcel Gibelin, *Juin 1936* (Paris: Les Editions Ouvrières, 1952); Val Lorwin, *The French Labor Movement* (Cambridge, Mass.: Harvard University Press, 1954); L. Bodin and J. Touchard, *Front populaire 1936* (Paris: Collection Kiosque, Vol. II, 1961).

act as a further brake, since any initiative on the part of one of the three *confédérations* can be immediately exploited and used against it by its competitors. Thus French unions, whatever the wishes of some of their leaders, must neglect their chances of intervening in the struggle at the plant and local level, and devote all their efforts, men, and money to maintain the national façade and the political and territorial contacts[31] which make it possible for them to participate according to their rank in the national game of the major social and economic groups. Within this routine, crises arise when pent-up frustrations must explode. They lead to some reforms, which are finally imposed and applied in a centralized and authoritarian way.

Thus, finally, the labor movement itself can be viewed as a reflection of our French model—authoritarian and absolute in its radical beliefs, weak and bureaucratic in day-to-day routine operations, avoiding face-to-face relationships, isolated from other social groups, not very cohesive itself, more ready for negative expressions of opposition than for constructive co-operative leadership, preferring finally to submit to impersonal rules and to appeal to a superior authority than to fight and to compromise in its own right. On the other hand, it should also be taken into account that it is a powerful reinforcing force for the French bureaucratic model. Because of its radicalism, because of the threat of uncontrollable explosions which it maintains, it is very difficult for the employers and for the state to relinquish their tight and inefficient patterns of social control—without which, they have some ground to fear, chaos would develop.

THE FRENCH POLITICO-ADMINISTRATIVE SYSTEM

One of the major characteristics of the French political system has always been the contrast between the permanent and efficient administrative bureaucracy, able to remain impervious to successive political crises, and the unstable governments unable to choose and to carry out consistent policy. This contrast has become a commonplace for the many who have written on France's political troubles. Yet few of them, we believe, have understood it correctly. It is no paradox. The institutional patterns are merely two sides of the same coin and tend to reproduce, at the level of the whole society, the opposition we have noted at the organizational level between the power of the central authority as regards routine and its helplessness as regards change. This contradiction may have been expressed

---

[31] Key spots in the French labor movement are still the territorial *unions dé-partementales,* whose counterparts in England, America, and Germany have long lacked any real importance.

differently after 1958, but it has persisted nevertheless under the fiction of the *pouvoir fort*.[32]

Society, of course, does not function as a close-knit organizational system, but this is not simply an analogy. Patterns of action operating at the organizational level have lasting effects on the system of interrelations prevailing at the global societal level, which itself relies on the same cultural traits. These correspondences were already apparent in the educational system and in the industrial relations system. They may be even clearer, if somewhat more complex, in the case of the political system, if one considers its functioning around the central issue of decision-making.

In the French political and administrative system, we should like to submit, decisions are made through the working of three different subsystems, all of them simultaneously closely interdependent and very far apart operationally: the administrative subsystem, responsible for all decisions that can fit into the multiple routines and programs already well elaborated; the deliberative policy-making subsystem, which takes care of all problems that go beyond the accepted routines; and, finally, the revolutionary grievance-settling subsystem, which forces decisions outside the approved legal framework.[33]

THE ADMINISTRATIVE SUBSYSTEM

We consider the administrative subsystem as the basic one—not only because it is regarded more or less as common law and most decisions fall under its jurisdiction, but also because it corresponds to the ideal pattern of decision-making in France, since the decisions it produces present the qualities of rationality, impersonality, and absoluteness that fit the basic French cultural traits.[34]

[32] The constitutional amendment calling for the direct election of the president by universal suffrage and the subsequent parliamentary election giving a clear majority in the UNR may, however, lay foundations for a much deeper change.

[33] This hypothesis should be discussed at much greater length. But we would like to consider it, for the moment, as a convenient way to explore the interrelationships between different, and even opposite, patterns on action in France.

[34] The term "administrative system," as used here, covers all the public administrations and all the semipublic organizations which must use the same administrative procedures. It is surprising to see that, in spite of its central importance for the political and social life of the country, the French administrative system has very seldom been studied from a sociological point of view. De Tocqueville and Taine have made a magistral analysis (in, respectively, *L'ancien régime et la Révolution* [Paris, 1857] and *Les Origines de la France contemporaine* [Paris, Calman Levy, 1877]). Since that time, however, one can point to only a few English-language investigations, such as the excellent thesis of Walter Rice Sharp on the functioning of French public administration in the 1920's (*The French Civil Service: Bureaucracy in Transition* [New York: Macmillan, 1931]); Brian Chapman's very good book on the *prefects* (*The Prefects and Provincial France* [London: Allen & Unwin, 1955]); and a more general and ambitious analysis

The administrative system operates through a complex network of public agencies which are deeply influenced by the bureaucratic traits of the French model. As such, it suffers from the same basic dysfunctions that are inherent in the model. Three major difficulties are apparent. First, decisions can never be really adequate, because people who have the power to decide remain far above the pressures of those who are affected by their decisions.[35] Second, the rigidity of each organization's relations with the environment and the parallel rigidity found in the relations between different organizations raise difficult problems of co-ordination. Finally, the over-all and recurrent problem of adjusting to change that plagues bureaucratic organizations cannot be satisfactorily solved.

To meet these problems, the administrative subsystem has elaborated special institutions and special patterns of action which entail general consequences for the whole political and administrative system. Let us take, for example, the problem of co-ordination. It is extremely difficult to solve, because of the fears of conflict and of face-to-face relationships that we analyzed earlier. French administrative organizations attempt to solve it, on the one hand, by exerting a great deal of self-restraint in order not to risk a conflict with another organization—this is the generalized fear of overlapping which is a characteristic paralyzing feature of French administration[36]—and, on the other hand, by calling for an over-all supra-organizational centralization.

by Alfred Diamant ("The French Administrative System," in William J. Siffin, *Toward the Comparative Study of Public Administrations* [Bloomington: Indiana University Press, 1959], pp. 182–218), which is, however, much too simplified and relies too heavily on the image of a static France popularized by Herbert Luethy. Numerous valuable works have appeared in France, but they give only a technical and narrow view of the field, whether written by jurists like Duguit and Hauriou or by administrative experts (see, e.g., the book by Roger Grégoire *La fonction publique* [Paris: Armand Colin, 1954], which centers on the technical aspects of the problems of personnel; and the book by Gabriel Ardant, *Techniques de l'Etat* [Paris: Presses Universitaires, 1953] which deals only with problems of efficiency).

[35] In order for a reform to be successful, it must be elaborated by people who are in a position to keep aloof from all pressure groups and thus also from all experts.

[36] French higher civil servants have a sort of panicky fear of possible overlapping. While American administrators do not mind setting up two or three competitive agencies whose conflicts will certainly entail waste, but which will also bring new ideas and interesting change, French administrators spend much of their time trying to avoid possible overlapping. They are motivated, we suggest, by their conception of authority as an absolute that cannot be shared, discussed, or compromised. If they prefer restraint to imperialism, this is not for co-operative purposes, but for the preservation of the integrity of the organization's power; this attitude tends, therefore, to result mostly in caution and conservatism, and to reinforce the pattern of over-all centralization which curtails the possibilities of initiative and autonomous development of each organization.

This pattern of co-ordination reinforces the lack of communication between strata and increases the remoteness from the field of decision-making. To meet this problem, administrative authorities multiply consultative committees at the middle and higher levels. This makes it possible to avoid gross inadequacies, but it also has negative consequences. Conflict cannot be solved within these committees. It can only be brought before the representatives of the responsible agency, which will later make its decision unilaterally. This means that the affected interests represented in these committees will be defended in a rigid and uncompromising way; every one of the participants will insist on his rights and principles for fear of his voice's being silenced by his antagonists.

All these pressures, finally, will tend to paralyze still further the responsible agency. We come to the following paradox: all these administrative practices have only entailed more detours, more delays, and more conservative pressures, so that reform-minded administrators tend to be contemptuous of the influence of the committees and to adopt a disrespectful attitude when they have to deal with them—which, of course, does not foster co-operation.

The more ancient institution of the *prefects* is more efficient in this respect.[37] The *prefects* are the only strong link between the local and field problems and the different bureaucratic systems of organization. This explains their strength and the prestige and influence they wield. Basically, however, their situation vis-à-vis the public and the local interests is not very different. They are extremely powerful in keeping order and insuring the maintenance of equilibrium between the ranks and privileges of all participating groups, but they cannot play a long-range innovating role, since they are not in a position to help solve conflicts dynamically.[38]

The consequences of these patterns of co-ordination and of decision-making together reinforce the extreme caution and routinism of the organization leaders, and the frustrations and lack of initiative of the lower echelons and the public that are characteristic of a bureaucratic system of organization. This indicates again that change is the basic problem of the whole administrative subsystem.

We have already discussed at length the pattern of routine and crisis that is the logical response of a bureaucratic organization to change. We have also noted that the French administrative estab-

---

[37] See Chapman, *op. cit.*; Diamant, *op. cit.*; and Crozier "Le Corps prefectoral en action," *Séminaire de Science Administrative* (Paris: Institut d'Etudes Politiques, 1960).

[38] The constructive aspect of their role consists in helping to rationalize administrative methods and to extend, to all parts of the country, initiative and progress that has been halted for various reasons.

lishment has developed, with the *Grands Corps*,[39] certain tight groups of higher civil servants, remote from all kind of pressures, who can act as agents of change capable of cushioning the difficulties of at least minor crises. This integration of change within the model and the existence of absorption-of-crises functions make for a much greater smoothness in the older administrative agencies, where the pattern has been better elaborated. But these rather esoteric interventions do not make for much participation on the part of the citizens. Administrative reforms develop only in the direction of more centralization, by extending the application of principles arrived at in earlier crises. Like the *prefects*, therefore, the *Grands Corps* cannot really play the role of prime mover. Their influence is exerted more in the interests of peace, order, and harmony than in the interests of experimentation and innovation. The administrative subsystem, therefore, must finally resort to the deliberative policy-making system. But it does so only at the highest level, and its preponderance at all other levels has direct consequences for the process of change, its timing, and its rhythm. Because of this arrangement, French policy-making authorities are too much estranged from the actual problems of the citizens and cannot play their role properly.

THE POLICY-MAKING SUBSYSTEM

There is nothing surprising, of course, in the fact that deliberative bodies and political figures are given the rights and duties of making decisions to promote new policies, i.e., to permit adjustment to change. This happens in all Western democracies. But until now there has been something peculiar in the French model. First, these functions were performed only at the very top level. Second, they were performed in an anarchistic and confused way without any kind of specialization. Parliamentary seeming omnipotence and simultaneous powerlessness reflected very well the central dilemma over authority which we have discussed and were, at the same time, consequences of the predominance of the administrative patterns of action.

Traditionally, the French policy-making system has been formed by the national parliament and the government. No other deliberative body of any importance has existed. They have all disappeared in the course of time during the long process of centralization, and the void was filled everywhere by administrative bodies. Having no rivals and no political authority with which to compete, parliament

[39] On the *Grands Corps* see above, p. 198, n. 25.

has had attention focused on it. However, its powers were not enhanced, because the predominance of Civil Service at the local and intermediate level has estranged it completely from actual conflicts. The curious paradox, however, is that this very narrow and centralized policy-making system has also been very much divided and almost anarchist. The main trouble has resided in the relations between the government and parliament. These institutions have been strongly interdependent and there has been considerable overlapping and confusion of roles between them. Finally the great difference of status between presidents and ex-presidents, ministers and ex-ministers, and at the bottom simple deputies has had a much deeper influence on the strategy of mass participants than their role as members of the majority or of the opposition.

Both institutions have had the same competence, since conflicts that could not be solved within parliament—and these have been all the important ones—were solved by bargaining and compromises within the government or by a change of government. The recurrence of such cycles has meant, at the same time, the predominance of the government, since matters could be settled only at the government level, and its helplessness, since parliament has been the constant arbiter of the intragovernmental struggles and has yielded to the government only for as long as necessary to handle the crisis it has been unable to solve alone.

This system can be considered a perfect method for institutionalizing the crises necessary to an omnipotent and centralized administrative power. It embodies once again the paradox of the helplessness of absolute bureaucratic authority when facing compromise and change. It has not, however, provided a satisfactory solution, inasmuch as it has met only partially the needs of mediation between the social forces at work at the local level and the administrative system.

This is due to the fact that the political class[40] has behaved according to the same cultural traits that are at the root of the development of the bureaucratic system of organization. The volatility and instability of the political game are, of course, far removed from the stability and strength of commitment necessary for the administrative game. Yet we can discover some exactly comparable traits. The "po-

⁴⁰ We use the expression of Nathan Leites, *Du Malaise politique en France* (Paris: Plon, 1958), p. 2 and *passim* (translated into English under the title, *On the Game of Politics in France* (Stanford: Stanford University Press, 1962). There have been many recent works on the attitudes of the French political class. We have consulted especially the pamphlet of Michel Debré, *Ces princes qui nous gouvernent* (Paris: Plon, 1957); and the more balanced studies of Jacques Fauvet, *La France déchirée* (Paris: Fayard, 1957); Roger Priouret, *La République des députés* (Paris: Grasset, 1959). On a more distant past see Robert de Jouvenel, *La République des camarades* (Paris: Grasset, 1927); Maurice Barrès, *Leurs figures* (Paris: Fasquelle, 1897).

litical class," just like the bureaucratic strata, has become an isolated group, extremely equalitarian, rebellious against any kind of authority, unable to build stable leadership and to engage in constructive collective action. Its main failure has been its inability to understand that it cannot deny the government the right to act independently, coupled with its refusal to assume its own share of responsibility.[41] The French political class has fought and debated endlessly—but on abstract principles and not bargaining realities. It has consented to compromise only at the last minute, when the force of circumstances could be invoked. Finally, the distance created by the complexity of the game has been equivalent to the distance created by impersonality and centralization. It has helped to preserve the isolation of the parliamentary stratum and of the possible ministers' stratum, preventing control by a higher authority, government, or electors, and insuring the fundamental autonomy and equality of each of its members.[42]

This isolation of the political class, its fear of face-to-face relationships, and its inability to solve conflicts have tended constantly to bring together the political and the administrative system, whose symbiosis has become nearly perfect. But the more the political system has become bureaucratic, the less has it been able to bring to the administrative system the renewal needed. Thus the very kind of sophistication that enabled the parliamentary game to institutionalize and to smooth over crises finally prevented the political system from answering the deeper questions and solving the deeper conflicts constantly developing in society.

Like all other French institutions marked by the bureaucratic patterns of action, the political system has been conservative, more preoccupied with safeguarding the elaborate equilibrium of rank and privilege than with experimenting with new policies. Mediation has been possible only for the very local problems, for whose solution members of parliament have been able to bargain with the administration on a sufficiently distant and abstract level. It has not been able to develop for national and even regional problems, from which parliament, and administration as well, have not felt sufficiently remote.

Such a game should not, however, be too severely judged. It was well suited to the problems of the bourgeois society of the late nineteenth century, for which Stanley Hoffmann has coined the very

[41] Leites, *op. cit.*, pp. 6–53.

[42] It remains to be seen whether the drastic reforms of the Fifth Republic will transform a model already very deeply entrenched. During the first four years of the regime, the struggle against responsibility has gone on as before. The decisive steps taken in 1962 toward a presidential and a majority system, however, have profoundly altered the rules of the game of the policy-making system; but, as will be seen later, as long as the predominance of the administrative system persists, the whole political system will remain unbalanced.

adequate term of the *stalemate society*.[43] The combination of a strong administrative system with an unstable policy-making system insured, in the smoothest possible way, the introduction of the exact amount of change that was tolerable without endangering the bourgeois equilibrium. Even at this period, however, it had three far-reaching drawbacks: (1) it allowed citizens to participate only in a very remote and indirect way;[44] (2) it deliberately excluded whole groups from any actual possibility of participation; and (3) it slowed down considerably the rhythm of economic and social change.

THE REVOLUTIONARY GRIEVANCE-SETTLING SUBSYSTEM

These drawbacks have assumed greater importance with the acceleration of change and with the general social evolution, which make it more difficult to accept the exclusion of one or several groups and increase the frustration of all citizens, since the functions of the state affect the latter increasingly without a comparable improvement in the possibilities of their participation. The development of the revolutionary grievance-settling system has been the answer to this difficult situation. It is the direct consequence of the failure of the policy-making system to make decisions and to associate all groups constructively in problem-solving. And it is the indirect consequence of the predominance of the administrative system, which prevents joint problem-solving at all but the highest levels.

We have already taken a side glance at this third method of decision-making when considering the industrial relations system. French working-class politics, which constitute the most elaborate part of this subsystem, derive directly from it. To start with, let us analyze the scheme we had elaborated in terms of a political game.

1. For the working class, the central state (administration and government) is the main decision-making center, even for problems of minor importance and of local scope. This does not mean that workers are actually prevented from reaching their goal. But it is easy to understand that they should feel frustrated by the cumbersomeness of the whole system and especially because it is impossible for them to participate in the discussion at the decisive level. Thus they naturally remain suspicious about the results they finally obtain, since they can never experiment themselves to find out to what extent these were the best possible.

[43] Stanley Hoffmann, "Paradoxes of the French Political Community," in *In Search of France* (Cambridge, Mass.: Center for International Affairs, Harvard University, 1963), p. 3.

[44] Complaints on this account have come repeatedly from the right as well as from the left. See e.g., André Tardieu, *Le Souverain captif* (Paris: Flammarion, 1937); and Maurice Duverger, *Demain la République* (Paris: Julliard, 1958).

2. Since the main decisions must be made at the political center, there is, even at the primary level, an overwhelming preoccupation with national politics and a sort of myth has developed around political power. Working-class militants are almost fascinated by political power as such. They do not care about power for what it can achieve. They are not worried about what kind of use can be made of it. They feel that political power is a cure-all, that if only they could get power everything would be settled. As a consequence, with them tactics take precedence over long-range and even short-range goals.[45]

3. Frustration with present-day, possible accomplishments and fascination with power are in accord with a radical approach toward politics and a revolutionary philosophy. The myth of revolution has been the only way for the French working class to mobilize its members into some kind of participation.[46] Even now, whenever the hold of the myth declines, so does participation in political activities at all levels and also the pressure on the central state and consequently the possibility of progress.

4. This revolutionary philosophy conceals and helps a shrewd if limited game played against the state that can be characterized as a general blackmailing strategy.[47]

In a country where the central state is the only authority responsible for the maintenance of law and order, and where there is an equal and pathological fear of anarchy and disorder on the one side, and of violent repressive measures on the other, the working class is in a good position to discredit the central governing authorities by making it impossible for them to preserve internal peace.[48]

[45] This may ostensibly be contradicted by the almost Byzantine disputes of working-class politicians over programs. But programs, in this as in many other contexts, are only tactical elements and cannot be considered as rational goals.

[46] This role of evolution as a mobilization myth for the working class had been understood long ago by Georges Sorel.

[47] The word "blackmail" can be used for the working-class strategy only if one accepts at the same time that power politics in any field always involves a good deal of blackmail.

[48] Let us take, for example, the very significant case of the struggle between Clemenceau, the strong man of pre–World War I French politics, and the postal workers. This was one of the most famous episodes of the labor history of the time. Postal workers had been organizing for a few years, and they were making decisive headway. Clemenceau, then a very strong premier, saw the importance of their progress and decided to fight. His postmaster general, Simyan, was instructed to go ahead. He started a long-range reform of the promotion system which could be used to deny advancement to labor people. The union struck in March, 1909. The whole labor movement came to its help. Taken aback, Simyan and Clemenceau had to play for time, and they accepted a compromise favorable to the strikers. A few weeks later, however, it appeared that they had only intended to prepare for a more decisive battle. Reorganization went on and the union had no other course but to strike again, but this was too much and in May the second general strike was a complete failure. It was followed by

Most observers of the French scene have explained some of these traits by the alienation of the French working class. This is partially true, but the expression may be misleading. The French working class is surely deeply alienated as regards participation in decision-making, but most French citizens are also somewhat alienated on this account. The difference is one of quantity and not of kind, and on most other counts it does not seem that the French working class is more alienated than the less revolutionary working classes of England, Germany, or Belgium.[49]

The behavior of the French working class can be analyzed much better in rational terms if one considers the conditions of the game it is playing with the higher-ups. French workers have learned, through long years of dealing with the national state, how to exploit their natural frustrations to obtain as many advantages as possible without endangering what they have already won. They try to make the higher authorities pay dearly for the tutelage which the latter are imposing on them, but they are not over-eager to change the rules of the game and consequently have many conservative reactions.[50]

It is true in a sense that French workers' one-day general strikes and warning manifestations are part of the traditional international working-class upheaval. But they can and must be analyzed also as a very specific pattern of action often witnessed within French society whenever a deprived group has felt unable to make its voice heard through the legal system of action. It has always been implicitly accepted that such behavior should be tolerated.

Notwithstanding the bloody episodes of civil war of 1848 and 1871, the interplay between the state and the working class in France has not been primarily one of oppression and revolt. As soon as the workers began acting as a relatively autonomous group on the political scene, the state tried to act as a tolerant arbitrator between

---

mass firing of strikers as the prelude to complete elimination of the union. What is very often overlooked, however, is that less than two months later, Clemenceau and, of course, Simyan, had to go, and the union finally won, because no political figure, even one as powerful as Clemenceau, had enough leeway to run the risk of antagonizing as small a group as the postal workers. Such a pattern was at first characteristic only of the Civil Service, but Civil Service unions were the first to succeed; and little by little the whole labor movement was pervaded by this philosophy. For the details of the struggle see Edouard Dolléans, *Histoire du mouvement ouvrier* (Paris: Armand Colin, 1953), II, 157–63.

[49] It can even be argued that on some important counts it is less alienated than most other European working classes; that social distance, for example, is not so overbearing in France as in England or Germany.

[50] The extraordinary formula used by the workers of the village described by Bernot and Blancard, who vote for some conservative notables at the village level, for a Socialist at the county level, and for a Communist at the national assembly level, is a limited case but it is representative of this kind of unconscious double talk (see Bernot and Blancard, *op. cit.,* p. 241).

them and the other groups. The Second Empire did not oppose trade unions, and protected the labor leaders who founded the First International. The Third Republic, but a few years removed from the terrible shock of the Commune, made strenuous efforts to integrate the rebel working class in the republican order. Not only did it legalize the trade unions, but it subsidized them indirectly by providing them with housing in the *Bourse du Travail* buildings.[51] It is true that the French working class responded very negatively; yet the contact was never broken completely. The threat of anarcho-syndicalism, the myth of the general strike, and even the ominous souvenirs of the repression of the Commune were used as a sort of indirect moral pressure in a general game of power politics that paid off in the long run, whatever the short-run emotional reactions of the politicians in power.[52]

This kind of strategy is not specific to the working class. Other deprived groups in France have acted at times in the same way, threatening and finally provoking some spectacular uproar to force the state into action. Wine-growers, for example, made a perfect demonstration of this mode of conduct in 1907. Its development, however, has been much greater since the end of World War II. In the case of the working class, it has become more and more elaborated and even abstract and, at the same time, it has tended to spread to other groups. Civil servants, teachers, shopkeepers, and peasants —to mention only the leading groups—resort to it more and more. This was finally also the basic strategy of the white settlers in Algeria and even of the Army officers.[53] Groups and individuals who cannot resort to such violent unrest because of their status have utilized it in a milder, attenuated form by staging spectacular, well-timed resignations supported by consistent group pressures and all sorts of ir-

[51] These labor exchanges built by municipalities with state subsidies housed many local unions and most local labor councils. It is no small paradox that the French labor movement, so jealous of its independence, was in very large part housed in buildings paid for by the bourgeois state.

[52] In the same period the German working class, even after the disappearance of Bismarck's exception laws against the Socialists, had to face a national state siding completely with the employers, while the English trade unions progressed half by bargaining with the employers and half by playing politics at the national level. These were three different games. In Germany, the working class had to bargain with the closely allied state and employers. In England, it bargained with the employers for the material stakes and with the state for improving the rules of the game. In France, it pressured a more aloof state into forcing the employers to yield.

[53] President de Gaulle has called off such blackmail, which had begun some years before his coming to power, by forcing the Army to choose between rebellion and yielding, fully convinced that as rebels the Army officers were bound to lose. But twice their cause regained momentum as soon as they had yielded, since De Gaulle continued to play the French political game of putting harmony first, pretending to ignore the officers' attempts at disrupting it.

responsible actions which can weaken a government whose main function is to maintain peace and order.[54]

This third subsystem, however uncontrolled it may appear, should not be considered only as a succession of haphazard explosions. It is, in a sense, a rather elaborate functional pattern that provides satisfactory solutions for the maintenance of the over-all system. It is the necessary substitute for the inadequate policy-making subsystem that tends always to become so perfect in its procedures that it is no longer able to assume responsibility and to provide the administrative subsystem with the necessary innovations. But it is also a very rough and imperfect method of social control, since it does not allow either good communication between the partners of the game or serious study of the issues involved. It inevitably engenders a much greater number of errors to both sides and fosters uncompromising radical attitudes.

We have, therefore, a curious balance between an overly esoteric political game that is losing its grip on the problems and a primitive revolutionary game that is too rough and unelaborated to favor sensible discussions and progressive compromises. Viewed in this way both subsystems may be characterized by a pattern of avoidance of serious face-to-face contacts. Evasion occurs in two opposite directions: either through the complexities of a game functioning only for specialists who lose touch with the conflicts they should mediate, or through the outrageous simplification of irresponsible explosions. Both methods, whatever their opposition, have this in common: they rely on and reinforce the basic patterns of the bureaucratic system of organization embodied in the administrative subsystem.

The three subsystems are interrelated not only through the basic cultural traits they have in common but also at the institutional level. They are directly and functionally interdependent, and it is this independence which is the basis of the equilibrium of the whole system. The pressure of the administrative system, through its patterns of co-ordination and centralization, tends to push decision-making to such a high level and to restrict its scope in such a way that policy-making becomes isolated from society's real problems. Thus government and parliament tend to be restricted to the role of an "omnipotent" yet helpless monarch which fits best a generalized bureaucratic society of the French type. But the more the policy-making subsystem comes close to the elaborate routine of the administrative system,

---

[54] Stanley Hoffmann has presented a very similar argument in a brilliant paper, "Protest in Modern France," in M. A. Kaplan (ed.), *The Revolution in World Politics* (New York: Wiley, 1962).

the more likely it is to omit problems that must be settled one way or another, thus making it necessary to resort to the explosions and extra-legal compromises of the revolutionary subsystem. The errors, frustrations, and fears generated by such a rough pattern of conflict-solving, however, strengthen the administrative subsystem and prevent progress in group participation and in more responsible policy-making methods.

The equilibrium between the three subsystems depends, of course, on a number of factors, and especially the rate of social and economic change, the stability of the social structure, and the problems which society must solve. The Third Republic before World War I was the chosen time of the preponderance of the deliberative methods. The Fifth Republic, with the decline of the parliament and the concomitant increase in extra-legal action, has offered us until now an extreme example of the predominance of blackmailing tactics. It seems reasonable to argue that periods of accelerated change will be marked by a greater development of extra-legal grievance-settling methods.

The traditional French deliberative system was too brittle and sophisticated to resist the tremendous pressure of a period of social upheaval. But a question immediately comes to mind. What will happen when the acceleration of change becomes the dominant trait of an industrial society whose rhythm of growth will be more and more qualitatively different? One may submit that then the equilibrium of the whole system will be called into question. The extra-legal system is efficient only when it is not used too frequently.[55] It loses its innovating properties when it becomes one of the rules of the game, and the last resort of the system thus disappears. Finally, the administrative system, as the cornerstone of the whole political system, has become much more vulnerable now, just at the time when it seems to supersede the deliberative system that had been actually protecting it. The political system will not change deeply as long as the bureaucratic patterns of action remain preponderant, but they are now, notwithstanding appearances, more directly threatened than ever before.[56]

THE FRENCH COLONIAL SYSTEM

The political and social organization brought by a Western country to the territories it has colonized, its methods of imposing and main-

---

[55] When all the groups resort to such tactics, the gain for each of them will be minimal, while the inconvenience for all of them will be more and more spectacular.

[56] This problem is discussed more fully in the last chapter.

taining that organization, the aims it pursues, all of these reflect closely, as in an enlarged sketch, its own patterns of social organization. Nowhere is this so apparent as in the case of virgin territory, where the metropolis must be built from nothing and the builders need not confront already existing societies and can, consequently, project their own image of the perfect society.[57]

Canada in the seventeenth and eighteenth centuries has been the most revealing of these endeavors for France. And the lesson of French colonization in Canada also points to the importance of the bureaucratic system of organization as an essential element for understanding the French ideal of the good society and the French way of life.

De Tocqueville, in one of his most penetrating footnotes, suggested that all the decisive characteristics of the royal administration that were to manifest themselves only later in France, had already been pushed to their extreme in Canada, where no municipal or provincial institutions were tolerated, where the most trivial collective action was prohibited, and where the administration took charge of all the activities of its subjects. For him the Canadian experiment was almost a limit case that was to be reproduced only in the second French large-scale settlement colony, Algeria. At the end of his remarks he wrote:

> In both places the government numbers as many heads as the people; it preponderates, acts, regulates, controls, undertakes everything, provides for everything, knows far more about the subject's business than he does himself—is, in short, incessantly active and sterile.[58]

A less impassioned researcher, the American historian Sigmund Diamond, who has studied carefully the colonization methods of the French and of the English in North America,[59] confirms this analysis. He gives many examples of the passion for detail of the centralized administration in Paris that decided even on disputes involving "a cow strayed in someone's garden, a brawl at a church door, the virtue of a certain lady " [60] its hostility to any kind of autonomous leadership, "for it is well that each should speak for himself and no one for all," [61] and its constant interference with the activities of its

---

[57] Alexis de Tocqueville made the point: "The physiognomy of governments can be best detected in their colonies, for there their features are magnified, and rendered more conspicuous." (*The Old Régime and the French Revolution* [New York: Doubleday, 1955], p. 127n.).

[58] *Ibid.*, p. 126n.

[59] Sigmund Diamond, "An Experiment in Feudalism: French Canada in the Seventeenth Century," *William and Mary Quarterly*, 1961, pp. 3–34.

[60] *Ibid.*, p. 8.

[61] Letter from Frontenac to Colbert, November 2, 1672, quoted by Diamond, *op. cit.*, p. 8.

subjects, obliging them to marry, giving them bonuses according to the number of their children, and prescribing what they had to cultivate.[62]

What was the rationale of these patterns of action? For Diamond

What above all characterizes the plan [of the French in Canada] is that it bore so clearly the stamp of that passion for rationality—the desire to achieve order, symmetry and harmony, which is the hall-mark of bureaucratic endeavor. It would be anachronistic and yet truthful to describe the objective of the French authorities in Canada, after 1663, not as the creation of a society to be governed by political means but as the creation of an administrative system, in which persons would have fixed positions in a table of organization, would behave in the way deemed appropriate for those positions and would be manipulated, deployed and disciplined by measures more compatible with the requirements of a formal organization than of a society.[63]

Such an interpretation, of course, is in accord with our own earlier analyses. The same bureaucratic system of organization we had seen influence the educational system, the industrial relations system, and the political system seems here to be applied to the functioning of the whole society. For the royal administration, the image of the perfect society revealed in these instructions is that of a giant bureaucratic organization. We will not go so far, however, as to contend that this model has been the guiding principle for the operation of French society as a whole. It is true that there seems to be a constant temptation in French theoretical and applied social thinking, as well as in the popular conception of the way things should be, to consider society as a closed organizational system. Administrators and reformers alike tend to disregard the human material that must always be adjusted to society, and not the reverse. Even ordinary people always talk of ranking, as if there should be a just ordering of functions and merits. For the French, things and men should be in their place and there should be a place for each of them. But whatever the strength and persistence of this tradition, it is a temptation more than a central guiding principle. The bureaucratic spirit in the French way of life has always been strong, but it has always found limits very soon.

In Canada, as Diamond shows, these limits appeared almost immediately. The plan did not succeed very well. But what is usually ignored is that its miscarriage was not due to the hostility of the environment, but to the apathy and the indifference of the members of the new society that were the direct consequences of the perfect system to which they were obliged to submit. Canadian settlers continually escaped the obligations of the bureaucratic world in order to

[62] *Ibid.*, pp. 10 and 27.
[63] *Ibid.*, p. 5.

engage in illegal or semi-legal fur trade and to live the independent and adventurous life of a *coureur de bois.* "At no time," states Diamond,

does the proportion of the adult male labor force engaged in trapping and hunting seem to have been less than one-quarter or one-fifth. Not only did they deplete an already inadequate labor force, but they infected those who remained with the example of their rebelliousness.[64]

Their motivation was characteristic. Diamond quotes Pierre Radisson, the most famous of them, as saying of their enterprises: "We were Caesars, there being nobody to contradict us." [65]

What is striking in this attitude is that it is so similar to the attitudes of the administration itself. There is not a very great ideological distance between the *coureur de bois* and the *intendant.* Both of them have the same absolutist conception of authority—a conception which is, as we have seen, basic if one is to understand the cultural traits underlying the French bureaucratic system of organization.

In this perspective, the Canadian example is very enlightening, inasmuch as it shows the bureaucratic patterns, as well as the individual rebellion, pushed to the extreme. No middle course existed between discipline and desertion, and desertion amounted to an actual curse for society.

At the same time and under equivalent conditions, the English colonies, developing without much planning or bureaucratic centralization, could rely on collective initiative and escape the wholesale desertion of the *coureur de bois.* The two patterns of action were almost opposite. On the French side, we find explorations, discoveries, individual contacts with the native tribes, and the temporary nominal conquest of the greatest part of the continent, pursued in an individualistic and adventurous way from a central establishment in Quebec characterized by an extremely weighty bureaucratic organization and by economic, social, and political stagnation. On the English side, we find much less adventure and conquest, but rapidly progressing autonomous settlements developing into a diversified society.[66]

This comparison puts into proper perspective the limits and contradictions of the French bureaucratic endeavor in Canada and the meaning of the French bureaucratic temptation itself. The temptation developed at that time in a society, still diverse and particularistic on many counts, that could not find the necessary unified leadership outside the centralized bureaucratic order. But the bureaucratic

---

[64] *Ibid.,* p. 30.
[65] *Ibid.*
[66] See Sigmund Diamond, "From Organization to Society: Virginia in the Seventeenth Century," *American Journal of Sociology,* LXIII (1957–58), 457–75.

system was able to grow only because it seemed a more satisfactory counterpart to other, less satisfactory, systems of human organization. It depended on the existence of the diversified, anarchistic, and feudal society it was fighting. What brought about its failure in Canada was the lack of vitality and the gradual dissolution of the feudal way of life. People rebelled not because their position had become worse —on the contrary, in Canada it was better—but because the system, unlike that of the metropolis, could not find an indirect legitimacy and guiding principle in the desire to tame and rationalize a society still profoundly marked by systems of obligations and privileges of a feudal nature.

In spite of the transformations and upheavals that have changed the social and political organization of French society, these two opposite traits, the rigorous and constraining bureaucratic centralization of collective action and the spontaneous vitality of individualistic adventure in exploring new territories and making contacts with old societies, remained until the end the two most permanent traits of the French colonial system. Their opposition was at the root of most of the contradictions that were to plague its development and make it so difficult for it to give way.

The most important of these contradictions concerns, of course, the problem of dealing with the native population. The *coureur de bois* tradition consisted of respecting the customs of the native population and dealing with it on an individual and human basis. The explorer could play the benevolent "Caesar" protecting the native culture and eventually defending it against the West.[67] In any case, he refused to consider seriously the inevitable consequences of his own action. He despised, and tried to ignore as much as possible, the acculturation process which the arrival of Europeans was bound to initiate.[68]

The bureaucratic tradition, at the same time, refused to recognize the existence of the native culture itself. Its avowed aims were to make Frenchmen out of these as yet uncivilized people. Both dimetrically opposite approaches had in common the same trait, that of refusing to understand realistically the problem of change. Neither individualistic explorers nor conformist bureaucrats could accept contacts with native societies as collective and human, implying actions and reactions on both sides. They were equally reluctant to accept hard face-to-face bargaining relationships. On the one side, the adventurer pretended that Western culture should not have any impact on primitive societies, their customs being as worthy of consideration as ours.

[67] Most of the time he was running away himself, trying to escape the constraints of Western society.

[68] The tremendous success of the novels of Pierre Loti at the time of the greatest French colonial expansion is a good indication of the diffusion of this attitude.

On the other side, the bureaucrat completely ignored the existence of the natives, as if there were, in fact, only one civilization. In this view, it was the duty of France to teach French civilization—i.e., "civilization"—to people who had not yet advanced very far on the road of progress, and to teach it to them individually.

The assimilationist approach has almost always been the official principle of the French colonial system. But the other approach has always persisted in the background, inspiring many little and sometimes great Caesars at the time of the conquest and many individualistic opponents of the system at the time of the consolidation and of the decline of the colonial endeavor.

The policy resulting from the coexistence of these approaches had its early successes and its final failures. Most French colonies were acquired with small expenditure through the initiative of daring individuals.[69]

The bureaucratic system of organization that followed rather quickly had many advantages for rapidly bringing peace and order to populations who needed them more than anything else, but it failed to develop strong new societies or to reinvigorate old ones. Finally, when the time of decolonization came, the very long refusal to tolerate the existence of representative authorities within the native population, the reluctance to face directly the conflicts with this population, made it inevitable that the native nationalists would resort to violence.

Assimilation—one must be fair to it—had many progressive aspects. It was generous and humane in theory and, to a certain extent, even in practice. But the complete lack of realism that prevailed in the relationships between the dominant and the subject cultures prevented the administration and white settlers from perceiving the motivations of the natives' behavior and from adjusting to them.[70] The assimilationist goals denied the existence of an autonomous personality to the native population. This provided a good rationale for direct administration methods and for refusing face-to-face relationships outside the teaching situation. But in so doing, the colonizing society was imposing a fraudulent world and a fraudulent language —of which it was also itself prisoner—on the natives. It was not amenable to discussion and therefore to change. Each blow to the

[69] This is one of the great paradoxes of French colonial history, that many territories were acquired for the French Empire with little support from the bureaucratic establishment, to be turned over to it by people who were themselves vigorous opponents of the bureaucratic system of *administration directe*. Lyautey was, at least in part, one of them. This contradiction can be explained in the terms of the dilemma of the French bureaucratic organization that needs the help of the lone authoritarian reformer to bring change.

[70] White settlers were often opposed to assimilation, but this was still in considering the natives within the assimilationist scheme.

system, being interpreted only in the terms of this fraudulent language, was likely to reinforce it. No wonder that French administrators and French settlers were to remain blind so long—their own system of social organization gave them no ways of understanding the natives as autonomous agents. Whether in good will or in bad faith, they could view them only as either unsuccessful or promising Frenchmen.[71]

[71] Algeria was a more complex problem, inasmuch as the European community was so important that it was a society by itself, and the Moslems were not primitive people, but could pride themselves on a brilliant civilization of their own. Yet, whatever the complexity of the three-cornered game between the administration, the European community, and the Moslem community, it is characteristic that the guiding principle at the last resort of the colonial system in Algeria was always direct administration and assimilation. The campaign for integration was the last misadventure of this colonial policy. It is true that it developed out of very special circumstances, but it could never have been so successful, had it not relied on such a long bureaucratic tradition. Soustelle's speeches echoed plans already well elaborated in Colbert's time, with the Black Code and the *francisation* policy of the American Indians. The rationale of this policy also remained practically the same. It was supposed to give legitimacy to the continuation of direct administration, i.e., the rule of Paris, that could offer at the same time a measure of theoretical equality between French and Moslems and the maintenance of strata isolation, i.e., segregation and the practical subordination of the Moslem stratum.

Chapter Ten

THE BOURGEOIS ENTREPRENEUR
AND BUREAUCRACY

THE LIMITS OF THE BUREAUCRATIC SYSTEM
AND THE ENTREPRENEURIAL ROLE

In the successive systems of French social relations and French social institutions that we have analyzed, we have discovered the same type of dysfunctions and the same kind of self-regulating patterns that were characteristic of the bureaucratic system.

These analyses have thus made it possible to show the importance of a "bureaucratic model" of human relations. They may, however, foster the illusion that the whole of French society tends to transform itself into a generalized integrated bureaucratic system. The problem with which we must now deal, in order to evaluate properly the role which bureaucratic patterns play within French society, is that of the existence of other models and of their possible counter-influence.

In our analysis of the politico-administrative system and, above all, of the colonial system, we have already noted the importance of other models of human relations for understanding how bureaucratic institutions themselves are able to develop and change. This concept is in accord with our earlier definition of a bureaucratic system as a system of organization unable to adjust without crises to the change of its environment and of its resources. We must now, however, look at the problem at the level of society as a whole, and ask ourselves what kind of sources of renewal and innovation the bureaucratic system must find outside itself in order to survive.

This new perspective should enable us to assess more realistically the importance of the bureaucratic system. We shall develop it by studying the field that seems at first glance to embody the opposite model of human relations, the business field. This field has been traditionally dominated by the entrepreneurial figure, who in the West has always been supposed to assume the role of innovator and agent of change. By opposing patterns of action specialized in innovation and change to the bureaucratic patterns of action devoted to stability and order, we should like to elucidate, first, the complex interdependence existing between types of rigidity and types of change processes, and, second, the structure of social stratification and the patterns of the social game that govern it.

Our remarks, however, must once again be qualified. They will remain general and speculative, inasmuch as there do not exist many works on the French system of enterprise that are valuable from this perspective. French economists have approached the problem only from a normative or narrowly descriptive point of view.[1] Historians are beginning to contribute interesting material on industrialization and the beginning of modern capitalism,[2] but their rather narrow contribution must be placed in a broader sociological perspective. French sociologists themselves have as yet tended to avoid the problem for the past as well as for the present.[3]

The problem had already been investigated in some unexpected quarters. In the pre-World War I years, trade unionists like Merrheim and Delaisi bitterly accused the French employers of the time of lacking dynamism and of not living up to their role of innovators.[4] These accusations were repeated again in the early 'twenties by political fringe figures like Lysis.[5] They disappeared completely during the long period of withdrawal and retraction of the depression and war years. But they appeared again, in even more violent terms, in a wide stream of thought inspired by Alfred Sauvy. Sauvy's fight has been against what he has called *malthusianism*. He received increasing recognition in the 'fifties, and his ideas have been some of the major tenets of the new left wing of this period, as exemplified in the magazine *l'Express*. Jean-Paul Sartre himself used them extensively in one of his most popular articles.[6] But these criticisms have always been uttered against the business community as the

[1] See, however, Jean Lhomme, *La Grande bourgeoisie au pouvoir* (1830–1880), *Essai sur l'histoire sociale de la France* (Paris: P.U.F., 1960); Charles Morazé, *Les bourgeois conquérants* (Paris: Armand Colin, 1957).

[2] P. Leon, *La Naissance de la grande industrie en Dauphiné* (Paris: PUF, 1954); C. Fohlen, *L'Industrie textile sous le second empire* (Paris: Plon, 1956); B. Gille, *Les Origines de la grande industrie métallurgique* (Paris: Domat Montchretien, 1948); and *Recherches sur la formation de la grande entreprise capitaliste* (Paris: Ecole Pratique des Hautes Etudes, 1959).

[3] A few articles have been published recently on the values of French entrepreneurs, especially by François Bourricaud, "Contributions à la sociologie du chef d'entreprise," *Revue Economique*, 1958, pp. 896–911; and "Malaise patronal," *Sociologie du Travail*, III (1961), 221–35, but they concern ideology only.

[4] Francis Delaisi, *La Démocratie et les financiers* (Paris: La Guerre Sociale, 1911); Adolphe Merrheim and Francis Delaisi, *La Métallurgie* (Paris: Federation C.G.T. des Métaux, 1913).

[5] Lysis, *Vers la démocratie nouvelle* (Paris: Payot, 1917).

[6] "Les Communistes et la paix," *Les Temps Modernes*, April, 1956. Jean-Paul Sartre, as a matter of fact, has relied more on a book by Michel Collinet, *La Condition ouvrière* (Paris: Les Editions Ouvrières, 1951) than on Sauvy's works, but his Manichean argumentation is similar to Sauvy's.

enemy: they are pleas against a regime considered unacceptable. They have therefore never developed into a comprehensive analysis. Whatever the intelligence of many of these censures, they have been distorted by an underlying desire to find a scapegoat for all the difficulties which reformers can find. None of the *antimalthusiens* has ever been able to acknowledge that, within the same social system, the uncompromisingness and intransigence of the revolutionary trade unionist, the class stereotypes of the bourgeois entrepreneur, and the absolutism of the Cartesian intellectual are as deeply interdependent as are bourgeois *malthusianism* and bureaucratic conservatism.

The most stimulating contributions to date have been made by a few foreign observers. They have tried to understand the French economic lag by venturing beyond the safe ground of geographic and technological determinism[7] to examine directly the problem of the human factors of development and, first, the entrepreneurial spirit. We shall rely on these studies to start our own analysis.

The ground was paved by David Landes in a fine technical article on the French entrepreneurial system published in 1949.[8] This article was followed by a few insightful papers by Landes himself and by John E. Sawyer. The more or less common thesis of both authors runs approximately as follows. France's economic lag in the nineteenth and early twentieth centuries was not due to the country's lack of material resources but to the behavior of its businessmen and, in the last analysis, to a social system that did not reward innovation and could even penalize it. French capitalism had been dominated far longer than that of other Western countries by family firms, whose objective had been the social success of the family and not individual profit or industrial expansion. The bourgeois family values hampered economic growth by preventing strong competition between family firms, by forcing businessmen to shun risks and making it difficult for innovations to succeed if they were capable of endangering the existing organizational system. Society itself did not reward success in business. Social prestige was still the preserve of more aristocratic achievements and, within the business world, there was a considerable difference of prestige between more noble activities where one did not have to deal directly with lower-class consumers, and those more despised ones where one had to submit to their

[7] The lack of coal, just at the time when the development of modern industry depended mostly on coal, was the main argument of several generations of historians and geographers. The problem has been discussed again in a fresh perspective by David Landes (see below) and in *France, crise du régime ou crise de la nation* (Paris: Economie et Humanisme, 1956).

[8] David Landes, "French Entrepreneurship and Industrial Growth in the Nineteenth Century," *Journal of Economic History*, IX (May, 1949), 43.

judgment. As a result, the best talents were drawn away not only from business pursuits in general but also, even within business, from its most dynamic aspects.

A few years later, another team of sociologists and economists studying management in Europe presented the same picture from a slightly different angle.[9] Their field was not the entrepreneur and the nineteenth and early twentieth centuries, but management and the 1950's. What struck them most in Europe, and especially in France, was the persistence, in the twentieth-century world of large-scale organizations, of some of the practices and patterns of behavior characteristic of the nineteenth century. The managerial function, even if one compares organizations of the same size, is much less developed in Europe than in America. In France especially, the decision-making system is centralized. The managers are overworked but glory in being in control of everything. The authors suspect that managers are likely to prevent organizations from growing too much for fear of having to relinquish some of their control. Such reactions are linked with the persistence of traditional values, which endure much longer than even the family firms.

Certainly the French economic lag has often been exaggerated.[10] But as regards the core of the problem, notwithstanding the numerous criticisms with which these studies have met in America as well as in France,[11] the basic facts on which their thesis relies and the basic relationships they try to establish have never been seriously contested.

The thesis, however, has a serious weakness. It proceeds from a basic assumption according to which there is only one possible form of development, exemplified by the American case. By restricting the comparison to France and the United States, its authors can present only a simplified over-all view of the relationships between a social system and the rhythm of economic development. This perspective is indeed indispensable at the start. It is very valuable and stimulating, at first, to use the American model as the model of a completely developed economy and to explain the European lag as a conse-

[9] F. H. Harbison and Eugen W. Burgess, "Modern Management in Western Europe," *American Journal of Sociology* LX (July, 1954), 15–23; Eugen W. Burgess, "Management in France," in F. H. Harbison and C. H. Myers, *Management in the Industrial World* (New York: McGraw-Hill, 1959).

[10] See, for example, the arguments presented by Rondo E. Cameron, *France and the Economic Development of Europe, 1800–1914* (Princeton: Princeton University Press, 1961); and the very good summary of the discussion by Charles Kindleberger in *In Search of France* (Cambridge, Mass.: Harvard University Press, 1963), pp. 118–59.

[11] See especially the polemics between Landes and Sawyer on one side and Gerschenkron on the other in *Explorations in Entrepreneurial History*, May, 1954; and Bernard Mottez, "Le Patronat français vu par les Américains," *Sociologie du Travail*, III (1961), 287.

quence of the paralyzing legacy of the past. But this does not make it possible to take into account the specificity of the French case and thus to understand the problem raised by differences in development. One should be able to explain why values and patterns of relations, in Germany and even in England, that seem at least as aristocratic as those in France, were able to support an economic growth more rapid than the French.[12]

BOURGEOIS STATUS AND THE ENTREPRENEURIAL SYSTEM

The French social system, in this perspective, presents a real paradox. It calls for certain egalitarian, impersonal, and universalistic patterns of action which are usually associated with industrialization, while remaining quite conservative in regard to economic values and business practices.

The best description of this paradox to date has been given by another American social scientist, Jesse R. Pitts. He has tried to explain the peculiarities of the French economic system by analyzing, in Parsonian terms, the French bourgeois family and its relationships with the traditional bourgeois enterprise.[13]

Three main points seem especially valuable in this effort. Pitts underlines (1) the importance and special properties of the aristocratic values persisting within French society; (2) the perfection of the patterns of social control that govern the traditional bourgeois family; and (3) the predominantly negative character of all collective behavior outside the family.

On the level of values, the French paradox lies in the close association between an egalitarian and universalistic tendency, whereby no discrimination can be accepted on the bases of birth or tradition, and an aristocratic tendency that calls for differentiation and hierarchy. The contradiction is solved through what Pitts calls the "cult of prowess," which is, according to him, one of the deep values on which all French classes and social groups will agree. The "cult of prowess" can be understood as the primacy given to the "conspicuous achievement of a unique individual in a unique situation."[14] This is certainly an individualist value and it is open to everyone, even the most modest. It can thus persist much longer than the more

---

[12] Landes understood the problem quite well and has called it to the attention of scientists.

[13] Jesse R. Pitts, "The Bourgeois Family and French Economic Retardation" (Ph.D. diss., Harvard University, 1957). A summary of his views has been published in *In Search of France*, pp. 235–304.

[14] See a definition of "prowess," *ibid.*, p. 241.

"particularistic" aristocratic values that prevailed in Germany and England. At the same time, however, it is a value that does not help develop an entrepreneurial spirit, since it is geared toward consumption and not toward production, assigning much more importance to manner and style than to results. It is also a value which fosters all kinds of resistance to standardization and the "disenchanting" of human relations. It helps maintain all economic and social particularisms and privileges, inasmuch as the kind of equality it calls for can be achieved only in the most abstract judicial field.

To these individualistic and even "anarchistic" values corresponds the most elaborated and rigid system of social control, one which is rather oppressive for the individual but allows these values to flourish. Pitts has presented a good and convincing analysis of the system of social control of the traditional French bourgeois family. The essential unit of social strategy is the family and not the individual. Business life is deeply influenced by the battle which bourgeois families sustain against each other in order to maintain and improve their respective positions. This game is extremely tight. It does not call for taking risks and moving ahead boldly; its natural economic consequence is the model of safe management (*père de famille* management). Traditional bourgeois businessmen would indulge simultaneously in petty economies and in conspicuous consumption, but would have difficulty embarking on an aggressive investment policy. Success came to those who knew how to prepare for advantageous marriages by living in the most proper way for their status and not to those who dared challenge the normal cautious business practices.[15] In this system, the firm's interests had to be subordinated to family imperatives and to the rules governing intra-family and inter-family relationships.

Family social control, furthermore, was not primarily a paternalistic and hierarchical control; it was much more indirect, and, like the bureaucratic system, it relied heavily on the egalitarian pressure of peer groups. The necessity of safeguarding equality between individuals and family branches was as powerful as the primacy of family interests in preventing the emergence of strong leadership, of clear-cut principles of authority and accountability, and of the divi-

[15] Pitts's criticisms may be excessive and are actually relevant only for pre-World War I France, but they are not one-sided, since Pitts insists on the human qualities which such a style of social relations allowed to develop. For him, the remarkable cultural blossoming of the France of the end of the nineteenth and the beginning of the twentieth centuries is due to this bourgeois family system, which would take its place in the "Pantheon of Organizations . . . next to the Catholic Church, the Roman Army, the German general staff, the American corporation and the British Commonwealth as a great creation of the human mind" (*ibid.*, p. 254).

sion and professionalization of work indispensable to organizational growth.[16]

For the individual himself, social action usually takes the form of the delinquent community. The head of a bourgeois family, according to Pitts, does not know how to participate in constructive collective action any more than do the high school children in the school delinquent community. The usual behavior of groups larger than the family tends to preserve equality between the members and to protect the group against change.

This analysis adds a new link to a more general theory. Between the realm of values and that of actual economic behavior, we discover a very specific system of human relations and ideological interests that seems to be more complex than the first hypotheses opposing a pre-industrial aristocratic society to the modern industrial world. From a rough historical interpretation, we progress toward a more sophisticated cultural interpretation. This new analysis, however, remains inadequate on two counts.

First, the model it presents is static, and cannot, therefore, account for the changes and progress that have been realized. It does enable us to understand why the French social system and the French bourgeois family resisted change. But change always comes in the end, and, however badly the French entrepreneur finally met his duties as an innovator, France after all progressed at a rate roughly comparable to that of its neighboring countries. If French economic progress is compared with the progress of the United States, the main question which must be raised is the problem of the French lag; if one compares French advances with those of the non-Western world, however, the main question becomes not why France has progressed so slowly, but why it has progressed so quickly. Pitts's analysis is not specific enough on this count, because it leads one to believe that the push toward progress is the same everywhere and that differences of achievement depend only on the greater or lesser importance of the factors of resistance. In effect, however, it is only after analyzing the peculiar processes of innovation of the French social system as well as its factors of resistance that one can both understand and measure the kind of equilibrium and the rate of dynamism of the model of economic development that is characteristic of it.

The second important point neglected by Pitts concerns the relations between the bourgeois entrepreneurial system and the state bu-

[16] This is why authoritarian patriarchal figures must of necessity appear, and why such figures are venerated. They alone are responsible for the progress of family firms. But, even if they did in fact appear more frequently than the authoritarian reformer of the bureaucratic system, contrary to the impression of many people, they were the exception rather than the rule.

reaucracy. Pitts, like Landes before him, talks about the "infantile" behavior of the French entrepreneur when dealing with the state. But for him it is only another personality trait of the bourgeois family. He does not grasp the meaning that this trait may have for the operation of the whole system. If the national centralized state can, as a matter of fact, play a paternalistic role in its relations with the local bourgeois family firms, this implies that its importance in the general economic system is considerable and that one cannot understand the bourgeois entrepreneurial system without referring constantly to the model of administrative action supplied by the state bureaucracy. We shall try to show that the key to the innovation processes of the French economic system lies primarily in the efficient management of these difficult relations.

The Opposition between the World of Free Enterprise and Paternalism and the World of State Bureaucracy

Before proposing our own tentative scheme for understanding these relationships and the model for innovation and change they tend to foster, we must draw attention to a very peculiar and decisively important phenomenon in the perspective we have adopted. We want to speak of the very deep gap still found in France between the paternalistic world of private business and the egalitarian world of the Civil Service and its dependents. Such oppositions exist everywhere in the West; everywhere a very numerous group of people complain about taxes and free-spending bureaucrats. Only in France, however, does one have the impression of two actually different and hostile worlds.

This situation is not new. Its roots can be traced to the late monarchy and its development, followed throughout the nineteenth century after the acceptance, by the reinstated Bourbons, of the Napoleonic legacy of the administrative state. It took its present shape with the definitive victory of the Republicans in the 1880's. Since World War II, the situation has become increasingly fluid. The two worlds interpenetrate and there has been a certain decrease of antagonism between them. But in no other Western country at present is the world of the Civil Service still so clearly set apart and raising so much opposition as well as personal identification.

Organizationally speaking, the two worlds are actually distinct. They have their separate bases of recruitment, their own channels of promotion, their clienteles, their political influences. This is reflected in their opposed ideologies, symbols, and even values.

As regards recruitment, the opposition is most conspicuous on a

geographical basis. The lower and middle ranks of the Civil Service[17] come mostly from the de-Christianized and economically underdeveloped southwest, while the white collar people with equivalent functions in Paris, when not from the city themselves, come from
the west, the north, and the east.[18] Socially, the opposition is not so
strong. There is, indeed, much recruitment within the same milieux
—i.e., the sons and daughters of civil servants become civil servants
themselves—but, for the rest, both business and Civil Service recruit from the same social strata (farmers, shopkeepers, artisans,
craftsmen, independent workers). It must be noted that the Civil
Service rarely recruits from the industrial worker group. Even here,
however, the greatest difference seems to arise from the religious
and geographical background rather than the social status.[19]

Much more important than the bases of recruitment are the separate and eventually antagonistic channels of promotion. This has
more direct and more enduring consequences, since it immediately
conditions the actual behavior of the two groups.

Private business has traditionally recruited its elites by using a
complex network of family and paternalistic relationships, often
with a strong clerical influence. There were, of course, a number of
diverse and antagonistic channels and the religious minority groups,
Protestants and Jews, had their own channels and were even more
jealously restrictive. In comparison with business, however, the Civil
Service was the world of open competition and of the equality of
opportunity. French social history of the last hundred years may be
viewed as a slow progression of the egalitarian pattern of promotion,
first within the Civil Service and then, as a consequence, within
business, because of the indirect influence of school and university
examinations. This history is quite different from that of other Western countries, and especially America, inasmuch as equality of opportunity was not understood in France as the ability to compete on
equal terms on an open economic and impersonal market, but as the
possibility of striving individually for selection within a very imper-

---

[17] The higher ranks, in contrast, are mostly of Parisian origin. See Thomas
Bottomore. "La mobilité sociale dans la haute Administration française," *Cahiers
Internationaux de Sociologie,* XIII (1952), 167–78.

[18] There is a well-established symbiosis between the secular left-wing southwest and a Civil Service of the same religious and political orientation. Almost
two-thirds of the girls coming to the Parisian Agency which we studied were born
in the southwest, and, among the others, many had parents from this region.
This seems to be true for the whole postal service and for primary schoolteachers,
who form the bulk of Civil Service employment.

[19] People from different backgrounds can adjust very well to the same situations
in a culture that has always been rather open and whose most important values
are widely diffused. There must still be, however, a statistical predominance of
"clerical" (Catholic) recruitment in the lower ranks of the bourgeois entrepreneurial hierarchy and of secular recruitment for the world of the Civil Service.

sonal but also hierarchical educational system. The decisive criteria for promotion have been the way of life and the intellectual attitudes of the candidate and not his spirit of enterprise and capacity to innovate. Greater importance is still attached in both worlds to prestige-filled competitive achievements, made very early in life and depending in large part on family background, than to later professional achievements. This attitude tends to maintain social distance and to reinforce the traditional model of social control of the bourgeois family.

Politically, the struggle between secular and Republican on the one side, clerical and right wing on the other—later between the radicals and the moderates; and now between the socialists and radical socialists on the one side, and the MRP and the independents on the other—has found a great deal of its organizational basis in the existence of these two antagonistic channels of promotion. Of course, there is not a simple correspondence between the "religious" side and private business, the secular side and the Civil Service. The Civil Service as such is a minority group, and its secularization was at first more a consequence than a cause of the success of the Republican party. Quite soon, however, it did become its organizational basis, and this evolution was well in line with the traditions of the centralized monarchy, where a *gallican,* if not anti-church, spirit, and a general bias against aristocratic clienteles can be distinguished early.

Since the reforms of the Liberation, the number of persons whose channel of promotion no longer depends on the clerical and paternalistic world of the traditional entrepreneurial system has increased greatly. With nationalizations, 15 per cent of the total active population—and, even more significant, 27 per cent of the salaried employees (agricultural labor excepted)[20]—depend directly on the state (civil servants with tenure and contractual salaried personnel). The balance is no longer so unequal as it was. On the other hand, Catholics have now entered the Civil Service in sizable groups, and their influence cannot be neglected, even if the basic secular hold remains. In counterpart, the influence of the public school system has spread over most of the business field with the development of the competitive and impersonal examination system, whose decisive importance has reinforced the egalitarian spirit.

Finally, both worlds have had their own symbols, their language, and their ideology.[21] The paternalistic business world valued tradi-

[20] Sources: *Resultats du sondage au 1/20 de mai 1954* (Paris: Imprimerie Nationale, 1958).

[21] These ideologies unfortunately have never been studied comparatively. For an analysis of the entrepreneurial middle-class value, see Georges Lavau, "Les Classes moyennes," *Partis politiques et classes sociales* (Paris: Armand Colin,

tion, hierarchy, the family, an integrated social order; and its patriotism was based on the occupation of territories.[22] The secular world of the *fonctionnaires* valued progress, the equality of opportunity, the individual; and its patriotism was based on the universalism of French culture. French intellectual circles have long resounded with the interminable quarrels of representatives of these two worlds, occasionally with famous feuds, like those of Anatole France and Paul Bourget, André Gide and Maurice Barrès.

The interpenetration of the two worlds, especially since 1945, and the concomitant weakening of their ideology, have strongly reduced the militancy of the rank and file and the polemical spirit on top. Organizationally, however, the opposition between the two separate worlds of business and Civil Service still remains one of the basic elements of French political and social life.[23]

Yet even at the time of their strongest opposition, in the 1900's, the basic values of the two worlds were similar. The elementary traits of our bureaucratic model—isolation of the hierarchical strata, individual equality within each stratum, and the fear of face-to-face relationships—were also dominant in the entrepreneurial world.

The entrepreneurial world was also heavily stratified; rank had a great importance and promotions were difficult. Each stratum tended to remain jealously isolated and thus could be considered as a barrier to communication. The pervasive influence of the bourgeois code of behavior fostered a sort of protective distance between them. Promotion required painful and anxiety-producing individual and family acculturation. The difficulty of the process and the high value placed on independence were partially due to the reluctance of the bourgeois entrepreneur to accept the members of his managerial force as equals. He thus diminished the interest of talented people in these positions while reducing those who worked with him to a subordinate status. Even between enterprises, stratification, while not so apparent, was extremely rigid. Altogether, the French business world even now has remained much narrower than one would anticipate from the development of the economy.

1955), pp. 49–84. For an analysis of the secular Civil Service see Georges Duveau, *Les Instituteurs* (Paris: Le Seuil, 1957).

[22] Because of the presence of private minority groups, the problem was actually much more complex, since it was not possible to propose an easy equivalence between the world of private business and clericalism. But the ideological opposition, even if restricted to one part of the business world, must be given great importance.

[23] There is a paradox in the fact that, although according to the traditional rules of the game, the organizational basis of the secular world should now be more powerful because of the nationalizations and the extension of the power of the state, its militancy has so decreased that the period has seen some long-awaited clerical successes.

The second principle of the Civil Service, equality between all members of the same stratum, also holds true, at least partially, in the entrepreneurial system. The delinquent-community behavior of the bourgeois entrepreneur insured the maintenance of a minimum of equality between firms. The laws of the market have been obeyed only to a certain point. The feeble have been protected and the traditional ranking preserved against the natural law of conflicting interests. Within the family itself, there can be discerned clearly the paradox of the combination of egalitarianism and respect for hierarchy that we found in bureaucratic organizations. It has been extremely difficult to resist the strong pressure for equality between different individuals and different branches of the family.[24] Between the stratum of owners and the stratum of retainers, the distance was enormous, but the existence of this gap made it possible to maintain equality between the owners. As a consequence, seniority and collegiate forms of leadership, while not weighing on the whole so heavily as within the bureaucratic system, tended to predominate most of the time, i.e., when the charismatic influence of the founder, the head of the dynasty, had disappeared.

The third principle, the avoidance of face-to-face relationships, also has had a great influence. We have analyzed the reluctance of French employers to talk directly with their workers. Pitts and Landes have shown their similar reluctance to accept possible dependence relationships with customers. The traditional bourgeois enterprise has tended to avoid contacts that could bring subordination or even conflict. On the other hand, it itself was founded on dependence relationships. Paternalism, which was its basic pattern of action as regards work, implied the existence of protector-protégé relationships. But such relationships, which have tended often to crystallize in forming quasi-permanent clientèles, are not so different from the parallel power relationships we have found in the bureaucratic system. In the business world, it is true, they have been the rule instead of remaining the unavowable exception.[25] But notwithstanding the numerous efforts to glorify them, they have never been viewed with equanimity even within the bourgeois culture. They are difficult and painful relationships and regarded as morally despicable.

The existence of these common traits makes it possible to understand why, in spite of continuous invocations to the spirit of free enterprise and to the principles of authority and responsibility, it has been almost as difficult to find strong leadership and strong collective

---

[24] Pitts notes that a few important families were thus led to elaborate a code of impersonal rules for allocating jobs and responsibilities within their firms.

[25] There are as painful examples in the administrative system for many similar ambiguous situations corresponding to the difficult acculturation necessary for promotion.

action within the entrepreneurial world as within the Civil Service. We tend to believe that these similarities stem from the existence, on both sides, of the same values and of the same basic patterns of action. For us, the paternalism of the French entrepreneur, like the impersonal rules of the bureaucratic patterns of organization, can be viewed as relying ultimately on the same absolute conception of authority and on the same idealization of individual mastery and control over oneself and one's environment, associated with a genuine feeling of equality that cannot be concealed by any recognized means of discrimination among human beings. In this perspective, the French bourgeois entrepreneurial system and the French bureaucratic system of organization appear to be two very elaborate answers of French society to the central dilemma posed by the management of large-scale collective action. Both answers, however different, are marked by a deep attachment to the same values.

This common substratum in the realm of values makes it possible to understand how these two antagonistic worlds can be complementary and almost indispensable to each other. The coexistence is only superficially the forced symbiosis of two unhappy partners. At a deeper level, it seems to be the best way of achieving a common way of life.

THE RELATIONSHIP BETWEEN THE TWO SYSTEMS AND THE PROBLEM OF INNOVATION

If we consider the stable equilibrium of that "stalemate society" of the end of the nineteenth century and the beginning of the twentieth that constitutes the classic period of the bourgeois state, it seems clear that the state bureaucracy, because of its organizational devotion to stability and its basic fear of anarchy, was able to provide the bourgeois social order and the bourgeois entrepreneurial system with the strong national framework and the protectionist and conservative economic policy necessary for enabling the family firm to retain its hold over the economy. More aggressive and business-minded governments would have taken risks and endangered the survival of the delicate bourgeois order by their successes as well as by their failures. This caution, however, did not prevent progress. France was not left behind by any means; but progress was to come only on her terms, i.e., in preserving the fundamental arrangements of status and the privileges to which French groups were attached. The French type of centralization has made it possible for France to keep pace with the general progress of the West while preserving very archaic organizational structures. Conversely, the family firms' co-operative way of absorbing the threatening uncertainties of the market allowed the French bureaucracy to isolate itself from overly urgent problems and thus to preserve its own perfect stationary equilibria.

The underlying symbiosis of these two antagonistic worlds can be understood by elaborating two complementary models corresponding to each system's functional point of view about the other.

The bureaucratic model of French economic life supposes the primacy of two basic aims: (1) stability, harmony, protection for all citizens; and, (2) development, so that France should not be left behind in the international power competition. Since collective action can very seldom be trusted to be constructive, and since groups have been trained only to be defensive and are thus unable to face the conflicts in which they are always engaged, the achievement of these aims requires the central state to intervene directly and at all levels in order to reach the minimum objectives on which everyone is agreed. Bureaucracy, therefore, must rule and make harmonious the entrepreneurial system; it must stimulate and favor different groups within it according to the priorities of the common aims. It cannot, on the other hand, intervene too far, because of its rigidity and its inability to adjust to change on a highly uncertain market. It must, therefore, be satisfied with applying very general pressures and relying, for the more concrete problems, on the bourgeois entrepreneurs. Only the latter can preserve the status quo, in spite of the risks imposed by the uncertainties of the market, because of their long tradition of undercover *ententes* and family alliances across different branches and different regions.

The strategic position of the entrepreneurial class, on the other hand, has enabled the bourgeois families to exact exorbitant privileges for all services they give. This is how they have been able to consolidate a number of dependence relationships around themselves. This privilege, however, has not been well accepted. French society has not tolerated great industrial empires as easily as England, Germany and the U.S.[26]

But the sheer persistence of those areas of paternalism that Frenchmen accepted has stirred up a violent pressure for equality and impersonality, to which the bureaucratic system has provided relief on two counts: (1) by offering a means of escape for people who could not face paternalistic relationships and their consequent frustrations; and (2) by protecting the entrepreneurial class against the consequences of its own lust for power and obliging it to adjust to

[26] These foreign industrial empires arouse a great deal of opposition from the two opposed groups; they affront bourgeois as well as bureaucratic ideology.

the progressing mores. The consequence of this type of intervention, however, has been to extend gradually the bureaucratic rule so that it began, little by little, to threaten, if not the bourgeois order, at least the bourgeois basic relationships. From an extreme bureaucratic point of view, the entrepreneurial system can thus be considered as the survival of non-rationalized areas around special zones of uncertainty that will progressively diminish—something to be tolerated but not acknowledged as having a legitimacy of its own.[27]

The entrepreneurial model of French economic life is the mirror image of this bureaucratic model. For the state bureaucracy, bourgeois entrepreneurship is a necessary cumbersome legacy of a paternalistic past; for the entrepreneurial class the state is a necessary evil, which can be held responsible for many difficulties but to which it has been necessary to resort because no common rule can be imposed by the weak and negativistic coalition of the entrepreneurs and because the resort to state action can be considered preferable to the rise of individual leadership over and within the autonomous bourgeois families. The state, at the same time, has protected the entrepreneurs against their own workers. It has made it possible for them to maintain the moral authority that comes with aloofness, inasmuch as they have never had to yield to anyone but the state. When offering avenues of promotion to potential trouble-makers, when imposing necessary compensations to deprived groups, the French bureaucracy, finally, has brought some very useful slack to the whole system.

The key point of the relationship, from the point of view of the entrepreneurial class, however, has been the problem of innovation. Innovation is necessary to the maintenance of the double system, because in a changing world, routine means decline and death. But if the central function of an entrepreneur concerns innovation, one must admit that the French entrepreneurial system does not favor it. It does not reward the innovator and it does not encourage the taking of risks, preferring stability and the upholding of everyone's privileges to all forms of venture, even when they may be successful.

Thus we find this contradiction: Change comes with great difficulty from the entrepreneurial class, while the entrepreneur's favorite role, the one for which he claims special treatment in society, is the role of change agent. In the traditional French entrepreneurial system, this contradiction is solved as follows. For large-scale organizations, at least, innovation comes only under the urging of the state, which represents collective aims and the underlying general interests which no one dares advocate alone for fear of upsetting the theo-

---

[27] This may be the rationale for the large moderate audience of a socialist creed quite compatible with otherwise bourgeois reactions.

retical equality between peers. But while the state alone pressures for change, it must rely on the entrepreneurial class to realize that change; and the entrepreneurial class consents only if it can use the opportunity to assert its prerogatives and to reinforce its privileges. Paradoxically, it is by resisting change that the entrepreneurial class is able to exact the most profit from its role of change agent. By sitting tight until a real emergency develops, it obliges the state to come to terms with and to reinforce the privileges of the bourgeois dynasties. Finally, this system of innovation has had still another advantage: it has provided acceptable opportunities for promotion. Bourgeois capitalist groups have founded their fortunes on state emergencies of all kinds. We note again the decisive role of crisis, the only way for an overly-rigid society to move. In earlier times, problems were predominantly financial, and the fortunes built on public misfortunes were financial fortunes. (Whatever the public outcry, swindling the state never seemed to be actually immoral.) With the rationalizing of state finances, state protection for innovating purposes, which became more and more honorable, was extended to all kinds of activities that appeared indispensable to the progress of society and especially to its survival in case of war. Such promotion of bourgeois dynasties that profited from the upheaval brought by war finally became considered more decent than the same innovating result achieved by ruthless competition on the market for the mere lure of money.[28] The state, therefore, plays a functional role for the entrepreneurial system in the innovation process, just as the entrepreneurial system has been functional for the state in meeting the dangerous uncertainty of the free market.[29]

The two systems have actually protected each other against change, and their joint action has made it possible for society as a whole to domesticate it. As we have already begun to notice, however, this whole interrelation has operated, slowly but continuously, to the prejudice of the entrepreneurial system. This was unavoidable in view of the general evolution toward impersonality and rationality, since the state alone was left to embody those qualities which the bourgeois entrepreneurial system refused to assume. Thus, by shunning the rationality of the market and direct contact with customers and workers, the bourgeois entrepreneurial class abandoned

[28] Even the great strides of the automobile industry, in France also the most dynamic episode of the industrial revolution of the twentieth century, owed much to the role which firms like Citroën and Renault played in the armament industry during World War I.

[29] We finally come to the following paradox: the bourgeois entrepreneurial class, which was declaring itself to be indispensable to society for introducing necessary innovations, was generally conservative and opposed to innovation and change, while the incompetent and routine-minded state bureaucracy was always progressive in spirit and urging people to progress.

the advantages of progressing to the state bureaucracy. This growing inferiority may explain why the rift between two worlds has sometimes developed into a bitter struggle. The bourgeois entrepreneurs have had to fight hard to prevent the interrelationship from becoming too disadvantageous to them. And it is the contemporary decline of bourgeois particularism and bourgeois status privileges in business that make it possible now for the business world to regain its influence and to become at least partially reconciled with the state.

THE FRENCH MODEL OF CHANGE AND ADJUSTMENT TO CHANGE

This brief analysis of the traditional opposition between bureaucratic and bourgeois patterns of action has brought into focus the problem of change as one of the problems most central to understanding the institutions of a society. Despite this opposition at the level of organizational structures and patterns of action, there seems actually to exist, at another level, an over-all model of change and adjustment to change.

A few more general hypotheses appear to be necessary for assessing the respective importance and meaning of our bureaucratic model and of its bourgeois counterpart.

We have frequently noted the similarities of the patterns of change we have discussed at different levels and in different systems. Three main patterns seem to be especially decisive: (1) the alternation of periods of routine and crisis and the need for crisis for breaking up the daily routine order; (2) the will and passion for planning, ordering, and equalizing all situations; and (3) the opposition between the negative and conservative behavior of all formal groupings, and the effervescence and intellectual, irresponsible creativity of individuals.

We have already dwelt at some length on the importance of crisis. We have shown how the alternation of long periods of routine and short periods of crisis was a necessary concomitant to the organizational tightness of both the bourgeois entrepreneurial system and the political and administrative system of France. None of the large complexes of interrelations, embracing in the same program of action so many heterogeneous situations, is able to adjust to change piecemeal and locally. In order to maintain the delicate and yet essential equilibrium among its parts, the whole system has to be reshuffled in order to make it possible for one part to change substantially. It could, of course, be imagined that the system might succeed in isolating itself from change. But such retreat was never possible nor sought in France; the French model may be extremely rigid as regards the maintenance of equilibrium and of the complex network of interrelations between roles and situations, but it is at the same time relatively flexible as regards the content of these roles and situations.[30]

The difference between France and other Western countries concerns much more the way change is achieved than the actual degree of change. To obtain a limited reform in France, one is always obliged to attack the whole "system," which is thus constantly called into question. This explains why the rules of the game can never be completely accepted. Reform can be brought about only by sweeping revolution. Reformists, in any case, cannot succeed without counting on the pressure generated by revolutionary or quasi-revolutionary movements. On the other hand, revolutionary utterances tend to have only a symbolic value, and they suffer a constant erosion.

The second trait, the will to order and equalize, we have analyzed only indirectly. It is a direct consequence of the egalitarian pressure we have seen operating within each stratum and of the hierarchic differentiation that simultaneously develops between them. Whenever a change occurs that enhances the situation of some persons or of some groups within the system, all peers of these persons or of these groups exert a similar pressure to preserve their own distance from them. This trait is more ambiguous than is initially apparent. It is one of the obvious rationales of the resistance to change, since it makes it more difficult for those who must make decisions and who foresee the consequences of their actions to assume the responsibility for very long chain reactions. On the other hand, the results are completely opposite whenever change has broken through in one place or another. Then the will to equalize, instead of working on the conservative side, will work to accelerate change and extend it to all possible situations. This is, of course, rather more regularizing and planning after the event than preparing for the future and ordering the adjustment to it, but the tendency should not cause us to dismiss this pattern as merely conservative.

The third and last trait, the creativeness of the individual, we have discovered and analyzed within the bourgeois entrepreneurial system. But we can find it everywhere; it is, indeed, the natural counterpart of the predominance of routine and the necessary preparation for the crisis period. It is, at the same time, a consequence of

---

[30] This combination of rigidity of the equilibrium and flexibility of the content of the social game exists in many other countries. It is especially noteworthy in Japan, where change occurred on a grand scale in extraordinarily short periods of crisis at the beginning of the Meiji period and during the American occupation. The difference from France would be that the crisis in Japan is affectively and intellectually minimized, and that it does not develop so much individual effervescence.

the fascination for revolutionary deeds that comes with the central importance of crisis as the constitutive act of any rational order. Members of the system suffer from the impersonal routine under which they must live, since it does not allow them to play a creative role and fosters many serious dysfunctions. At the same time, they enjoy the protection of a social system whose main objective is to guarantee each individual his independence and freedom of expression; and this protection makes it possible for them to escape their frustrations by resisting the established order and asserting their will to change.

Such concordant pressures naturally lead to the development of effervescence and of an irresponsible form of intellectual creativity. Most individuals, of course, do not actually think that they have a chance to play a great revolutionary role. However, they accept the individualistic values according to which the only great deeds (and the only examples of freely welcomed leadership) have come about in time of crisis. Last but not least, the model of competition between individuals at any level is based on the scorn for present arrangements and on the distinction which can be gained by outsmarting one's peers in disparaging these arrangements and in proposing new ones, even in an irresponsible way.[31]

Whatever their irresponsibility, these social games are very important in the long run. They are necessary for achieving change; they are part of the French pattern of constructive crisis. Crises and changes are brought about also, to quite an extent, by the violent pressure of individuals irresponsibly expressing their frustrations caused by the dysfunctions of the present equilibrium, while all their responsible group actions, which remain conservative and negative, make it impossible to cope with these dysfunctions.

The development of this trait makes it possible to explain the importance which has finally accrued to the intellectual world in France. De Tocqueville, in a brilliant chapter of *L'ancien régime*,[32] had already shown how the lack of responsible political life in the provinces, as well as its narrowness in the center, resulted in writers' enjoying a tremendous influence and practically securing the leadership of public opinion. This is, of course, no longer true today, but some of the same basic pattern still persists. Since decision-making seems to be blocked in daily routine for the preservation of the delicate equilibrium between all groups and privileges, and since groups are incapable of constructive co-operative action, the initiative must

[31] This is, for example, the favorite pastime of the maintenance men in the Industrial Monopoly.

[32] De Tocqueville, "Comment vers le milieu du XVIIIᵉ siècle les hommes de lettres devinrent les principaux hommes politiques et des effets qui en résultèrent," *L'ancien régime et la Révolution*, I, 193–201.

be left to individuals, and it takes the form of intellectual expression. Thus many men of action in France are also intellectuals in their own more or less partial way—i.e., persons who give priority to intellectual creativity over the restraints of collective action; they succeed because of their qualities of brilliance and not because of their actual achievements.

On the social scene, the intellectual milieux and the intellectual elite who control the channels of expression and who can appeal to each individual's own self-reserved creative domain have secured a tremendous, if very brittle, influence. Only they are able to create the climate of opinion that will bring about a crisis and thus make change possible.[33]

This cycle, with its periods of routine and crisis, corresponding to the alternation of the regular hold of the negative-minded group and the temporary breakthroughs of individual creativity, must be viewed, however, within the larger context of the rapidly changing world in which it occurs. The apparent contradiction between these two successive phases makes it possible to understand why France has been analyzed by certain authors as an arch-conservative country, the China of Europe, and by others as one of the beacons of human civilization. It is both at the same time; the emphasis on one or the other image depends only on whether one considers the tightness of the mechanism of the social system and the barriers which they oppose to change or the individual achievements in the domain of creativity. Many Frenchmen live the contradiction in themselves, being simultaneously extremely conservative as members of one or more egalitarian groups, and very progressive and creative anarchists as individuals within their own personal domains, which they are able to preserve because of the protection of these same groups.

This contradiction has led to two characteristic phases of French culture: the prevailing, at times even obsessive, skepticism about man's influence, implying either that change does not have much importance—"Plus ça change et plus c'est la même chose" [34]—or that change is completely independent of man's will and that human actions always have consequences opposite to the actors' aims;[35] and

---

[33] There are also many important individual and group interests in the intellectual world. The intellectual world itself, inasmuch as it has acquired a recognized importance, has also become plagued with the same egalitarian and routine pressures as the other French systems of interrelations. One can analyze its internal functioning also as the functioning of a stratified and routinized system of action with crises bringing change and new leadership. But the intellectual game must remain much more fluid, and change, therefore, is always present.

[34] "The more things change, the more they remain the same."

[35] There are good comments by Martha Wolfenstein on the French children's world as pictured in the movies, where a decisive importance is given to disillusion as the central experience of a Frenchman's world. See Margaret Mead and

the hidden individual megalomaniac will to transform and reorder the world according to one's own rational scheme.[36]

What is involved, if one wants to measure the stability of these processes and of the systems of social organization to which they correspond, is not any special kind of attachment to routine—although routine is the most important phase of the cycle—but more basic values, such as the conception of the self and especially the insistence of the individual on his own autonomy and his refusal of all dependence relationships.

The preservation of this individual autonomy and creativity may indeed be considered as one of the latent functions of the routine-crisis cycle. Its negative phase, routine, protects the individual against arbitrary decisions and leads him to criticize the existing order and to invent for and contribute to the positive phase of the cycle, crisis, which offers exciting possibilities of action to a few people while taking on, for the others, the appearance of a *force majeure*.[37] Change thus finally comes without having to resort to the dependence relationships implied by a gradual, reasonable, and conscious adjustment.

Let us return to the entrepreneurial system and to the role of the bureaucratic system within French economic life. By using the model which we have just elaborated of French patterns of change and of adjustment to change, we shall be able to understand the paradoxical contrast so often emphasized, especially by the American authors we have quoted, between the technical maturity of the French elite and the abundance of talent and invention of all sorts on which they can rely, on the one side, and the constant lag of the economy, on the other.[38]

Innovation has been difficult in the traditional bourgeois entrepreneurial system, not because candidates for the role of innovator have been lacking—on the contrary, it may be argued that they have been more numerous here than anywhere—and not because those who have succeeded are not rewarded—they have received as many

Martha Wolfenstein (eds.), *Childhood in Contemporary Cultures* (Chicago: University of Chicago Press, 1955).

[36] The Marxist view of change is quite well suited to a synthesis of the two phases, the hard skepticism as regards man's possibilities to do good and the merciless attacks on well-wishers and do-gooders, on the one side, and the marvelous framework of the future post-revolutionary world in which to project one's own rational schemes, on the other. This may be one of the reasons for the paradoxical hold of Marxism in a country whose stage of economic development does not correspond to this kind of revolutionary politics.

[37] Circumstances outside one's control.

[38] We are not contradicting here our earlier statement about France's always keeping up with other countries. We only mean that she has never pioneered, and has waited for others to pave the way.

if not more honors as anyone—but because it has been much more difficult to succeed in France, in view of the extreme rigidity of the organizational model with which one must comply.

Immediately beyond the stage of individual effervescence is the stage of routine, the well-oiled conservative mechanisms of the perfect bourgeois family organizations and of the perfect bureaucratic system. These mechanisms have prevented any individual, whatever his personal achievements, from crossing the social barrier as long as he does not meet the necessary requirements of conformity to the cultural and way-of-life patterns of the bourgeois group.[39] Because of such egalitarian and hierarchical obsessions, French society until recently made the most inefficient use of all the individual efforts which its devotion to intellectual creativity has stirred up. Besides enthusiasm for progress, it has manifested apathy, indifference, and revolt. This routine, whatever the normal increment it was bound to produce, could not help but bring retardation; and, since French society as a whole has not been able to accept it, emergency crises have been indispensable. And the instinctive belief in crisis as the only solution has reinforced the stability of the routine periods, since every one of the factors has not wanted to take undue risks by trying to go forward before the rest of the crowd.

On a more practical level, the French model of change has been directly embodied in the dichotomy between the world of business and the world of state bureaucracy we have described. The two worlds show the same opposition between the creative effervescence of individuals and the conservatism of groups. The distance between them and the hostility they have manifested to each other have created the conditions necessary for their adhering to the same model. They have thus been at the same time similar and complementary.

The impersonal bureaucracy has served as regulator and moderator, at times slowing down the rate of change and at other times accelerating it. The world of business has been dominated by the well-protected experts of the bourgeois families who alone have been able to face the difficulties raised by the economic progress necessary for meeting the aspirations of the whole society. The fact that these two roles have been separated and antagonistic has made it impossible for a role of mover and animator, i.e., a pattern of leadership, to develop. Leading, propelling functions could not be institutional-

---

[39] This does not mean that the individual efforts of inventors and pioneers have not brought them rewards. They have brought them consideration and eventually successive bourgeois promotions for their scientific prowess and for their technological *tours de force*, but without permitting them to exert the organizational influence they would have in other countries. This has tended to lead the bulk of them away from the more immediately rewarding applied fields.

ized. They have been indirectly assumed by the revolutionary pressure of individuals, and also to some extent by the example of foreign countries. This dichotomy entails great inefficiency, considerable detours and complexities; it fosters contradiction and waste. At the same time, these same dysfunctions insure the permanence of the model of change and adjustment to change and thus give the individuals the protection they require.

Society, however, as we have emphasized, is not entirely bound by the existence of cultural patterns. It learns constantly through the different organizational experiences to which its members resort to reach its general ends and their own particular ones. The difficulty of communication, the misunderstandings, and the hostility existing between two separate and complementary worlds which could not act without one another, were necessary for the French model of change to persist.[40] New experiences of an easier kind of relationship between these two worlds will then tend to react on the model. By experimenting with better-integrated organizational processes, French society can overcome its model of change. This is why the interpenetration of the two worlds, which characterizes the period since the end of World War II, constitutes such a decisive development for the future. As communications and understanding become easier between business leaders and higher civil servants, adjustment to change will not involve crises so profound as before. Groups will not give so high a priority to protecting themselves, they may become more constructive, and, finally, individuals will therefore find it easier to overcome social barriers and will slowly accustom themselves to the constraints of actual action. The orgaizational experience which France is undergoing now, because of the pressure of the world of efficiency, may tend to transform the cultural model that had shaped and bound it at first. The successive models we

---

[40] It can be argued that dualism has been one of the most permanent features of the development of French modern society. In the *ancien régime,* there was a constant dualism between the aristocratic rule and the rule of bureaucracy. To the aristocracy went the honors and the monetary rewards, but to the bureaucracy accrued the realities of power. This took place under the pressure of the rise to pre-eminence of the bourgeoisie; since the aristocracy did not want to face any direct pressure, the bureaucracy had to mediate between it and all other groups; and thus, finally, it came to tame the aristocracy itself. When the bourgeoisie came to power, in turn, the same process was repeated in regard to it. And the bureaucracy, that had been once identified with the rising bourgeoisie, had to dissociate itself from the entrepreneurial system so as to be able to mediate between this new conspicuous group and the other classes, especially the workers. Such dualism may generate endless and at times bitter conflicts, but these conflicts cannot go too far, and they serve to conceal other conflicts, which could not otherwise be dealt with so easily, given the French basic values and patterns of action.

have proposed must not be considered, therefore, as the immutable principles of action of French society, but only as the provisory models it has used until now.[41]

[41] We shall develop this discussion more fully in the concluding chapter.

Chapter Eleven

THE BUREAUCRATIC PHENOMENON AND THE "FRENCH MODEL" AS PART OF THE OVER-ALL DEVELOPMENT OF INDUSTRIAL SOCIETY

THE PROBLEM TO BE SOLVED

The models we have elaborated are functionalist models, whether we look at them from the point of view of the theory of organizations or from the point of view of cultural analysis. Instead of describing bureaucratic dysfunctions merely as the automatic consequence of the ordering of human and technical factors necessary for achieving a superior form of rationality, we have tried to understand them as the elements of more complex equilibria affecting the patterns of action, the power relationships, and the basic personality traits characteristic of the cultural and of the institutional systems of a given society. In this perspective, the bureaucratic phenomenon has appeared to be an indispensable means of protection which individuals need all the more as they depend most exclusively on brutal and coercive means for co-ordinating those activities necessary for achieving their ends. But we stated at first that we were dismissing the genetic and historical viewpoints only temporarily. In order to prove our point, we must now show that our analysis may be used as a decisive cue for the better understanding of the conditions of development of modern rationality and the factors active in its evolution.

This endeavor leads us still farther away from our original investigations, but it is rewarding even from the point of view of our earlier analyses and theoretical schemes. For functionalists always run the risk of indulging in a self-deceiving, conservative, and complacent commentary on the status quo. When analyzing the tendency to remain stable and to perpetuate itself manifested by a complex system of interrelationships, they often forget how such a system has developed and how and why it will ultimately have to change. They have the right to claim priority for understanding the daily routine state of affairs before trying to understand what is changing and what is going to change, but they should never be misled by this methodological [1] priority into believing that they have solved a problem when they have only described all its relevant parts.

The crucial point, which has direct implications for the meaning of research results themselves, concerns the actual limits of the self-reinforcing schemes which have been discovered. Functionalists usually forget to discuss why, when, how, and under what circumstances strains that had heretofore reinforced the hold of the central pattern become too burdensome for it and force it to transform itself or even to disappear.

In this book we have tried to avoid the temptation to describe and celebrate the temporary equilibrium, the harmony of the moment, as the sole possible system. We have always studied the relevant problems in the perspective of change. This approach has led us to broaden increasingly our scheme of interpretation and to consider the bureaucratic phenomenon, finally, as a global answer of the whole of a given society to this very problem of change. But if this effort has made it possible for us to overstep a superficial description of the present equilibrium and to discover some deeper and more meaningful regularities, it has not enabled us to succeed in avoiding the fundamental functionalist problem. We have analyzed how change has been integrated within the system but not how the system itself could change. In order to meet our first requirements, we must assess the extent to which our general model is a rigid and permanent one, the extent to which it can change and develop, and the kinds of pressure to which it is now submitted.

We shall not be able, of course, to give entirely satisfactory answers to these questions. In order to resolve them, we should need a number of new findings, the results of a quite different type of research from that which has been pursued until now. We should, however, by drawing all the possible conclusions from our tentative theory, be able to present a few useful remarks and thus set the problem in its proper context.

We personally believe that the domain of organizational structures and organizational patterns of action is one of the most central, if not the most central, domain where human groups and human societies can learn and constantly re-elaborate their social and cultural systems. We also believe that this domain can be studied seriously only through a very comprehensive, i.e., "functionalist," theory of organizational systems. For it is only through action, and through a kind

---

[1] Methodologically, however, functionalists have a very good point, and the position of Dahrendorf attacking Parsons' devotion to stability does not seem to us to be very solid. See Ralf Dahrendorf, "Out of Utopia," *American Sociological Review*, September, 1958. Even Marxism, after all, relies on a series of functionalist schemes which made it possible for Marx to overcome the usual extrapolations of the traditional philosophies of history.

of action that cannot be carried out without resorting to organizational models, that human groups and human societies can set new objectives for themselves and thus learn by obtaining the sanction of the environment. It is only through these sanctions, i.e., in view of their successes and failures, that they can change. Changes, we are inclined to believe, appear first at the level of the praxis and second only at the level of the values. It is true that cultural and organizational systems are too stable to allow groups to learn just anything. But within the limits fixed by the conditions of equilibrium of these systems, they can and actually do learn. The sanction of the environment, furthermore, does not stop at this stage; it tends to eliminate inadequate patterns of action and, finally, feeds back on cultural traits and basic behavioral attitudes.

To discuss the margin of freedom and of innovation or, better, the possibilities of learning still offered by these complex systems, we shall employ the theory we submitted about their conditions of equilibrium. Even less than in the technical field can one discover, in this domain, a *one best way* to be accepted by everyone, and there is no point in looking for the linear growth of a unidimensional rationality. This does not mean, however, that it is impossible to predict the evolution of the systems of interdependent elements of which we have tried to understand the latent functions. In this final perspective, our models will appear no longer as ends in themselves but as so many stages necessary both for understanding the general orientation of this evolution and for setting the problems in their proper context.

We shall study successively the development of bureaucratic rigidities according to the evolution of industrial society and the special place of the French model within this evolution. In conclusion, we shall examine, in the more concrete case of French public administration, how the forces of resistance and the forces of change can be roughly appraised in terms of action.

BUREAUCRATIC SYSTEMS OF ORGANIZATION AND THE EVOLUTION OF INDUSTRIAL SOCIETY

Two general factors, in our opinion, influence the evolution of organizational patterns in modern society in a way Weber did not foresee. These factors, whose importance we have already stressed in our discussion of the ways in which an organization achieves conformity, are (1) the constant progress in the techniques of prediction and organization; and (2) the growing sophistication of the individual in an increasingly complex culture. Organizational progress has made it possible to be more tolerant of the personal needs and idiosyncrasies of individual members: one can obtain the wanted results from them without having to control their behavior so narrowly as before. Cultural sophistication, on the other hand, has increased the individual's capacity for accommodation and at the same time, as a consequence, his possibilities of independence. People can now measure their contribution to the organization in a more precise way; they are no longer obliged to bargain for all or nothing. Participation is much less dangerous for them, since they have learned to be more flexible and since they can participate without committing themselves quite so much. The cost of quitting and finding a substitute participation is, in any case, both psychically and materially much less heavy than before. The more tolerant modern organizations demand much less from their members, and the latters' freedom and flexibility allow them also to demand much less in return. If pressure from both sides can diminish as both parties become less demanding, rigidity will tend generally to decrease. The number and the complexity of the rules may increase tremendously—modern organizational patterns will be more flexible, much less "bureaucratic" than before. Organizations will be content with a more temporary loyalty from their members, even at the highest echelons, and individuals will not press the organization to protect them by using the rules in the most binding way. With pressures from the top and counter-pressures from below decreasing, rigidity as described in our model will tend to diminish.[2]

Many authors, we are aware, have adopted a different view of modern organizations. William H. Whyte, Jr.,[3] who has been among the more outstanding, argues, for example, that modern organization man is above all a conformist, that the new ethic which the development of large-scale organizations is creating is an ethic of conformism, in contrast to the Protestant and capitalist ethic of individual responsibility. His arguments, however, are not very convincing even if limited to the short run. It might be true that our social system still needs more individual responsibility than the present trend allows us to manifest. But this does not mean that our society is more conformist than that of even thirty years ago. The "well-rounded" per-

[2] Starting from a different point of view, the British social psychologist Tom Burns has recently presented a similar argument. For him, the growing acceleration of change in modern industrial society tends to impose a type of *organistic* management against the usual *mechanistic* type. See Tom Burns and G. M. Stalker, *The Management of Innovation* (London: Pergamon Press, 1961).

[3] William H. Whyte, Jr., *The Organization Man* (New York: Simon & Schuster, 1956).

sonality which Whyte so attacks is the mark of a flexible individual always ready to compromise and generally more socially-minded than his more assertive counterpart of thirty years ago. Does this mean that organizational men in general are now more conformist? Certainly not; the confusion comes from Whyte's focusing on the top, successful individual. The Protestant ethic was supportive for the successful executive who could be extremely assertive in the name of individual responsibility. But this kind of independence meant more submissiveness on the part of his subordinates and the retreatism and ritualism necessary to alleviate it. The social values of today's organization man are conducive to better possibilities of adjusting in a more independent way, if not the top, but the average member is considered.[4] Certainly, the extension of those values to other domains where individual creativity is the decisive factor can become a deterrent to progress, but in the paramount domain of social action the price which had to be paid for maintaining the authoritarian hero of former times was such that the flexible, tolerant, and well-rounded conformist manager of the organization era seems, in comparison, to be a model of efficiency.

Moreover, as Dalton has shown, the complex human relations and power relations system of a modern organization imposes on its executive the need to take initiative constantly and to be creative more subtly.[5] Instead of assuming the full responsibility of command in a general climate of uncertainty, they must settle conflicting claims in a maze of rules, arbitrate between opposing forms of rationality, and face the difficult moral issues of the ambiguity of means and ends. They are becoming political leaders instead of risk-taking entrepreneurs.

Considering only these general tendencies, we could conclude that bureaucratic systems founded on those vicious circles of dysfunctional elements which we have analyzed are bound to become less conspicuous. Contrary to the fear of so many humanists and revolutionary prophets of doom, we can expect more promises of liberalization than threats of standardization.

Such optimism, however, must be considerably moderated, since we must also take into account the general progress of rationalization that constantly diminishes the challenge of uncertainty, thus allowing organizations to escape reality. The existence of this long-range trend toward rationalization that so impressed Weber does not mean that organizations are becoming more "bureaucratic" in our

---

[4] Notwithstanding the difficult situation of several layers in the hierarchical pyramid, and especially the lower supervisors and foremen.
[5] Melville Dalton, *Men Who Manage* (New York: Wiley, 1959).

dysfunctional sense, but that men's activities are increasingly processed through formal organizations, i.e., that bureaucratization in the Weberian sense is truly increasing, perhaps at an accelerated rate, but without entailing the dysfunctional consequences that Weber feared and all his successor prophesied. We come then to the following paradox. That greater flexibility which makes it easier for individuals to participate in the standardized and controlled activities of large-scale organizations is responsible for the development of "bureaucratization." In other words, the elimination of the "bureaucratic systems of organization" in the dysfunctional sense is the condition for the growth of "bureaucratization" in the Weberian sense.

Finally, as is most often the case, the optimist's and the pessimist's views equally should both be dismissed. Neither the logic of standardization nor the logic of liberalization is applicable alone if one tries to envisage the total picture. Both are valid at that level. Man seems to push the logic of standardization, i.e., the goals of efficiency, as much as the successes of the logic of liberalization will permit him. New equilibria are constantly formed in place of the older ones. They give man both the advantages and the burdens of greater sophistication and more complex entanglements.

Within this very general framework, it can be shown that, at the operational level, it is only when large-scale organizations become more flexible and can eliminate some of their bureaucratic vicious circles that they can overstep significant stages of growth. Recent research in the field of large-scale organization history has made this point clear.[6] Decentralization now seems, to shrewd observers of the business scene, to be the necessary condition for further growth.[7]

This outcome, however, is not a simple linear process, and present systems of organization are still to a large extent "bureaucratic." Progress in the organizational field meets a strong passive resistance. Bureaucratic systems persist and always find news forms. This is the result of two opposite and yet convergent pressures. On the one side, each individual, each group and category within an organization, will always struggle to prevent the rationalization and maintain the unpredictability of their own task and function. Their power, the influence they can wield, depend, as we have demonstrated, on their amount of discretion, and, finally, on the uncertainty they have to face. One can thus understand that they will fight rationalization in

[6] See, among a number of articles published in the *Administrative Science Quarterly*, Ernest Dale, "Contribution to Administration of Alfred P. Sloan, Jr., and G. M.," I (June, 1956), 30–62.

[7] Ralph R. Cordiner, *New Frontiers for Professional Managers* (New York: McGraw-Hill, 1956).

their own field while trying to further it in other fields. On the other side, the constant progress of rationalization offers the possibility and the temptation, to those responsible for it, to push planning and standardization further than is rationally feasible.

Two kinds of privileges and vicious circles, therefore, tend to develop. The former correspond to the resistance of groups trying to preserve their positions of strength which can be weakened by technical progress, and the latter to the desire of other groups to impose a rationalization which is not yet warranted by this progress. Those two forces very often reinforce each other. A premature centralization can create the best protection for local privileges; conversely, a coalition of such privileges will eventually fight to impose a rationalization which will protect them and even enhance their status temporarily by eliminating other privileges.

The success of these two maneuvers depends on the organization's capacity to isolate itself from the rest of society. Since the persistence of bureaucratic vicious circles will entail, as a primary consequence, difficulty of contact with the environment, those activities in which it is easier to remain isolated from outside pressures are most likely to allow the development of bureaucratic systems of organization.

We should like thus to argue that the fears of technocracy expressed by so many authors are not founded on fact. When progress accelerates, the power of the expert is diminished and managerial power becomes more and more a political and judicial power rather than a technical one. Managers' success depends on their human qualities as leaders and not on their scientific know-how. As science invades the domain of the experts, those aspects of their roles which it affects decrease in importance.

We may emphasize, as a last paradox, that bureaucratic forms in the dysfunctional sense correspond to the impossibility of eliminating all elements of charismatic power from the functioning of large-scale organizations. Bureaucratic privileges and vicious circles follow from the necessity of resorting to charismatic-like power in an otherwise ever more rationalized world.

The Growing Threats to the French Bureaucratic Patterns

Let us now analyze the place and meaning of the French model in this general context. We have shown that its temporary and local dysfunctions could only reinforce its general hold. The system as a whole seems to be functional, inasmuch as it relies on a number of cultural traits and basic patterns of behavior that have been constant throughout the modern history of French society. These traits and these behavioral patterns, however, cannot be considered as given once and for all. Whatever their stability, they have also to submit to the necessity of a minimum of equilibrium with the environment. And we now must ask ourselves whether or not, in view of the extraordinary upheaval brought about by the rise and the development of mass-consumption society, the whole complex of bureaucratic patterns, processes of change, and the basic primary traits will not finally become gravely dysfunctional and whether or not the pressure of necessity will not oblige French society to learn new patterns of behavior that will tend to influence and transform basic traits which could until now be considered immutable.

Until the present, the pressures of the outside world have led only to a reinforcement of the system. There had been constant progress in flexibility, but this was offset by a general growth of centralization and a wider diffusion of the bureaucratic patterns. French society met the challenge of the modern world by extending its own special type of organizational rationality and pushing it to the extreme. There are now signs, however, that the limit of possible developments has been reached, that the system does not have the necessary resources to solve the increasingly difficult problems which it will confront if it extends still further. We may now approach a breaking point, from which point on the basic stability of the system will be threatened.

The threat comes from two sets of convergent pressures. On the one hand, the requirements of efficiency of modern industrial society, that cannot be met as in earlier times by resorting to greater centralization, force the elimination of some of the bureaucratic rigidity. Role differentiation, the complexity of the co-operative process, and sheer organizational growth require that individuals and groups have more personal contacts, participate better in the decision-making system, and be part, finally, of more fluid equilibria of newer relationships. On the other hand, the modern mass-consumption techniques seem to present new possibilities of meeting French basic needs at lower cost and more rationally. This convergence makes it possible to meet the two basic conditions for successful change: urgent necessity and the material and moral possibility of adjusting to it.

Let us be more specific. We emphasized, in the preceding section, that the whole tendency of modern organizational development has had to be toward more flexible patterns and that decentralization at certain decisive stages has been prerequisite for further growth. This problem has been especially misunderstood in France, where modern organizational development has often been resisted under the pretext that it is bureaucratic. To be sure, many voices have denounced, time and again, the errors and failures caused by the French patterns of organization. But most of the time this has been done in a very partial and ultimately reactionary way, since the critics have refused to understand the price which would have to be paid to eliminate the dysfunctions about which they complain so bitterly. Finally, there has been a deep consensus about the relative excellence of the French system, to which most Frenchmen, revolutionaries and conservatives, radical and moderates, alike have instinctively adhered.

They have had some justification for this opinion, since the French system has been able to claim, within the context of bourgeois and traditional Europe, all the tangible advantages that we have analyzed of stability, reliability, protection of individual independence. At the same time, it has seemed to bring, in its own way, a very sufficient measure of efficiency, while appearing, in a nation deeply influenced by the ups and downs of a turbulent history, as the best system for safeguarding the unity of purpose and the permanence of national society and insuring a quick mobilization of resources in case of war.

The consequences of the ensuing organizational lag have not been very worrying, since the lag could not be embodied in practical terms. On the contrary, most responsible Frenchmen have been very proud of the success of an organizational system that could make it possible to benefit from all the progress of modern technical civilization without having to obey the imperatives of standardization, concentration, and discipline already stifling the spirit of the other Western nations. But the lesser efficiency of French organizations can be compensated for by the gains brought by centralization, only as long as planning, prediction, and development activities remain extremely uncertain, arbitrary, and hazardous, thus making the activities of control and regulation the decisive administrative functions. Now, when a more rational view of man's influence in shaping future events can be maintained and an increasing number of organizations are becoming able to make more conscious choices, the centralized administrative state and all organizations and branches of activities influenced by bureaucratic patterns are, curiously enough, becoming more conservative than their less integrated counterparts. They may be bigger and more sophisticated, but they are paralyzed by egalitarianism, by the weight of their own impersonal rules, and, above all, they are unable to master the necessary pressure for imposing change upon resisting groups. Centralization, once a certain stage has been definitely overstepped, cannot any longer bring useful rewards. It seems even to have become self-defeating in the French cultural context, where socialist solutions are not able to escape the dilemma of stagnation or totalitarianism.[8]

At the same time, when there seems to be no escape within the system itself, pressures from without become increasingly stronger. The different para-bureaucratic systems disintegrate. The bourgeois entrepreneurial system is no longer able to compete with the more flexible modern managerial organizations. The educational system cannot any longer promote the highest learning and research achievement. The colonial system is unable to give way to another, better-adjusted type of political influence. Pressures to disrupt all these entrenched patterns are finally threatening the bureaucratic system of organization itself.

From another and perhaps more profound perspective, the possibility of the emergence of a new form of rationality not compatible with the bureaucratic tradition seems extremely difficult to discard in a country which has always prided itself in keeping in the vanguard of rational achievement.

French bureaucratic rationality has relied on individual effervescence and competition to produce new and more elaborate models of routine activities to be carried out on an egalitarian and impersonal basis after having overcome the resistance of groups. This has meant no competition and no co-operation at the group level; state and group quasi-monopolies have imposed the *one best way* through egalitarian pressures against individual resistance. This procedure makes planning extremely difficult, because planning ahead implies organizational experimentation, exchange of information, and statistical analysis—all contrary to the philosophy of the *one best way* and the negative practices of groups. It also requires a co-operative attitude on the part of individuals that cannot be obtained when the dominant behavior of the central and group authorities is one of control and repression.

Now, when managerial planning for growth both in private and public organizations has definitely taken precedence over state and group attempts at controlling or regularizing the blind forces of the market, when organizations come to recognize that it is better to allow a large tolerance for calculated waste and human deviances and imperfections than to sacrifice growth to thrift and the pursuit of possible overlapping, waste, and corruption, the rationale of the traditional system of organization crumbles. The French bureaucratic system of organization, as we have described and analyzed it, cannot

---

[8] The model of state socialism, once rather progressive, seems now increasingly to be associated with inefficiency, corruption, and waste (the Middle East, Latin America, Spain), unless it becomes totalitarian, while the only success of socialism in modern times has been obtained in countries with strong tendencies to self-government.

easily adjust to this new form of rationality. It is not fit for planning ahead, but for regularizing, after the fact, the results of group struggles over the proposals of individuals. Planned growth implies greater trust in human motivations, fostering initiative at all levels, more co-operation between individuals, and more competition between groups.

If everything is taken into account, it no longer seems possible to maintain the rate of development required by modern industrial society without resorting to this new strategy of action. And French society, as a matter of fact, has been moving steadily in this direction. The first sign of a significant change was the creation of the Planning Commission just after the Liberation, and the subsequent elaboration, in its midst, by younger higher civil servants and the most progressive business leaders, of first the practices, and then the philosophy, of *économie concertée*.[9]

Economie concertée has many weaknesses in practice and is only very partially fulfilling its ideals. It retains many of the anterior practices. The state still keeps some of its authoritarian and negative attitudes, and it is only by manipulating the different pressure systems that it can succeed in obliging private groups to act. Private groups, on the other hand, maintain their infantile attitude and consent to co-operate only when they feel that the state agrees to pay a heavy price for their co-operation. Yet *économie concertée* is a significant departure, since many positive results have been achieved without the traditional controls, and both the private managerial elite and the state bureaucratic elite are gradually but definitely being won over to the new kind of rationality. These groups are thus increasingly able to bargain realistically without resorting to the traditional mixture and alternation of repressive control on the one side, and secretiveness, resistance, and apathy on the other.

[9] This is what Henry W. Ehrmann, in an otherwise extremely perceptive article on *économie concertée*, fails to understand when reviewing the theory and practice of recent French bureaucratic intervention in the economy. He is judging according to the American standards of a trust-busting and competitive philosophy. For him, therefore, *économie concertée* has much in common with the Vichy attempts at corporatism and traditional European protective tendencies. This is quite true but represents only a part of the picture. That picture may be good, but the comparisons, we believe, are not relevant. The defects of *économie concertée* to which Ehrmann is pointing concern practices that were flourishing earlier in different forms. And what is more significant for assessing the change brought by *économie concertée* is not a comparison with American but with earlier French practices which have been hampering the growth of the nation. Measured against the latter, the new attitudes toward co-operation and planning ahead, the diffusion of the new managerial rationality, are extremely important and revolutionary factors. (See Henry W. Ehrmann, "French Bureaucracy and Organized Interests," *Administrative Science Quarterly*, V, No. 4 [March, 1961], 534–53; and Club Jean Moulin, *L'Etat et le citoyen* [Paris: Le Seuil, 1961], pp. 354–70.)

While the pressures for new organizational patterns become stronger and more difficult to resist because of the lure of progress, efficiency, and a broader kind of rationality, there are also signs that the cumulative changes brought about by the emergence in France of a mass-consumption society are beginning to offer new possibilities, outside the bureaucratic system of organization, of meeting basic individual demands. In the pre-mass-consumption era, the satisfaction of the individual needs for autonomy, individual control over the environment, equality, and freedom from direct dependence relationships required the combination of a stratified society and a centralized system of decision-making. Stratification made it possible to safeguard equality, while centralization made the consequence of stratification impersonal and allowed the individual to escape the difficulties of hierarchical relationships.[10] But with mass consumption, stratification becomes less rigid. More and more people can participate in ever wider cultural influences. The greater complexity of the whole culture does not seem to entail a greater degree of hierarchy but engenders, on the contrary, greater and greater specialization and the breakdown of the old hierarchical order. Impersonality, equality, and individual autonomy, therefore, become possible outside the protection of the strata, and direct interpersonal contacts become less threatening. We do not want to imply that the pressure for avoiding face-to-face relations will cease, all at once, to be an important element of French social relations, but we do believe that the emergence of mass consumption is already lessening this pressure.

French society has resisted the diffusion of the new cultural models of mass society, which for this reason have developed less quickly in France than in the neighboring countries.[11] But this resistance amounts only to rearguard delaying tactics.

A national, all-encompassing market is emerging in France slowly but with increasing rapidity, in the field of culture as well as in the fields of material products and services. It may even be argued that the more rational and universalistic culture of the French has fewer possibilities of resistance than more particularistic and "deferent"

---

[10] The protection brought by social stratification is still important in France. We believe one can find an indirect proof of this in the strong limitations imposed by spontaneous group references· to the expectations of individuals. These limitations appear to be much greater than in America and the other Western countries closer to the model of mass society. See Stern and Keller, "Spontaneous Group References in France," *Public Opinion Quarterly*, XVII (1953), 208–17.

[11] The temporary but important lag in the diffusion of television in France in the 1950's is a good case in point. This lag cannot be explained by economic and financial reasons, as the French standard of living in this period was high enough and still growing—it was caused by the general resistance to change generated by the French system of social relations.

cultures.[12] The open and egalitarian French culture has been able to maintain stratification only with the use of artificial distances.[13] Once such distances appear anachronistic and ludicrous, no possible basis of discrimination remains.[14]

The consequences of these new developments are already apparent. The basic rules of the game of French human relations have already changed greatly in many fields, as can readily be verified.

Changes in class relations are the most conspicuous. Social distance has diminished considerably. Class lines are increasingly blurred. Only the widest social distances are apparent. Centralization has both focused attention on them and helped to lend strategic importance to the opposition of groups at the end of the social spectrum. But the game is played, on both sides, with more sophistication and less passion than earlier. Employers and employees understand each other better and are becoming more tolerant. Parallel progress in the organizational field, finally, makes the complex game of polite avoidance and indirect bargaining seem hollow and useless.

Cultural differences, however, still remain as difficult a barrier to overcome as the traditional bureaucratic rationality; but they also are tending to crumble under the pressure of mass culture. A great loss of faith in the most discriminating aspects of bourgeois culture is already manifest. Even the baccalaureate, that old symbol of bourgeois status whose sacred character Goblot emphasized, is about to disappear in the relative indifference of public opinion. Correlated with this loss of faith in social discrimination, and running much deeper, is the change that is slowly gathering momentum in parent-child relationships, which will have a decisive influence upon the patterns of authority.

The impact of the mass media has already made possible the development of a youth culture outside the parental orbit, and the diminishing influence of traditional social discriminaton has greatly alleviated the pressure on the younger generation. French parental

[12] We use the term as suggested by S. M. Lipset in his analysis of present-day British society. See Lipset, "Democracy and the Social System," in *The First New Nation* (New York: Basic Books, 1963).

[13] Inferiors did not internalize their inferiority as in England; they were kept at a distance only by the vertical stratification of cultural patterns, the difficulty of promotion and crossing over the social barrier, and the resulting fear of face-to-face contacts and of humiliation.

[14] The disintegration of the traditional system of cultural stratification is quite apparent already when comparing the theater and movie public in Paris. The hierarchic differences in public, still very strong in the theater, have not persisted for the movies, in spite of the frantic efforts of the holders of high-brow culture to impose more sophisticated aesthetic standards. See Crozier, "Employés et petits fonctionnaires, note sur le loisir comme moyen de participation aux valeurs de la société bourgeoise," *Esprit*, June, 1959.

authority is still far from being permissive, but the self-perpetuating conflict over authority can be expected to lose one of its indispensable sources, the family system.[15]

These new social and cultural developments may account for the emergence and the significant progress of new patterns of action opposed to the bureaucratic spirit. We shall cite only two of them. First, as we have stated, a new managerial spirit is flourishing that is breaking away from the traditional bourgeois pattern and pervades the entrepreneurial system as well as the higher strata of the Civil Service. Good observers might still find many remnants of the bourgeois patterns in this new spirit. But, here again, the important thing is the departure from entrenched patterns of action and the tendency to give more importance to the values of growth, co-operation, and service to the community than to the values of stability, individual control, and class discrimination. Another new and interesting phenomenon has been the increase in autonomous co-operative group action in a number of different domains, ranging widely in the fields of economic and political action, among students, peasants, entrepreneurs, and religious milieux. Many aspects of these new group activities, it is true, also retain some of the characteristic negative features of the French tradition.[16] Yet we believe that there has been a significant departure from the traditional group passivity of the French bureaucratic and bourgeois system. The change that is occurring in the peasantry, especially, is an extraordinary revolution which no one would have dared to predict twenty years ago and which puts to the question many aspects of the traditional equilibrium of French bourgeois society.

All these changes and their consequences feed back vigorously on the spirit of youth and have finally brought in a new intellectual climate whose importance, although fogged by the passions and violence of the Algerian war, should not be underestimated.[17] A greater

---

[15] Another very important element of the French family system has changed significantly, namely, the attitude and behavior toward procreation. The change in the birth rate is not very great and may seem, at first glance, to be accounted for by too many factors to be relevant to our discussion. Yet we believe that this change is very important, because it concerns basic attitudes toward life and therefore must be associated with the general transformation of French society. The behavior of self-restraint that the French people were the first to impose on themselves in the nineteenth century was quite an unusual human achievement, and it can be considered as a milestone in human rationality typical, after all, of the bureaucratic spirit. A relaxation of this restraint is thus very significant. It corresponds in our opinion to a moré trustful and future-oriented view of the human condition that is well in tune with the new forms of rationality.

[16] E.g., the activity of the students' union and of the farmers' associations in the years 1959–61 has often been extraordinarily irresponsible.

[17] The decisive breaking point seems to have been the Mendès-France experiment in 1954.

concern for empirical knowledge, a greater disregard for abstract theories, a reformist and action-oriented philosophy, have marked a student body whose enthusiasm and radiance have not been matched since the first half of the nineteenth century. The educational system has not yet changed; but the climate which is shaping the learning process of the elite of French youth[18] also calls for the acceleration of the disintegration of the traditional bourgeois and bureaucratic order.

The Model's Possibilities of Resistance:
The Case of French Public Administration

In considering the growing threat to the French bureaucratic and para-bureaucratic patterns, we have taken into account only the changes in values and modes of action effected by the accelerating development of industrial civilization. We have thus easily concluded that these patterns are likely to recede inasmuch as their latent functions lose their importance. These conclusions may be considered as probable hypotheses for the long run, but they do not seem adequately relevant to the present and the near future. For they do not give proper importance to the possibilities of resistance to change of all-encompassing and yet self-contained and tightly controlled systems of organization. It may be argued that such systems can outlive the disappearance of their traditional latent functions. Because of their possibilities of action upon their own environment, they can reshape the latter, create a new kind of equilibrium, and develop new latent functions for maintaining the basic behavioral patterns necessary to their survival.

We shall discuss these possibilities of resistance in the most central and decisive case for France, that of public administration. The bureaucratic system of organization of French public administration is certainly one of the most entrenched of such closed systems of social action that has existed in the modern world. It contributed heavily to the shaping of its own environment in the past, and many of the patterns of action that support it at present have developed under its influence.[19] Our problem is to assess whether and to what extent it is still able to exert such influence in the mass-consumption era.

---

[18] This climate is all the more important, since the content of the curriculum is formalistic and uninspiring.

[19] De Tocqueville has argued, for example, that the lack of independent group action and the strata isolation in French communities were due to the king's municipal and fiscal policies. See Alexis de Tocqueville, *L'ancien régime et la Révolution, passim* and especially I, 115–22.

It is self-evident that most nations are now much more interdependent than they were, and that France is no longer able to pursue its own bureaucratic experiment by isolating itself from the rest of the world. Once it was possible for parallel social systems to take their own courses in a rather independent way. Today, however, there are too many organizational links and too many intellectual contacts to allow a nation to remain isolated. Only Russia and the Communist countries can preserve such isolation, but they are a world unto themselves and have to pay a heavy price for it. France, in any case, cannot conduct its bureaucratic experiment while ignoring the rest of the world. The failure of its colonial system, the end of its "civilizing mission," have taken away the last buffer against foreign contacts that it had elaborated. France has had to recognize that its organizational system is not only not universal but has proved inferior, at least in the organizational competition within the Western world.

This over-all analysis, however, is still adequate only for the long run. The relative inferiority of an organizational system does not make it impossible for this system to resist change if it is able to maintain its equilibrium or to find a new equilibrium with its environment. From this point of view, we believe that three main areas of contact are decisive for assessing the possibilities of resistance to change of the French bureaucratic system of organization: the area of policy-making (the orientation of the system); the area of personnel recruitment (the human basis of the system); and the area of the bureaucratic functions (the services given to the larger community).

The first area of contact of the bureaucracy with the outside world concerns, of course, general policy-making. We have shown how difficult this problem can be for a bureaucratic system that always tends to transfer major decisions further up. French public administration has set aside special categories of higher civil servants separately recruited and trained, relieved from the usual organizational requirements, who alone can confront these problems and thus become the system's change agents. The role of these members of the *Grands Corps* has become increasingly important as the gap between the bureaucratic system and its environment has widened, for they have become the necessary mediators between the bureaucracy and the environment, especially at times of crisis. This is why the present change of outlook of the younger generation of higher civil servants should not be neglected. They have been deeply influenced by the new intellectual climate of the student world and by the experiments in economic action made possible by the nationalization of various enterprises and the growth of *économie concertée.*[20] As a consequence, they have lost most of their attachment to the bureaucratic system as an ideal of perfection.[21] They have become empiricists, more devoted to economic growth than to purity of style and, especially, financial purity. Their heroes are no longer the perfectionists but the doers.

This great change, however, has not as yet greatly influenced the internal functioning of the system.[22] At this level, the values and perspective of the new managerial leaders are not entirely decisive. According to the scheme we have proposed, the "directors" are all-powerful in maintaining the status quo and finding ways of readjusting the system to new conditions, but very weak in operating basic reforms or even changes affecting interrelationships between different groups. Yet it must be recognized that some margin of action is granted them, especially during crises and because of their strategic situation as mediators. In the short run, it is true, a higher civil servant who wants to initiate reform must resort to an authoritarian show of force that, in the end, defeats its own purpose and reinforces the whole system. In the long run, however, the diffusion of a reformist spirit among most of the higher civil servants must have decisive consequences. When the breaking point is reached, it will no longer be possible to maintain the bureaucratic faith in the middle ranks while the upper ranks disown it.[23] From then on, groups' resistance to reforms will be less and less easy.

The second area of contact is the domain of personnel recruitment. No organizational system can survive without achieving a proper equilibrium with the community in which it is developing and which must provide it with a reasonable flow of new members. This condition is even more restrictive for the French public service, since it relies on a tight stratification system that functions well only if there is enough pressure for entering it at the bottom.

Yet this is now one of the weak points of the French bureaucratic system. The crisis of recruitment that began after World War II has become increasingly more acute. Contrary to a very long tradition, there seems to be a decreasing interest in state employment at the

[20] This may be only vicarious participation. The Renault experiment is considered by many younger higher civil servants as one of the outstanding successes of their new philosophy, although almost none of them has been active in it.

[21] Although, in practice, fewer of the present than of the past generations of higher civil servants leave the service.

[22] Very curious double standards seem to have emerged. The bureaucracy is progressive when dealing with the outside world and extremely conservative in regard to its own patterns of action and internal functioning.

[23] The bureaucratic faith has already much declined among young middle-rank civil servants.

lower and middle ranks.[24] There are now fewer candidates for many competitive examinations than there are jobs offered.

This situation, which is beginning to undermine the whole system, has many causes. General factors that have devaluated the traditional advantages of the Civil Service are the universal downgrading of routine clerical occupations, the growing stability, security, and even independence guaranteed by private employment. But more specific factors may have had as much importance, especially the insistence of the French bureaucratic establishment[25] on maintaining and even extending its rigorous selective system, with its high and at times irrelevant standards, and the climate of cramped outlook and narrow bickering that has discredited petty civil servants in the community.

Here again, instead of the bureaucracy's influencing its own environment, as in earlier times, and slowly reshaping it in accord with its own wants and requirements, the community is beginning to put pressure upon the bureaucracy by refusing the bureaucratic patterns. This second area of contact is also an area where the bureaucracy is in an inferior position, more likely to be influenced than to influence.

The system has been able to maintain itself up to now by tapping new human resources. Lower civil servants, once predominantly male and recruited from all over France,[26] have become increasingly female and originate mostly from the underdeveloped Southwest. Such a new symbiosis with the community, however successful it may be in the short run, inevitably involves two risks. First, it is only temporary; the Southwest also will industrialize (it is already doing so), and there are limits to the number of women who seek employment outside the home. Second, it accentuates the inferior situation of the bureaucracy, increasingly staffed by people who are clearly ranked much lower than their counterparts in private employment.

At the same time, other pressures are exerted during the employment life of civil servants. Civil servants are no longer so isolated as they once were. They are, therefore, much less committed to the Service. The rate of departure may still be low, but there is already much more alternative employment offered, and this is causing unrest. Public service will have increasingly to compete with other possible employment in order to keep its personnel. This will become

---

[24] Because of their general social and intellectual prestige, the higher ranks still attract the best talent.

[25] The pressure, as we have shown, does not come from the policy-making ranks but from all the groups interested.

[26] There were, of course, already many important distortions of geographical distribution, but no such focusing on only one region as exists now.

extremely difficult if public service maintains the egalitarian guarantees that make it impossible to discriminate between employees.

Finally, the pressure for change we have seen developing in the higher ranks has its counterpart in the lower ranks. There, however, it is likely to be expressed through movements making rather simple claims, whose objectives are likely to be even more conservative in regard to the system. This has already been marked in the successive strikes and social movements that have plagued the Civil Service in the last fifteen years and that played their part in the troubles of the Fourth Republic.[27] But we are also close to a breaking point, inasmuch as the system is pushed into more and more contradictions and can no longer find its equilibrium.

The last and third area of contact of the bureaucracy with the outside world is the area of the bureaucratic functions. This is not so dynamic a domain as the first two, but it will also, in the long run, generate a pressure for change that will be difficult to resist. Change in this area comes from the universally increased importance of the role of the state and the growing demands of the community for public services. This trend is disturbing the traditional French equilibrium between the state and the citizen. The citizen, who once refused state intervention as much as he could, is now continually asking for more services. Thus servicing in the balance of activities of the bureaucracy is taking the precedence over controlling. Increasing numbers of new roles must therefore be created which do not fit into the old scheme. The system is tending to disintegrate because it has had to overextend. Specialization and differentiation, as we have seen, entail another logic of bureaucracy that can be reconciled with the logic of centralization only in the short run. In the long run, and we are already seeing many consequences of these new developments, the general equilibrium of the system is completely disturbed, and this engenders another kind of pressure for change.

In all three of these areas, the same scheme operates that we have so briefly reviewed. The pressure of the general community, which is much more open than the bureaucracy to the new patterns of action brought by mass production and the mass-consumption society, becomes the leading force, and the balance between the state and society is reversed. In the major areas of contact, the French Civil Service seems unable any longer to shape its own environment; it appears, on the other hand, to be fighting a rear-guard battle to escape the outside influences conveyed by this environment. The French bureaucratic system of organization is desperately trying to

---

[27] We are still within the vicious circle. The malaise originating in the application of the system gives rise to movements that claim, and partially succeed in imposing, an extension of this system.

cope with ever expanding responsibilities, and with new functions and a new managerial spirit not easily compatible with its principles, while the community refuses to give it proper recognition and to staff it adequately.[28] In so doing, without understanding it very well, French society is paving the way for a much deeper crisis, or at least for a change of a much greater magnitude, whose repercussions will bear in their turn on the French model of change and adjustment to change and on its usual patterns of action.

THE FRENCH BUREAUCRATIC CONTRIBUTION

No such deeply stabilized system as the French bureaucratic system of organization can disappear without shaping profoundly the patterns succeeding it. The more practical question, therefore, which should be asked is not whether or not change will come, but what is likely to remain from the traditional bureaucratic system. Or, in more elaborate terms, what new equilibrium, what new system of relationships, can be evolved in, and well adjusted to, the modern world, to preserve the advantages of the original French bureaucratic contribution.[29]

We have already discussed the advantages for the individual of the French bureaucratic system,[30] and what was at stake in the individual's attachment to it. Examining these advantages again from a general and comparative point of view, we should like to argue that the basic benefit the French bureaucratic system brought to the individual was the possibility it offered to all its members, even the most humble, of participating on a wide and egalitarian basis in a style of life that featured especially a great deal of personal independence, the possibility of detaching oneself from the pressure of circumstances, and great freedom and lucidity. These achievements should not be minimized. They may be considered as one of the best parts of the contribution of the French culture to the Western world. At different stages they have been decisive for the progress of Western civilization. They are maintained now in a very expensive

[28] One should also take into account that the new functions and the new opportunities offered by these changes will lure away the most brilliant of the civil servants, by weakening resistance that would otherwise be very difficult to break. It can be hypothesized, finally, that resistance will come mostly from the middle and lower middle ranks that are best identified with the system and less open to exterior influences.

[29] We tend to believe that older systems influence new ones by imposing on them the requirements of securing at least equivalent benefits for most people concerned. This means that one of the decisive starting points in our prospective orientation would be to ascertain what was the basic contribution of the French bureaucratic system to the general Western culture in which it has developed.

[30] See above, pp. 198–203.

and inefficient way, and the whole balance of French society is affected by the relative failure of these traditional patterns. At the same time, however, there are enough elements in modern mass production and mass-consumption society that can be utilized by French society to elaborate new patterns enabling it to maintain and to renew its traditional and necessary contribution.

Such a problem presents a very deep challenge to a society, but it is not insuperable. One should point out also that nowhere else has a satisfactory balance as yet been achieved between individual and organized activity. Modern organization man is groping for a new culture, open to all and thus a mass culture, yet lively and creative enough to encourage each individual to participate with the best of himself. It is not so surprising that France, whose bureaucratic and bourgeois system permitted the blossoming of one of the most elaborate individual cultures of the pre-industrial era, should remain attached to it somewhat longer than other nations. But we can hope that when change comes, as it now does, the challenge offered to French ingenuity may be met by a positive contribution to the new humanism that must develop in the context of the new organizational rationality.

SUBJECT INDEX

INDEX OF NAMES

PHOENIX BOOKS
in Sociology